CREATIVE FASHION PRESENTATIONS

SECOND EDITION

CREATIVE FASHION PRESENTATIONS

POLLY GUÉRIN

Fashion Institute of Technology

FAIRCHILD PUBLICATIONS, INC.
New York

Executive Editor: Olga T. Kontzias
Acquisitions Editor: Joseph Miranda
Assistant Acquisitions Editor: Jason Moring
Art Director: Adam B. Bohannon
Director of Production: Priscilla Taguer
Associate Production Editor: Beth Applebome
Assistant Editor: Suzette Lam
Publishing Assistant: Jaclyn Bergeron
Copyeditor: Chernow Editorial Services, Inc.
Interior Design: Renato Stanisic
Cover Design: Adam B. Bohannon

Cover images, left to right, courtesy of the following: Rachel Herbst, Alexander Doll Company, Melissa Moylan, and Fairchild Publications, Inc.

Library of Congress Catalog Card Number: 2002113442

ISBN: 1-56367-250-2

GST R 133004424

Printed in the United States of America

Contents

Extended Contents

Preface

Creative Fashion Presentations was conceived as a basic text that would cover the entire spectrum of creative productions developed by diverse industries in the fashion theater. The first edition met with an enthusiastic response, but developments and changes in research services, trends, and fashion shows, as well as the impact of technology in all areas and the expansion of E-commerce, made a new edition essential—and exciting to prepare. Thus, this second edition, which employs creative tools and techniques to introduce new trends or collections and even soft sell a product, may well be the most comprehensive textbook on the subject of creative presentations.

Creative Fashion Presentations is directed primarily to the young man or woman, whether undergraduate or graduate, who is interested in preparing for a career in one of the fashion industries. By reviewing the examples in this book, students will understand the increasing complexity of fashion presentations and will begin to appreciate the many career opportunities available to them. In addition, academic faculty and professionals in the fashion business will find the book essential for acquiring an overall view of creative presentations—from the initial research steps to the final presentations.

This second edition has several new features that further emphasize developments and current trends in the fashion industries. The first is a series of industry profiles that are based on interviews conducted by the author with key executives and major players in diverse industries. These profiles, showcasing a significant person, provide an insider's view on the creative process. The author thanks these professionals for their time and interest and for contributing the erudite knowledge that makes this book a "how to," easy-to-read primer. The second new feature consists of selected readings from periodicals and newspapers that augment the text with current industry information. Then, sidebars are scattered throughout the text to provide additional information on subjects of special interest. Finally, each chapter ends with a list of terms with which the reader should be familiar.

In addition, an entirely new selection of illustrations furthers the learning experience. The author is particularly proud of the color insert, which consists of presentation boards created by two undergraduate students as part of their course work at the Fashion Institute of Technology.

Creative Fashion Presentations begins with a discussion of forecasting and moves on to creative presentations given by fiber and fabric companies, fashion show producers, trade associations, fiber promotion organizations, the apparel marts, cosmetics and fragrances, men's wear, the toy industry, and E-retailing. Fashion presentations by the Haute Couture and the Prêt-à-Porter are examined, along with other spectacular fashion shows in the global marketplace.

The first chapters explore the research necessary to begin the creative process. They take the reader on a fashion expedition, a tour if you will, of the resources ideal for market research and inspiration immersion. A proper appreciation of these resources is the first step in analyzing and compiling trend information. The discussion examines the importance of observational research in creating the inspiration for presentations. Such research includes the wide arena of MTV, videos, movies, theater, television, and a myriad of other areas, including fashion magazines, collections, and simply "people watching." The creative presentation and the storyboard process is then further explored in discussions of tools and techniques used by professionals to create industry presentations. Using new technology, audiovisuals, videos, and Internet sites, creative fashion presentations introduce new concept collections that affect the markets for fibers, fabrics, apparel, accessories, beauty products, men's wear, and even toys.

Emphasis is placed on the role of fashion forecasting and the vital part it plays in the initial research of colors and trends that will impact the sale of apparel and products. It shows how every level of the fashion and auxiliary industries, from high-end to low-end product lines, relies on a fashion forecast company's sophisticated trend predictions as a guideline for accurate and timely business decisions. Working eighteen months to two years ahead of a selling season, these prognosticators of trend information project the global aspects of merchandising with input from a network of worldwide sources.

This leads into a discussion of creative fashion presentations by the leather and fur industries, as well as the fiber and textile mills. These presentations range from the elaborate and entertaining to the practical application of storyboards as an integral part of their marketing process to promote a brand to an impressive array of industry end uses.

The ever-changing career profile of the fashion director at retail is the focus of the chapter on the retail challenge. It uses current examples to illustrate how retailers are vying for market share through creative promotions and tie-ins with popular movies, artists, or musicians. The changing and demanding role of the fashion director is demonstrated through trend tracking techniques that keep buyers in tune and current with color and fabric trends that emulate the image of a store.

The text then devotes several chapters to market expansion, which is the top priority of the international trade shows in an increasingly global marketplace. These chapters highlight the major trade shows and exhibitions, including Première Vision, which pinpoints emerging trends and gathers exclusive data on new lifestyles around the world. Première Vision presents it all in creative presentations and fashion show productions.

The Fashion Show Circuit is one of the most exciting chapters in the book. It covers fashion weeks in New York, London, Paris, and Milan, and also highlights the fashion extravaganzas in Hong Kong, Antwerp, Madrid, and Montreal. Most interesting is the "how to" of fashion show production, which illustrates how to plot out fashion shows that come to life through these pages. This material should inspire professionals in their respective fields to try the "new" and "unexpected" and, in essence, to take the most "creative" route. The fashion activities of the regional merchandise marts include fashion office responsibilities as prognosticators of trend information each season.

The French Connection introduces the Haute Couture and Prêt-à-Porter activities represented by the Fédération Française de la Couture and gives a frank discussion of the creative catwalk productions. The sidebar, Toujours Couture, is a soupçon, a bit of history about the couture, and provides readers with an understanding of what made the city of Paris the ambassador of fashion.

Next, the book addresses the auxiliary industries, beginning with cosmetic and fragrance. This discussion focuses on how products are researched, created, launched, and presented in elaborate promotions or star personality endorsements. The information on the fragrance industry also highlights the industry's important trade organization, The Fragrance Foundation.

Expanding areas in the men's wear industry introduce readers to creative presentations in the global marketplace, including major players in the American market scene, as well as renowned foreign presenters, such as London's Savile Row and Pitti Imagine Uomo, which is held in Florence. Spotlighted are the NAMSB trade organization and its trend projections, as well as Elyse Kroll's The Collective. These trade shows give readers an insight into the dramatization of men's wear in creative presentations and fashion shows.

A completely new chapter on the toy industry presents the tidal wave of creativity that sparked the production of high-tech interactive toys and games. Creative presentations in traditional product lines are also explored, including the teddy bear phenomenon and a doll's legacy. The latter features the creative team at Madame Alexander Dolls and shows how the members work synergistically together.

Finally, another new chapter—this one on the Internet. It introduces the subject of creative Web site design for major fashion designers and forecast firms. It also illustrates how E-commerce has become yet another important tool for creative presentations. A special feature shows readers step-by-step how to create effective Web sites, including the necessary tools and techniques, the skills needed to evaluate a good Web site, and the know how to drive traffic to that Web site.

The appendices provide a sampling of employment opportunities, as well as listings of industry services and associations useful to anyone creating a fashion presentation.

Another new feature, a color insert, includes boards prepared by two students in my Creative Presentations Class at the Fashion Institute of Technology. We wanted to show what today's talented students can achieve after learning from the materials presented in this book.

Thus, in its broadest sense, this book is a comprehensive compendium of creative presentations, which tantalize and sell fashion or products through show-biz techniques across all industry levels. It systematically outlines the steps necessary to produce creative story boards, promotions, and tie-ins and to produce fashion shows, while simultaneously coordinating the activities of a host of individuals who must be galvanized into action to meet pressing deadlines.

Instructor's Guide

An instructor's guide is available and contains general suggestions for teaching the course. This is a project-driven course, and the assignments relate specifically to the chapters in the book. A midterm is included, as well as a mini quiz.

Instructors may wish to adapt chapters that best suit their curricula. Project suggestions are industry specific. However, instructors may choose to develop their own projects based on their areas of expertise or industry experience. The instructor's manual includes additional readings that augment the chapters.

Acknowledgments

The author is indebted to the diverse numbers of industry firms and professionals, who through their generous contribution provided the first-hand, market-specific information in this book, making it one of the most up-to-date references on the exciting dramatization of fashion and products. It is these companies and individuals, too numerous to list here but well represented in the book, who have brought the multifaceted business of creative fashion presentation to its finest summation in this book.

Completely new content for this book was developed by the author through interviews with industry executives and by acquiring illustrations materials that augment the text. Profiles of industry professionals and readings further enhance the presentation.

The author also wishes to thank Executive Editor Olga Kontzias, and especially her colleague, Beth Applebome, whose assistance in acquiring permissions for material in the book was exemplary.

To Barbara A. Chernow of Chernow Editorial Services, Inc., I also extend a very special "thank you" for taking on the enormous task of shaping this book into a one-of-a-kind compendium of creative fashion presentations.

Readers selected by the publisher include Cynthia H. Baker, University of Wisconsin; Michele Granger, Southwest Missouri State University; Teresa Howe, Fisher College; and Lynda Poloian, Southern New Hampshire University.

As a training tool, *Creative Fashion Presentations* inspires and educates, but most of all it reveals the enormously vital creative process both here and abroad.

As always, I welcome comments and can be reached through Fairchild Publications or at my Internet address: www.pollytalk.com.

Polly Guérin
Adjunct Assistant Professor
Fashion Institute of Technology
State University of New York
New York, NY

CREATIVE FASHION PRESENTATIONS

1

A Visual Marketing Tool

In the highly competitive business arena, fashion industry firms eager to sell their merchandise, products, or services rely on the dynamics of creative fashion presentations as a valuable, visual marketing tool. The technique may vary from one market to the other, but in general, companies know that success requires more than simply introducing a new product. It takes storyboards, slides, videos, and computer-generated presentations to dramatize their messages.

PRESENTATION ANALYSIS

An effective industry presentation serves as an inspirational platform on which seasonal forecasts on color, fabrics, and silhouettes are unified by an overall theme and identified by creative subthemes each season. To create such a presentation a company needs the resources to analyze forecasting trends and determine the components for the most effective presentation.

In its broadest meaning, forecasting is the analysis of what is going on in the global fashion society and the trends that emerge based on professional experience and assessment of people's evolving tastes, changes in consumer buying habits, and economic conditions. Forecast projections differ from market to market. They may be long-range, short-term, or immediate. A sales presentation then communicates these new ideas using a "sell message" that introduces new products or seasonal merchandise in an exciting and memorable way.

THE MARKETING PROCESS

The fashion industry consists of a wide span of companies, from fiber houses and mills to manufacturers, product developers, retail fashion offices, and fashion forecasting firms. For all of them, fashion presentations are a major component of the marketing process.

Segments of the Market

Fashion presentations occur in a logical sequence, beginning with fabric selection and ending with retailing. The market has four basic segments.

1. Leather, Fiber, and Textile Mills. Creative fashion trend presentations begin at this level. These companies are assisted by the activities of fiber promotion organizations, such as Cotton Inc. Products are displayed to manufacturers and designers at trade shows, such as the International Fashion Fabric Exhibition.
2. Designers and Manufacturers. The producers of fashion apparel—children's, boys', men's wear, and accessories—then market their lines to buyers. Venues also include the apparel trade shows, such as Designer's Collective, the Boutique Show, and MAGIC, which also present trend reports, and fashion shows.
3. Auxiliary Fashion Industries. These companies market their own services to the other three segments of the industry so that each segment can better market its own products. It is the only segment of the fashion business that functions simultaneously with all the other segments. Auxiliary industries include fashion consulting firms, forecasting firms, advertising and public relations industries, trade show organizers, and trade publications and fashion magazines.

4. Retailers. This group, which markets to the public, includes buying offices, department and specialty stores, boutiques, chains, online retailers, catalogs, and discounters.

Scheduling Industry Presentations

The timing of creative fashion presentations is another important factor. Scheduling the presentation for the trade depends upon the firm's position in the production channel, which moves from fiber to fabric selection to manufacturing to retail. Another factor is the lead time needed for a presentation, which is influenced by whether production occurs overseas or in the domestic market. The entire fashion calendar for a particular product line or season runs approximately two years.

The calendar begins with presentations by the leather and fiber industries approximately two to one and a half years before the selling season to introduce their new product lines to the textile mills. Presentations at the textile mills follow, usually one year before a selling season. Six months before a selling season, designer and apparel producers give their presentations. At retail, the fashion office presentations for the store's merchants are introduced to serve as a buying guideline ahead of a selling season.

PRESENTATION FORMATS

In general creative presentations consist of the following elements and products:

- Boards: Trends/Images
- Color Cards/Color Reports
- Fabric Books/Fabric Reports
- Silhouette Trend Reports
- Audio Visual/Slide Trend Reports
- Prototype or Sample Garments

BALANCED • FABRICS / PATTERNS

Balanced

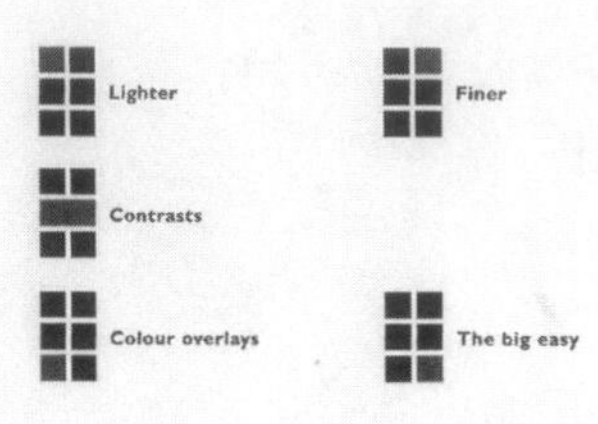

FABRICS outerwear weights that are light but compact. The overall effect should feel as gentle as possible with lots of sanded and powdered finishes. The focus is on poplins, the finest of twills and gabardines in cotton or lightweight wool. Cotton/wool blends are used for very smart but deconstructed suits. Cotton/nylon is important for outerwear where the coatings are getting much lighter. Also artisanal touches brought on by printed or space-dyed yarns in subtle multicolored combinations.

PATTERNS oversized simple checks. Also degradés and softly washed or water stained effects with gentle discolouration.

Photography: David Burton

36 COLOUR PLANNER SUMMER 2002

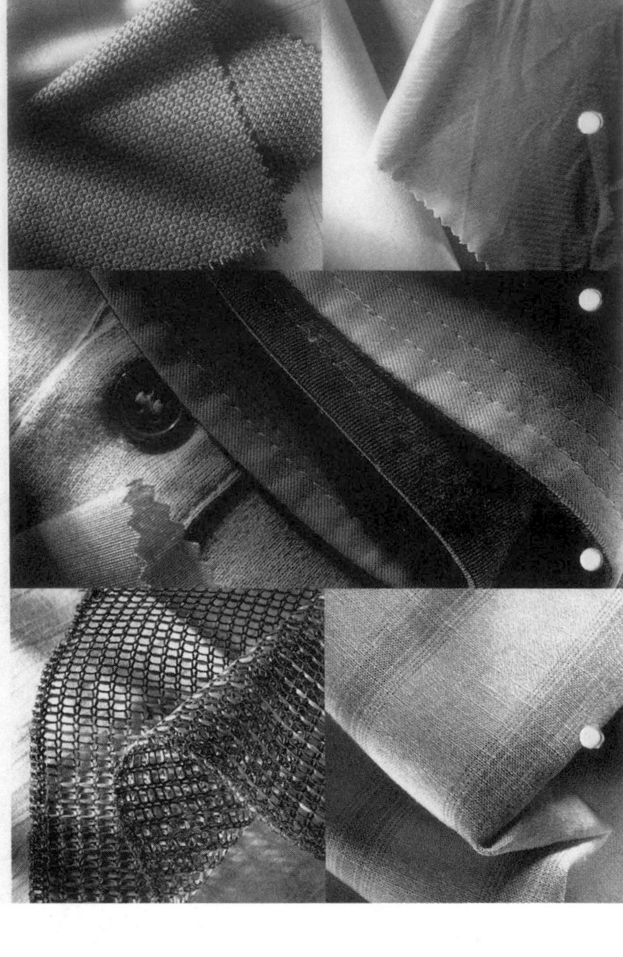

The Pantone® View Colour Planner for 2002 included four color directives. Here, the search for a new sense of emotional and physical balance is revealed in fabrics, patterns, harmonies, and proportions. Note how this unusual color palette reflects this balance between lightness and emotion.

Different segments of the industry use boards to present color, fabric, and silhouette trends and may also showcase concept garments to promote or sell their products to a specific market. For example, a fiber company pitching the swimwear market would not only include its fiber brands and color cards, but would also showcase concept or prototype garments in its creative fashion presentation. These garments illustrate fashion forward trend ideas that the swimwear manufacturers, who attend the fiber company's presentation, can review and adapt for new swimwear collections.

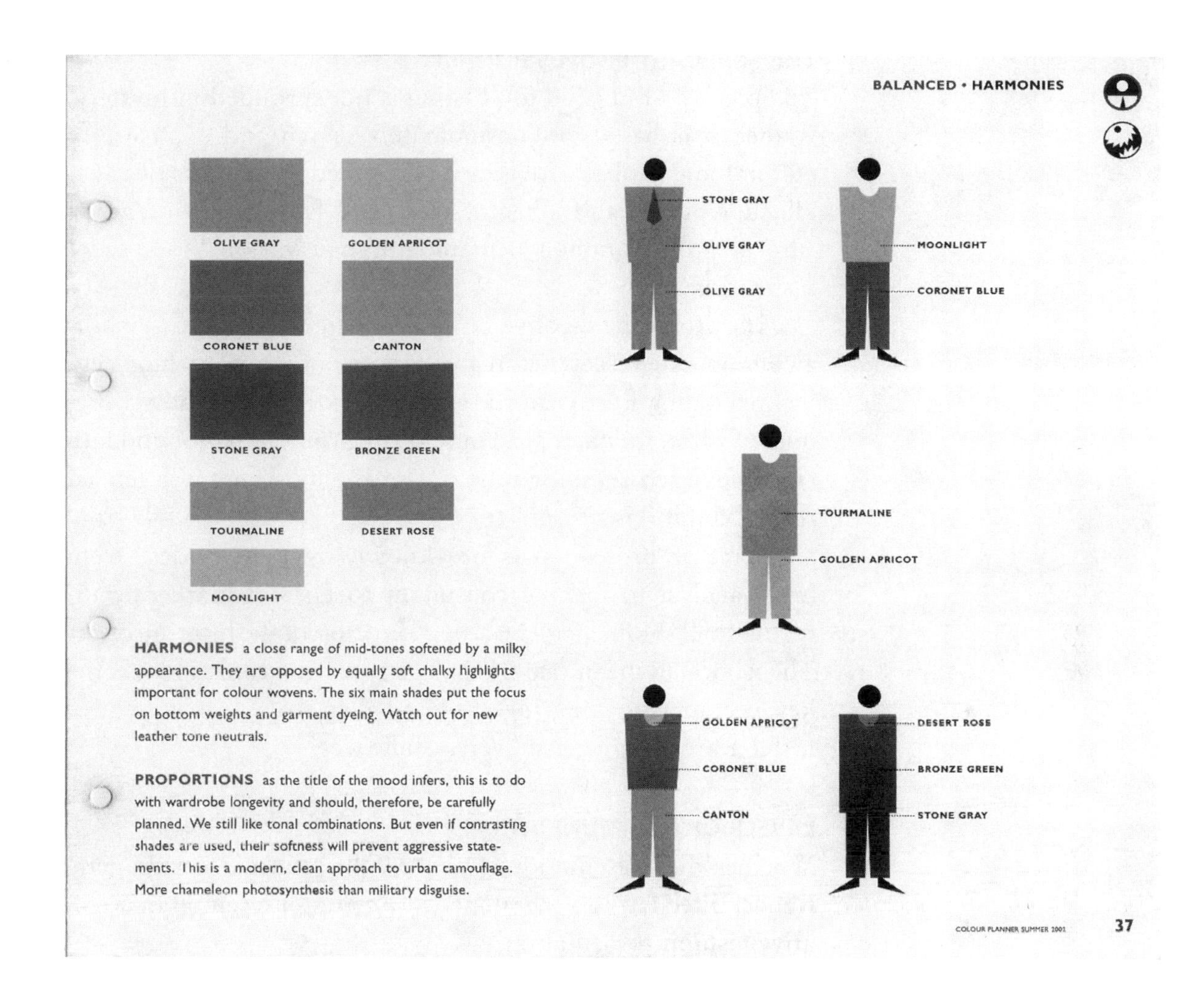

Similarly, creative fashion presentations at the trade level benefit from various visual aids, particularly storyboards, that identify and dramatize the trends or "sell" message. Presentations by forecast companies may be as client specific as a one-on-one consultation. Informal presentations may also be given for a select group of industry clients in the firm's offices or showroom. A more formal venue may be programmed for larger industry audience at such locations as a hotel's ballroom or the auditorium of a theater.

THE FORECAST PROFESSIONAL

The process of fashion forecasting is not shrouded in mystery. Rather, it is based on consummate research and exposure to cultural and global activities. If the trend is alligator leather, alligator prints, and alligator embossed faux fur, you can be sure that the common denominator had various sources of inspiration.

Therefore, the creative fashion presentation professional is a consummate researcher in a wide scope of global fashion centers, including European runway and textile trade shows. Premiere Vision, for example, consciously promotes color and fabric trends each season and is one of the most highly attended trade exhibitions.

Forecast professionals are known by many titles, from trend analyst to fashion consultant to fashion marketing director to fashion merchandising director or fashion director. The names all mean one thing. The forecast professional is the key person who puts together and delivers a firm's creative fashion presentation to diverse audiences.

LEVELS OF COMMUNICATION

Whether the presentation is about color, fabric, or silhouette trends, three levels of communication are represented in a creative fashion presentation.

1. Visual. Boards have the greatest visual impact because the images and decorative elements on the board convey the trend or sell the message through artistic renderings that are in context with a specific creative theme. Video, slides, and computer-generated presentations are other visual means of communicating the message.
2. Written word. A written synopsis of the overall theme and the subthemes reinforces the creative board presentation. It may be either a capsulated short paragraph

INDUSTRY PROFILE 1-1 | Neville Bean Designs

Present ideas in a provocative way. That's the advice of Neville Bean, trend analyst *par excellence* and owner of Neville Bean Designs (NBD), a comprehensive trends-based studio. With a specialty in fashion, the company focuses on trend analysis and line development by presenting seasonal direction in color, silhouette, and theme. In the process, Ms. Bean creates dramatic and creative presentation boards that feature trend stories for a wide range of fashion industry companies.

Ms. Bean has been in business for twenty-five years, and her professional fashion career as a designer, entrepreneur, and product developer has served her well in customizing presentations for her clients. As a creative problem solver with a hands-on, production-savvy approach, Neville Bean's consulting services are custom tailored to the individual client's needs.

"A creative board designer has to communicate a story and project ideas from a real-life prospectus," notes Ms. Bean. In addition to having an innate creative ability and a background in art and fashion history, she suggests that courses in psychology will contribute to developing a person's ability to conceptualize ideas for trend board design.

Neville Bean adds, "However, you can create a much stronger presentation if you work within structured themes. For example, if you use a tropical theme, what does that mean in terms of color, fabric, decorative elements, and rendering?"

Ms. Bean stresses that you have to present creative board designs that are in the context of the specific theme or story. For example, does a "tropical" theme mean Hawaii, Caribbean, or rain forest? You have to ask yourself the big "WHAT." What exactly is it—an ethnic look, a cruise, yachting, an island, a resort, travel—what are you trying to convey? For creative boards you must be aware of innovative materials that fuel ideas. If the theme for an architectural firm is light and transparency, the use of a translucent concrete block, if available, will tell the story. Creative boards must reflect the interests of the times, like handmade and handcrafted, which are key trends pointing toward a balance in nature.

"In order to sell buyers and retailers, you have to present ideas in a provocative way so that the information will filter down to the ultimate consumer," advises Bean. "Don't underestimate the consumer's awareness of what's happening in color, textiles, or fashion. They may not be able to articulate it but they feel it. It's important, therefore, to be 'on trend' because the consumer is 'on trend' and knows what's going on and can see what's fresh and right."

"Images, illustrations from magazines, or photographs must reflect the main concept of the season. In designing the boards it is important to look for defining image elements. Is the message one of transparency, luminosity, or spiritualism? Lifestyle influences leave you open to be creative. Look at ideas in a literal way. Then speculate on how these could be applied to your industry and translate it for the target market."

She further advises that you step out of your tunnel vision into the big picture. Look at everything, but especially elements from society. Watch what's happening everywhere, from the performance aspect

Neville Bean's creativity and philosophy has made her one of the most successful fashion trend analysts.

Examples from Neville Bean reports include vibrant and exciting trend boards, with actual yarn samples. In 2001, the boards brought to life the themes of Travel, Currents, and Cunima.

of the new boutique hotels, such as the W with its white serenity and ceiling-to-floor curtains, to the performance art of skateboarders and music and MTV personalities. Remember that rappers create style. Bigger concepts can emerge from the study of multiculturalism, the mixing and clashing of cultures in our society, and the media bombardment of ideas expressing individualism. For example, people watching celebrities and singers, such as Jennifer Lopez, indicate the Latino influence and trend direction.

Ms. Bean concludes by saying, "The way trends and ideas evolve is cyclical, and trends influence each other. You have to ask what are the overriding trends. Don't just check the competition in the same industry, but look elsewhere into the big picture."

Neville Bean's inspirational "Demystifying Fashion Forecasting" talks are a feature in the seminar department at the Fashion Institute of Technology and are given at industry trade shows as well as for private clients.

or a more detailed report that highlights, theme by theme, the color or trend message.

3. Spoken word. The presenter's sounds and words should reinforce the written message. The presenter should be a skilled professional who is confident before an audience of any size. Like an actor, the presenter must deliver the creative fashion presentation with a certain degree of pizzazz. Without becoming too flamboyant, the presenter should be able to exhibit through speech and manner a spirit of enthusiasm that provides a convincing sell message on trend, product development, or merchandise presentation. As Fran Yoshioka, fashion director of Sears Roebuck and Co., said, "What good is technology if you can't present creatively."

THE AUDIENCE

Who Attends

Qualified professionals from diverse areas of the industry attend creative presentations in different market areas to glean, in advance, the color, fabric, silhouette, and trend information that will aid them in producing successful lines or making sound retail decisions. They include:

- Apparel Designers
- Buyers/Merchants
- Creative Staff Personnel
- Design Teams
- Divisional Merchandise Managers
- Fashion Consultants
- Fashion Directors
- General Merchandise Managers
- Private Label Manufacturers
- Product Development Personnel
- Retail Executives
- Trade Press
- Trend Analysts

Invitations

Presentations by the fiber firms, textile producers, or fiber promotion organizations are "free" to industry guests. The presentation is considered a service, an added value, because most of the audience consists of the fiber company's customers to whom the company hopes to promote or sell its fiber or textile products.

Similarly, fashion and color forecast firms also do not charge their clients. The fee charged to clients for consulting services includes the privilege of attending the presentation.

Some firms, like the fashion forecast division of a buying office, may extend invitations to a broader industry audience and charge a nominal fee to attend a trend presentation. For an industry professional to qualify for an invitation to a presentation, the presenter/firm may require a "request to attend" on company letterhead. In some cases a telephone call may suffice.

The firm may also sell its trend books and color/fabric swatch cards to industry professionals, who purchase them for their research.

PRESENTATION DECISIONS

Industry professionals doing research on trends and color must determine which presentations are appropriate to attend. In other words, an industry professional does not attend every presentation. Rather, the professional is selective and chooses presentations that will best accommodate a company's needs. When the research is completed, all the collected color cards and trend information must be analyzed and digested into one common denominator of trends in color and fabric and silhouette for a specific target market. A design team for a major manufacturer or designer, for example, would apply the edited color, fabric, and silhouette information to its line of production.

Trade Terminology

Forecasting
Inspiration
Lead time
Levels of communication
Market research
Presentation analysis
Sell message
Storyboards
Trend books
Visual impact

READING 1-1

Secrets of an MTV Fashion Director

SUSAN BAUER, FASHION BUYING AND MERCHANDISING '92 DRESSES THE STARS AND SETS THE STYLE OF MTV

BY ROBERT KNAFO

So you're the MTV fashion director, and you see this show biz celebrity show up to tape a segment of something or other, and this person is dressed, shall we say . . . hideously, or just plain tastelessly, or, god forbid, wearing red stripes. (Red stripes are a double television no-no, as red bleeds and stripes warp). We're talking about a VIP here, mind you—someone conditioned by years of posterior kissing to thinking that he/she has achieved a kind of infallibility that is perhaps only rivaled by the Pope. But you, being the MTV fashion director, are responsible for on-air stylishness. And therefore, you must separate this great talent from her unfortunate get-up. By any means necessary.

But how?

It's simple, if you're Susan Bauer: You 1) tell the celebrity that he/she looks absolutely fabulous. (Do not, she emphasizes, *ever* skip step one). 2) You nonetheless suggest a visit to the MTV fashion closet—"just for fun"—where innumerable wonders await, by the name of Prada, Gucci, and Dolce and Gabbana. Within a minute or so, you should have the celebrity *out* of the red stripes and preening in some *truly* fabulous outfit. 3) You then tell the celebrity that as much as the personal stylist in his/her employ has done a *fabulous* job with that red-stripe number, this other outfit makes him/her look even *more* fabulous—if that is indeed possible. 4) You then tell the celebrity (who should be nodding and smiling at him/herself in the mirror by now), that—oops—he/she's due on the set *now.* 5) You nudge the freshly re-attired celebrity toward the cameras.

MTV Studio Fashion Director Susan Bauer has mastered the celebrity styling switcheroo, as well as a thousand other solutions for the sundry snags, snafus, hitches, and *situations* that inevitably come up when fashion, television, entertainment, and big egos come together on everybody's favorite music channel. Sure, Bauer is bright and personable, and tall and blond and attractive, and she's got great style chops, and a gazillion fashion industry contacts, and the ability to sew on a stray button or hike up a hem in world-class time. But what may be the most important part of her job—what makes her really qualified to be the MTV fashion director—is a combination of tact and cunning that would make our nation's diplomats stand up and nod in acknowledgement at a fellow pro. On the day I come to visit at MTV studios at 1515 Broadway, Bauer has to do a favor for a company vice president who's going to give a talk at his high school reunion, and who needs a little guidance on dressing up in the right theme tux. The theme being the stylistically challenged Seventies. Bauer has dug up various cheesy and strangely colored formal wear. She and the VP are now standing in a walk-in closet and pondering the possibilities: plain vanilla (one tux is actually vanilla-toned), or the tie-dyed purple number? Frilly scarlet shirt or "simple" white? This gentleman may be one of the key personnel at a billion-dollar entertainment conglomerate, but he seems completely at a loss in that typical male-before-fashion sort of way. Bauer deftly eases him toward the fateful decision: "Maybe you can just take a couple home and try them on with your wife and see," she breezily suggests, Getting his wife's take on the matter and color coordinating with *her* retro Seventies outfit strikes the VP as an excellent idea. By the end of the brief consultation, he is fingering the lapel of the purple tux and thanking Bauer very, very much for her help. Hey, no problem, her shrug and easy smile seem to say.

Bauer came to fashion, and FIT, in a roundabout way—via Delaware. She was, she recalls, variously "pre-law" and "in restaurant management," at the University of Delaware before she realized that her interests really lay in the fashion world. After three years at Delaware, she spent a year at FIT—a "3-and-1" program that allowed her to get both a BA from her home school and an associate's degree in Fashion Buying and Merchandising from FIT. While at FIT she interned at a photography studio that specialized in clothing catalogues. "They shot Avon and J.C. Penney fashion," she remembers. Graduating in 1992, she took a job as an assistant stylist with the same studio. "It was great, because I had the opportunity to assist 20 different stylists," Bauer recalls. She was soon asked to cast the models and pick the locations as well, thereby gaining a comprehensive education in putting together a fashion shoot in her very first job out of school. "I was 23, 24 years old, and I was running the entire fashion department," she says with a trace of amazement at her good fortune, and maybe a dash of pride in her precociousness. After nine months of "doing the job of four people, I was burned," she remembers. Bauer went on to freelance for MTV as an entry-level assistant. While there she heard of an opening as a stylist at VH1. She got that job, and then subsequent positions at *Mirabella* and *W* magazines before coming back to VH1 as a senior fashion stylist, and then getting her present position at MTV.

So how did a personal sense of style figure in the success of someone who dresses other people for a living? I look at what Bauer's wearing: Nice brown knit top, stylishly low-cut-jeans, expensive-looking but inconspicuous spiky tan heels. Her clothes don't shout out a particular style so much as a kind of low-key, go-anywhere good taste. I ask her if she has a particular style or fashion point of view. She reflects an unusually long time before answering this question. "I think one thing that has been a strong point of mine is that I'm very versatile. I'm like a chameleon," she finally says, divulging what perhaps is another of her secrets to fashion director success. "I can do hip-hop, 1930s, 1970s, everything." This is a woman who also knows her resources. "I have a photographic memory," she explains. "I know every store to get anything, and I know the people who can make anything." She adds matter-of-factly. But how did she go about accumulating this invaluable fashion industry knowledge, you may wonder. "I read every magazine possible and everyone's credits, so I knew who was doing what out there." She also admits to borrowing a few sources from colleagues. Thus prepared, Bauer went on to a successful three-year stint as VH1 senior fashion stylist, running the wardrobe department for the channel before getting hired back again by Viacom older sibling MTV.

Bauer's formal responsibilities as fashion director include setting the style direction for the channel (as well as for MTV2), managing relationships with the fashion world, keeping the channels on the cutting edge of style trends, and dressing celebrities, as well as designing costumes for sketches and theme shows—"the very creative part that I love," she says.

Sometimes Bauer"s creativity is taken to the limit: at MTV's recent Spring Break show in Cancun, Mexico, she had to dress a celebrity (who must remain nameless) in the mandatory fun beach wear. But the celeb, Bauer says delicately, "needed a little help in the cleavage area." So she took the bikini top she had selected for this special guest and performed some quick emergency work. "I opened the seams on the inside, and put in raw chicken cutlets, which move with the body like the real thing. The cutlets made the breasts look bigger and fixed the cleavage issue. And the show started on time."

Bauer is happy to share many of her hard-won professional secrets with today's FIT students in the internship class she teaches at the college. In the class, Bauer explains, she helps her students "prepare to enter the job force by strengthening their negotiating skills, networking skills, and defining and prioritizing their values." She loves teaching, she says. As for the students absorbing Bauer's expertise in career development, they are, It's safe to say, in the hands of a master.

Source: *FIT Network* magazine, Spring 2002, pp. 14–15. Reproduced with permission of *FIT Network* magazine.

READING 1-2 | Lights, Camera, Fashion BY SAMANTHA CONTI

From the day Ava Gardner demanded that all her movie costumes be made by Rome's Sorelle Fontana, and far beyond the night Richard Gere stripped off his Armani suit and seduced Lauren Hutton in "American Gigolo," the relationship between Italian designers and the film industry has been one big *cinema paradiso*. The affair stretches back to the days of Hollywood on the Tiber and still rages today, as the best of Milan fight to dress the brightest lights in Los Angeles.

"The Italians get a genuine kick out of dressing celebrities. They love it. You can tell they're having as much fun as we are," said Phillip Bloch, a Hollywood stylist who's draped his clients in Armani, Versace and Valentino. "And we all know they make unforgettable dresses."

The love story began right after World War II, when American film producers, in search of exotic locations, solid production facilities and low costs, flocked to Cinecittá, the film studios built by Mussolini in the Thirties and the only place in Europe with the full range of production facilities—and some of the largest studio spaces in the world.

When Hollywood and its divas arrived, Rome's fashion scenes changed forever. The city's *salta moda* designers, used to catering to the city's stuffy nobility with knockoffs of French designs, all of a sudden had a whole new roster of young clients—Ava Gardner, Kim Novak, Ingrid Bergman, Elizabeth Taylor and Audrey Hepburn—with an appetite for elegant, but wearable fashion.

"The Americans were practical, they wanted something they could wear on the street, and we gave it to them," said Micol Fontana, who with her two sisters, Zoe and Giovanna, opened her atelier after the war.

"Our initial success was thanks to the actresses who wore our clothes on-screen and off," said Fontana during an interview in her Rome offices. "And once we made the wedding gown for Linda Christian, everyone in Hollywood knew who we were," she added, referring to Tyrone Power's bride. The Sorelle Fontana made the costumes for 15 films between 1937 and 1995, including "The Barefoot Contessa," "The Sun Also Rises" and "The Bible," all of which starred Ava Gardner. The actress once said that if you weren't dressed in Sorelle Fontana, "you simply weren't dressed."

Another Roman designer that tacked her hemline to Hollywood was Fernanda Gattinoni, whose roster of clients in the Fifties read like roll call at Twentieth Century Fox. Ingrid Bergman was one of her favorites and she made sure that the actress's skirts were wide enough so that her large feet wouldn't look so big. Gattinoni also outfitted Bergman in many of the films she made with Roberto Rossellini, including "Stromboli" and "Europa 51."

Gattinoni, nominated for an Academy Award for her costume designs in the 1956 film "War and Peace," was credited with bringing the Empire style back into fashion. That moment in fashion was a big one for Italians, for it was the time when Gattinoni softened Gina Lollobrigida's hourglass curves with Empire dresses.

"Those were the days," said the 95-year-old Gattinoni, whose fashion house is still thriving under the guidance of a new designer, "when a woman wore at least four outfits a day."

The films of the Fifties brought Italian fashion to the world's attention. The decade's neo-realism period—the heyday of Vittorio de Sica, Luchino Visconti and Roberto Rossellini—gave Italian fashion a lasting legacy of poor, gritty, street urchin sensuality.

"You can see it in the fashions of Dolce & Gabbana and Mariella Burani," said Natasha Celati, the director of the master's program in fashion design at the Milan fashion school, Domus Academy. "It's a woman-in-the-market type fashion: poor, simple and sensual."

Other films—Fellini's "La Dolce Vita," with Anita Ekberg busting out of her wet halter top, and "Yesterday, Today and Tomorrow," where Sophia Loren strips off her black garters in front of Marcello Mastroianni—still inspire Rome's *alta moda* designers. And, of course, there was Loren sashaying around in a peasant blouse in "Gold of Naples."

"The grotesque glamour of those years, that overdone Hollywood look, is still present on Rome's runways today," Celati added.

Indeed, many of Rome's current designers are used to dressing Italian TV starlets with dimensions more or less like those of Ekberg and Loren.

Salvatore Ferragamo, founder of the renowned accessories house, actually moved to Hollywood to make his name. Born in southern Italy, he moved to Santa Barbara in 1914 to join his brothers, who had a shoe-repair shop. In 1923 he moved to Hollywood and began making shoes for films—mostly cowboy boots and Greek and Egyptian sandals for Cecil B. DeMille's costume blockbusters.

Soon enough, Rudolph Valentino, Gloria Swanson and Joan Crawford were asking for custom-made shoes they could wear off-screen. Four years later, Ferragamo moved back to Italy—choosing Florence as his new home because of its leather crafting tradition—and set up his shoe manufacturing business.

He made red, rhinestone-encrusted stilettos for Marilyn Monroe, ballerina flats for Audrey Hepburn and chunky, open-toed shoes for Evita Peron. Later, Drew Barrymore and Madonna would be asking the company for shoes similar to the ones they wore in "Ever After: A Cinderella Story," and "Evita."

After laying low in the Sixties and focusing on the industrial sides of their business in the Seventies, the Italians were back with ferocity by 1980. That was the year Giorgio Armani made his Hollywood debut with "American Gigolo" and ushered in a new era of product placement and celebrity dressing.

"He was the designer who first recognized the value of Hollywood," said Madeline Leonard, head booker at Cloutier, a top Los Angeles stylist agency. "He had offices out here way back in the early Eighties. No one ever had any problem getting Armani clothes."

Even today, the designer will fly stars—and their stylists—to his fashion shows in Milan. Sophia Loren is walking, talking evidence of Armani's power in Hollywood. Garters and peasant blouses tossed to the wind, Loren is now one of Armani's biggest fans.

"When you dress in Armani, you can be sure you'll never look like a Christmas tree," she told *WWD* after the designer's spring-summer 2000 fashion show last year.

Armani's exclusive didn't last long: by the early Nineties, other Italian designers had high-tailed it to Hollywood and were fighting to dress stars on-screen and for their premieres and awards ceremonies: the Golden Globes, Emmys, and, of course, the Oscars.

"That is the climax. It's what we work all year for," said Piera Blodwell, whose Beverly Hills-based firm, PRB, represents Krizia, Missoni, Gruppo Genny and other Italian houses.

Indeed, getting a dress on the right celebrity is becoming as important as staging a fashion show or unveiling a stunning ad campaign.

Some credit Uma Thurman's custom lavender Prada ensemble at the 1995 Oscars with creating a Hollywood fervor for the Italian collection: Soon after, Sigourney Weaver, Nicole Kidman, Leonardo DiCaprio and Brad Pitt were wearing Prada.

Valentino, Versace, Gucci and Dolce & Gabbana have also won starring roles in Hollywood wardrobes—and basked in the glory of it all.

"When Elizabeth Hurley first wore that Versace 'pin' gown, Versace's name reached a whole new level," said Leonard of Cloutier, referring to the busty black number Hurley wore to the premiere of "Four Weddings and a Funeral."

The designers, however, downplay the importance of dressing celebrities, and claim they're just "dressing friends" for an event.

"Of course, we're flattered when celebrities wear our clothes," said Donatella Versace, who has dressed everyone from Madonna to Courtney Love to Wynona Rider." But dressing celebrities is not a priority, and it's not the goal of the company."

The Italians are ever pumping up their presence in films. Nino Cerruti is perhaps the forefather of Italian product placement—his clothes began appearing in films at the end of the Fifties. Today, companies like Ferragamo, Fendi, Bulgari and Tod's are all making sure their products are front-and-center in films.

"Hollywood is a marketing machine, and the Italians have understood that," said Reuben Igielko-Herrlich, an owner of Geneva-based Propaganda, a company which specializes in product placement and special events. "They are the most aggressive Europeans in Hollywood, and they know that a film is simply another event they can use to their benefit."

Source: *Italy, the Fashion Makers* (*WWD* supplement), February 2000, pp. 48–50. Courtesy of Fairchild Publications, Inc.

2

The Fashion Forecasting Process

In today's fast-moving global marketplace, the process of determining fashion trends has changed dramatically. This is a direct reflection of changes in the individual's role in society and the diverse international cultures and economies that are now influencing fashion.

To many people fashion looks like a revolving door. In one season, out the next, then back again for a second or third introduction. However, trend predictions do not just come out of nowhere; they evolve seasonally and yearly. They are based on concrete research that will influence the creation of exciting and timely fashion, home furnishings, and product lines.

Fashion forecasting emerged as an industry in the 1960s out of the need for trend information. However, forecasting today is propelled by modern communications that pull the industry forward with unprecedented speed. Take your eyes off it for a minute and wham—fashion is completely different.

THE FASHION FORECAST COMPANIES

Fashion forecast companies have become a major source of trend information that impacts the success of diverse industries—from women's, men's, and children's wear to active sportswear, swimwear, accessories, beauty products, footwear, home furnishings, and industrial products. Doneger Creative Services, for example, services firms at the high end of the market, firms that look at fashion in more esoteric terms.

Fashion forecasting includes home furnishings, as well as apparel and accessories. The use of geometrics and op-art patterns with diagonal cuts and shapes are reflected in these patterns.

The structure of a fashion forecast company is multidimensional, including services for realists who regard fashion as a business, not an art form. They are profit-producing businesses that charge for their services and operate in a highly competitive marketplace.

Forecasting companies produce multidiversified trend products. Prices vary, ranging from hundreds to tens of thousands of dollars, depending on the combination of consulting services a manufacturer, designer, or retailer purchases to meet its needs and budget. Most fashion forecasting services price their services comparably. Thus, it is not a bargain hunt to find one service cheaper than another. Rather, it is a matter of evaluating which forecasting company's products effectively satisfy the trend needs of a particular designer/manufacturer, product development team, or retailer.

Subscribers may purchase more than one service to cross-reference and confirm commonalties in color, fabric, and trend information. It depends on a firm's budgetary limitations; only the fashion industry professional can decide which service will produce the best commercial results for a product line.

Tuned into the World

Effective fashion forecasters are tuned into all influential areas of research in the global marketplace. This vast network allows a forecaster to develop a keen eye to track trends and be aware of the potential for global business.

A network of correspondents based in the fashion capitals of the world also facilitates the fashion forecast company's ability to forecast trends on an international basis. Through satellite communications, these correspondents file reports on international fashion shows and trade fairs, designer profiles, and what's happening on the streets and in retail environments. With the click of a mouse, information is analyzed, dissected, and interpreted for the global market.

Diversified Presentation of Trend Information

The complex business of forecasting trends benefits those industry professionals—designers, manufacturers, product de-

SIDEBAR 2-1 | **How to Interpret Trend Information**

When you look at trend presentation, how do you interpret what is new? What is the fabric or silhouette story? The best way to interpret the trend report is to compare it with the forecast report from the same season one year ago. Look for the differences and changes in silhouette and fabrications. You may be surprised to find that fashion does not change drastically and that some of the trends forecasted earlier may continue into another year. If you are looking at the Spring season, another checkpoint is to look at the previous Fall's trends to assess what ideas have been carried forward. This analysis will enable you to formulate trend direction for your target market.

When you attend a slide show trend presentation given by a fashion authority, you should take notes that capture the key phrases and tips that cue you into the fashion buzzwords and themes of the season.

The choice of fashion forecasting service is entirely your decision. It should be one that will satisfy the needs of the company you represent. Although general forecast company presentations are right on target with trend information, each one offers different services. A first time industry guest might attend several presentations to decide which of the forecasts is the most satisfying for trend analysis.

velopers, buyers, and fashion directors—whose firms would not have the budget or the personnel to perform such research.

Fashion forecasting companies offer a diverse mix of products and services, including:

- Audio/Visual Trend Slide Shows
- Client Consultations
- Color Cards/Color Consulting
- Concept Garments
- Fabric Library
- Fabric Trend Books
- Fashion Silhouette/Books and Reports
- Hot Items at Retail
- Industrywide Audiovisual Presentations
- International Street Scene Reports
- International Fashion and Fabric Trade Fair Reports
- Newsletters
- One-on-One Consultations
- Pictorial Fashion Trend Summaries
- Computer-Generated Presentations
- Prêt-à-Porter and Haute Couture Collection Summaries
- Product Development
- Promotion Programs
- Prototype Garments from Worldwide Sources
- Worldwide Retail Selling Trends

The Subscribers/The Audience

Every level of the fashion and auxiliary industries relies on a fashion forecast company's extremely sophisticated trend predictions as a guideline for accurate and timely business decisions. The firms that subscribe to these services range from Seventh Avenue designers and manufacturers from high fashion to moderate and popular price points, fiber producers, textile mills, mass merchandisers, retailers, catalog houses, fashion Internet sites, cosmetics and accessories companies, home furnishings manufacturers, and industrial product producers. A firm either subscribes to a forecast company as a member client or attends seasonal presentations on a pay-as-you-attend basis.

Creative fashion presentations on color, fabric, and silhouette at Doneger Creative Services, for example, are usually given fourteen to sixteen months before a Spring or Fall selling season. Spring 2006 would be presented in January/February 2005, and Fall 2006 would be presented in June 2005. However, the scheduling of creative fashion presentations depends on the production cycles of individual markets and the products forecasters sell, and may differ from these time frames.

The Trend Forecasters

The creative fashion presentations given by forecast companies provide a comprehensive general overview of an upcoming season not only for the apparel and home furnishings industries, but also for hard goods lines, such as appliances and automobiles. Many of the companies in nonfashion-related industries are also interested in trend information from a lifestyle standpoint.

These trend forecasts differ from presentations given by firms in the primary market because the fiber firm's primary interest is forecasting trends with a specific fiber focus. The forecast company's role is far more general and diversified and may include product development, retail promotion programs, and retail selling strategies.

Similarities mainly relate to the creative way trends are presented. Like the fiber company presentations, forecast companies also create a central theme, an overall concept that unites several subthemes in silhouette, fabric, and color trend direction. They present these themes on boards, in audiovisual shows, and in hands-on seminars that serve as an inspiration for design direction. Subscribers can implement these directives in their color, fabric, or garment collections. For a list of companies, see Table 2-1.

TABLE 2-1	MAJOR FASHION FORECASTING SERVICES

Committee for Colour & Trends
Doneger Creative Services
Edelkoort Studio
Ellen Sideri Partnership
Here and There
IMPRINTS NY Trend Reports
Promostyl
The Trend Curve
The Fashion Service (a member of The Doneger Group)
Tobé
Trend Union
Worth Global Style Network

For contact information for these companies, see Appendix B.

PROMOSTYL

The first fashion forecasting company to have an international office, Promostyl's fashion headquarters for trend research and project development has been in business for more than twenty-five years. With offices in Paris, London, New York, and Tokyo, Promostyl's team of market coordinators, stylists, and designers collaborate to help companies adapt to changing lifestyle, cultural, and fashion trends, and use these trends to strategic advantage.

Trend Forecasting Services

In addressing its clients' demands, Promostyl brings to the task a team, a structure, and a methodology. A worldwide network of twenty-two agents provides fashion forecast feedback on a daily basis. Fueled by the communications from its international agents, Promostyl's clients profit from this worldwide knowledge. According to Jayne Mountford, senior trend consultant, "More and more clients want to know what's happening in other parts of the world."

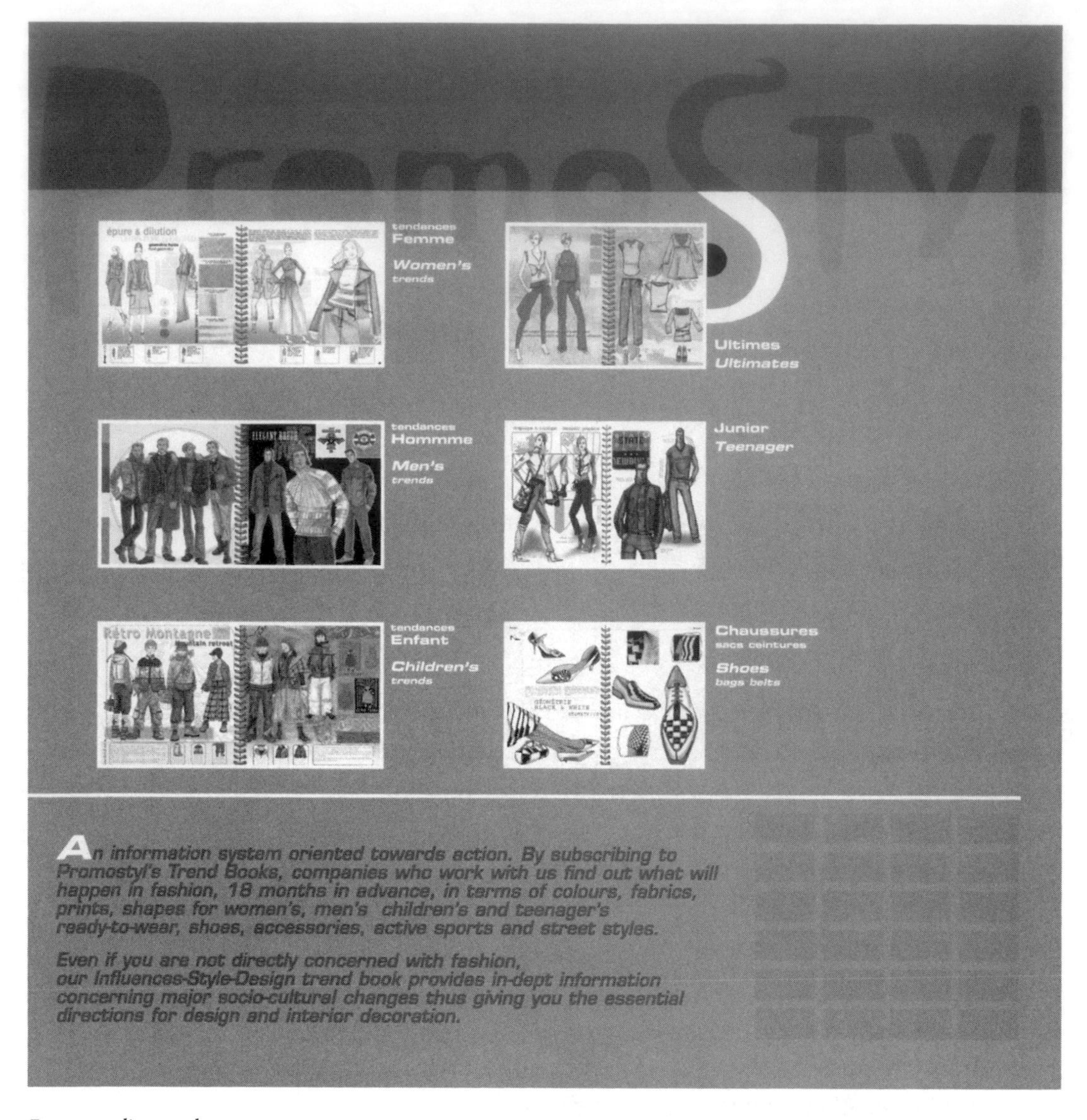

Promostyl's trend books forecast fashion colors, fabrics, prints, and shapes eighteen months before the season begins.

Promostyl's methodology is to understand a client's requests by studying the changing lifestyles and cultures belonging to the client's market. One-on-one consultations that adapt trends to each client's specific needs are available at Promostyl's four main offices.

Promostyl's services to its clients include trend conferences on marketable themes.

The firm also publishes trend books twice a year, eighteen months ahead on color, fabrics, sports, baby, children's, teen, men's, and women's fashions and accessories. These trend books analyze the major sociocultural trends that will influence fashion and design and provide essential color and fabric information for elaborating a collection. Between publications, Promostyl provides supplements for subscribers. For each market, Promostyl offers a silhouette trend book structured by the season's themes. Each theme is developed in numerous product lines for different consumer types.

Promostyl also conducts industrywide trend conferences that highlight marketable themes in an audiovisual presentation for the Spring or Fall selling season. Promostyl's clients and industry guests attend these events.

In addition, Promostyl produces a newsletter that contains key information on trend news worldwide. In particular, it covers events from the showing of European designer collections and trade fairs to displays at stores, on the streets, and related events.

Finally, Promostyl's subscribers also have access to fabric libraries in the Paris and New York offices, which contain woven, knit, print, and trimming collections that are constantly updated by the most innovative European and American mills.

Other Services

Although fashion forecasting is a major part of Promostyl's business, it also offers clients the following services:

Promostyl's 2005 forecasts show a balance between the need to be part of the group and the desire for self-expression. Again, these trends are reflected in both personal and home furnishings.

- Brand Strategy and Positioning
- Design and Packaging
- Line Development
- Merchandising Concepts
- Media Design and Production
- Store Concepts

- Industry Organization
- Fair Planning

Brand Positioning

An international Asian electronics company (Casio of Japan) wanted to increase consumer awareness in Europe for its watch brand (G-Shock, Baby-G). The watch had considerable success in Asia, but was not well known in Europe.

Promostyl's collaboration established a positioning and relaunching strategy based on extreme sports and fashion. Staff members studied retail outlets for the young in three European countries and designed avant-garde looking catalogs to be distributed in stores. They organized parties in fashionable locations, had designers feature "the watch" in the Paris runway shows, and had their client sponsor a recurrent fashion event. The result: Brand awareness was increased with the "street," "extreme," and "fashion" approaches.

Industry Organization and Fair Planning

The industry organization and fair planning client was a French textile industry organization, Fédération Française de la Maille, which managed a lingerie and swimwear trade fair. Promostyl created four trend books for the client. The books explained the strong points of the each manufacturer's line during the lingerie fairs in Lyon and Paris. Promostyl also assisted manufacturers with their runway shows.

TOBÉ

Fashion's retail consultants since 1927, Tobé Associates, Inc., specializes in merchandising analysis, customized consulting projects, and the *TobéNext Forecasting* service. Clients who benefit from these services range from multibillion-dollar home and beauty businesses to fashion retailers and manufacturers.

Tobé's fashion/merchandising service is subscribed to by the highest level merchants in retailing, including CEOs, presidents, general merchandise managers, divisional merchandise managers, and corporate fashion directors. Clients range from top-line department and specialty stores to mass merchants, chain stores, the fashion press, colleges, and universities, as well as the U.S. government and financial institutions.

A page from The Tobé Report *in 2003 reveals the explosion of polka dots in tailored women's wear. The jackets and sensual flair of the skirts make these fashions appropriate for both business and social occasions.*

The Tobé Report

The Tobé Report is the industry's most recognized authority on the opinions and trends that will impact the success of retail sales. The report is published thirty-eight times per year and is subscribed to by clients throughout the United States, Canada, Europe, Asia, Africa, Australia, and Latin America. Unlike other industry services that only report fashion news and trends, Tobé's primary focus is the retail customer. It is the one un-biased source of fashion analysis.

Tobé's editors research every facet of the women's, men's, and children's apparel and accessories business for its clients in a search to uncover the hot items and new trends as they are developing.

Tobé keeps its clients informed and on target with the following communications:

- The Weekly Report: Realistic, well-researched input on evolving business opportunities
- Fashion Flashes: What is hot and what is trendy
- Resource Alerts: New vendor resources
- Reorder Flashes: Best-selling items at retail
- Market Departments: Key items, color and fabric trends, and the manufacturers that best capture these elements

The firm's sources of critical research matter are quite diversified and include special reports on the European and New York designer runway shows and the European and American designer color trend report.

TobéNext Forecasting

TobéNext Forecasting is a trend and color workbook published several times a year. It contains saleable themes eighteen to twenty-four months in advance of a season. Specifically geared to product and brand development, it includes color swatches. For Fall 2002, for example, the themes and trends featured were Coquette, Jock-e, and Cartoon Culture. Each trend was accompanied by color photos to illustrate the looks.

Outer Mongolia, for example, took its cue from the region between Russia and China and from films such as *Crouching Tiger, Hidden Dragon*. The key looks included a shearling vest with curly hair, ethnic mountain jacquard sweaters, Dr. Zhivago hats, and patchwork panel skirts and floral print insets.

Key to interpreting these trends are one-on-one client consultations with Tobé's market editors, who are considered authorities. They cover and report on a wide scope of the fashion market, from contemporary/better sportswear to children's wear, moderate sportswear, and dresses, contemporary/better dresses, intimate apparel, accessories, footwear, men's wear, outerwear, suits, swimwear, and furs.

DONEGER CREATIVE SERVICES

Doneger Creative Services is the fashion forecast division of The Doneger Group, a major buying office located on Fashion Avenue in New York City. This firm is on the cutting edge of fashion information and translates it into money-making concepts for product development and merchandising.

According to Abbey Doneger, president, "The right decisions must be made at the right time. You cannot be in the marketplace every day, visit every showroom, read every trade publication, and continually meet with industry leaders. You need a knowledgeable partner who feels the pulse of the industry, one who has the expertise and resources to help you generate greater sales, increase profits, gain market share, and realize your full potential. That partner is The Doneger Group."

Doneger Creative Services provides its member clients in the women's, men's, and children's industries with cutting-edge color and trend forecasting. Its broad scope of women's, men's, and children's fashion trend services includes:

- Color Forecasts
- Fashion Trend Forecasts
- Personal Forecast Consultations
- Newsletters
- Slide Presentations
- Slide Library/Slide Packs
- Workbooks

Merchandising Experts

Doing business internationally is an intricate business. The Doneger merchandising experts tap into the inside track by traveling to major fashion destinations coast to coast in the United States, and to London, Paris, Milan, Barcelona, and other hot spots in the world, such as St. Tropez, a trendy fishing village in the south of France.

They attend trade and fashion shows not only across town, but across the country and even around the globe, such as Premiere Vision in Paris, the Couture collections, and the Prêt-à-Porter shows in London, Paris, and Milan.

In the United States, these professionals attend trade shows and also may give the Doneger trend presentations at such exhibitions as Magic in Las Vegas, the International Fashion and Fabrics Exhibition, and the Coterie and Boutique shows in New York City.

These merchandise experts read every major trade and fashion publication, not only industry-related material, but the *Wall Street Journal, The New York Times,* the *Chicago Tribune,* and the *International Herald Tribune.* These watchdogs track a trend and see it develop on television shows such as *Sex and the City, Will and Grace,* and *Friends*, and at award events, such as the Oscars.

As a subscriber to Doneger Creative Services, clients have a world of retailing and merchandising tools, networking opportunities, and fashion forecasting information at their fingertips.

Creative Fashion Presentations

Every creative presentation, whether the focus is on color, fabric, or silhouette, is based on the "sell message" that enables clients to understand the trends that will help them succeed in today's retail environment. Color and lifestyle trends are presented three times a year in men's and women's wear and twice a year for children's wear.

Creative boards with trend themes feature image swipes and fashion illustrations. These are used in one-on-one consultations to show clients the color, print, fabric, and silhouette trends eighteen months before a selling season. A past presentation, "The Ladylike Trend," for example, took its cue from movie star icons, such as Grace Kelly, Vivian Leigh, and Audrey Hepburn. It was subdivided into the Well-Dressed Lady, the Sophisticated Lady, the Suburban Lady, the Sweet & Pretty Lady, and the 40s Swing Lady. Each theme was defined by color, fabric, and silhouette nuances that identified with a trend and lifestyle message.

Slide Shows

The Doneger Creative Services slide shows are by invitation and draw a large audience of industry guests. If not a client subscriber to Doneger, an individual is required to pay an entrance fee to attend the presentations.

Industry professionals, including buyers, fashion directors, designers, manufacturers, and retailers, rely on the intensely researched and prophetic Doneger trends as part of their market research. Appropriate fashion forecasting trends will then be edited and defined for each firm into marketable product development and buying decisions in fashion, accessories, or home furnishings.

As you can see, The Doneger Group is truly unique as both a major buying office and fashion forecast service. The firm offers its members services and opportunities in one convenient source to succeed in today's retail environment and prepare for the future.

COMMITTEE FOR COLOUR & TRENDS

The Committee for Colour & Trends (CCT) is an international forecasting service with a product specific focus that specializes in color and trend analysis for footwear and all accessory classifications.

INDUSTRY PROFILE 2-1 | David Wolfe

David Wolfe, one of the most dynamic authorities on fashion trends, is known for his exciting on target slide presentations, a "must see" for industry professionals.

Doneger Creative Services' Spring, Fall, and St. Tropez Summer audiovisual presentations are spearheaded by David Wolfe, Doneger's fashion guru and consummate fashion authority and showman, who provides a lively commentary describing the trends.

To develop current trend direction in visual form, Mr. Wolfe travels extensively on fashion photo shoots to create slide presentations of trends worldwide. He writes the script and with his creative team develops an overall theme and subtheme stories. These forward trends are then presented in the audiovisual presentation that highlights the season's color, print, texture, and fashion silhouettes in prophetic themes.

Case in point: In the Spring/Summer 2002 Forecast Slide Show, Wolfe's overview states "Re-Think the Way You Think About Trends" and alludes to the fact that trends come and go very quickly. They turn on a dime and rarely do they affect the entire industry as they once did.

The following themes projected The Big Picture idea:

The Big Picture Idea #l: Volume—Bigger shapes and silhouettes, wider cuts, and graceful flowing lines.

The Big Picture Idea #2: Contrast—Contrasting colors, contrasting textures, contrasting prints/patterns.

The Big Picture Idea #3: Exposure

The Big Picture Idea #4: Pre-plan and round out the theme subjects.

The report also includes V.I.F.s (Very Important Fabrics) and V.I.C.s (Very Important Colors).

For Fall 2004, the big picture focuses on "The Search for Fashion Intelligence in a Universe of Style Spam" and the splintering of the consumer population.

THE BIG PICTURE **FOR FALL 2004...** and Beyond

Presented by David Wolfe, Creative Director, Doneger Creative Services

THE SEARCH for FASHION INTELLIGENCE in a Universe of Style Spam
Style spam means style that pops up and we don't really want it.
Spam also means TMI... too much information, too much assortment, all directions at once.

SPLINTERED CONSUMER POPULATION
Connections Create Customers
Beehiving is the new behavioral pattern that makes small groups cling together.

IMPORTANT BEEHIVES:

Brand Buyers
Money in the bank... just waiting for China growth to resuscitate luxury brands.
Rare now, but still possible to initiate a new brand powerhouse such as Marc Jacobs.

Teen Tribes
Short attention span means need for fast turnover of trend-after-trend.
Important to communicate change quickly, maximize and move on.

Hub Drones
Simple, nondescript, comfortable, unisex wear-everywhere-wear.
Only growth area now is casualwear for women ages 50 - 64.

CLASSIC COP-OUTS
Replays with a twist as fashion begins to become polished again.
Traditional tailoring for classic items such as Chanel suit, Burberry raincoat.
Eternal items: ladybag, sweater, white shirt, tailored jacket.

STAR GAZERS
Celebrity worship continues as consumers emulate their movie/TV idols.
Fresh, younger, foreign, celebrities need to keep gristmill grinding out fashion role models.

MULTI-DIVERSITY means the END of the MASS MARKET MELTING POT

Multi-*Generational*
Boomer Power puts the over-50 consumer in the economic driver's seat.
Age-appropriate? No such thing anymore. Body appropriate is what matters.

Multi-*National*
Many groups: Asian, African-American, Russian.
Most important now! Latin... doubling, 70 million by 2025.

Multi-*Sexual*
Gays assimilated into mainstream... influencing new Metrosexuals.
Trend and designer brand awareness for new generations of male style consumers.

Multi-*Physical*
Now more acceptance of varying physical types (though thin is most desired).
Diet, yoga and sport influence design, fabric choice and end-use.

Multi-*Subcultural*
Renegade bands of consumers bound together by common cultural interests. Special needs.
Skate, surf, music, extreme sport, collectors, ebay-addicts, bookworms, travelers.

ACROSS CONSUMER CULTURES
FALL 2004 COLOR FORECAST

Changeable!
Dust Storms... grayed, soft, misted pale colors.
Snowstorms... lightened, whitened neutrals.
Dark Eclipses... heavily saturated deep hues.
Sunny Intervals... bright, bold, energizing eye-poppers.

FRICTION creates FASHION!
Extreme Opposites almost Obliterate the Middle Mainstream

Decadent/*Innocent*
Decadent continues to project oversexed images.
Black is the color of decadence.
Decadent materials include lace, leather and satin.
Innocent images are based on childlike naïveté, cartoons.
White and light pastels are the colors of innocence.
Innocent materials include sheers, denim, dainty prints, crisp wovens.

Modern/*Rustic*
Modernism means simplified forms for all aspects of dressing.
Modern materials include metallics, tech and non-wovens.
Graphic color combinations emulate modern abstract art.
Rustics are directly lifted from Mother Nature.
Wood, fur, tweed and plaids are rustic materials.
Rustic moods can be sophisticated or down-to-earth.

Simple/*Excess*
Simplicity divests design of all superfluous elements.
Simple, generic styles are timeless and universal.
Oversize clothing is simple and comfortable.
Excess exhibits extrovert, expensive, show-off style.
Lavish prints offer excessive artistry.
Excessories are the over-done accessories.

MANY LITTLE PICTURES add up to *THE BIG PICTURE for FALL 2004... and beyond!*

DONEGERCREATIVE*services*

463 Seventh Avenue · NY, NY · 10018 · 212.564.1266 · www.doneger.com   For Doneger Creative Services please phone 212.560.3721

The program for Wolfe's Fall 2004 presentation illustrates his clever choice of trend themes, such as "Teen Tribes" and "Hub Drones," and the thoroughness of his coverage.

This firm researches fashion and lifestyle trends and conducts customized consultations on a one-on-one basis that are personalized to meet a client's target audience. The audiovisual color and ready-to-wear overview provides insight into how ready-to-wear trends will affect the design of footwear, handbags, belts, hair accessories, watches, eyewear, and leather goods. CCT addresses fashions for the adult and junior customer, as well as all accessory classifications, from head to toe. Trend track presentations and reports are given seasonally for Spring and Fall.

This advance trend information is critical to the production of fashion accessories, which are merchandised in important (and expensive) retail real estate on the main floor of department stores, specialty stores, and boutiques.

The dates for CCT's forecast publications are:

Spring forecast issue: January of the preceding year

Spring confirmation issue: April of the preceding year

Fall forecast issue: July of the preceding year

Fall confirmation issue: October of the preceding year

CCT's format consists of committees whose members are professionals in accessories merchandise classifications. At strategic meetings, these specialists contribute information especially organized for designers, merchandisers, manufacturers, wholesalers, importers, buying offices, and retailers.

For example, consider that leather is a major material for fashion accessories. As a result, CCT addresses this classification for industry subscribers. Twice a year, CCT publishes a *Leather Colour, Textures and Materials Forecast Guide*. The color story is swatched in Pantone textile chips of actual leathers developed in Europe with different tanners and nonleathers.

The focus is on shades and materials applicable to footwear and accessories complementing incoming ready-to-wear trends.

Publication dates for the guide are:

Spring/Summer issue: January of the preceding year

Fall/Winter issue: July of the preceding year

CCT's *Fashion Facts Folio* newsletter, a comprehensive report of fashion and accessory trends, keeps retail clients in the loop of what is hot. It also features a calendar of important accessory trade fairs, including Accessories Circuit, FFANY Shoe Expo, WSA Footwear, Las Vegas, Accessories Market Week, and JA Jewelry.

THE TREND CURVE™

The Trend Curve specializes in forecasting trends for the home furnishings industries, which represents a wide range of furniture, home, and lifestyle products. "Even if it is perfectly designed, color can make or break a product," says Michelle Lamb, senior editor.

To guide firms in the right direction, *The Trend Curve* provides a comprehensive look at the most up to date projections of the key directions that will impact business for manufacturers, retailers, interior designers, custom home builders, and anyone else interested in the future of home furnishing trends.

FutureHome 2004™ presents the details of the most significant home furnishing trends and explains how important they will be for the next twelve to fourteen months. It includes a written color forecast (by color family as well as by palette), plus a detailed design report covering both major and emerging themes. The report is packed with more than one hundred full-color photographs that will help businesses recognize trends and implement them in product and design decisions.

Each spring, Michelle Lamb and her staff of editorial correspondents travel to European trade fairs to search for clues to future trends for the U.S. market. She writes with a depth of understanding that comes from years of experience in home furnishings and color forecasting.

The Trend Curve newsletter, published six times a year, includes information on major markets and trade fairs, such as Heimtextil, Paperworld, Christmasworld, Ambiente, and Domotex.

As a recognized spokesperson for this industry Ms. Lamb is also called upon to speak at the High Point Furniture Market, the American Lighting Association Conference held in Las Vegas, and the La-Z-Boy's Furniture Galleries Conference in Las Vegas.

WORTH GLOBAL STYLE NETWORK

Worth Global Style Network (WGSN) is in a class by itself as one of the first worldwide on-line news and fashion forecast services. It offers subscribers in the fashion and style industries immediate access to all aspects of style information on international color, fabric, fashion, and cutting-edge trends.

Founded in 1998, WGSN is now one of the most dynamic Internet business-to-business ventures. In addition to its commercial site, www.wgsn.com, for industry subscribers, WGSN also offers a student initiative, www.wgsn-edu.com, to which all students with proper identification may subscribe.

The WGSN news and information service is a powerful online business tool created to aid and inspire every organization involved in the fast-moving and interrelated style industries. WGSN counts among its clients many of the world's leading names in fashion, retailing, and manufacturing. The service is targeted at buyers, designers, manufacturers, retailers, marketing companies, and industry observers. WGSN is also used by many other related industries that benefit from up-to-date

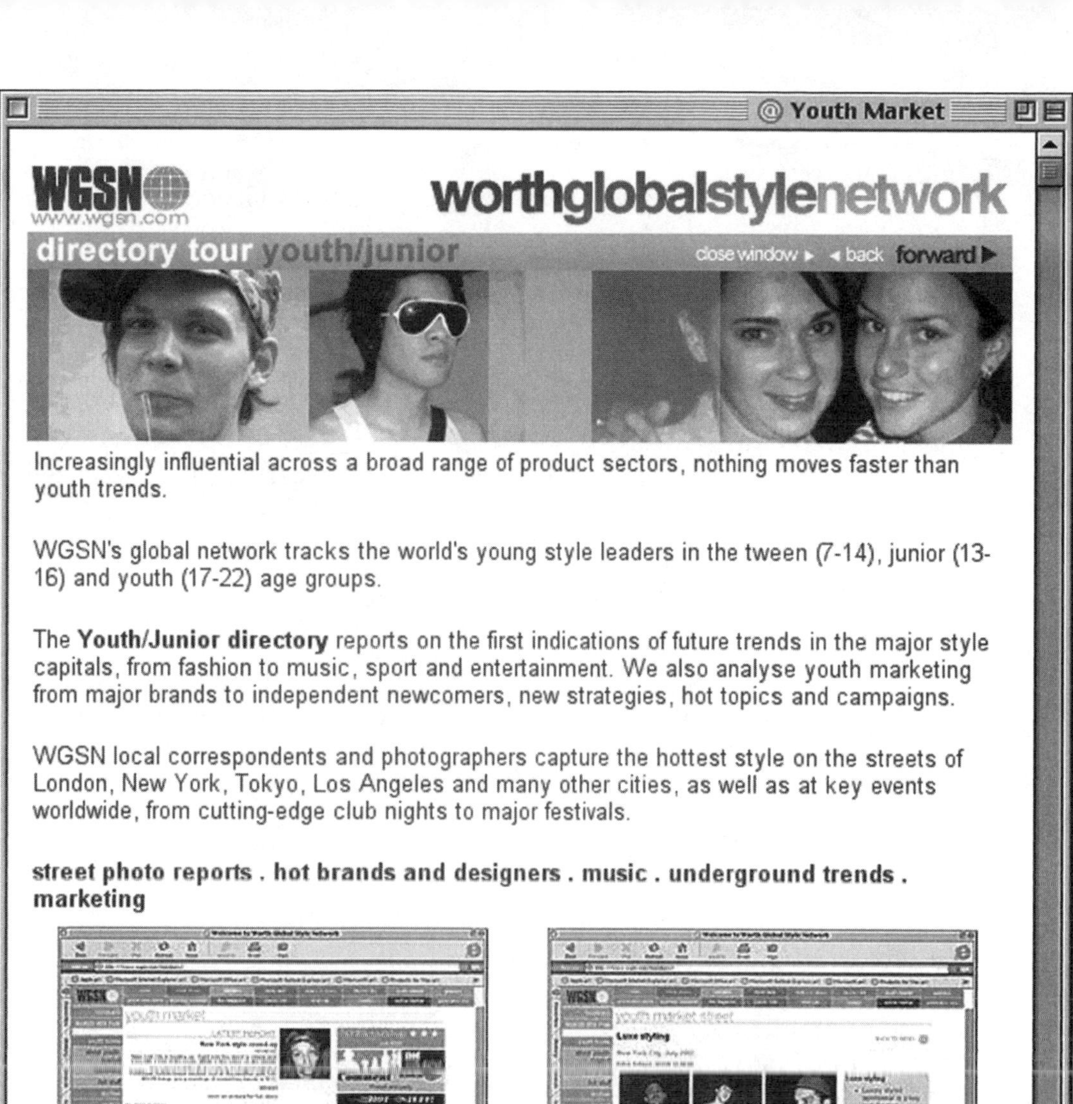

WGSN's clients can find the most up-to-date information on international trends in all areas of fashion. Its youth market directory reports the latest styles in the major cities of the world, including brands, designers, and on-the-street photos.

information on emerging trends, such as General Motors and Motorola.

Navigate the Site

Subscribers worldwide can easily navigate the site for fashion news and trends, watch runway shows taking place in the fashion capitals of New York, London, Paris, and Milan, view store windows, and see what women are wearing on the streets in twenty cities. Within hours of a designer catwalk show, the service can broadcast hundreds of pictures to its subscribers.

The site also offers reports on the marketing strategies of key retailers, such as H&M, the cheap-but-chic fashion chain from Sweden. Designer access to season colors and an extensive textile section shows fabrics along with vendors and phone numbers.

Subscriber Comments

Customer comments say it all. "WGSN helps us to be wiser about the current industry trends and developments. It again underscores the power of the Internet today in providing real time information that in the past would have taken days if not weeks to obtain," says Robert Triefus, corporate vice president of Giorgio Armani. "The catwalk overview is particularly useful. I can get graphic representation of a specific garment idea which can then be shared with the designers," writes Mark Hopkins, ladieswear buyer for Marks & Spencer.

Just a click of a computer mouse links subscribers to what is hip on the streets of London, enables them to view fashion, children's wear, or interior trends, or find information on what is happening in the youth market. Although WGSN's information cannot totally take the place of actually shopping in the markets or trade shows, it allows for cost-cutting measures. For instance, in the site's Trade Show section, fabric previews and swatches are posted for major fabric shows such as Première Vision.

The WGSN Team

Based at WGSN headquarters in London and at offices in New York, Los Angeles, Paris, Madrid, Frankfurt, and Tokyo, more than two hundred designers, reporters, and technicians cooperate closely with a dedicated network of photographers and research contributors around the world. Hard facts, news, reviews, and inspiration from top industry players worldwide bring more than 350,000 pages of invaluable style information to a subscriber's fingertips.

Trade Terminology

Audiovisuals
Brand positioning
Committee for Colour & Trends (CCT)
Concept garments/Sample garments
Doneger Creative Services
Haute Couture
Hot items
On-line business tools
Prêt-à-porter
Product development
Promostyl
Research
Street scene reports
Tobé
Trade fairs
Trend forecasters
Trend predictions
Trend reports
Worth Global Style Network (WGSN)

READING 2-1 | Rat Pack BY DAVID CAPLAN

NEW YORK—Whether it's "The Mashed Potato," "The Bird," "The Bug" or another finger-snapping, hip-shifting dance routine that the hair-ratting cast of "Hairspray" performs, costume designer William Ivey Long has a suitable—and appropriately campy—ensemble.

But for the musical version of "Hairspray," which begins in previews Thursday night and opens Aug. 15 at Manhattan's Neil Simon Theatre, the fashions differ from those featured in the 1988 John Waters film, which is set in Baltimore in 1962.

"When I do what I call 'previously owned vehicles,' meaning from a film, I ask the director if we are going to be inspired by, or should we not look at, the movie," says Long, who has earned Tony Awards for his work on "The Producers," "Nine" and "Crazy For You." "There was a general sense of 'no, we are different from the film, but we want you to look at it.' So I purchased the movie and I watched it a total of once and I thought, 'OK, I have committed this to memory. If I watch it twice, I will not be able to be creative.' "

Long says there is a key difference between the cinematic and theatrical versions of "Hairspray," the latter of which is directed by Jack O'Brien and choreographed by Jerry Mitchell: "For the movie, I think John wanted to be real; we're being surreal," he explains.

For the musical, he created approximately 300 pieces of clothing, footwear and accessories.

"I'm starting from [the movie], but I think we've gone quite far," he adds. "I've added color—characters have different color schemes. Velma Von Tussle has metallics and Motormouth Mabel is in purples and golds, for example."

Long's "hands-down favorite" scene to work on was "Welcome Sixties," during which dowdy homemaker Edna Turnblad, played by Harvey Fierstein, receives a fashion makeover at Mr. Pinky's Hefty Hideaway boutique. Edna visits the shop with her daughter Tracy, played by Marissa Jaret Winokur, an overweight socially shunned teen branded a "hair-hopper" by those who scoff at her ratted hair-dos.

"[Edna] gains confidence; she also changes her clothing, her hair and her fingernails—but not her shape," Long says, laughing.

Color-coding is integral to the costuming of the show's villainesses, Amber Von Tussle and her mother, Velma, who match each other in every scene. "But the daughter is in more femmy girl looks, while the mother will be in a sort of tailored metallic brocade suit or dress," says Long. "So metallic means villain in this show."

Long also cherishes a piece of wisdom imparted by Waters about the villains: "He says when these women went shopping at the grocery store, they dressed like they were going to a ball at Versailles. So all you have to do is hear John say that once, and you go 'OK, she's copying Jackie Kennedy.' Now add 10 details to this pared silhouette and it's like, how do you ruin it? So I have ruffles and buttons and I even have ruffles around buttons. I have kick pleats and there is a nice box pleat inside the kick pleat."

Long sought design inspiration by flipping through the pages of publications from the late Fifties and early Sixties, including

Jet magazine and *Good Housekeeping,* as well as Montgomery Ward and Sears, Roebuck & Co. catalogs. He also cut out photos and sketched over each image, creating a series of collages he describes as "sort of Rauchenberg," depicting the outfits of each scene.

When he signed on as costume designer for the musical, Long bonded with Waters over the duo's similar lineage, which also helped the designer prepare for the gig.

"My mother is from Baltimore, so I think once you have any Baltimore connection in your blood, you bond," says Long, who was raised in North Carolina. "And I must say, I grew up on that outrageousness."

Source: *Women's Wear Daily,* July 17, 2002, p. 6. Courtesy of Fairchild Publications, Inc.

READING 2-2 | Trend Spotters Play It Safe BY VALERIE SECKLER

NEW YORK—Call it trend spotting's reality check.

True, it's a premise that, at first blush, seems something of a contradiction in terms. After all, aren't most trends supposed to have an edgy, fantastical element; a romantic hue, or at least a sense of cynical nihilism about them?

Whereas so many of them did so as recently as two years ago, the trends driving today's fashion and lifestyle options are becoming anchored more firmly in the reality of people's day-to-day lives. That's because marketers are having a harder time capturing the fancy of a finicky consumer, one whose shifting set of priorities has only accelerated further in the year since Sept. 11. And at the same time, those businesses are coming under increasing pressure to produce bottomline profits from virtually all of the trends they serve up. It is no longer enough to simply stir some excitement or augment sales.

The consumer's evolving mind-set and corporate America's new sobriety have prompted a hasty retreat from the days of hunting for fashions and lifestyle trends so cool that almost no one had ever heard of them. Many of those trends were unable to create demand and drive business. It's not that cool has died; rather, industry's search for the offbeat increasingly is being grounded by a new requirement: the addition of hard-core market research to project its commercial potential. This, in turn, means marketers are in the throes of redefining cool trends as those that are, by and large, less esoteric, safer and, in the end, more broadly appealing.

"When trying to identify trends, a group tends to be a lot more valuable than an outstanding, leading-edge person, whether it's the edgiest kid in a high school or Chloë Sevigny—people who are just too out there for most Americans," advised Irma Zandl, president of market researcher Zandl Group. For example, she noted: "In trying to find trends for high schoolers, it's better to track the most popular kids [rather than the edgiest ones] who shop at stores such as Abercrombie & Fitch. To have broad commercial appeal, trends need to percolate from the mainstream."

Forming the foundation of such marketable trends is data being gleaned through traditional methods, like surveying consumers and analyzing census data and focus group sessions, as well as via anthropological approaches, many of which provide the illuminating one-on-one contact with their subjects that's favored by trend scouts and analysts, as well as their clients. The latter include conducting: "crib" chats, a take on "MTV Cribs," in which marketers videotape teens talking about the things in their bedrooms; studies of closets and medicine cabinets, affording people a chance to chat about their wardrobes and personal care items at home, where they choose and use those items daily; slumber parties with teens and shop-alongs with a variety of consumers, in order to observe product preferences and shopping behaviors; and video and Web-cam recordings of people using products.

"Now, trend spotting is about going to fashion shows to find out what is going to sell," offered The Doneger Group's creative director, David Wolfe. "Before, it was about business with a capital 'F': spotting what was fabulous at fashion shows. It has become more bottom-line oriented, less creative, more challenging, more fun."

For now, though, consultants and researchers are playing out that notion in a range of ways to clients in search of a hot, marketable trend.

Zandl, for one, says the businesses she's dealing with are looking for profitable sales of $10 million to $100 million annually from mining a particular fashion or lifestyle trend, which are dynamics, she noted, that typically last at least five years and often twice that long. Zandl cited khakis and baggy hip-hop looks as examples of styles that have recently enjoyed no less than a 10-year run.

In contrast, trend analyst Edie Weiner, principal of Weiner Edrich Brown, said she and her colleagues have been identifying six major themes per quarter, or 24 emerging trends per year, for the past 32 years. "We don't milk a trend for 10 years," Weiner said of a process in which she and two colleagues regularly analyze and synthesize information from 60 or so mostly monthly publications, to produce 60–90 abstracts, from which the half-dozen themes are drawn each quarter. The titles scoured range from Mother Jones and the Utne Reader to the Harvard Business Review and The National Review, and from The Economist to New Times.

"Coming up with six themes a quarter is ball-breaking work, but our view is that these themes are a motion picture, not a snapshot," Weiner said of the grueling research. It's a process used by Weiner Edrich Brown to identify four primary dynamics:

- Is there anything new here? "That's a really tough one when you've been in business 32 years," Weiner admitted.
- Pattern recognition, or the connection of seemingly unrelated trends to fill in pieces of a puzzle. For example, a new technology and changing demographic may combine to create a new group, like digital grannies—parents of the oldest baby boomers, who often are more interested than those boomers are in the Internet.

- The surprising source, or a person who is unlikely to take a particular stand, such as a doctor who endorses a high-fat diet.
- The glaring contradiction, that is, anything well expressed and well documented that contradicts what Weiner Edrich Brown had been telling its clients thus far.

As more and more trend advisers embrace an increasingly research-driven approach, the phrase "trend spotting" has, ironically, taken on a negative connotation for some, such as Wendy Liebmann, president of retail and marketing consultant WSL Strategic Retail. Instead, she insisted, it's all about consumer research versus an allegiance to the cult of celebrity. "We tend to shy away from the term, as it has developed such a bad reputation over the past four or five years," Liebmann stated. "Trend spotting suggests the notion of celebrities as kingpins of marketing, but for us, it's all about talking with and/or watching the shopper, and measuring changes in quantitative and qualitative ways.

"The only thing we are doing differently now is we are listening to consumers in a quantitative way more frequently—monthly or bimonthly," Liebmann continued. "The process needs to be ongoing in order to see how people have behaved over the past five to 10 years. If we don't understand that context, we could be leading people down a garden path." For example, Liebmann said, WSL may begin to ask consumers if reading the allegations over Martha Stewart's financial activities is having a spillover effect on how her products are viewed. And, if it has, perhaps WSL would ask if the phenomenon has had an affect on their trust in other branded or celebrity-endorsed items and whether more effort should be focused on playing up a company's heritage.

One who hasn't shrunk away from the trend-spotting phrase is author Richard Laermer, whose study of the practice, entitled "Trend Spotting," was published this March by Perigee. However, Laermer has joined in the chorus about the negative influence of the cult of celebrity. And he's taking the notion a step further, suggesting that the celebrity influence is now having a detrimental effect on the business of fashion. "When I tried to get people to talk about fashion, they tended to want to talk about other things, like economics, politics, technology," Laermer said in relating his experience while interviewing approximately 100 people for his book.

"It seems like Hollywood has cheapened fashion's image," he continued. "It's almost like everything is an eyeroller, these days, because the celebrity thing tends to be about a J.Lo, a Jennifer Aniston, rather than the luxurious association of Hollywood and fashion in the Thirties and Forties. Now, the [public's] mimicry is not wholehearted."

Doneger's Wolfe took the thought a step further, telling Laermer in "Trend Spotting" that entertainment's influence on fashion is bad because "nothing is being originally created for the movies. Clothes are bought off the rack and put together by stylists. Those clothes are a year old. That is why so much of fashion is at a standstill."

And in an interview, Wolfe expanded the thought, remarking: "We are not in a time of creativity or originality. We are in a time of marketing. A lot of looks are derivative; we are in a time of recycling. Gallagher's, a used-magazine-and-book store in the East Village, is a huge resource for designers."

Wolfe's observation hints at a minor theme sounded by trend analysts and market researchers: Companies may be playing it safer with trends but there is the peril of playing it too safe, and thus becoming boring to the consumer. There is still a window open—if a narrower one—for, say, the $70 candle that will make someone feel great about their home environment, or music by Detroit thrash rocker Andrew W.K., whose CD cover portrays him looking dazed after bashing his nose into a cinder block. That more extreme CD was recently highlighted in "True View," a trend report published by Northbrook, Ill.-based Teen Research Unlimited, which generally has been veering more mainstream, noted the firm's trend manager, Rob Callender.

Still, today's climate portends it's the Vanilla Cokes of the world that are destined to be businesses' bell ringers rather than some edgy drink no one has ever heard of, Zandl said. Indeed, she estimated the combined volume produced by Vanilla Coca-Cola and Diet Vanilla Coca-Cola this year will be close to $1 billion.

"Its success is not a surprise, given vanilla's popularity," Zandl said. "Should Coca-Cola have done Blood Orange Coke or Ginseng Coke because they're more edgy? They wouldn't have sold, because hardly anyone's heard of those flavors," she projected. "Meanwhile, Vanilla Coke is currently outselling Diet Coke."

Source: *Women's Wear Daily*, August 21, 2002, p. 8. Courtesy of Fairchild Publications, Inc.

3

Color Forecasting

When a designer sketches a new shoe, a manufacturer prepares a seasonal line, or a retailer programs its merchandise mix, the first and most important decision is color selection. Flip through any fashion catalog, and you will see how the names of colors become more complex each day. The language of color and its psychological impact are prime reasons why shoppers at retail respond to a product in a positive or negative way.

THE INFLUENCE OF COLOR

Why is color so important? Because the ultimate consumer is quick to decide on color. If consumers like the color, the product is a giant step closer to the cash register; if they do not, the same item is a giant step closer to a markdown. Designers, manufacturers, and retailers cannot afford to be wrong about color selection. While cosmetic companies rely strongly on color names to sell their products, the sales success of other classifications of merchandise, from fashion to home furnishings, industrial products, and automobiles, is also based on the color.

For this reason, color marketers develop a palette and search for creative names to identify colors that will tap into a consumer's emotional makeup. Think about it. If colors were merely named red, brown, or green, which would consumers choose? The way we refer to color has to do with status. If color has a creative name, the consumers are more willing to pay more for it.

Look at a few examples. One season fashion color names such as Espresso, Mud Brown, and Mocha reflect America's penchant for coffee. Another time, Feng Shui influenced a color palette theme by evoking society's interest in ancient philosophies. At cosmetic counters, color romances the customer with wine names, such as Beaujolais, Chianti, and Merlot. Paint colors go ethnic with names that suggest an "Out of Africa" inspiration.

Color palettes for the American market may differ from those for the international marketplace. Color is based on light and New York City light, for example, reflects a brighter, more intense palette because of the enormous amount of sunlight. By contrast, European cities have an overcast sky with less intensive light. This results in colors that are not as sharp. Therefore, people look right wearing Loden. It sells well in Europe but not in the United States, because it does not look right here.

THE COLOR FORECASTING COMPANIES

To demystify color, the color forecasting companies are in the business of determining which colors will be the big trend and best sellers in showroom collections and at retail. For a list of the major color forecasting companies, see Table 3-1.

Color forecasting companies are in business to sell color trends and predictions to a large client base of product end users. The intensive research required to produce color cards and trend color boards is time consuming and expensive. It involves every aspect of design, references to historical textiles and fashion, as well as research on current sources of inspiration, such as culture, architecture, movies, television, and environmental and political issues.

When military spending increases, greater emphasis is placed on military colors and military styling. People react to it by dressing in a military theme. Camouflage is a continuation of this theme.

TABLE 3-1	MAJOR COLOR FORECASTING COMPANIES
Color Association of the United States (CAUS)	
Color Box	
Color by Design Options	
Color Marketing Group	
Color Portfolio	
Creative Solutions	
Design Options	
Huepoint	
Pantone Inc.	
The International Color Authority (ICA)	
Trend Curve Colors™	
View on Colour	

For contact information for these companies, see Appendix B.

Color Cards/Presentations

Creative color presentations are conducted eighteen months to one year before the season being projected; they come out twice a year in the Spring/Summer and Fall/Winter for women's and children's wear. Some services put out a third forecast of colors for the holiday/resort season. Individual color directives may be given separately for the tween/youth, men's wear, and home furnishings and hard-line industries. Thus, mills, manufacturers, and product developers have sufficient time to consult with a color forecasting company and evaluate the color direction in which their company will go for the season.

Although color cards and creative boards provide an overall view of color trends, color consultancy is usually customized to address a client's specific price point and market. In addition, slide show presentations may highlight silhouette and color trends.

INDUSTRY PROFILE 3-1 | Margaret Walch

Margaret Walch is an international spokesperson for color standards and forecasting trends. Here, she is surrounded by seasonal color presentation boards.

Margaret Walch, director of Color Association of the United States (CAUS), has not only spearheaded the phenomenal growth of color standards throughout diverse industries, but she is a highly sought after spokesperson.

"The reputation of CAUS in the marketplace is one of high color integrity," notes Ms. Walch. "Major firms rely upon the CAUS forecast services as the quintessential reference and color authority. In early November 2002, for example, Centro de Moda, a fashion exposition in Rio de Janeiro, Brazil, invited me to present the American forecast colors for the Spring/Summer 2003 season."

With archives dating back to 1915, the year CAUS was established, longevity makes this firm one of the most reliable sources of color trends for the American markets. An index of color names, also dating to 1915, is available for research. This historical color information includes millinery, hosiery, shoe, leather and accessory color cards, and U.S. military standards.

Ms. Walch's no-nonsense approach to color stems from a long tenure as director in which she has witnessed vast changes in color standardization. "Before World War I no standards existed for military colors," she says. "CAUS is the depository that holds the U.S. Armed Forces colors, approved and accepted by the Institute of Heraldry, U.S. Army, as being in accordance with the standards on file in that office."

CAUS is a membership-based organization. As such, its forecasts are determined by design and fashion-and-textile industry professionals in a time-proven process of color consensus. "Our members, therefore, can rest assured that each forecast represents a reliable projection of future colors," notes Ms. Walch.

For the latest edition of an Activewear Color Card, the typical Activewear Color Committee consists of professionals recognized by the industry, such as Monika Tilley, chair, Monika Tilley Ltd.; Roseann Forde, INVISTA (formerly DuPont Textiles & Interiors); Katherine Gordy-Novakavic, Cotton Inc., James Siewert, Celanese Acetate, Phil Shroff, Solutia, and a guest contributor, Noris Solano, Brookwood Co., Inc.

"The application of each color forecast to specific markets, regionally, nationally and globally, is available to each member on a one-on-one basis with the CAUS staff."

The Color Association issues seasonal fashion forecasts in three categories—women's, men's, and children's—as well as an annual forecast in the field of environmental/interior design. Past issues can be reviewed online at www.colorassociation.com.

Color forecasts are released twenty months in advance of a season. In apparel, the two seasonal forecasts are displayed in color yarns or fabrics; in interior/environmental design, the yearly forecast is shown in silk-screen paper and fabric.

Membership in CAUS provides subscribers with additional benefits, such as discounts on all publications, including *The Standard Color Reference of America, Living Colors, The Color Compendium, The Activewear Color Card,* and the *U.S. Armed Forces Color Card.* "CAUS conducts monthly seminars to keep members informed of new developments," adds Ms. Walch. "The CAUS bimonthly newsletter is issued to members and up to five individuals with a member's company. The newsletter reports on the Association's forecasts, digests all seminars and keeps members informed of exhibitions and events in New York City that are relevant to future color design."

CAUS offers student memberships. Contact CAUS at www.colorassociation.com.

HUEPOINT

"No one system can fill all your needs. A designer may subscribe to two or three services to reinforce color information," notes Amy Aspland of Huepoint, Inc. "Designers don't have the time to do a lot of early research needed to steer their company's product lines in the right direction and build sales. Color forecasting is the answer."

Huepoint's color forecast for Spring 2004 illustrates color trends for its themes with more than just photographs. The box includes test tube vials with actual colored yarns.

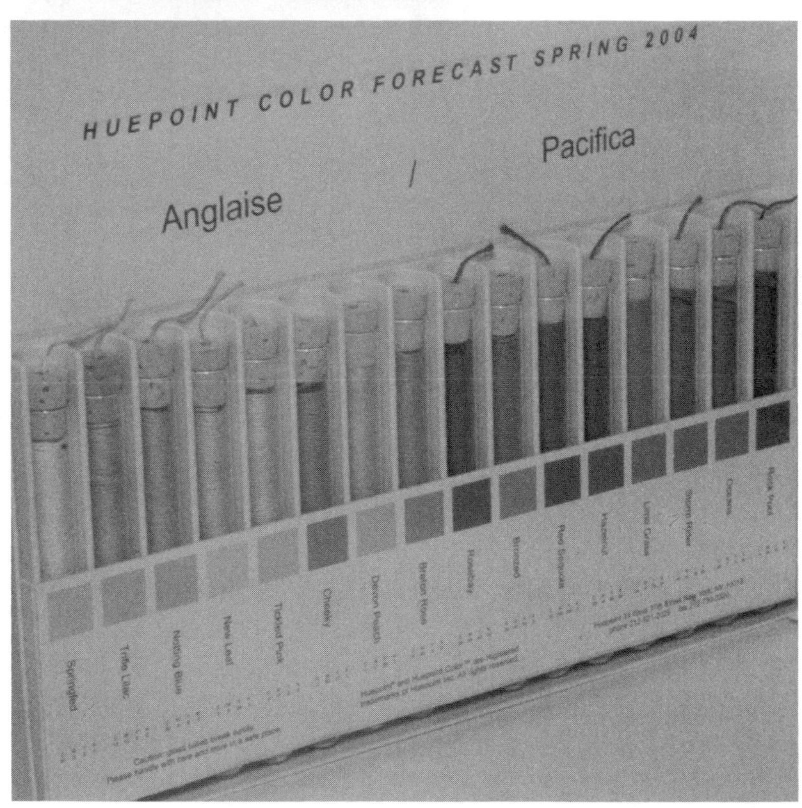

Huepoint's Macks and Wellies creative board is a good example of a themed board.

Huepoint's colors are presented on natural fiber yarns that are encased in test tubes, which suggest a more scientific approach to color trends. The firm aims to make its seasonal color standards as clear as possible for applications in the men's, women's, children's, and sportswear markets. The test tubes are showcased in a double box containing thirty-two test tubes with color names such as Tickled Pink, New Leaf, and Devon Peach, to name a few.

Huepoint believes that there never is enough color and has developed an extensive color library that contains more than 2,000 colors from the firm's archives, which are in stock at its offices. The Color Store changes seasonally and is filled with yarns handpicked from color selections around the world. Here, designers and product development teams can sit in a quiet workspace and develop their color programs.

Creative color presentations not only include the test tube color ranges, but also creative image boards that visually tell the color story in themes, such as Macks and Wellies, Vagabond, Sweet Chic, and Vintage Modern. Each color story features a color palette that is associated with the theme and photo images that illustrate the source of inspiration. Colorways are also included in combinations of two or three colors to provide design inspiration.

For example, in Macks and Wellies, the story reads, "Fly fishing colors, wet from trough streams and thunderstorms are Fall's strong base colors. We know we'll wear them for boots to bottom weights and their all-terrain appeal goes straight from authentic sporting gear to urban basics. Combine our three indigos with Macks and Wellies colors for newly minted rugged gear. We've added Hunting Red to this palette, because these deep, dark reds just look better every season."

THE COLOR BOX

The Color Box began business in the late 1970s with Jane Resnick's Color Box, which formerly housed colors on movable yarn pompoms in a series of palette stories accompanied by a written report. Today, the firm produces color notebooks in a ringbinder format that present an overview of trends and color palettes in braided wands of color. It has also expanded its service to include a one-stop menu of trend forecasting and computer-aided design (CAD) for its worldwide clients. The Color Box not only researches the global marketplace, but also advises international clients on what to sell to the American market.

Creative trend boards are industry specific for men's, women's, and children's wear. Meetings are custom coordinated for each client. A theme is created to illustrate the trend message, while additional boards pull the trend forward with subtheme titles and images that convey the trend. The Color Box's library of more than 3,000 colors is indexed and market specific from kids to juniors, women's and men's apparel to home furnishings.

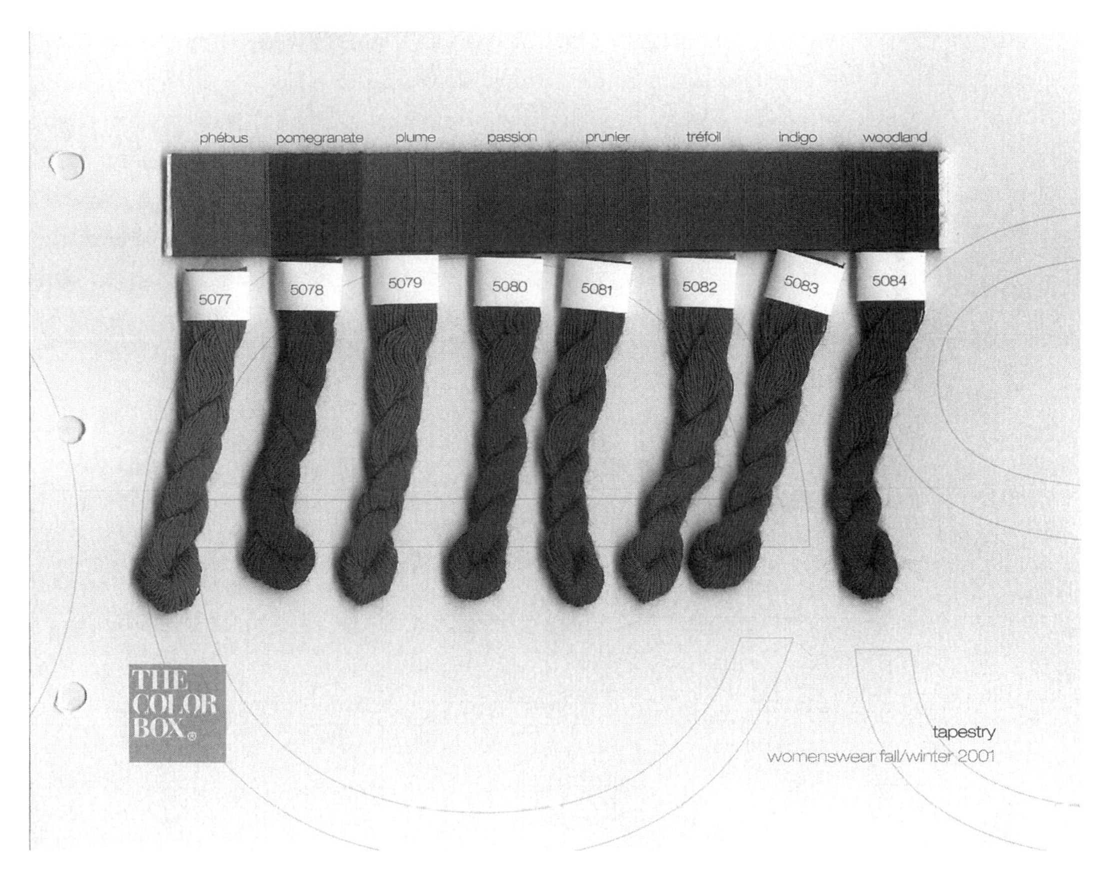

The Color Box's innovative presentation of braided wands of color. These samples are for a Fall/Winter 2001 women's wear collection, entitled Tapestry.

The trend notebooks with illustrations, photos, and magazine swipes present trend direction and report on color, fabrics, and silhouettes that provide clients with documentation on moneymaking ideas. The men's wear trend notebook, for example, highlights what is happening in prints and knits and features design concepts in the different product categories, from shirts and slacks to outerwear and casual apparel.

Timing of Color Box presentations depends on the industry. Mills, catalogs, and costume jewelry subscribers that must make color decisions earlier than other fashion industries attend presentations approximately eighteen months ahead of the season. In general, the manufacturers and designers view presentations a year ahead: For the year 2006, they will attend presentations in December 2004.

In addition to its color library, the firm has installed the CAD Service Studio to give clients yet another way to individualize lines. The CAD facility develops prints for computer interpretation. Old antique swatches of fabric, hand-painted designs, florals, abstracts, and pictorials can be scanned and the repeat pattern configured.

COLOR PORTFOLIO

Color Portfolio tracked the selling pattern of color from fiber to mill and through all other industries. The firm kept tabs on the influences of color from such diverse sources as the stock market, the Grammys, the Oscars, and MTV. All these impact future business.

Carole D'Arconte, owner of Creative Solutions, is former owner of Color Portfolio. She says, "If you need colors for the prom dress market you have to know where the trend is coming from. You have to be open to everything. Practical observation is a must. Whether at a football game, movie, theatre or any other entertainment venue, trends emerge right before our eyes. Color and trend stories at retail must also entertain and pull the consumer in to check the merchandise."

The firm's research and analysis of color and trends was digested and mixed into homogeneous color and silhouette stories in several products.

- Trend Posters, such as trend boards, featured colorful photographs that illustrated important fashion trends. *The Trend Report* provided individual breakdowns of men's, women's, kids, junior's, young men's, golf, swim apparel trends, style details, color, and color combinations.
- The forecast featured six merchandise color groups directed toward outerwear, bottom weights, and better sportswear.

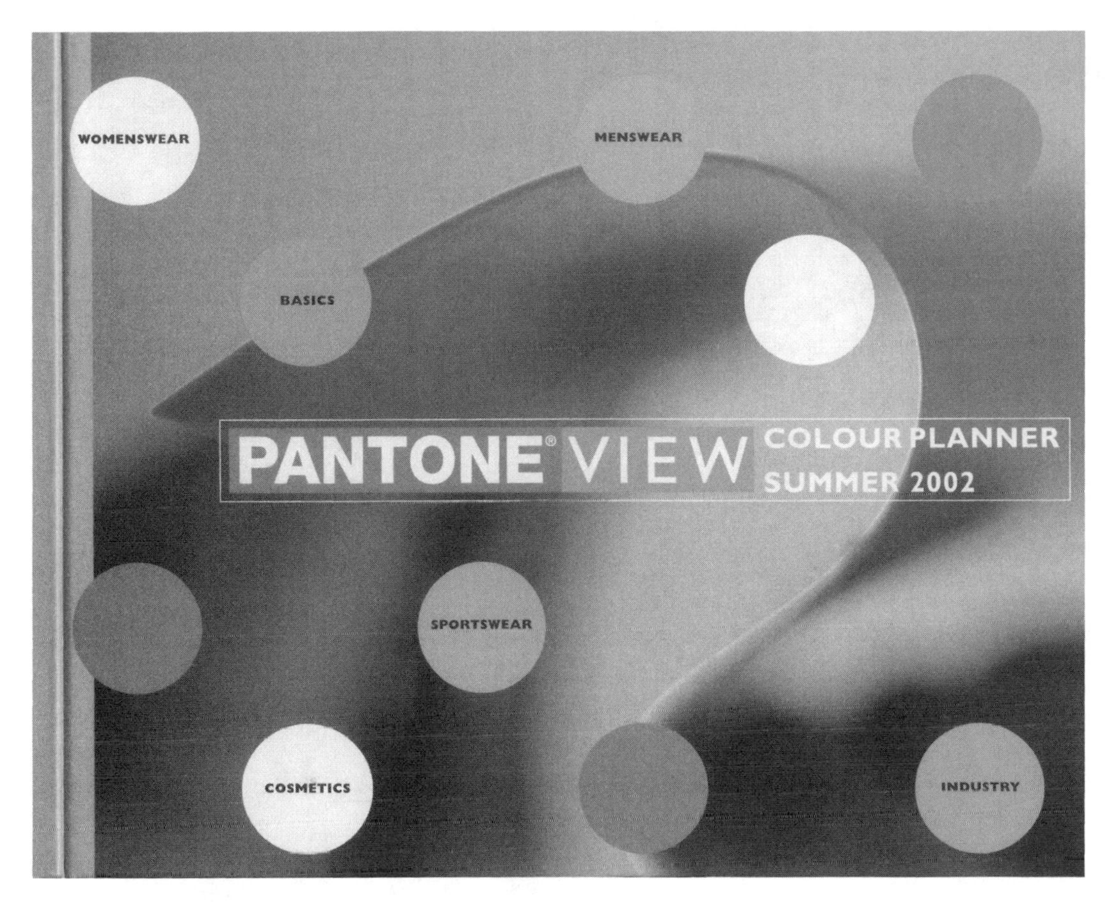

Above and next two pages: *The Pantone® View Colour Planner for Summer 2002 tied together Pantone's definitive color system with its forecasting trends. In the Bliss theme, for example, separates with striped patterns in cottons and iridescent poplins are presented in such shimmering colors as meadow mist, starlight blue, and sweet lavender.*

- The Youth/Active report had high-impact colors for young men, juniors, and tweens apparel and activewear and swimwear.

In addition to its domestic clients, Color Portfolio also engineered global color trend information for foreign firms who wanted to merchandise their lines in the United States.

PANTONE, INC.

For the past 40 years, Pantone, Inc., the globally recognized authority on color and a provider of professional color standards, has created a unified language of color communication

BLISS • FABRICS / PATTERNS

Bliss

Candy madrasi

Side seams

Big is beautiful

The spice route

FABRICS this is mainly a shirt, separates and knitwear look. All eyes on new shirtings in very fine cottons and iridescent poplins with a generally fresh and clean appearance. Separates favour hopsack type wovens and flammé cottons in wool/silk/linen blends. When mixed with polyamide, the touch gets a little drier - more natural, less techno.

PATTERNS a lot of stripes - rainbow, vertical, horizontal and diagonal, giant or fine. Checks are also there, but usually on a large tablecloth scale.

Photography: David Burton

54 COLOUR PLANNER SUMMER 2002

for every industry professional to understand. If a firm is producing a collection in Hong Kong, you just can't say, "Make the garments geranium pink." That color may have no meaning—or a different meaning—in Hong Kong than it does in the United States. That is why Pantone's color system is the primary source for color reference that ensures consistency across worldwide production channels. Every color is identified by a unique number; specify the number, and you know exactly what color you will see in your product.

In partnership with the National Retail Federation (NRF), Pantone will now be mapping its copyrighted numbering sys-

tem to NRF's Standard Color Codes for general merchandise and apparel products. This will bridge existing business processes from text-based to Web-enabled ones. Pantone's inclusion of the NRF Standard Color Codes in the Pantone Textile Color System® will also better serve the customers, as it will improve the way vendors monitor sales and tract trends.

Pantone Textile Color System

The Pantone Textile Color System is unique in its ability to speak across both vendor and product lines and is used by apparel and home furnishings/interior design professionals around the world to select, specify, control, and communicate color from design through production for fashion and in the home. Available in both paper and cotton formats, each chip or swatch is numerically referenced to the Pantone Textile Color System. This system of communicating color enables fast and more accurate communication, resulting in a higher rate of on-time delivery and fashion-right merchandise. To date, the Pantone Textile Color System has been hailed as the ultimate color authority used by professionals, trade shows, and the editorial press around the world.

Pantone View Colour Planner

Teaming up with Metropolitan Publishing BV, publishers of *Textile View* and *Viewpoint* magazines, Pantone's first color forecast, the Pantone® View Colour Planner, made its debut for Spring/Summer 2002. Using the language of the Pantone Textile Color System, this is a comprehensive color forecasting publication offering color and trend direction for men's, women's, and activewear markets, including accessories, shoes, cosmetics, and industrial design.

Colors are segmented to key color directives, fabric viewpoints are highlighted, and palette overviews and color harmonies are provided. As all forecasted information is designated by the individual Pantone color number, the Colour Planner allows the Pantone Textile Color System to be used in a directional way for a seamless process of choosing and specifying color based on forecasted information.

Through Pantone's focus on color trends and forecasting and its background and expertise with color, Pantone, Inc. and its Pantone Textile Color System are recognized by the industry as the definitive color standard. Pantone currently markets and sells its professional products in sixty-five countries worldwide.

DESIGN OPTIONS

Fran Sude says, "As an ex-retailer I understand that it is not only important to provide the right seasonal colors, but also to make sure the right color is delivered to the stores at the right time. This is not the case in other color services. There are many companies with extremely creative people, but there is quite a difference between being a trend setter and being a successful business person."

Ms. Sude ought to know because Design Options' California-based firm is the only color service that is broken down by in-store delivery dates for fall/winter, spring/summer, and early spring. The focus is on the American marketplace, with a decidedly California perspective.

With the California point-of-view, the service provides reorder reports on color every six to eight weeks. A Power Palette includes a range of eight of the most commercial colors. It is coordinated to Pantone's Textile Color system of color references, which enables major retailers, textile converters, and manufacturers, who are CAD focused, to communicate internationally with color accuracy. A news flash keeps clients on target with current color developments.

The Design Options service includes:

- Color yarn box, extra yarn, and a traveling Pantone pack.
- Newsletter for communicating with clients
- *Lifestyle Report* for home furnishing trends
- Color palettes for retailers, manufacturers, and converters

A consummate researcher, Ms. Sude acknowledges that you cannot be everything to everyone but you can get mileage out of a color if you know your customer. If blue is hot, for example, the question is, "How does the retailer take it forward

SIDEBAR 3-1 | How to Interpret Color Forecast Material

Everyone agrees that color is an essential factor in the success of a product line. That is why designers, manufacturers, design teams, retail fashion directors, store merchants/buyers, home furnishings experts, and interior consultants may subscribe to not one but several color forecasting services to verify color trends. In so doing, they must analyze, edit, and define the commonalties in seasonal color cards that will impact the sale of their products at the consumer level.

When you look at a color card, the best way to understand how color has evolved is to look for differences between this year's color card and the same forecast service's cards for the same season one year ago. A color range may appear totally different because it has been arranged as the newest colors of the season. Best-selling colors may have been carried over from a previous season and reinvented as a tint, lighter for spring, or as a shade, darker for fall.

These are questions to ask:

1. If you look at several color services, which colors pop out as commonalties across all the cards?
2. Are these the dominant colors, the new colors of the season?
3. Does the repetition of a color range on several color cards verify the direction in which color is moving for a season?
4. What color or color range that was not there last season appears as a new trend?
5. How many colors are in the cool color family?
6. How many colors are in the warm color family?
7. This assessment will indicate whether it is going to be a cool or hot color season.
8. Do not be fooled. Do the colors appear different because they are arranged on a different ground color?
9. Does the color service indicate new ways to combine the colors? Innovative arrangements and combinations will also create new ideas.
10. What material are the colors made of? This will greatly affect your perception of a color.

Remember when you look at a color card, it is not the final word. The color choices represent a color service's point of view. In doing research for a particular company, color cards mainly serve as a guide to make intelligent color decisions for a specific market.

and evolve it further to the ultimate consumer? Design Options shows them the path."

As fashion and home furnishings trends have evolved almost simultaneously, the need for timely direction has become acute. Design Options' *Lifestyle Report,* for one, bridges the gap between apparel and home. In the firm's Photographic Journey for Spring/Summer and Fall/Winter, photographs depict six key trends that illustrate how to take the trends from apparel to home.

COLOR MARKETING GROUP

The Color Marketing Group (CMG), another major source of color specifications, is an international, not-for-profit association of 1,700 color designers. Color designers come from diverse industries and are professionals who enhance the function, salability, and/or quality of a product through their knowledge and appropriate application of color. CMG members forecast color directions one to three years in advance for all industries, manufactured products, and services. These consumer/residential and contract/commercial products include interior/home, architectural/building, communications/graphics, fashion, action/recreation, and environments for retail, hospitality/entertainment, office, and health care industries. CMG professionals meet on a regular basis to validate a consensus of color for industry-specific use.

Trade Terminology

Color card
Color library
Color range
Color stories
Color themes
Color registry
Hue
Palette
Pantone
Standard color codes
Trend analysis

READING 3-1 | Color Symposium

AN EXCLUSIVE REPORT BY LIZ MECHEM

Once again, there was a great turnout for the Margit Publications Color Symposium, held at F.I.T. We were treated to the usual suspects, Margit's posse of color mavens: Tod Shulman of Pantone View Colour Planner, Paul Pelssers of Paul Pelssers Early Color and Trend Directions, and Lousmijn van den Akker of L.A. Colors from Amsterdam. They were joined this year by Marilyn White, representing The Mix Fashion/The Mix Interior. While each presenter spoke to different themes, their presentations seemed to point to a similar direction. In hard economic times such as we have now, people often turn to a renewed sense of opulence, of creativity, of quiet indulgence. The new color palettes reflect this artistic take on the sensibilities of the past merged with the possibilities of the future.

Pantone View Colour Planner

Tod Shulman took the stage first with a very focused and relevant presentation. The news from Pantone is that the color books are now arranged in chromatic order, which is a new direction for the company. This will aid designers in finding just the right color of choice, without looking in two or even three sections of a particular color. So all the reds, for example, from coolest to warmest, will now be found grouped together. "Treating Yourself" is the name of this season's Pantone roundup of colors. As Tod pointed out, with fragile political and economic conditions, the consumer feels the need for a little self-indulgence. We seek out what is comforting and nurturing to offset some of the uncertainty that we feel. This indulgence is anything but ostentatious or excessive, rather it's about doing things that make us feel good, about buying products that are special and important to us. Color, textile and styling all come together to make something new and different, offering balance and a pleasing calm. *Following are the seven color stories:*

Focused Contrast, Peaceful, Mystery. This group works out from the basic black and white mix, with a different spin. The feeling is stark, cold, with shades of ombre blue, caviar, forest, set against pale gray and white for illumination. We see the play of light and dark for a three-dimensional effect. For Menswear, this color balance finds its way in a number of different looks: formal, casual, classic or activewear. Fabrics are shiny or treated, with zippered or belted details. Looks can be luxe, techno or tonal. This colorway is very masculine looking in all its applications. For Womenswear, the somewhat morbid tones can be used for very dramatic, sexy or sporty effects. Flip skirts return, as does veiling, where sheers are used over opaques, adding three-dimensional interest.

Treats Bright winter colors are fun and whimsical. This palette works best when mixed with darker or more muted hues to tone them down, make them appropriate to the season. This group takes its inspiration from synthetic, industrial materials, and lends a light note to what is usually a more somber season. For Menswear, the lime, citron and raspberry are a fun and youthful way to play up darker colors. We see this palette worked into groups of stripes, or engineered stripes. Use these brights in outerwear, as a liner, a trim, a placket, a hood. This would work well with the myriad cardigans we're still seeing, as well as utility or gas station jackets. Also, try a little twist on tradition with bright business shirtings, a group that performs consistently well. In Womenswear, the pallette can be more intentionally bold, marrying converse looks. We'll still see lots of '60s influences, from the Mod to the ladylike, from A-line dresses, patent leather and swirled prints to leggings and knee socks, for a schoolgirl look. Treats work well with deconstructed, bohemian or proper ladylike styles.

Comforting Ease and simplicity. These warm, natural shades can be either soothing and consoling, or intriguing, almost flashy. The palette is built on warm-based yellows against cold grays and taupes. An especially new way to use these colors is with very heavy-weight fabrics. The total effect of Comforting is lazy and understated. For Menswear, the classic prevails, with heavier fabrics which are textured, patterned, tonally mixed. Look for chunky, soft touch fabrics. The cool colors prevail, set against yellow or ivory neutrals. For Womenswear, the emphasis shifts to the yellows in the palette, used for a rugged but practical effect. Try these colors as a singular look, or for bicolor treatments. The mood is relaxed, rugged, with detailing that is sportswear-inspired.

Grace This group is based on brown, for a more elegant, balanced and gentle appearance. Accented with delicate washed pinks and pale, faded copper, these darks look new. Try the summery tones in heavier, winter-weight fabrics for a fresh look. For Menswear, think Saville Row, where tailoring is classic. We take inspiration from vintage looks, always with an eye for comfort. These are classic colors, used with a youthful approach. Color, of course, can be used to define a look, and this is especially true with this palette, in which all combines for an effect of comfortable elegance. For Womenswear, there is a timelessness to this style, with the eternal use of colors from nature, used to mimic natural contrasts. This palette extends well to lingerie, as well as the continued trend of the mini-cardigan. Don't forget, leather is still a popular seller.

Pleasing A pampered, decadent mood prevails here, with grayed-down fondants of mauve, green, and gray set against leather brown for contrast. We see retro patterns and luscious colors for a naughty and sweet charge to the general darkness of the season. For Menswear, these colors work best for a younger, more daring market. Think cyber-punk, acrylic, performance, being tough, being different. Here, the styling can be more fun, active, casually inspired. Try these colors with fleece, for jackets, patterned woven shirts. As ever, for men, color works best for tops rather than bottoms. For womenswear, this group lets girls enjoy being girls. We see influences from the '20s and the '60s, both decades of sexual revolution and social change. There's the sweetness of the candy fondant colors, which can be mixed with darks for a naughtier look, or for contrast. Think of fur trim on a sweet cardigan, for example.

Recharging The landscape is a major influence in this group, which is based on yellow mixed with dark brown and spruce green. When metallics and shiny fabrics enter the picture, the effect becomes theatrical, dramatic, glowing. For menswear, add color in stripes, or try on some of the collegiate influences. Mix up brushed corduroy with nylon, for example, or tweeds worked in modern silhouettes. For womenswear, the yellow works well with metallized bronze and dark brown. Texture and shine make the difference here. Influences are from the '40s, '60s, '70s and the '80s, always with an eye toward glamour. Bronzed, textured and shiny, color combinations are inspired by nature.

Nourishing A deep and lush mix of full-bodied colors. Orange illuminates dark brown, reds, and blues. Growth and imagination are nurtured from the warmth of these rich tonalities, which give an outdoorsy feeling to city looks. For menswear, the look is artistic, blocked, patchwork. We see heavy fabrics against light, ordinary against extraordinary. Set these fashion colors against very dark backgrounds for an urbane effect. Again, the zippered cardigan will be important, worn over or under a jacket or sportcoat. For womenswear, the look is seductive, blurring the lines between city and country. Look for heavy, piled fabrics in lush tones, and tweedy or brushed fabrics. These colors work well when used with leather, distressed leather and rugged materials.

Paul Pelssers Early Color and Trend Directions

"Color is the new black," began Paul Pelssers, quoting a recent New York Times article. After seeing the variety and richness of tonalities as Paul outlined them, all in attendance were sure to agree. Paul pointed to the success of the Gap pink raincoat, a bestseller this spring. Fall/Winter is one of the most colorful cool-weather seasons in quite a while. While Paul presented the men's and women's directions together, we are separating them out here for ease of reference.

Womenswear: Fall/Winter 2004/05

Is a season of warm, enveloping fabrics, created with artistic sensuality. The creativity expressed in these fabrics links past, present and future. Color will appear as bright and theatrical or subtle and earthy. These new fabrics and colors reflect a sense of history, the patina of time, much like aged wood, clay or metals.

Decorative Midtone pastel shades, such as sea foam, pink, brown and dusty yellow are combined with neutrals. Yellow will be an important color and will show up in patterns, which are extremely important this season. Fabrics will range from gloss to satin to many knits. We'll see the return of sweater knits, with lots of texture. The '60s Chelsea Girl influence continues, and we'll see patterns like reinterpreted plaids and checks, multicolored crazy stripes, vintage floral prints and lots of tweed, sometimes very colorful. Corduroy will also make a comeback, with wide wales or very soft corduroy with drape.

Floral Rich and velvety floral tones, from dark rose to pink to plum, accented with sky blue are inspired by all things antique, renaissance or patinated. We'll see bouclés and lingerie fabrics like georgettes, chiffons, and feminine ruffles. Pleats look new and exciting, as do flip skirts and skirts with godets. There will be renewed emphasis on the leg, and leggings appear again for a "Let's get physical" look. This group can be interpreted with very plush fabrics, from velvets to mattes to brilliant gloss, from smooth to textured.

Utilitarian This group makes the camouflage aesthetic urban and feminine. Green-tinted khakis working back to peach and chocolate brown show up in cottons like moleskin and corduroy, as well as sumptuous fabrics like duchess satin and tapestries inspired by furnishing fabrics. We'll even see tinted furs, as the fur trend, both real and faux, continues. And there's life in denim yet, which still veers to the washed and aged, as do most other sportswear fabrics. We'll see jean and motorcycle jacket styling in fabrics ranging from corduroy to plaids and tartans.

Golden Honey-blond neutrals and browns are accented with bright yellow and of course, metallic gold. Looks are warm and authentic, or enriched and highly decorated. Jacquard, damask and other dressy fabrics have a renaissance inspiration and metallic shine, while we see innovations in tweed and plasticized fabrics, sometimes with frayed finishes and a dry, rough look. Prints work well with brown/yellow combinations and are often graphic, Pucci-inspired, as we see with Paul Smith and Marni's recent collections.

Total This is the group of monotones and duotones, with white and black showing up in head-to toe looks or combined for graphic impact. Add red to this for more punch. Monochromes look new when one color shows up in matte/sheen combinations. White will be a big color for fur this season, and we'll even see some bold red head-to-toe dressing. Look out for oversized, large-scale plaids.

Primary Remember the Benetton color palette from the '80s? This group plays with these brights, taking influence from the '60s and '70s as well. These are colors which are bright and assertive, and work well with color-blocking treatments, with Kelly green an important accent. We'll see cotton with coated or resinated or waxed finishes used as outerwear, as well as geometric knits, and classic patterns worked in cartoon colors. Quirky, whimsical and upbeat, this group stands out in a season of color.

Metallic Silver is everywhere in this cool and elegant group. Silvery metallics with grey to dark charcoals are warmed by flesh-pink accents. Here we see classic menswear inspired patterns in fine weave wools, and winter-weight cottons. Goddess styling continues to have impact, along with diagonal weaves and ornamental prints and jacquards. These colors were shown in the Prada collections, showing up with shorter jackets and 3/4 length coats.

Pristine: A late winter group which takes its cue from pristine snow-capped tones. Soft yellows, violets, pinks and eggshell make up a palette that is feminine yet perfect for new sportswear shapes. We see the continued importance of luxe activewear, with sweater knits and multicolored stripes. The colors in this group are often heathered, hazy and blurred through the use of cross dying, tweed and marled yarns or sheer layering.

Womenswear Trends:

New Proportions Influenced by decades past in retro-inspired items and looks. Mini, micro-mini, sleeveless layered pinafore dresses, big over small, as in the '80s, cropped 3/4 lengths, leggings, boleros, oversized sweatshirts.

Sheer and Shine Glossy, high-shine fabrics, plasticized satins, shiny silks, mirror-like surfaces, lace effects, metallic lace. Inspiration from vintage lingerie and corsetry.

Masculine Classic pinstripes, two-piece matched dressing, suiting, tweed, herringbone, used in highly feminine silhouettes. Inspiration ranges from Edwardian dandies to Oscar Wilde eccentrics.

Plaid Play Eternal favorites such as Tartan, Prince of Wales checks, houndstooth and plaids are reconfigured, resized and re-patterned. Windowpane checks in very large scale, lumberjack flannel shirts, plaids with embroidery, textured yarns and slubs.

Coats Oversized and extra long in shaggy sheepskins, folkloric inspiration, kimono with obi-sash details, plastic finishes, satin edges, old and granny-like in tweeds, patterns, and decorated fabrics. Coats can be quilted, belted, or short and tailored. Color in coats will be strong.

Fur Fur trim on everything, from coats to sweaters. Real or artificial, we'll see fur everywhere, from natural, colored and totally white sheepskin shearlings, to shorn, shorthaired glossy fur. Fur in sleeveless vests, recycled fur, reconstructed old fur coats.

Sweater Knits Layers of sweater knits, different stitches, multicolored or graphic patterns, black and white, jacquards, intarsia. Lots of motifs, from cats to butterflies to novelty items. Chenilles, plush, thick and thin. Fur and ruffle trims.

Jeanswear The bootcut continues, but the ultra-low rise seems to be abating. Alternative fabrics, pigment-dyed, 3/4 lengths, reversible. Black denim is on the rise, washed or dark.

Menswear Fall/Winter 2004/05
Is a season in which color provides the main inspiration. Harmonies are gentle, nuances are subtle and tonalities are grayed. Earthy brown tones are important, while extremely pale tones can seem to almost disappear under bright light. We'll see intense, deep darks contrasted with transparent light tints. Black is ever present, surrounding and anchoring all colors this season.

True Blue An upfront, new color group, in which brighter turquoise plays with navy and more subdued grays, from light to dark. Cotton is strong, in woven shirts, checks, plaids, sweatshirting. We'll see the use of coatings and resinated finishes which add sheen and tonal interest. Twill, cavalry twill and, of course, denim will be important.

Urban Fatigues Green-tinted khakis combine with neutrals and dark chocolate for a camouflage story that bespeaks urban utility. Washed, cotton-textured fabrics, brushed surfaces, fine herringbone and coated outerwear make for a very texture-rich melange. Doodads abound, from straps and toggles to drawstrings and cargo pockets. Camouflage inspiration comes in the form of sweater knits, tweeds and camo prints, which now veer toward the abstract.

Berry Reds Warm, rich and deep tones of plum, pink, and red are set off against chocolate brown and ochre for a menswear pink story. Here the pinks are mostly heathered or tweeded for a more masculine look, or are used as accent colors. Textured stripes, matte/sheen effects and natural/tech combinations are key.

Tonal Greys From dove to charcoal, these greys run the gamut across the spectrum. Accented with red and pale blue, and worked in traditional English fabrics, this group takes on a comfortable look. Layering and head-to-toe grey looks are seen alongside tonal stripes and engineered stripes. French terry and Fair Isle sweaters show up in this colorway, sometimes with an oversized, '80s proportion, as well as traditional coats and jackets.

Vegetal Ochre hues that take inspiration from both vegetal and mineral tones are the starting point for this palette. Natural, colored or all-white shearling appear with aged, cracked leathers and soft, rich suede tones. Fabrics include corduroy and utility materials, used in parkas, zip jackets and hoodies. We'll see placement prints, appliqués and lots of practical pockets.

Leather Brown A range of natural browns with grey and rust accents takes its cues from a folkloric and eclectic range of inspirations, from Eastern European, South American/Andes and Scandinavian themes. Chunky, handmade knits, and weaves, striped pants, ticking or mattress stripes will all be the key. Look for plenty of bonded fabrics, including bonded leather, suede and even faux shearling.

Black/White Worn in head-to-toe looks, these non-colors take on strength and new harmonies. Several shades of black or white worn together look new. All-black takes on pensive and sensual qualities, with washed out, satinized softness and luminosity from glazing and bonding. White veers toward the antique or greyed-down tones. In denim, we still see black, but with less washing and whiskering effects as in previous seasons.

Paradise Bright '80s influences combine with bird-of-paradise jolts of color for an intense and vivid palette. Working off neutrals, these brights show off best in imaginative knitwear patterns, which could well be the signature look of the season.

Key Trends

Sweater Knits Knitwear makes a long awaited return, showing up in chunky or fine-gauge looks, handknit, ribbed, stripes and patterns, lots of Fair Isle. Zip-front cardigans are a key look, and we'll see lots of value-added detail, such as leather or trims. Sleeveless vests return.

The Parka Hooded, coated, resinated, in neutrals or colors, the parka will be a key, versatile look. The proportions are getting more extreme, overscaled or underscaled, big over small. Fur trims and zip-out linings are important details.

Sheepskin and Fur Fur is back in a major way, with faux as important as real, reconciling ecological concerns with style options. Sheepskin is shaggy or bonded, colored, white or natural. The fur vest worn under the jacket or coat looks new.

English Traditions Inspired by the English dandy, this trend includes chalk stripes, pinstripes, windowpane, Fair Isle, drawing-room jacquards, stripes, velvets, satins. Herringbone, houndstooth, tweed and slubbed fabrics work well next to natural cottons.

Sport Think David Beckham. The international football look, with team influences from England, Ireland, Italy, South America. Colorblocking, traditional sweatshirting, item pants and item sweatshirts, oversized. Vintage fabrication and styling.

Urban Fatigues Street styling comes into its own, with twills, herringbones, drill, ripstop, ringspun textures, bedfords and pronounced diagonals. Fabrics are felted, peached, for moleskin and textured effects. Boiled wools combine with cottons, oversized sweatshirts return.

L.A. Colors from Amsterdam

To hear it from Lousmijn van den Akker, the irrepressible visionary behind L.A. Colors from Amsterdam, the world is a supple and sensual place which uses the beauty of nature and the wonders of global culture to bounce back from crisis mode. Lousmijn closed the show with her usual energy, humor and insight, and surely won many converts to her optimistic worldview. Many indicators point to the recession coming to a close. And if it's not, here are Lousmijn's six ways to handle the downturn:

1. **Dream,** escape to fairy tales, with dreams of clouds, floating in the ether.
2. **Be creative,** take up brush and easel and paint.
3. **Bring romance to situation,** imagine that it's actually wonderful to be poor, and revel in the charm of the basics.
4. **Believe in the future,** believe that some positive change will come out of warfare, such as technical innovations.
5. **Engage in total denial:** "Crisis? What Crisis?" Revel in opera, drama, luxury, and velvets.
5. **Keep an eye on the bright heights,** feel the joy of survival, the rhythm of life, the power of color.

And here is how these coping mechanisms translate to new color directions for Fall/Winter 2004/05. This season, L.A. Colors from Amsterdam will be presented in a new format: La black box, a new and intriguing case for all the wonders contained within. Like Pandora's box, only not quite as dangerous.

1. The Perfumed Garden The sunrise over a wintry Taj Mahal is the starting point for this group of soft, peaceful colors, golden hues mixed with pastel colors. Embroidery of the Ottoman Empire, the old culture of the Middle East, the delicacy of Persian Miniature paintings—all these elements of a poetic life, a sense of indulgence and decoration. We see silks, many levels of luster, from the glow of marble to the shine of silk with a golden glow. Indian Bridal Saris, miniature patterns like inlaid flowers, paisleys, and small, fine ribbings all add up to a rich and indulgent sensibility. This translates well to lace, to modern lingerie dressing, like Stella McCartney's "sweet nothings," and lingerie style used for streetwear. Pashminas, intricate jacquards, Mother-of-pearl pigment powder is used in yarn-dyes for added luster, iridescence. The palette goes from golden to cool as well, incorporating silver lace, double-woven or polyester silk with icy overtones. The total escapist fantasy, living on a cloud, adorned in the softest, most ethereal of colors.

2. Bloomsbury Boudoir The setting is in Sussex, England, at Charleston House, circa 1900. Virginia Woolf, Vanessa Bell, and Duncan Grant are gathered here with the other members of the Bloomsbury Group, painting, writing, composing, living an artistic, revolutionary, slightly decadent life. They've hand-painted everything, from the furniture to the walls to the floorboards. The palette is warm intense pastels mixed with autumnal, berry darks, all drawn from nature, from the English countryside. Tweeds, herringbones, checks, multicolor, gain intensity from nubs and slubs in the yarns. Velvet is the fabric of choice, hand-painted, embroidered, iridescent velvets. Mohair velvet makes a comeback, as does the velvet suit for men. Wiener Werkstätte patterns are right at home here, with the decorative sensibility rendered in warm, cozy, landscape colors.

3. The Salt Nomads We're in Tibet, in the Himalayas, covered by snow, white, omnipresent. The nomadic people go on their pilgrimage for salt, following ancient trade routes through India, Nepal, Bhutan, China. Colors range from tan to white to grey to copper, with taupe, black, and red—"Rinpoche red." These are the colors of burlap, jute, coarse wool, of earth, air, water, fire, and salt. Fabrics mohair, alpaca, camel, Mongolian lamb and even fluffy fake-fur knits. We see poor-looking wool, cracked leathers, suede, moleskin, corduroy; hand spun, coarse yarns, crude, raw materials. Tribal influences from all over the world converge on these trade routes, so we see ethnic patterns, striped wool blankets, patchwork, coins and jewelry woven into the clothing. Dark, cakey neutrals with ice white—the essential colors, the essentials of life. These are the colors of the kilim, with all its intricacy, richness and history.

4. Stainless Steel Better living through technology is the optimistic credo of this palette, which takes us back to the future with the romance of metallics. Blue, olive, bronze nod to the influence of modern architecture, Frank Gehry and Rem Koolhaas; cool colors with the jolt of yellow remind us of urban gladiators, aluminum, plastic, and the space-age designs of NASA. Architectural materials influence fabrications; from steel, wire, and wavy metallics come shiny metallic jerseys, denim with metallic films, high-tech materials like black rubber, neoprene, reflective, rubberized and coated materials. Think of the industrial origami of Japanese fabrics, with their quilting, pleating, crinkling. Think Pierre Cardin, Courrèges, the '60s of neons and fluorescent greens, yellows, emergency brights. Holographic effects, fabrics coated with crystal from Swarovski—this is the high-tech, futuristic glean of Stainless Steel.

5. Courtly Splendor Here we visit the Italian Renaissance in Florence and Venice, with its rich colors, brocades, silks, dark gold, every shade of red. Deep tones of Burgundy, reddish brown and green are borrowed from still-life paintings and the jewel-toned Bayeux tapestries, illuminated manuscripts and glassbeaded embroidery. We take our inspirations from the court of the Medici, from heradlry—tooled leather and leather stitched to look like armor, to the richest velvets, which drape and move as if fluid, in colors from black cherry into eggplant. The ornamental is everywhere, in burned out velvets, jacquards, flocking and sumptuous cashmere. The richness even makes it to the street, as we see flocking on denim, black lace, and warm, deep, heavy fabrics.

6. Bright Heights The highest reaches of the Andes are home to the ethnic beauties of Peru, where brightness falls on everything. The palette is nearly neon in its brightness, optimistic in mood, folkloric in inspiration. We see Navajo blankets, ethnic embroidery, fuchsia into lime green, sulfur yellow and brightest turquoise. The simple things in life are culled from many ethnic and folk traditions, from the Andes to the Alps, from Peru to Mexico, from Eastern Europe to Russia, stopping at Switzerland and Austrla. Russian hand-painted roses share space with tweed, wool, felted materials. Roses are everywhere, knitted, crocheted, printed, wood-blocked. This is the exuberance of color, the joy of the simple, modern tech meets handmade, straight out of Macchu Picchu.

Source: *MP News Newsletter*, June–July 2003, pp. 1–8. Courtesy of Margit Publications, a division of The Doneger Group.

READING 3-2 | Speaking Color BASIC COLOR TERMINOLOGY

Hue Color and hue are synonymous and can be used interchangeably. Red, yellow and blue are the primary colors. Green, orange and violet are the secondary colors and tertiary colors are a mixture of two secondary colors.

Saturation The intensity of a color is described as saturation or chroma. Saturation is determined by how little or how much gray a color contains. In its purest form a hue is at maximum chroma; these are colors that are not "grayed." They are described as: clear, pure, brilliant, bright, rich, bold, vivid and/or true. The grayer or more neutral a color is, the less its saturation. Less saturated colors are described as soft, muted, subtle, toned-down, misty, dull or dusty.

Value The lightness or darkness of a color is called its value. Lightened values are tints, darkened values are shades and medium value colors are described as midtones. A variation in the light to dark arrangement or design is called a "value pattern." Keeping the value pattern minimized within a limited range creates an understated, subtle and restrained look that is seen as calm and quiet. Colors close in value have "soft edges" between them, while excitement and drama are suggested by sharp changes in value. Surrounding a focal point with extremes of dark and light contrast will draw the eye immediately to the center of attention.

The perception of a color is affected greatly by its value or saturation; in planning a color combination, value and saturation are as important as the hue. For example, in the red family, a darkened value of burgundy imparts more power than a lighter value of rose pink. A vividly saturated turquoise is more exciting than a pale grayed aqua.

An important graphic tool for creating color combinations, the color wheel is a circular arrangement of the primary, secondary and tertiary colors. It visually illustrates color "temperature"—warm vs. cool—as vital psychological components in delivering a specific color's message. Colors are perceived as warm or cool because of ancient and universal associations. Red, orange and yellow are associated with the warmth of fire and sun while blue, green and violet connect in the mind's eye with the coolness of sea, sky, foliage and outer space.

But changing an undertone can alter the temperature somewhat. Yellow-reds are hotter than blue-reds. The redder the purple, the hotter it gets. Blue-greens are as cool as the water that inspires the liquid-like shades, but yellowed earthy greens are decidedly warmer.

Combinations of warm colors send a more energetic, outgoing, aggressive, active message that demands attention while cool colors are more restrained, reserved and calm—more contemplative than physical. But cool colors show less restraint when they are brightened: as cools become more vibrant, so do their personalities.

Color Schemes

Monotone The use of a single neutral color describes a monotone scheme. This includes light to medium grays, beiges, taupes and off-whites that will impart a calm, quiet quality, or a classic understated look.

The subtlety can be very appealing for use in more expensive products, but in signage, packaging, advertising or any other graphic application, monotones can be so subtle that they appear unreadable, so some contrast in color or texture is necessary.

Monochromatics The use of one color family in various values or intensities is called a monochromatic color scheme. These combinations can be very effective in imparting subtle nuances such as the refreshing quality of contrasting green foliage or the deliciousness of rich chocolate brown melting into a creamy mocha color.

Analogous Analogous colors are neighboring families on the color wheel. If the combination spans only one-fourth of the color wheel, they are always harmonious as they share the same undertones, for example: blue, blue-green and green. But total harmony is not necessarily a goal because a too-subtle use of color may lack impact. Expanding the analogous group somewhat by adding touches of another neighboring color (green, blue-green, blue and blue-purple, for example) will garner more attention.

Complementary Complementary colors means just that—they are total opposites on the color wheel that enhance each other when used as a pair; they "complete" each other. The red family will appear even redder when contrasted with green, as will orange with blue or yellow with purple. They balance each other as they are opposites, one hue is warm and the other is cool. Called simultaneous contrast, each complement seems to vibrate along the periphery of the area where they meet. In their brightest intensities, they literally command attention, so they are especially effective when used in packaging, advertising, at point of purchase, banners, sports uniforms or any other usage where exuberant and instant attention is important. If softer or deeper values of complements are used, the effect is more subtle.

Source: Extracted from *Pantone® Guide to Communicating with Color,* pp. 10-12. Courtesy of Grafix Press, an imprint of Design Books International.

4

Creative Visual Boards

Why are boards the major feature of a creative fashion presentation? The reason is quite simple. As a visual marketing tool, the role of creative boards is clearly defined. They are a frequently used creative form of communication between the seller and the buyer (e.g., between fiber firm and mill). The technique of creative visual boards provides information and promotes a firm's exclusive point of view. Creative fashion presentations may also serve as a strategy to enhance the reputation of a firm in the industry.

COST

The production of creative fashion presentations can be a costly investment, but one with a significant goal. The firm's objective is to stimulate industry interest and to accelerate the production of the product or merchandise for sale to the ultimate consumer. As such, the cost of a creative fashion presentation is justified on several levels. The main point is that no matter how colorful or fashion forward the merchandise or product, dynamic creative fashion presentations can convey messages in such a dramatic way that the goods become even more appealing and saleable.

Therefore, presentations play a major role in the fashion industry because the information directly influences the merchandising of fiber, textiles, apparel, and accessories—and how well they sell.

VISUAL DYNAMICS

The old Chinese proverb, "One picture is worth more than ten thousand words," may well apply to creative board presentations. This visual marketing tool primarily illustrates a particular firm's point of view on color, fabric, or silhouette trends as it applies to its specific merchandise or product. The visual boards augment the sounds and words and written report of a firm's executive presenter, fashion director, consultant, or trade show lecturer. The boards, coordinated and related to specific topics discussed by the presenter, reinforce a firm's "sell" message. Effective visual presentations inform and inspire, as well as help to maintain audience attention.

In short, presentation boards are creative and artistic renderings that create visual word pictures that illustrate themes. Board designers may have hundreds of foreign and domestic fashion, travel, and architecture magazines in their resource file. When it comes time to find appropriate images, they tear out the page. The images that best represent the trends will be superimposed on the boards with related decorative objects that augment the board's theme.

THE BOARD DESIGNER

Effective boards are creative works that usually require artistic rendering by a skilled board designer. Many firms hire outside professional board designers to produce highly professional boards. These individuals usually have a craft or art background or may also be graphic artists. Some businesses may have talented in-house individuals who provide a valued "insider" service. Other "insiders" may work for a trend analyst or forecast firm. The designer, may well be immersed in a firm's trend outlook, but also develops concept ideas for boards. Primarily the board designer must have a strong conceptual ability to translate the "sell" message that a particular firm wishes to convey to its audience.

SIDEBAR 4-1 | Check List for a Professional Presentation

Your Appearance
The impression you create by your appearance will contribute to the success of your presentation.

A. Do you look the part of a fashion representative of your company or the market level you represent?
B. Have you checked every grooming detail?
C. Have you taken off distracting jangling bracelets and earrings?
D. Does your attire represent the merchandise you are discussing? If you are representing a dress firm, be sure to wear a garment from the firm's collection.

The Commentary
Voice tone, enthusiasm, and a convincing message are essential ingredients for a successful delivery of the fashion or sell message.

A. Memorize the script so that you can speak in a conversational manner.
B. Make a tape recording before the event. Then, play it back to check style and speech.
C. Cue cards are good, but only as a point of reference. Do not read to the audience.
D. Maintain eye contact with the audience.
E. Pause and pace information.
F. Speak clearly and pronounce unusual or foreign words correctly.
G. Use a microphone.
H. Use a podium if it makes you more at ease.
I. Rehearse, rehearse, rehearse to establish poise and control.

Boards: Plan Ahead
Planning all visual boards or slide shows ahead is the sign of a professional.

A. Check the sequential order of the boards as it relates to your commentary. Number the boards at the back for easy reference.
B. Relate to the boards in an interactive manner.
C. Use a pointer to emphasize and reinforce your message.

Slides: Plan Ahead
Although slides of the Prêt à Porter or runway couture shows can be purchased from various services, many firms prefer to take their own slides of street scenes and windows to augment the board presentation. Slide shows may also feature catwalk fashion shows. If you plan to augment your presentation with a slide show be sure in advance that everything mechanical is working.

A. Recheck all technical aspects of the presentation with the audiovisual technician.
B. Rerun the slide show.
C. Be sure the slide tray lid is secure.
D. On the day of show, recheck the projector and do a run-through before the audience arrives to avoid technical mishaps.
E. Check the screen setup.

Camera Tips

Learning how to use a camera is a plus. Keep one handy as a window of opportunity may occur, and you do not want to miss a shot of an avant-garde or emerging trend. Here are some tips:

A. Learn how to use a 35-mm camera using color slide film or a very high-quality digital camera.
B. If the camera is not digital, be sure it is loaded with film.
C. Take the cover lid off the lens before shooting.
D. Check batteries (take extra batteries for long trips).
E. Carry a camera wherever you go so you do not miss a photo opportunity.
F. Always be camera ready. On international trips, take extra film to avoid delays.

However, almost everyone can learn board design technique and apply it to creative board presentations. As a case in point, students particularly use visual boards for various classroom projects related to creative fashion presentations, board designs, and product development or retail sales communication.

Novice Board Designers

For the novice board designer, the following guidelines provide the key to creating interesting, imaginative, and exciting boards.

1. Color interplay must make sense and augment the theme. Consideration should be given to hue, value, and intensity.
2. Graphic balance is essential. Squares, ovals, or oversized elements must be in proportion to the board.

INDUSTRY PROFILE 4-1 | Rachel S. Herbst and Melissa Moylan

*Rachel Herbst (**left**) unveiled her presentation of fashions for the urban traveler. Her themes are highlighted by clever and witty color descriptions for her "Hip Altitudes" theme (opposite page; see the color insert).*

As part of Polly Guérin's creative presentation class at New York's Fashion Institute of Technology, each student assumes the role of fashion director, trend analyst, or merchandiser. As such, they represent an apparel line and prepare a presentation as if they worked for a real company. As a springboard to creativity, students use diverse research resources, including fashion forecasting company references, to create an overall theme and prepare a trend presentation for a particular season. Each student presents a new silhouette and color trend storyboards, which are augmented with a written report on the fashions, color, and fabrics. While the industry usually uses several storyboards, in this abbreviated project students create one board on silhouettes and another board on the new season's colors. They also name each silhouette as well as one of the fashion forward, fashion favorite, and basic colors to correspond to the overall theme. Each presentation is made to the class, with the other students acting as the firm's design team or an audience of buyers. The Spring 2003 class produced creative and imaginative presentations, and two of them are being profiled here.

Rachel S. Herbst: Hip Altitudes

Rachel's interest in fashion began in elementary school, when she would trace and draw fashion garments and accessories

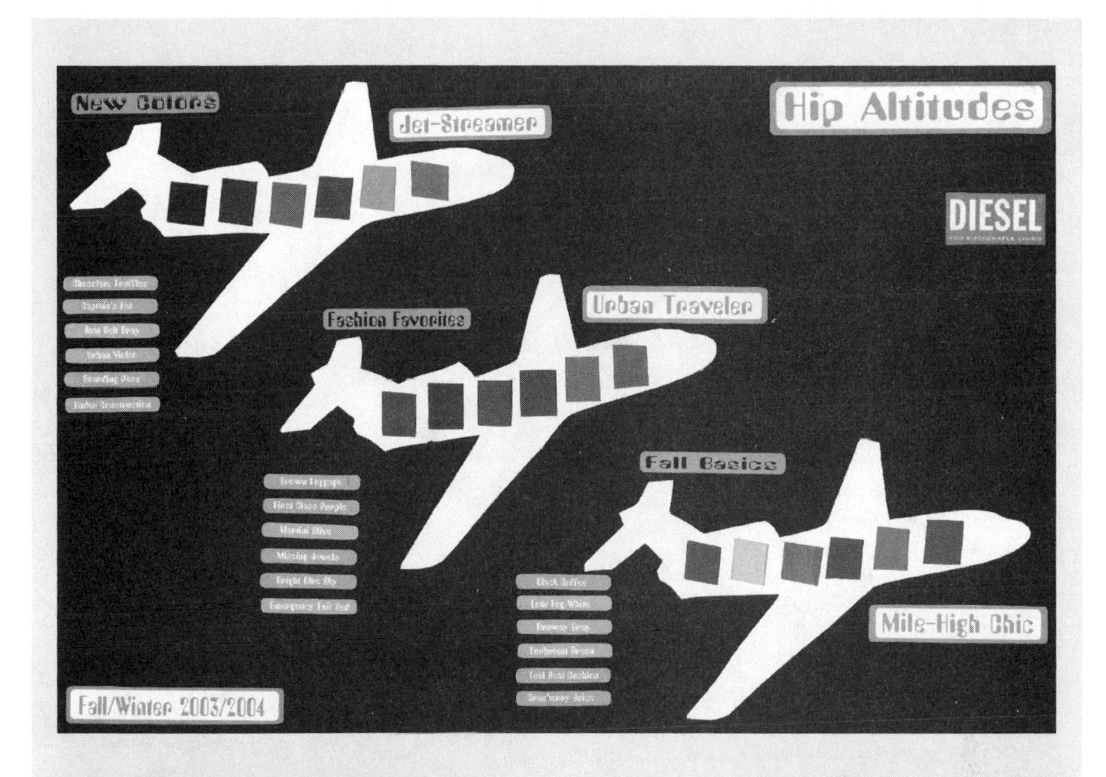
New Colors
Jet-Streamer
Hip Altitudes
DIESEL
Fashion Favorites
Urban Traveler
Fall Basics
Mile-High Chic
Fall/Winter 2003/2004

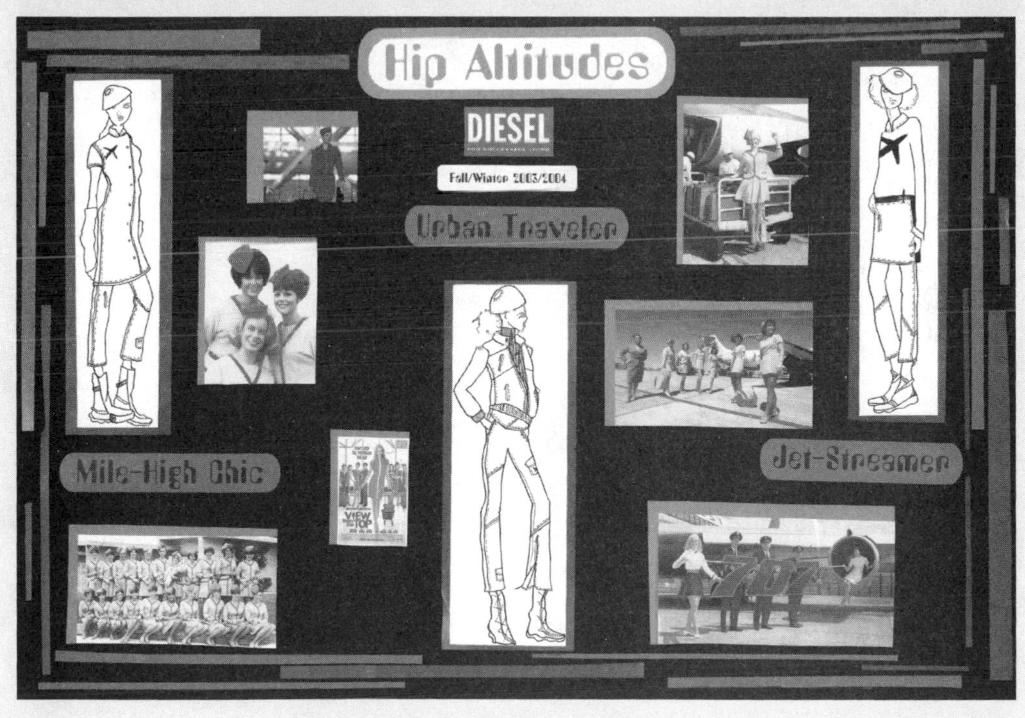
Hip Altitudes
DIESEL
Fall/Winter 2003/2004
Urban Traveler
Mile-High Chic
Jet-Streamer

using artists' kits. She enjoyed mixing and matching different styles and drawing unique ensembles. Her sewing skills enabled her to develop new approaches and to use nontraditional materials.

The inspiration for her FIT presentation came from magazines and people watching. She began to study the uniforms worn by flight attendants—and how they have been transformed into a polo shirt with khaki slacks or skirts. As she researched the different design periods of uniforms, she was drawn to the sleek form-fitting silhouettes and mod styling of the 1960s.

With her strong interest in the DIESEL clothing lines, she chose her project theme: to encourage DIESEL to create a line of clothing that would double as uniforms and street apparel so that the flight attendant could go to work and enjoy time off in style. Rachel researched her subject on the Internet, checked Doneger's forecasting services, and used basic silhouettes from the fashion forecasting books. The designs and colors came from her imagination. She then compiled her drawings, images, and color swatches into presentation boards using computer graphics, decorative paper, and three-dimensional elements of design.

Rachel's goal is a career in product development, so she can create a line of clothing that brings high style and quality together at an affordable price.

*Melissa Moylan's (**above**) presentation was based on three Picasso paintings. Her interpretations resulted in sleek men's wear silhouettes in warm and provocative colors (opposite page; see the color insert).*

Melissa Moylan: Modern Day Picasso

Melissa Moylan's interest in fashion combines her artistic talent with a love for shopping. She was always on the lookout for the hottest trends. At first, she wanted to study at FIT to become a buyer, but as her experiences grew, she decided to combine her artistic talent with business savvy. That means learning how to prepare a creative presentation.

Melissa's presentation was inspired by the Matisse/Picasso exhibit at the Metropolitan Museum of Art in New York City. She noted that Picasso's artwork evolved from the form of a line, and she paralleled that evolution in a clothing concept of new silhouette ideas for BCBG Max Azria by incorporating revolutionary and traditionalist approaches.

First, Melissa picked three Picasso paintings and incorporated them into three themes for the Spring season: Hip Harlequin, Man Before a Mirror, and Fine Shadow. She then created silhouettes and colors that reflected Picasso's original work

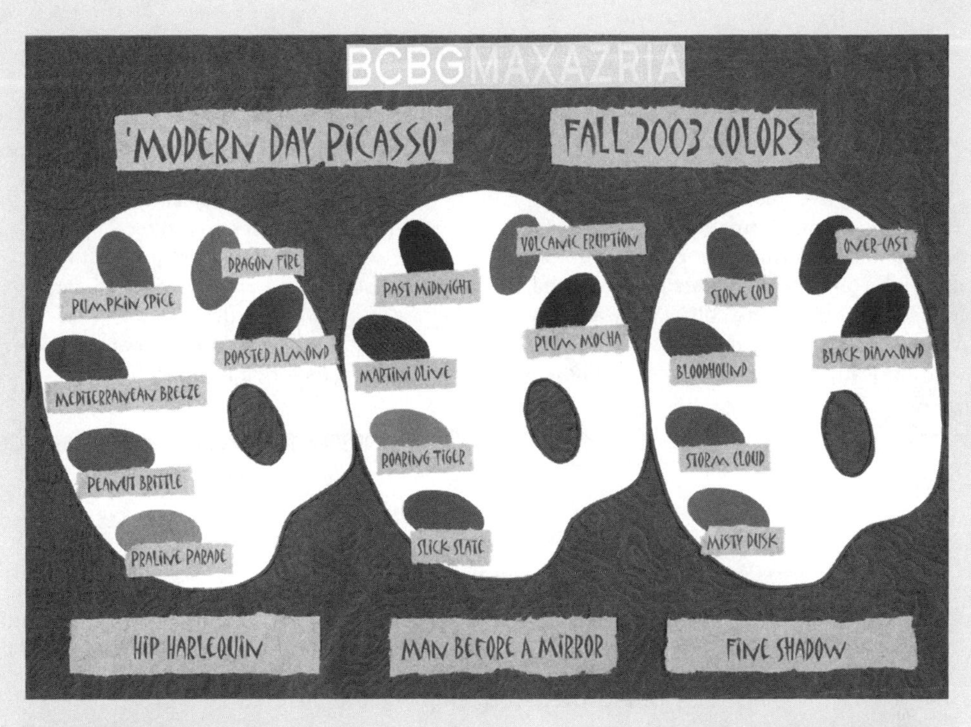
BCBGMAXAZRIA
'MODERN DAY PICASSO'
FALL 2003 COLORS
PUMPKIN SPICE
DRAGON FIRE
ROASTED ALMOND
MEDITERRANEAN BREEZE
PEANUT BRITTLE
PRALINE PARADE
PAST MIDNIGHT
VOLCANIC ERUPTION
PLUM MOCHA
MARTINI OLIVE
ROARING TIGER
SLICK SLATE
STONE COLD
OVER-CAST
BLACK DIAMOND
BLOODHOUND
STORM CLOUD
MISTY DUSK
HIP HARLEQUIN
MAN BEFORE A MIRROR
FINE SHADOW

BCBGMAXAZRIA
'MODERN DAY PICASSO'
MENSWEAR FALL 2003
HIP HARLEQUIN
MAN BEFORE A MIRROR
FINE SHADOW

and trends adapted from services such as Doneger and Here and There.

Thus, Picasso's overlapping motif in *Harlequin* is transformed into Azria's "Hip Harlequin." As Picasso embraces ambiguity through complex fragmented forms, Azria applies a remix to the collection. Hip Harlequin is all about newness and mixing different fabrics with one another. In addition, it redefines the identity of men's wear by combining casual with formal.

As a result of this project, Melissa's goal is to become a creative director for a designer or leading manufacturer. In that capacity, she will be able to conceptualize themes and work with designers or a design team to project fashion forward silhouettes and trends for collections.

3. Images should all speak the mood of the trend the designer is trying to describe.
4. Small platforms can be built to mount photos, magazine images, fabrics, or silhouettes and to give the layout dimension, depth, and interest.
5. Simplicity can also convey a major story. Therefore, boards should not be overloaded or montaged with too many elements.
6. Avoid haphazard or random arrangements that can be confusing and unintelligible.
7. Cut a straight edge.
8. Strive for clean, creative boards.

As a case in point: In a modernistic approach, a fabric house makes an impact with a theme called "Spare," using a metallic background with a nailhead frame anchored into a concrete block. The minimalistic images pay homage to the cool, clean, quiet surfaces of fabrics in cool shades of blues, violets, and steel grays accented by smoky greens.

Design Inspiration

Inspiration for conceptual board ideas may come from diverse sources, such as observational research, a vast knowledge of historical fashion, and styles in art and architecture. The board designer must be tuned in to what is happening in the worlds of art, music, theater, street life, high fashion, politics, the environment, consumer lifestyles, and even the economy. Their professional training should enable them to establish a theme for each board that creatively and directly relates to a firm's product or merchandise.

Conceptualization

The board designer must have a certain degree of talent or creative flair to develop the shape, dimension, and placement of elements on the board. Whether the board designer is an inhouse creative individual or a hired professional, the first step in creative visual board design is meeting with the client or the firm's decision makers to discuss the firm's point of view and the "sell" message. From this pivotal discussion, the board designer will conceptualize a theme or story line for the presentation boards. These concept ideas will be presented to the client or firm for approval, before the go-ahead is given and the boards are actually produced.

Creating a Theme

Case in point: "Americana," produced for Milliken & Company's forecast, is not an ordinary cardboard board, but a large six-foot barn siding background. It was chosen for its rugged rural reference to America's heartland and the quality of the firm's fabrics. The board is superimposed with vintage advertising signs, a pair of old sneakers, collectible travel photographs, miniature American flags, and a rag doll. These decorative elements say it all. Americana is clearly showcased with icons of human heritage placed on the board to give it three-dimensional character. Most unusual are the antique Coke bottles in their original wooden cases and a rare Route 66 emblem. Most of these objects are flea market finds collected by the board designer to convey the Americana theme. The fabrics are applied to square shapes that create a multidimen-

Milliken's Americana board uses popular culture icons and the illusion of depth to create a strong fabric statement.

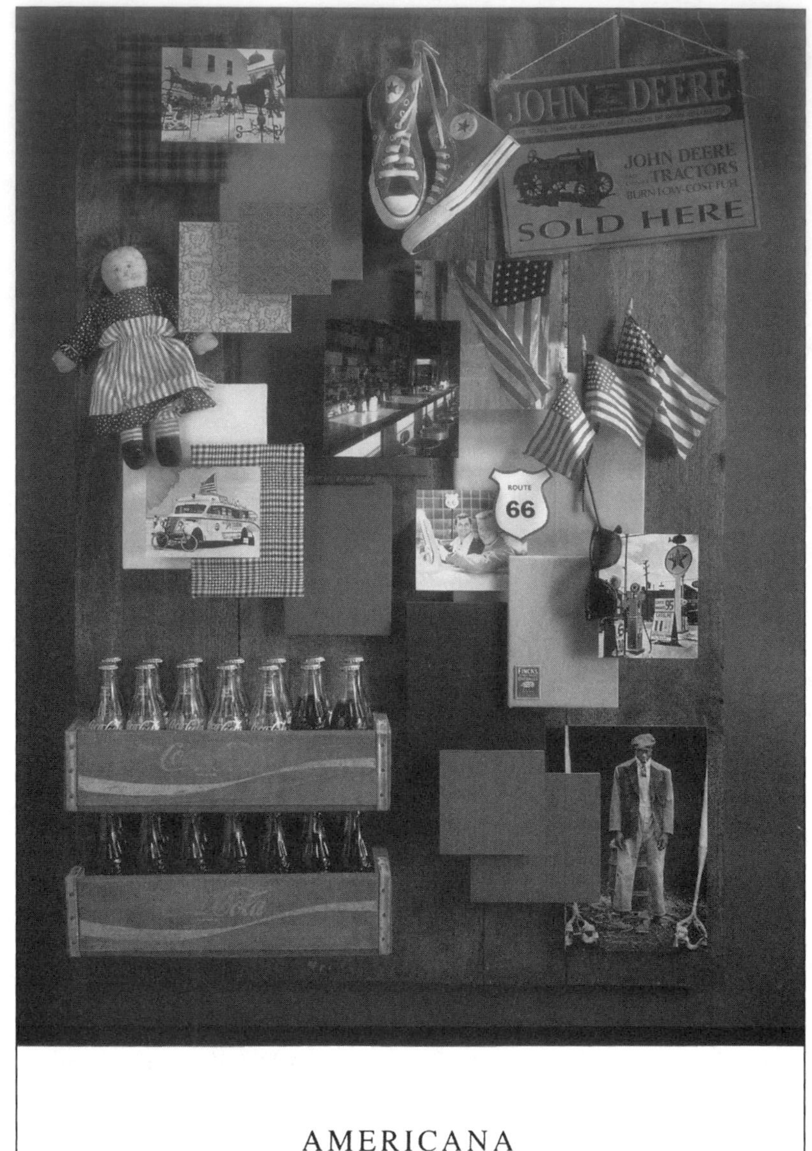

sional effect because they are raised above the surface of the barn board.

The number of boards used in a presentation will vary and depend on the purpose of the presentation. The 20″ × 30″ board size is usual, but the size will depend on the firm's "sell"

Milliken's men's wear-inspired board uses masculine imagery to illustrate its vintage influence on women's wear fabrics.

message. The size of the boards is a decision entirely up to the presenter. Keep in mind that the viewing capacity of the audience must be taken into consideration. Obviously, if the audience is large, boards that are too small will be difficult to see and therefore ineffective.

Board Elements

Board designers concede that one of the most important and sometimes the most difficult part of the creative process is coming up with an effective background and decorative elements to augment the theme on the board. The board designer must always be alert to the discovery of new objects which may be found in flea markets, thrift shops, hardware and craft stores—just about anywhere where there is a novelty chain or even a yarn or ribbon shop.

An effective board presentation should have the following three components:

- Visibility: Visibility includes the images and decorative elements placed on the board in landscape or portrait manner. The size of the elements and their placement should reflect balance and proportion. The layout should be logical and aesthetically pleasing.
- Portability: Portability means that it is feasible to ship or transport the boards out of town to other regional showrooms or trade shows. Three-part hinged boards that open up like a theater curtain are a good idea for travel and provide more space to display the theme.
- Durability: Durability is the quality of the board and the permanence of the application of the images and elements. The boards must survive considerable daily use over an extended period of time, not only in the firm's showroom, but also for out-of-town client presentations and for use at trade shows.

Board Assemblage

Like any artistic endeavor, board design requires adequate working space. Preferably the workstation should be an oversized, long table with all equipment assembled within easy reach. By now, the designer should have established the major theme name and subtheme names for the number of boards that will be used in the presentation. The main theme for an activewear line of fabrics might be called, for example, Rejuvenation, and corresponding theme names for other boards might be Springboard, Facelift, Power Punch, Escape, Shape, and so on. Good designers outline the theme names and "sell" message on paper so that they have an overall picture of the layout. Taking a cue from the theme names, the board designer can start to assemble the images and creative elements needed for each board.

Although many board designers work independently, some hire a production artist to assemble the various elements for the board and mechanically put them together according to the board designer's instructions.

Planning the Layout

Before starting the construction of the boards, first plan the layout. This is essential to avoid making mistakes in judgment and possibly ruining a potentially good presentation.

Therefore, creative elements should not immediately be permanently glued on multiple board presentations. Before mechanically finalizing the project, the decorative elements should be put down in temporary positions, so that the overall effectiveness of a multiple board presentation can be assessed as a continuous, coherent flow of information. At this stage, the elements can be moved or shifted into a more favorable position for balance and appealing contrast.

Another aspect of preliminary preparation planning is to create a diagram of the board layout. Designers place a large sheet of tracing paper over the board and create a template—an outline of the decorative elements. This tracing paper layout serves to visually verify placement of objects and images.

Unify the Theme

Unity is the board's bonding agent. This means that although the board may be composed of many different elements, those elements must relate to one another in a harmonious assemblage that immediately identifies with the theme.

A floral fashion theme may give a greenhouse impression with a miniature white fence border or trellis work, miniature gardener's tools, and watering hose from a hardware or craft store. A media theme may be constructed with a miniature television playing a men's wear fashion show. If the theme is based on manual labor, the boards may be made more unusual by fastening costume jewelry in the shape of a shovel, pitchfork, and spade to the board. In this case, the board designer found the costume jewelry in a vintage shop. Square shapes pasted with appropriate images that depict manual labor would further augment the theme.

The final assessment of the board is to look at all the elements and to be sure that they support the theme.

Supplies/Novelties

Supplies may be purchased in most art supply stores. Here are some of the materials that a designer may need to create boards.

1. Large boards, approximately 20″ × 30″. Designers prefer boards of a sturdy quality that will rest easily on an easel or can be propped up without falling down. The size of the boards depends on the size of the audience. If appropriate, gatefold boards and accordion fold boards may also be used.
2. The background color of the mounting board must effectively showcase the decorative elements, fabrics, or silhouettes. A black background may be dramatic, but it may not show the elements to best advantage.
3. A large metal ruler, a T-Square, or an L-shape ruler for accurate placement and alignment of decorative elements or lettering
4. Hot glue gun
5. A new mat knife
6. Sponges and erasers
7. Spray mount that allows tearsheets, magazine images, or photos to be pasted down but easily lifted and remounted, in case of a mistake or a desired change.

8. Paint
9. Other materials, such as sand and glitter, may be used to add surface interest to the board.
10. If the boards have text, designers may use handlettering, computer-generated lettering, or press out letters.

CONCLUSION

Creating boards requires considerable physical work, especially if the board designer is creating such special effects as imitating an old, beat-up Italian wall for the background. Innovative ideas are a must; so the board designer is challenged to create a work of art that has lasting appeal. The background and elements must be permanently placed, and the boards, which will be in constant use from six months to a year, must not fall apart. The most frequent use of creative boards as a marketing tool is during advance presentations made in Spring/Summer or Fall/Winter market weeks and at trade shows. Later the boards may be put on display in a showroom or exhibited on the walls of a firm's executive offices. At the retail level, multiple board presentations are often used to illustrate brand lines or product development programs.

Trade Terminology

Board designer
Conceptualization
Creative fashion presentation
Durability
Elements
Images
Layout
Point of view
Portability
Production artist
Theme
Subtheme
Visibility
Visual marketing tool
Visual dynamics

READING 4-1 | Peclers: Mixing It Up for Fall BY DANIELA GILBERT

NEW YORK—Trends for the upcoming Fall 2003 season will be a mixture of urban sexiness, men's wear-inspired classics, rustic chic and cool elegance, according to Peclers' latest trend forecast, presented recently in New York by Dominique Gilbert, senior stylist from the firm's Paris headquarters.

The four trends that the international trend and forecasting agency expected would dominate the season are: Sexy Mouse, Nouvelle Vague, Luxe Povera and Cool Appeal.

The first, Sexy Mouse, combines looks that are fluid yet still maintain a slightly rounded shape.

"It's really a move toward soft, ergonomic sportswear," said Gilbert. "There's a touch of preciousness in the fabrics. Soft and plush looks, such as velvet, give a cozy feel."

In this trend, shapes are ample, and colors are muted and monochromatic and include blue- and mauve-tinted grays. "It's a tonal range with touches of white," she added.

Nouvelle Vague is a slightly retro group with a masculine feel.

The silhouette, according to Gilbert, is "lanky." Inspirations include rockabilly. "There are roomy volumes with shifted constructions," she said. The group's colors are antiqued sepia-like tones such as a group of grays with a violet cast.

Luxe Povera, meanwhile, takes a turn toward "chic, rustic allure," said Gilbert. Shapes are again relaxed but feature a precious ethnic feel. "The influence is Morocco but something nicer than a bazaar feel," she added. Handcrafted looks reign with special weave effects and embroidery details. Subtly oxidized metallics make up the color range which includes soft, pinkish gold.

The last group, Cool Appeal, is "elegant softwear," according to Gilbert. "There's an Eighties influence that is sporty, yet it's ready-to-wear."

Geared toward a younger customer, the group features a combination of activewear and hip-hop-inspired looks that include the use of parachute fabric, as well as casual Americana looks. There's also a feel for glam looks from the Forties in the way of satin pajama styles.

Savory pastels and caramel beiges make up the color range.

"The colors are creamy, sugary and soft and used on a variety of fabrics such as distressed cottons and slippery silks," she said.

Source: *Women's Wear Daily*, July 9, 2002. Courtesy of Fairchild Publications, Inc.

5

Romancing Leather and Fur

The passion for leather apparel as a major fashion statement has reaped nothing but success for the fashion industries, not only among women's and men's apparel producers, but also manufacturers of girls' and boys' apparel and almost all accessories. Creative fashion presentations, therefore, are an important marketing tool to introduce new season leather offerings to manufacturers and designers. Dramatic visual presentation boards and written reports highlight color, texture, and fashion direction for the promotion of leather across all borders of fashion as well as home furnishings.

LEATHER INNOVATIONS

Driven by the demand for leather apparel, designers have been seduced by the wide variety of available types of leather. This has made it possible to incorporate leather into both Fall/Winter and Spring/Summer ready-to-wear collections. As a result, leather has become an all-season fabric and is being used in designs for everything from T-shirts and shorts to dresses and suits, as well as the more traditional outerwear.

Leather Variations

Leather has become an important category in the materials of fashion and is part of all the fabrications that the garment industry uses to create seasonal fashions. The newest innovations include cutting-edge leather treatments that create whisper thin suedes, sumptuously mellow leathers, antique patent, metallic shine, embossed or printed crocodile and lizard, perforated leathers that resemble lace, and glamorous floral, abstract, or conversational prints. The leather industry trends are in sync with fashion. When paisley is popular, leather will be printed to reflect the trend.

Shortened Tanning Process

Leather today is an "on-time" product. With new technology in the tanning processing of leather, the "wet blue" product (the raw leather or suede) is available at the tannery and prepared to be finished with color or texture in a mere three weeks turnover time.

In addition, leather is available in a broad price range, thereby making it accessible to consumers of all ages. Another factor contributing to the popularity of leather is that modern technologies have made caring for leather easier than ever before. As a case in point, there is now even stretchable leather and washable leather.

INTERNATIONAL FOCUS

In the global marketplace, leather fashions are clearly in the spotlight. Top designers, including Michael Kors and Calvin Klein, use leather prominently in their collections. "The ability to use leather like a fabric has been enormously important," said Angelo Uslenghi, a European trend forecaster. "Today's finishes give leather a new edge in apparel—drapability."

He presented the Spring 2002 leather trends, the Natural Sensations report, at a presentation hosted by the Genuine Italian Vegetable Tanned Leather Consortium in New York City. The consortium's presentation focused on Italian leather products. Uslenghi identified three trends based on the Spring/Summer 2002 season: Poetic, Dissonant, and Spontaneous. In 2002/2003, Frivolity was a theme. An excerpt from his 2004 report is at the end of this chapter.

The Italian Vegetable Tanned Leather Consortium's Autumn/Winter 2002/2003 sample book cover includes the trademark tag. Inside, color swatches illustrate the theme of Frivolity.

INDUSTRY PROFILE 5-1 | Faina Golub

336 336 336 336

This page and opposite page: *Faina Golub's creative energy pervades her working environment. These samples illustrate how she creates boards that are not only visually exciting, but also convey a total design image involving color and texture.*

9420 RUSTY
EXTRAVAGANCE
VELVETY
82
82
82
82

Faina Golub, vice president of Leather.Suede.Skins, Inc., based in New York City, is as fashion forward looking as her creative fashion presentations for designers and manufacturers. Interviewed wearing a beige cowl-draped sleeveless suede top and printed neckpiece, pearlized caramel leather pants, a complementary scarf sarong around her waist, and printed caramel/brown plaid patent pointed shoes, Faina exudes the ultimate fashion statement. She is the creative force behind her family's leather business, and she honed her creative skills at the Fashion Institute of Technology, where she studied fashion design.

"Leather has become another way for designers and manufacturers to express new fashions," says Faina. "Today everyone is in leather and suede, and a leather manufacturer can't just cold sell the product, but has to present it in a creative venue."

Faina practices what she preaches. Her creative fashion presentations utilize the visual technique of boards to montage color ranges in themes with appropriate pictorial images. "Many of the designers and manufacturers have done their research, but when they come in, our creative board presentations further confirm the "sell message" of a particular color range or textural treatment. A designer doesn't just make a leather jacket, there's usually five coordinate pieces involved combining leather and fabric. They need coordinated ideas to fuel their imagination."

In addition to the firm's comprehensive collection of skins, Faina puts together color-related sets by coordinating leathers and suedes for design inspiration. For example, in the lime to dark green color range, the coordinated choices include wafer thin suede, pearlized leather, printed floral suede, perforated leather, embossed or printed leathers, genuine skins, double faced leathers, stretch leathers, and matching fox fur. This coordinated assortment provides an all-in-one color and texture concept that designers can adapt. The firm also custom coordinates an assortment according to a designer's inspiration. In addition, depending on the size of the order, the firm offers designers exclusive use of a print. In stock at all times are more than eighty-five color ranges.

To augment the board presentations, Faina also uses color cards and a theme book to stimulate design creativity. "This excites the designer," notes Faina. For a theme called "Spiritual Relax," serene blues and pictorial images of stones and a monk meditating evoke a sense of calm. For another theme, called Miraculous Roots, sienna and brown colors are shown with pictorial images of plant roots and earth.

Who says there can't be creativity in trimmings? Faina knows that romancing leather can be given a new take with unique names. The firm offers more than 500 leather trimmings and, remaining true to its creative instinct, each trim is given the name of a particular pasta, like Angel Hair for a very thin cord, to Spaghetti 1, 2, and 3 or Mini Fettuccini as the trim sizes go up. Rosettes in all types of leathers and suedes have been given a woman's name. "It's all part of the creative process," says Faina. "So when orders are placed the designer may ask for the Mini Fettuccini trim and Jacqueline for a pearlized rose."

"I do not look at my business as work, the creative end comes naturally," Faina admits. "I'm a tear-out artist and collect pictorial images from all kinds of magazines all the time for future use. No one thing triggers an idea or theme. Looking at architecture could inspire me. I visualize texture."

Faina's creative fashion presentation boards, representing her firm's product offerings, are also used at trade shows including the International Fashion Fabric Exhibition in New York City, the Los Angeles Textile Show, and the Material World in Miami.

She travels worldwide to attend trade shows, including Linea Pelle which is held twice a year in Bologne, Italy, and Semaine de Cuir, held in Paris, where tanners present information on their textures, finishes, and colors, one to two years ahead of a selling season.

Research at these trade shows also provides advance color and trend direction for fashion directors, fashion consultants, and fashion forecasters. These prognosticators of fashion will analyze color and trend direction gleaned from these trade shows and may incorporate some of their findings into their own creative fashion presentations.

Ancient Greece influences the Poetic group. The colors are slightly pearlized and the finish is a bit sueded and glazed, ideal for pleating or draping. In the Dissonant group, the colors include a touch of black, which Mr. Uslenghi says creates a look that is crackled, dried out, and a bit ethnic. Finally, candy colors abound in the Spontaneous group. "They're not sophisticated in any way and the palette represents a childlike world," he said. "Leather is an enormous trend," he concluded, "and going forward for luxurious fashions and accessories."

Sharing the limelight is Ruffo Research, with boutiques on via della Spiga in the heart of Milan's fashion district and on via del Babuino, Rome. Ruffo leather fashions are also sold in many exclusive department stores and boutiques worldwide. Ruffo's production is situated in the Tuscan countryside in Calcinaia, a short distance from Florence. The company prides itself on its tradition of producing luxury leathers and using artisans to create many of the prized leather garments, accessories, and luggage with hand-finished details. In addition to its own line, Ruffo has made leather and suede pieces for the most revered designers, including Gianni Versace and Jil Sander.

VOICES OF THE U.S. INDUSTRY

Leather Apparel Association

Leather is at the very center of fashion's upscale statement, and the unifying voice of the leather industry in the United States is the Leather Apparel Association (LAA). Established in 1990, LAA is a not-for-profit trade organization of tanners, cleaners, suppliers, manufacturers, and retailers across the United States, who together represent nearly 60 percent of America's retail dollar volume in leather apparel. LAA helps to generate higher sales, improve profitability, and unite the industry under one recognizable moniker.

LAA is the industry's authoritative source for information on the leather apparel industry. As such, the organization works with more than 600 fashion editors of newspapers and magazines to encourage media coverage. As the leather industry's representative, the organization also addresses controversial issues. Its goal is to enhance the prestige of leather, provide consumer education, and increase consumer awareness and demand for leather. The LAA emblem, with its easily recognizable coat hanger logo, can be found on members' apparel hangtags and on stickers in the windows of retail members' establishments.

The LAA state-of-the-art Web site, www.leatherassociation.com, is the portal for information for consumer, trade, and member information. The comprehensive resource provides diverse sales and industry information in the trade sec-

TABLE 5-1 | MAGAZINES FEATURING LEATHER PRODUCTS

Progetti Moda Pelle
Il Mondo della Pelletteria
Idea Pelle Handbag
Outerwear Magazine
Vogue Pelle

TABLE 5-2 | TRADE SHOWS FEATURING LEATHER

International Fashion Fabrics Exposition, New York
Linea Pelle, Bologne, Italy
Los Angeles Textile Show, Los Angeles
The Material World, Miami
Pan Am Leather Fair, Miami Beach Convention Center, Miami Beach, FL
Semaine de Cuir, Paris

tion, while consumers can learn about the association, the latest fashion trends, care tips, and buying advice. The LAA member link provides a buyer's hotline, a bulletin board, and job listings. For magazines specializing in leather products, see Table 5-1. For a listing of trade shows featuring leather, see Table 5-2.

THE FUR INDUSTRY

Fur as status, fur as a paragon of chic, fur as glamour and the ultimate fashion statement—this is the hallmark of luxury apparel for women worldwide. To stimulate business, furriers continue to experiment with new technology to make fur coats more elegant and colorful or to make them look and feel like corduroy for casual dressing. They want their high-end sophisticated customers to return to glamour and to buy a wardrobe of furs for every daytime, sport, or evening occasion. They also want the career woman to invest in fur fashions and the young girl who is on the go to embrace the fashion for fur with hip-hop inspired coats and skiwear.

Fur as ready-to-wear is another trend exemplified by the firm J. Mendel, which focuses on producing a collection of not only coats, but also suits and dresses. A jersey minidress with mink sleeves, a silk chiffon blouse with ermine collar and cuffs, and a supersheared mink suit were bestsellers at a trunk show held at Bergdorf Goodman.

Fur Information Council of America

To promote the fur business, the Fur Information Council of America (FICA) kicks off Fur Fashion Week in New York City in May of each year with fur collections that will appear in specialty stores and retail department stores in Fall/Winter of the same year.

One FICA group fashion show featured leading fur designers, plus a fur home décor installation and a still-life exhibit. The show paid tribute to Hollywood glamour in a luxurious style that showed the best of the best in opulence by such designers as Donald Deal for Kyros Furs, Imperial Sable, and Zandra Rhodes for Pologeorgis. Chic furs on parade included Eric Gaskins for Miller & Berkowitz and a burst of colorful coats by designers that included David Goodman for Buonuomo. Fresh new takes on fur were presented by Oscar de la Renta for Alixandre Furs.

Licensing Agreements

According to FICA, fur sales increased by more than 21 percent in the year 2000, reaching $1.69 billion. Contributing factors to the increase in fur sales is the fact that the number of fashion designers working with fur has increased and more designers use fur as their fabric of choice. More than 300 well-known fashion designers include fur in their collections. However, because the finished fur garment requires specialized skill and machinery, a fashion designer's luxury fur collection is actually produced through licensing agreements with the market's leading fur manufacturers. For example, Alixandre Furs holds the Oscar de la Renta license, Alexandros Furs produces the Halston fur collection, Kyros Furs produces the Donald Deal line, and Pologeorgis produces the Michael Kors fur line.

A new fur collection by Chado Ralph Rucci is also under license with Pologeorgis featuring coats in mink, lynx, and zorina, a type of South American skunk.

FICA Trade Association

FICA is the fur industry trade association representing fur retailers, designers, and manufacturers across the country, who collectively account for more than 80 percent of U.S. fur sales. FICA provides the public with information on the fur industry, wildlife conservation, and responsible animal care to which the fur industry is committed.

Press Relations

FICA is the only fur trade association that employs a full-time fashion promotion team. Editors of major media and fashion publications rely on FICA's expertise for distinct and reliable fur information and fashion trends year round. Some of FICA's products are:

- Fur fashion trend kits
- Images and slides of the most current designer fur fashions
- Facts on the fur industry and related statistics
- Access to the marketplace via FICA'S promotion team
- Previews of leading international fur designs
- Remodeling, fur care, and storage information
- Consumer information: FICA tracks consumer buying habits and trends for an annual fur report
- Information on fur trade issues such as conservation and animal rights

The Fur District

The fur district in New York has a distinct character all its own and extends from Twenty-seventh to Thirtieth Streets on

Seventh Avenue, spanning out into the side streets between Sixth and Eighth Avenues. One cannot avoid the flurry of activity as workers dart across the streets rushing through the throng of people carrying expensive pelts on the arms in open view. Although some fur garments are made by manufacturers on the premises in New York, escalating production and labor costs have driven these activities outside the city—and even the country.

When buyers are not attending shows, they remain in the fur district reviewing lines for the next season. The pace is hectic during these market weeks, and fur houses hire additional models for in-house presentations. The shows held outside are more elaborately staged and require the expertise of a fashion show producer or public relations firm that will handle publicity and show coordination. A major fur industry fashion show is usually held in April each year. Leather and fur industry events are also featured in *Women's Wear Daily.*

SUMMARY

Clearly, research in the leather and fur markets provides invaluable color and silhouette trend direction to fashion directors in other industries. It also influences predictions made by the fashion forecasting firms, magazines, associations, pattern catalog companies, and the color and styling in the accessories markets. For magazines specializing in fur products, see Table 5-3. For a listing of fur trade shows, see Table 5-4.

TABLE 5-3 | MAGAZINES FEATURING FUR PRODUCTS

Infur
Outerwear
Fur World
Sandy Parker Reports
Textile View

ARDWALK

Sandcastle

Red Wagon

Splash

Powdered Sugar

Sunshine

ue waves and white clouds
n a sun splashed beach

ed pails full of toys carried by
hildren in bright swimsuits

ainbow confections and treats
usted with powdered sugar

old print umbrellas dot the sand
carefree color combinations

vely sports inspire bold graphics
or active lifestyles

MEL'S DINER

Grease

Seltzer

Peach Cobbler

Brown Bag-it

Bottle Green

- Subtle sentiments of happier days and simpler times
- Chrome bar stools, soda pop bottles and charred burgers on a greasy grill
- Pale shades of pastels create a retro feel
- Optical illusions in black and white
- A return to classic colors for bottomweight fabrics

AL FRESCO

Everglade

Fresh Cut

Mirage

Deep End

Starry Night

- Evenings spent at an outdoor cafe beneath a starry sky
- Twilight bleeds into moody shades of pale blue and deep indigo
- Summertime picnics on an open lawn in the park
- Natural greens of fresh-cut herbs and salads
- Sophisticated palette for new denim options

STURDY ELEMENTS

Classic Red

Uniform

Sterling

Burlap

Straw

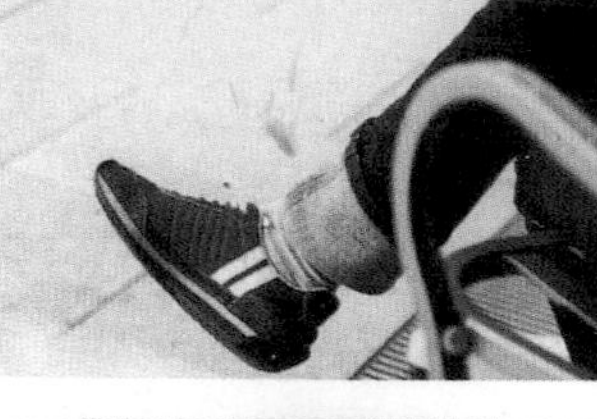

- Uneven texture of burlap sacks
- Traditional and dependable fabrics with hi-tech touches
- Shades of blue with time-honored red
- Base colors on textured weave
- Shades of indigo in fine corduroy

PLATE ONE Four of Cotton Inc.'s color trends for 2005.

PLATE TWO Rachel Herbst, a student at the Fashion Institute of Technology, based her presentation on fashions for the urban traveler. Her themes are highlighted by clever and witty color descriptions for her "Hip Altitudes" theme.

PLATE THREE Melissa Moylan, also a student at the Fashion Institute of Technology, prepared a presentation based on three Picasso paintings. Her interpretations resulted in sleek men's wear silhouettes in warm and provocative colors.

PLATE FOUR Additional color predictions for 2005 from Cotton, Inc.

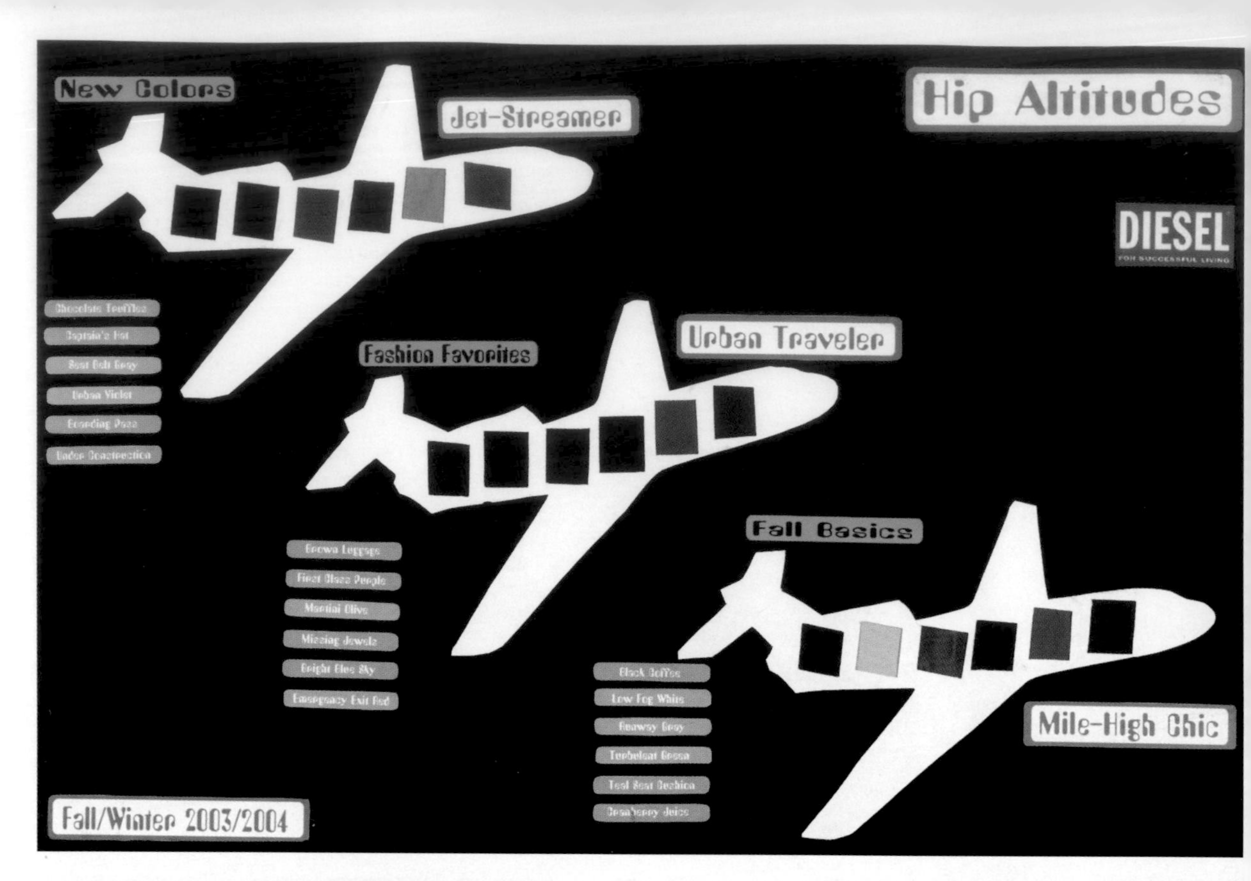
New Colors
Jet-Streamer
Hip Altitudes
DIESEL
FOR SUCCESSFUL LIVING
Chocolate Truffles
Captain's Hat
Seat Belt Gray
Urban Violet
Boarding Pass
Under Construction
Fashion Favorites
Urban Traveler
Brown Luggage
First Class Purple
Martini Olive
Missing Jewels
Bright Blue Sky
Emergency Exit Red
Fall Basics
Black Coffee
Low Fog White
Runway Gray
Turbulent Green
Teal Seat Cushion
Cranberry Juice
Mile-High Chic
Fall/Winter 2003/2004

Hip Altitudes
DIESEL
FOR SUCCESSFUL LIVING
Fall/Winter 2003/2004
Urban Traveler
Mile-High Chic
VIEW FROM THE TOP
Jet-Streamer
707

BCBGMAXAZRIA
'MODERN DAY PICASSO'
FALL 2003 COLORS
PUMPKIN SPICE
DRAGON FIRE
ROASTED ALMOND
MEDITERRANEAN BREEZE
PEANUT BRITTLE
PRALINE PARADE
PAST MIDNIGHT
VOLCANIC ERUPTION
PLUM MOCHA
MARTINI OLIVE
ROARING TIGER
SLICK SLATE
STONE COLD
OVER-CAST
BLACK DIAMOND
BLOODHOUND
STORM CLOUD
MISTY DUSK
HIP HARLEQUIN
MAN BEFORE A MIRROR
FINE SHADOW

BCBGMAXAZRIA
'MODERN DAY PICASSO'
MENSWEAR FALL 2003
HIP HARLEQUIN
MAN BEFORE A MIRROR
FINE SHADOW

VICTORIAN ENCHANTMENT

- Tea Rose
- Amethyst
- Citrine
- Patina
- Port

- Elegance of fairytale watercolors
- Fine motifs from porcelain dishes and wallpaper
- Inspiration from home furnishings
- Antiqued colors with charming fresh accents
- Soft pastels grounded by saturated shades of wine

TRIBAL HYBRID

- Masquerade
- Avocado
- Thai Spice
- Purple Lotus
- Orchid

- Seductive and primal, exotic and wild
- Masquerades, masks and face paint
- A celebration of ethnic cultures and heritage
- Enticing colors of peacock feathers
- Tropical flowers and raw earth elements

BAIT & TACKLE

- Stream
- Night Crawler
- Caution
- Goldfish
- Rubberband

- Crystal blue streams, the vibrant colors of lures in a tacklebox
- Escape from civilization, enjoy the leisure life
- Lifejackets and fishing caps in electric summer brights
- Energizing print accents
- Fluorescent stripes update yarn dyes and trims

spring / summer 2005

TABLE 5-4 FUR TRADE SHOWS

NAFFEM, Montreal, Canada
Mifur, Milan, Italy
Industry 212, New York
Coterie, New York
Magic, Las Vegas, Nevada

Trade Terminology

Antique patent
Embossed
Fur care
Fur District
Fur storage
Licensing agreements
Marketing tool
Metallic shine
Pearlized
Pelle
Pelts
Perforated
Printed leather
Suede
Tannery
Wet blue
Wildlife conservation

READING 5-1 | Uslenghi Report

Research for the Fall/Winter 2004–05 season focuses on prime values of today's society: security and protection, tenderness and warmth in addition to a more daring and inspiring imagination. The Consortium presents three main themes: Shielding—Sensitive—Striking.

Shielding

Medium to thick cowhide featuring relief, layering, incisions in addition to corroded and abrasive treatments for a rugged sense of protection and defense.
Colors: Dense, thick, ironlike, vegetable, and mineral, but even decorative, upholstery, abstract art.
Concreteness and craftsmanship convey feelings of security.

Thickness and Relief Earth crust, topographic maps, vegetal, calcareous, mineral layers. Sense of depth, 3-D effects with shading and hatching, earthy and rocky aspects. Embossing recalls ploughed lands, flowing rivers and streams. Flaky effects resemble layered rocks, lava deposits, crevices. Incisions like streaked pebbles, gravel. Moss effects alternating with lichens, incrustations like tundra.

Metallic Defense Armor, protective shields. Futuristic and medieval, cosmonaut and crusader, Joan of Arc and *Star Wars,* aeronautics and steel industry. Metallic pigments include lead, tin, zinc, pewter, steel, iron. Burnished, oxidized, antiqued finishing. Hammered effect workmanship. Ornamental incisions in curved, rounded, swirled patterns. Soldered aspects with darkened outline. Branding, corrugated sheet-iron effects. Xerographic prints with nails, bolts, screws, iron remnants. Plated, galvanized, glazed treatments.

Shock Proof Shock-absorption, packaging, wrapping. Leather features antique finishing on luggage, bags, satchels, retro trunks. Resort stamps, marks, travel emblems. Decorative reinforcements like metallic studs and straps. Topstitching, contrast and saddle stitching. Corrugated, ribbed and veined effects. Embossing imitates reptile skin with large or small scales. Scaffolding, framework, structured xerographic. Geometries recall Soviet Constructivism of Malevich, Rodchenko, Tatlin.

Decorative Covering Embellishment and support on the inside. Tapestry, wallpaper, lining, tiles, parquet, carpets. Interior design styles. Reproduction of different precious woods featuring Art Déco inlay in herringbone, diamond patterns. Weaves resemble bamboo and wicker workmanship. Embossing recalls symmetric tile patterns. Geometries and graphics inspired by modern art imitate carpet designs. Xerographic and engraved prints in Victorian style à la William Morris feature garlands, festoons, florals, leaf and animal compositions.

Sensitive

Medium to thin cowhide, full grain, nappa finish, milled and oiled to soften, enhancing suppleness and flexibility.
Colors: Warm, opulent, natural, creamy, but also fruity, pulpy, candy shades.
Refine and soften to encourage intimacy and warmth.

Softened Classic Traditional vegetable-tanned cowhide with a nappa touch. Colors reflect a discreet richness: hazelnut, chestnut, tan, blonde, beige. Finest quality, smooth surface, regular grain. Vegetable tanning at its best featuring slight shading, veining, imperfections. The naturalness of leather is emphasized and enhanced. "Wet milling" treatments for a worn look that seems to mold, take shape.

Velvety Touch Softness is accentuated by brushed, emerized, buffed treatments on both sides. Suede aspects often partial and irregular to "velvetize" inner and outer surfaces. Raised effects. Workmanship, slight incisions featuring circular movements. Whipped cream peaks with shading. Hand-coloring in overlapping layers with diluted tones in circular, blended effects.

Puffed Surfaces Fleshy, pulpy sensations. Workmanship features porous aspects, like tiny cells, honeycombs. Puffy rolls and cylinders. Natural, accordion pleats, organ pipes. Embossing with raised air bubble effects. Flounced or sectional work resembling parachute construction. Quilting in geometric designs features slightly chirred stitching.

Super Oily Slippery touch, extra brilliance, lubricated surfaces. Grease, oil, wax, silicone to mold without hardening. Use of grease, gel for wet aspects. Oily streaks, stains with iridescent borders. Designs, incisions often partially erased as if "consumed" by grease. Tiny drops of oil sprayed to create dotted effects.

Striking
Cowhide reflects maximum creativity with contrasting aspects and workmanship often to extremes, confirming the versatility and vitality of vegetable-tanned leather.
Colors: Nocturnal, darkened, dim, obscure but also acid, flashing, fluorescent. Audacious creativity to stimulate a bit of eccentricity.

Day/Night Positive and negative. Dark grounds with stunning highlights. Rays, flames, flashes and glowing, fluorescent, cathode arrows pierce total darkness. Inlays, engraving, luminous geometric inserts, recalling 1960s optical style. Beams of light, daybreak, dusk. Eclipse effect with circle of light, lunar phases. Gleaming rays to illuminate the night.

Summer/Winter Summer memories transported to Winter. Marine life including shells, starfish, jellyfish on dark grounds. Hazy, dim, obscured sunlight. Tropical flowers in dark shades. Beach chair stripes in black/acid tones. Tart, acidic shades feature grey blotches. Straw and basketweaves tinted with dark colors. Mock perforations form arabesque motifs in dark tints. Black netting, mesh on black or colored grounds.

Mini/Maxi Leathers to coordinate, mix and match. Identical workmanship and motifs in micro and macro versions. Spray and pigment-jet techniques create big blotches and tiny drops of color. Embossing, raised surfaces, large and small reptile scales. Coarse spiral placed effects create unique motifs. Geometric patterns include large squares, diamonds, triangles teamed with micro version. Inspiration: Op Art, Vasarely, Riley, Albers. Inlay of large and small squares.

New/Antique Craftsmanship and technology confront one other. Smooth, even, shiny aspects alternate with wrinkled, crumpled, opaque effects on the same leather. Lacquers and shiny wax combine or overlap with dull buffing. Partial embossing features crinkled, antiqued effects used on smooth leathers. Metallic pigments with antiqued, oxidized effects contrast with clean, shiny grounds. Hand-coloring in bright, dense tones alternates with faded, discolored, bleached aspects.

Source: Fall/Winter 2004/2005 Uslenghi report. Courtesy of Italian Vegetable Tanned Leather Consortium (English only)

6

Creative Presentations at the Fiber, Fabric, and Manufacturing Level

THE FIBER INNOVATORS

As an integral part of their marketing process, the large chemical producers are the big players in forecasting trends. Their main objective is to create design inspirations and promote their brands to an impressive variety of industry end uses. These strong-arm prognosticators command a giant slice of market share by aggressively promoting their fibers in creative fiber/fabric/fashion presentations. The first round of trend presentations is geared to guide textile mills, using new technology and concept ideas in color and fabric direction. The presentation's goal is to generate trade awareness and convey the silent "sell" message about a particular fiber company's family of fibers. A creative fashion presentation is also the vehicle that drives the promotion of the fiber company's brand name both at the trade and consumer levels. The fiber industry promotes itself through industry newspapers (see Table 6-1) and textile trade shows (Table 6-2).

For example, INVISTA (formerly DuPont Textiles & Interiors) is a global, branded business that brings innovation to diverse end uses through brands such as Lycra® elastane, Tactel® nylon, and CoolMax® performance fabrics. Aggressive advertising campaigns, generic for the trade or in concert with a designer/manufacturer, promote consumer awareness of the brand name.

TABLE 6-1 FIBER INDUSTRY NEWSPAPERS AND MAGAZINES

Bobbin
1500 Hampton Street
Columbia, SC 29201
(www.bobbin.com)

California Apparel News
California Mart
110 East 9th Street
Los Angeles, CA 90079
(www.apparelnews.com)

Daily News Record
7 West 34th Street
New York, NY 10001
(www.dnrnews.com)

Textile World
Textile Industries Media Group
2100 Powers Ferry Road
Atlanta, GA 30339
(www.textileindustries.com)

Women's Wear Daily
7 West 34th Street
New York, NY 10001
(www.wwd.com)

Trade Shows

Attendees

Fiber companies conduct their presentations on two levels. They first work two years ahead of a season with the textile mills, which are the fiber producers' primary customer base. Advance presentations give the mills sufficient time for fabric development and mill production for the new season.

At the second level, presentations are held one year ahead of a season for the designers and manufacturers, who attend fiber company presentations for color and fabric direction and

TABLE 6-2 TEXTILE TRADE SHOWS

Bobbin World, Orlando, FL
CPD Fabrics, Düsseldorf, Germany
Expofil Yarn and Fibers, Paris, France
Ideacomo, Como, Italy
International Fashion and Fabric Exhibition, Jacob Javits Convention Center, New York City
Los Angeles International Textile Show, California Mart, Los Angeles, CA
Lyon Mode City/Interfilière, Lyon, France
Première Vision, Parc d'Expositions, Paris, France
Salon International de la Lingerie/Interfilière, Paris France
Texitalia, Milan, Italy
Tissue Premiere, Grand Palais, Lille, France
The Material World, Miami, FL
Yarn Fair International and CAD Expo, New York Hilton Hotel and Towers, New York, NY

to see the concept garments. In addition, the audience may consist of other fashion industry personnel, such as fashion directors, fashion consultants, product developers, design teams, stylists, retailers, and the trade press.

No-Charge Presentations

A fiber company's presentation is free to qualified industry personnel. The advantage to the attendee is that in this world of high-tech communications and fast-breaking trends, the fiber company has done all the research for them on color, fabric, and concept garments. A fashion director or design team representing a manufacturer therefore can draw on a wide variety of market data, analyze the research, and interpret the information for a firm's particular classification of merchandise and target customer. When they attend several different fiber firm presentations, the repeat information confirms the right trend direction. INVISTA, Celanese, Monsanto, TENCEL®,

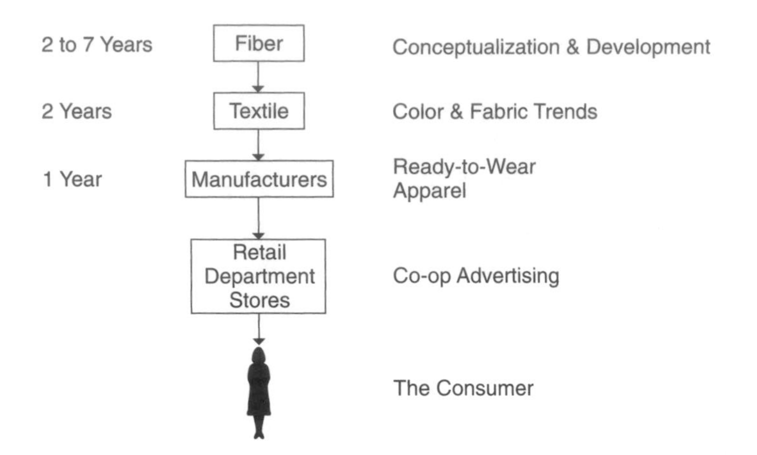

The route for creative fashion presentations

and Bayer are among the major presenters of seasonal Spring/Summer and Fall/Winter trend forecasts.

Creative presentations are usually held at a firm's executive offices in New York City. In some cases, a presentation may be given in other major cities. A company may also stage an extravaganza at an outside venue to kick off a major new fiber introduction. However, economic conditions and budget restraints have resulted in a decrease in expenditures on such major outside productions.

Fashion Research

Some fashion aficionados say that fashion starts with the fiber, where filament innovations will affect the look and texture of textiles, the construction of clothing, and what the consumer will ultimately wear. The point may be arguable, but the statement deserves examination. Case in point is that when stretch was introduced as a key ingredient in ready-to-wear activewear and sportswear, it appealed to society's lifestyle preferences for comfort and easy fit. Stretch is not just fashion driven. Today we take stretch for granted. You can feel the stretch but you cannot see it, because it is an invisible component in fabrications.

Quest for New Fibers

In early manufactured synthetics, wrinkle resistance, wash and wear, and permanent pleats were given factors. Today fiber producers, competitive to the very core of their existence, continue the quest for new fiber development by investing in high-tech equipment to create innovative new fibers.

The fiber company's laboratory research department, therefore, is on the cutting edge of developing new fashion-forward filaments that can perform with more texture and character. The textile mills then incorporate new fiber improvements and innovations into fabrications, thereby responding to the consumers' desire for comfort and fashion. Fiber development is a costly process that may have a gestation period of two to seven years. It is even longer until fiber realization.

Many influences are driving technological developments. Increasingly, consumers will be wearing fabrics made from fibers created in the laboratory using space age technologies. The future will bring fabrics with stronger ultraviolet protection; fabrics that adjust to changes in climate by regulating temperature; and fabrics that, like a chameleon, will change color depending on the lighting system. Eventually, a computer chip inserted in the fabric will change its pattern, and the surface will dry clean itself. The future is now, because some of these concepts are already available and look just like conventional fabrics.

Promotion Techniques

To introduce new fiber innovations and promote their established fiber brands, fiber producers consider creative fiber/fabric/fashion presentations a necessary marketing tool. Fabric mills can plan their fabric development cycle so that manufacturers and designers can glean trend inspiration. From a promotional perspective, trend presentations are an added value service for customers.

An Intimate Workshop

The INVISTA workshop, for example, gears its semiannual Intimate Apparel Workshop in New York City to a specific market audience—the intimate apparel, foundation, and swimwear designers and manufacturers. Iris LeBron, INVISTA's fashion director of intimate apparel, swimwear, and activewear hones her research skills and travels the globe in search of the newest, most innovative trends. She also attends major trade shows, such as the Lyon Mode City exhibit in France, featuring lingerie, swimwear, and fabrics; Intimo Intimare, highlighting swimwear and lingerie at the Bologna Fairgrounds in Italy; and the Salon International de la Lingerie Interfilière held in Paris. Once her research is compiled, she prepares a presentation for INVISTA's partners, such as mills, manufacturers, and retailers. Ms. LeBron's advance research helps her to identify intimate apparel trends and to establish and develop pertinent themes for both the firm's trend booklet and workshop presentation.

In addition to the creative board presentations featuring color ranges and fabric swatches, a video highlighting the trends illustrates the themes of the season. A global concept garment collection of trendy prototype fashions from Europe, North America, South America, and Asia pulls together innovative fabrics and incorporates them into new looks or styles. These garments include dozens of bra and bottom coordinates, as well as bodysuits, bodyshapers, camisoles, and matching pants.

The intimate apparel fashions help to inspire the imagination of manufacturers by showing the many creative applications of the firm's fiber brands. INVISTA also offers the latest developments in color direction as part of the trend forecast. The palette includes an extensive color card featuring approximately twenty to thirty colors per season.

Creative Themes

Theatricality combined with product information is a major component of a fiber company's presentation. It is part entertainment with the practical application of inspiration and interpretation of trend information. The fashion director is a creative individual who each season develops a new theme for the trend workshop.

With an overall theme such as As the World Turns, INVISTA's LeBron highlights not only the global aspects of the collections, but dramatizes the creative fashion presentation by tying in with popular television shows. Her findings are divided into three distinct categories, each after one of the U.S.'s daytime soap operas—*The Bold and the Beautiful, Days of Our Lives,* and *The Young and the Restless.* These three categories highlight a different trend and lifestyle.

1. *The Bold and the Beautiful:* This trend is all about luxury, and the concept garments feature colors that are bold and sophisticated. The fabric emphasis is on INVISTA's fiber Tactel®, which offers fashion-forward finishes in deep colors, and Lycra®, which provides a shapely and smooth fit.
2. *Days of Our Lives:* This trend is more about comfort, but it does not sacrifice style. Technology plays a big role, with a focus on seam-free looks and such details as laser cuts with daywear trends such as camisoles and coordinated bottoms, with emphasis on Supplex® and Lycra® Soft for shaping and Tactel® for an exceptionally smooth hand.
3. *The Young and the Restless:* The third theme is inspired by the patterns and colors in the swimwear market. Fabrics are easy care and allow for movement, such as cotton/Lycra® blends and Tactel®.

Celanese Acetate: The Fabric Library

Most fiber producers maintain a comprehensive archive of their fiber brands in mill fabrications in a fabric library for customer research and inspiration. The fabric library is therefore another

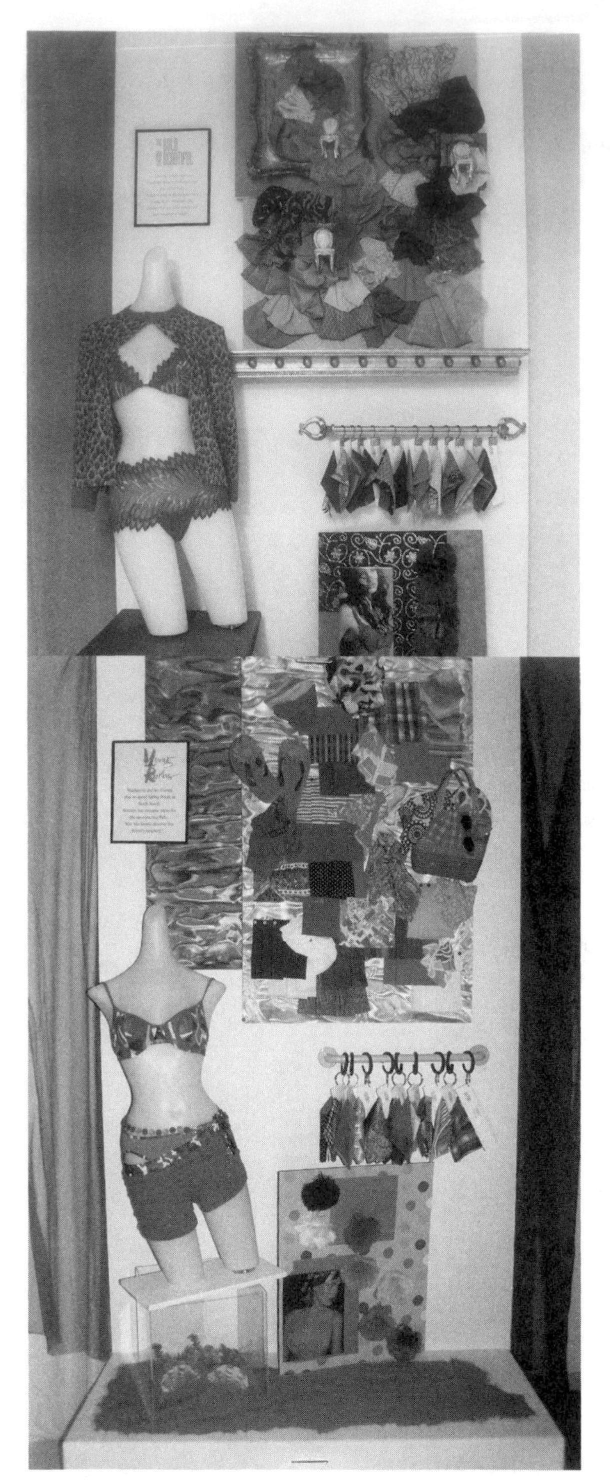

A familiar theme can provide an exciting backdrop to a presentation. INVISTA's use of soap operas, with the theme As the World Turns, highlights the drama associated with the world's many cultures. The Bold and the Beautiful *(top left), based on the character Brooke and her travels to Italy, is all about luxury.* Days of Our Lives *(top right) is inspired by the character Marlena and her spa getaway; the theme is comfort with style. Finally,* The Young and the Restless *(bottom), inspired by the character Mackenzie and her glamorous vacation to South Beach, is all about fun.*

marketing tool used to increase the sales potential of a fiber company's product lines. The library also serves as an important point of reference and gives manufacturers and retailers a hands-on opportunity to review established and new fabric offerings made exclusively of the fiber company's brands. Fabrics may be displayed on large boards, hung on racks, or categorized in trays on a conference room table.

THE GLOBAL STUDIO

Fiber producer Celanese Acetate is part of Celanese AG, the world's largest cellulose acetate filament producer. Its products, Celanese acetate and triacetate yarn and MicroSafe fiber, are found in women's and men's apparel fashions, linings, home furnishings, and industrial end uses. Celanese knows the value of its fabric library for research, inspiration, and marketing of its acetate brands. The library, a 270-square-foot space, is called Celanese Acetate Global studios. It is a permanent fixture at the firm's midtown Manhattan offices and houses a global collection of both men's and women's fashions, home furnishings, and lining swatches from more than seventy-five converters and knitters.

The purpose of the library is to offer retailers and apparel manufacturers a one-stop-shopping opportunity to review the different textures and uses of the company's fiber brand, Celanese Acetate. The swatches are updated every Spring and Fall with a brand new collection of commercial fabrics from the United States, Mexico, Asia, and Europe. In the fabric development stage, Celanese works with mills and converters fifteen to eighteen months ahead of a season.

In addition to the global fabric library, James Siewert, Celanese Acetate's international trend/forecast analyst, presents seasonal creative fashion presentations, which are given one year ahead of the Fall/Winter or Spring/Summer season for an audience of designers, manufacturers, and retail private label personnel.

INDUSTRY PROFILE 6-1 | Roseann Forde

Roseann Forde advising a mill client using a presentation board of concept fabrics and silhouettes.

Roseann Forde, former fashion director at INVISTA, was an influential spokesperson for the fiber giant. Her prognostications provided major color stories and concept fabrics and garments featuring INVISTA fibers in two workshops each season for its mills and manufacturing partners. "These hands-on workshops are considered to be an added value service that we provide our customers," noted Ms. Forde.

The first trend workshop was given for INVISTA's textile mill customers. The forecast presentation was tailored to meet the needs of each partner and was often most effective when conducted with one mill and its staff. Ms. Forde had been an instrumental force in developing product at the mill workshop in New York, which was given each year for the Spring/Summer and Fall/Winter seasons. The second presentation was a separate ready-to-wear trend workshop for the fashion apparel, plus size, and children's wear manufacturers throughout North America.

"Having served as fashion director for the past fifteen years, I have played an integral role in the design concepts and fabric development created by DuPont [INVISTA] and its customers," said Ms. Forde.

Working with the Mills

In one of her major roles as fashion director, she represented the fiber giant's global

The cover to the Spring/Summer 2002 workshop "Attitudes" reflects the theme perfectly. No words are necessary.

branded business, which is linked to INVISTA's goal to increase its introduction of innovative fabrics to the U.S. market. The mill trend presentation was based on research gathered from the various global INVISTA partners, market consultants, fashion forecast experts, and consumer reports.

Ms. Forde's trends workshop was given first and foremost for the spinners, weavers, knitters, and mills who are INVISTA's prime customers. INVISTA's connections with textile mills bring new innovative fabrics, developed in tandem with the trend findings, to all categories of apparel, accessories, home, and industrial textiles through brands like Lycra® elastane, Tactel® textile nylon, and CoolMax® performance fabrics, to name a few.

"I work with the mills two years in advance of a season on a one-on-one or group basis. The mills may bring in several of their product development people, the fabric stylists, and anyone else from the firm who would benefit from the color and fabric development information," said Ms. Forde. "Although many mills visit DuPont's [INVISTA's] flagship offices in New York City, my work also involves a great deal of

Illustrations of the three attitude themes: power (left), sensuality (center), and freedom (right).

travel to mills in other states, as well as the international sectors of DuPont's [INVISTA's] global community," added Ms. Forde.

Creative Inspiration

Ms. Forde put together boards that she used in a creative presentation to illustrate color, yarn, and fabric trends. The color and fabric boards featured key directional stories in creative themes that conveyed patterns, luxe elements, airy impressions, and tactile and dimensional effects.

She bridged the gap between creative inspiration and concrete product development of new textiles by showing mills samples of fabrics that she had acquired from international sources during her travel expeditions in the global marketplace. The idea was to demonstrate to the mills different end uses using INVISTA's family of fibers.

In addition, INVISTA has a group of international fabric development experts, who create an array of new knit and woven fabrics that utilize the latest fiber technology invented by INVISTA. Roseann and her counterparts throughout Europe, Asia, and South America presented these fabrics to the mill customers for product development.

"Color direction is also an important ingredient in mill presentations," added Ms. Forde. "I research color through many sources on a domestic and international level. Travel worldwide helps me to keep my pulse on what's happening by attending major textile trade shows such as Première Vision and Expofil, the yarn and fiber expo in France, and Texitalia in Italy."

Ms. Forde had a reputation as a fashion, fiber, and textile authority and brought to her role as global fashion director seasoned expertise as a fiber producer professional. She also served on various fashion committees and was president of the Roundtable of Fashion Executives, an "insider" group of industry professionals that meet to discuss trend topics or to hear about the latest industry developments. She also contributed to and participates in trend meetings at the Color Association of the United States and is on the advisory board of American Color and Trends for the International Fashion Fabric Exhibition.

The Attitudes Workshop

Ms. Forde pulled inspiration for creative fashion presentations from many sources. In general she was keenly aware of developments in all segments of the fashion industry and kept abreast about what was happening in society and the world.

After working with the mills Ms. Forde focused on the ready-to-wear workshop presented for the fashion industry designers, manufacturers, design teams, and product development personnel. Other industry guests might have included retailers, stylists, fashion directors, fashion editors, and any qualified industry professional whose job includes research in the INVISTA fabric library.

Ms. Forde zeroed in on a main theme to creatively present fabric and concept garment ideas. "No matter what type of attitude your customer wants to project, whether it's power, sensuality, or freedom, this season's wide range of fabric and silhouettes puts her in an independent frame of mind." This was the introduction to Ms. Forde's "Attitudes," theme for INVISTA's Spring/Summer 2002 ready-to-wear workshop.

To celebrate this liberation, Ms. Forde focused on three distinct feelings in fabric color and silhouette. Under an overall "Attitudes" theme, the three corresponding signature themes were Power, Sensuality, and Freedom. The Attitudes workshop also included an audiovisual presentation and a trends portfolio containing a ready-to-wear color card and a separate fabric resource list. The portfolio illustrated prototype garments and a vast array of commercially available fabrics from domestic and international mills. The INVISTA ready-to-wear workshop also introduced new garments (either concept styles or fashions bought abroad). Creative boards, placed around the workshop room, further emphasized the color, fabric, and silhouette trends. Ms. Forde then discussed the season's theme.

"Attitudes is a posture. It announces loud and clear, this is who I am," stated Forde. "Today's woman exudes attitude, she is unabashed in her sense of self and what she wants to convey. The trends for this season augment this notion with the use of Diverse INVISTA fibers such as Lycra® elastane, Micromattique™, Dacron® polyester, and Tactel® nylon."

The "Power" trend placed the focus on strong colors and bold apparel in a rich array of textures and patterns. "A woman of power loves the movement Lycra® brings to her obi wrapped jackets, pleated skirts, shirt dressing, asymmetric knit tops, and halter dresses," noted Ms. Forde, as she shows the concept garments to the audience.

For "Sensuality," the mood was softer, more provocative and feminine. Harmonious blends of Lycra® and Tactel® personify sensuality in printed sheer blouses and sequined skirts, embroidered cardigans and updated peasant blouses working their way into the trend.

"Freedom," according to Ms. Forde, promoted a younger lighthearted fashion attitude with stretch leather pants, bias cut skirts, and sculptural wrap dresses and tops. The colors for Freedom were more vivid, clean brights paired with dusty shades.

The concept designs and directional garments in the Attitudes ready-to-wear workshop indicated INVISTA's key trends for industry inspiration.

Called "Directives," the presentation is a review of the international fashion collections and focuses on trends in color, pattern, and fabric. Concept garments that demonstrate new and unusual uses of acetate knits and wovens are also shown. Directives seminars are available by appointment to qualified industry professionals (www.CelaneseAcetate.com).

Fashion Director's Research

To be a prognosticator of international trends, James Siewert has become a consummate researcher who attends major fiber/fabric trade fairs both in the U.S. and global marketplaces, including Texitalia in Milan, Italy, and Première Vision in Paris.

"A fashion director at a fiber company must not only have excellent oral communication skills, but the ability to write succinct reports on fashion and color trends," notes Mr. Siewert.

To introduce the color stories for the Spring/Summer 2002 Celanese Acetate color card, Siewert created six themes—Desert Shades, Beach Shades, Park Shades, Island Shades, Urban Shades, and Pool Shades—each accompanied by a description and market end use. For example, here's the description for the first theme:

> Desert Shades: The inclusion of Bleached White starts this group. As a pure base or an accent, white works in this group with all six categories as a necessary color. Add Sand, Slate, and Wood to the mix as solids with texture or sheen and use the Moss for more contemporary designs. This group will work for both men's and women's wear—as a casual separates story or in a more tailored mood.

In addition to seminars for Celanese, Mr. Siewert is a lecturer on the international circuit. He gives trend direction speeches in Mexico and Belgium where Celanese Acetate filaments are manufactured. As an industry authority he serves as chairman of the men's committee of the Color Association of the United States and is a sought-after speaker for the Fashion News Workshop and the Fashion Group International.

Tencel Inc. Presents

Fiber producers, vying for market share, also use other venues for creative fashion/fabric presentations. A lecture series format is the way that Tencel Inc. introduces major trends for its TENCEL® fiber brand. At the fiber firm's Global Fabric Fair, a guest lecture series was the focal point for presenting key trends to an attendance that topped 253 guests from the retail and manufacturing sectors of the business. TENCEL has the advantage of being made from the natural cellulose found in wood pulp. Because it is produced in a nonchemical manner, TENCEL is economical in its use of energy and natural resources and is fully biodegradable. This is an advantageous message when retailing to consumers.

The Global Fabric Fair is held twice yearly and is seasonally driven, one year in advance of the selling season. For example, Spring 2002 was presented in April 2001 and Fall/Winter 2002/2003 at the end of October 2001.

Guest speaker Sandy MacLennan of East Central Studios, an international fashion authority, discussed major color and fabric trends reflecting Tencel's importance in the marketplace. His presentation emphasized fabric concepts seen at Première Vision, as well as a directional viewpoint for the TENCEL fiber brand, particularly denim, natural stretch, and knitwear.

The lecture series provided a creative energy sparked by other scheduled speakers. Carole D'Arconte, president of Creative Solutions presented color and silhouette trends for men and women in a slide format; Elaine Flowers, trend director of Dillard's, Inc., offered a directional point of view and trends from retail; and Wendell Brown, fashion director of the *Daily News Record (DNR)* gave an editor's perspective of the runway shows in men's wear.

The Tencel Fabric Room's waterfall wall display of fabrics and colors provides designers and fabric researchers with a directional and global point of view of fabrics made in the fiber brand. To further augment the sell message of Tencel, the firm offers a resource list of the broad range of mills and converters of TENCEL-based textiles for men's and women's styling, upholstery fabrics, and home fashions in sheets and towels. Theme boards display fabric swatches and pictorial images called Lounge, Urban Kitten, and Oxygen as indicators of trend direction.

Taking a global approach, the firm's directional color card, called a Colour Narrative, is printed in French, Italian, English, Spanish, and German. It concentrates on a collection of thoughts with distinct themes like Naive, colors of generous innocence; Vintage, secret garden colors; Escape, therapeutic and refreshed colors; and Breathe, colors of energy.

At retail the firm's active coop advertising and hangtag program is designed to increase consumer awareness of the TENCEL products.

Bayer: Technology and Imagination

The Bayer Corporation, with headquarters in Pittsburgh, is a member of the worldwide Bayer Group based in Leverkusen, Germany, with U.S. offices in Charleston, South Carolina. Since 1964, Bayer has been identified as a major alternate spandex supplier. Bayer's technologically advanced fiber production facility is located in Bushy Park, South Carolina.

With sourcing a global issue and spandex demand increasing, creative fashion/fiber presentations give mills and manufacturers new technologies to create new possibilities and end uses in a fiber brand. "Spandex growth is a way of life for the comfort and active mobility it affords today's consumer lifestyles. To successfully meet this new demand, Dorlastan production has been doubled," says Jan Nolen, Bayer marketing and merchandising manager.

As fashion trends continue to dictate stretch and functionality, meeting the needs for stretch wovens and knits grows enormously important. At the same time, disseminating a high level of trend information to mills, apparel manufacturers, and retailers includes a mix of technology, imagination, and the recognition of customers' demands. One mouse click connects producer and consumer in a few seconds. Meeting the challenge the Bayer Corporation puts substantial emphasis on annual forecast presentations.

BAYER'S TREND EXPERT

Talk to anyone in the lingerie and hosiery industries about Marian de Ruyter, and their eyes light up. Ms. de Ruyter, a

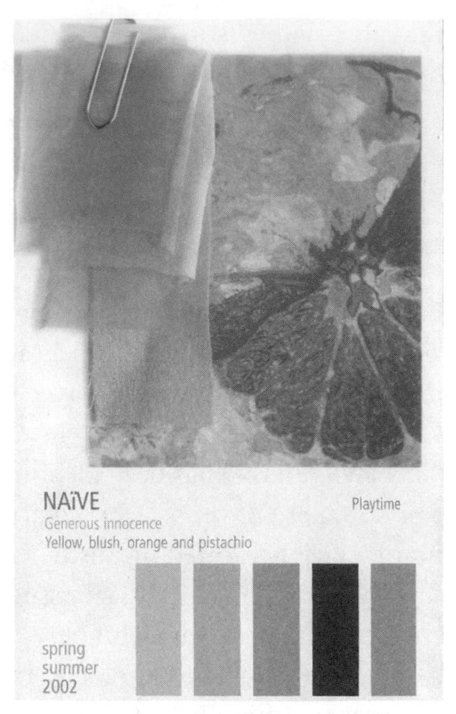

This page and opposite page: *For its Spring/Summer 2002 color narrative, Tencel's themes were Naïve, Intimate, Eye Candy, Escape, Breathe, and Vintage. The color card skilllfully blends the weight, color, and texture of the fabrics.*

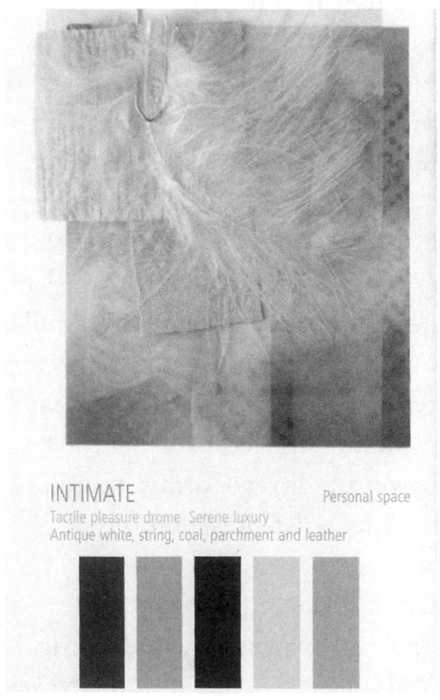

EYE CANDY
Delicious and vibrant A taste for warmer tones
Reds, pinks and browns
ESCAPE
Therapeutic and refreshed
Cool graduation and contrast Fluo yellow, cool turquoise and ecru
BREATHE
The colours of energy Clear and strong
Oxygen blues and white
VINTAGE
The secret garden
Calm and soothing Lyrical and organic Greyed and accented
TENCEL®

revered and respected consultant for the Bayer Corporation's global business, specializes in creating design ideas using Dorlastan® spandex. She produces trend sketch books on swimwear, hosiery, lingerie, and outerwear.

Ms. Nolen says, "Her guidance has helped Bayer bring added value to its customers by leading them into new design realms with ideas that lead to new fabrications and inspire the minds of today's customer."

At Bayer's annual forecasting presentation, Ms. de Ruyter introduces new concepts and challenges the industry with thought-provoking starter ideas in new fiber development. The Dorlastan bodyfashion Trendvision 2002, for example, is a comprehensive illustrated and written presentation on bodyfashions and hosiery colors, fabrics, atmospheres, inspiration, and styling for Dorlastan elastan and elastic fibers. These presentations are held annually for the mills two years ahead of a season. For example, Bayer's 2003 presentation is given in March 2001. Manufacturers and designers see the presentation one year ahead of a season.

Ms. de Ruyter's trends forecast is based on her innate foresight of what the market will expect in terms of style, comfort, and color. Sketches of concept garments include new seamless technology that creates another way for designers and manufacturers to create beautiful, fashionable, and functional fashion for all body types. Ms. de Ruyter's prediction that the demand for seamless will grow is supported by Bayer's installation of Santoni® (a registered trademark of Gruppo Lonati of Italy) seamless equipment. This equipment enables the Dorlastan technical teams in North America and Europe to collaborate with customers on product development ideas that will meet the needs of the marketplace. A seamless bodysuit is a typical example. Corsetry-inspired sketches project futuristic designs, as well as figure-flattering and hidden seam construction.

Above left: *Dorlastan's color vision for 2003/2004 emphasizes fiber, fabric, and color trends that are emotion driven. In "Free Spirit," the colors are graphic and the style playful.*

Above right: *For 2004/2005, the theme "Once upon a Time" brought a dreamlike look, with peaceful colors and seductive designs.*

Promotional Themes

Ms. de Ruyter's trend illustrations in Dorlastan's large black trends book represent a printed version of the theme boards with concept garments. Each illustration is given a theme name to inspire and promote the use of Dorlastan. The Organic theme uses ideas illustrating the imaginative power of nature and associations with mother earth with silhouettes for natural bodyforming seamfree garments. The Nude and Naked theme takes inspiration from the second skin approach with fluid silhouettes built on transparent layers. The Love for Decoration theme represents personalization and a move from "mass customization" to individual customized solutions with handcrafted looks. These themes ignite inspiration and promote Dorlastan in spandex solutions.

Industry Organizations

The Intimate Apparel Council (IAC) is a division of the American Apparel and Footwear Association (AAFA), the national trade association for apparel and footwear industries. The IAC is the intimate apparel industry's most prestigious organization and is comprised of the leading designers, manufacturers, and suppliers of intimate apparel products.

THE FIBER PROMOTION ORGANIZATIONS

Fiber promotion organizations, such as Cotton Incorporated's Cottonworks® and Masters of Linen, are also represented in the first segment of creative fashion presentations and provide another area for trend research. These organizations are member supported, and their prime goal is to provide a concentrated focus on a specific genre of natural fiber in trends that will impact the business of their members. The associations do not produce any fiber or fabric. They primarily disseminate information through diverse promotion programs to heighten trade and consumer awareness of natural fibers. The commercial aim is to capture market share for natural fibers in the international textile marketplace and to compete successfully with the manufactured fiber giants.

Fiber promotion organizations evolved in the 1960s when the natural fiber producers realized that their market share was being eroded under the assault of the new synthetic fibers. The cotton growers, for one, realized that they had to start thinking about trade promotion, and that realization led to the formation of Cotton Incorporated. That history is chronicled in a book commissioned by Cotton Incorporated, entitled *Cotton's Renaissance: A Study in Market Innovation,* written by Timothy Curtis Jacobson and George David Smith of the Winthrop Group, a Cambridge, Massachusetts-based

MASTERS OF LINEN, EUROPEAN LINEN OF QUALITY
You are cordially invited to attend

SPRING/SUMMER 2002
FABRIC AND COLOR TRENDS PRESENTED BY ORNELLA BIGNAMI
plus
An audio-visual review of linen fashions from leading international designers

Tuesday, March 13, 2001 at 4 p.m.

Fashion Institute of Technology
Katie Murphy Auditorium
Seventh Avenue at 27th Street • New York, New York

Exhibit: Masters of Linen fabric collections for apparel and the home.

Cocktail Reception Follows

R.S.V.P. Tel: (212)734-3640 Fax: (212) 734-3648 Email: USMastersOfLinen@aol.com

Invitation to Masters of Linen Spring/Summer 2002 presentation, along with linen swatches.

consulting company. The book details the history of the U.S. cotton industry and the role that the fiber promotion group played in it.

On the trade level, every planner in the chain of command—from president to merchandiser, designer/manufacturer, fashion director, and home furnishings analyst—attends a fiber promotion organization's creative fashion presentations. These professionals collect color, fabric, and silhouette trend data that will be used to make color, fabric, fashion, and home product decisions each season.

Services of Fiber Promotion Organizations

Fabric Library

The fiber promotion organization's fabric library provides a comprehensive collection of mill samples as well as concept fabrics that are a rich source of inspiration for product development. A newsletter keeps industry clients informed about trends and new fabric developments.

New Talent Showcases

As a showcase for new designer talent, fiber promotion organizations may also endorse young designers' interpretations of textile innovation through garment presentations of avant-garde fashions. These innovative styles by young designers illustrate to mills, manufacturers, and retailers the design possibilities of the natural fibers/fabrics.

Public Awareness

In tandem with forecasting services, the fiber promotion organizations also encourage public awareness of natural fibers by disseminating educational material to consumers through advertising and hangtag promotions. As a case in point, Cotton Incorporated introduced a new trade advertising campaign consisting of four-color advertisements featuring silicone figures in indoor and outdoor settings wearing all-cotton clothes.

INDUSTRY PROFILE 6-2 | Christian David Kozaki

Christian David Kozaki with his "Les Belles Choses" collection (top left) and a Cotton Inc. advertisement of Kozaki's wedding gown made of cotton (top right). At the bottom, his "Roman Holiday in Palm Beach" storyboard for evening wear is sultry and stylish.

In a special venue, The Cottonworks Fabric Library introduced Christian David Kozaki, designer of "Les Belles Choses," a premiere collection of cotton-inspired gowns and daytime fashions to the press and invited industry guests.

Mr. Kozaki brings couture style to women's sportswear and eveningwear, utilizing such all-American fabrics as denim, gingham, and piqué. In his Resort 2002 collection, he displayed his garments in a creative fashion presentation, with the overall theme, "Roman Holiday in Palm Beach." The theme was projected on storyboards with fashion illustrations and Roman Holiday images that related to a famous movie star. Audrey Hepburn was his muse, and fetching, too, was a 100 percent cotton A-line dress with polka dot ribbon appliqué. Sportswear concepts were jeune fille in pink or navy gingham, as was the white jacquard pique minishort.

To show the versatility of cotton denim, his navy denim ball gown with Sabrina neckline took one's breath away with a burst of pink organdy inserts fashioned into godets in the skirt. Innovative use of a cotton/silk blend also included a long sheath gown with trumpet skirt and a high waist princess seam dress with gold plated jewel ornamentation at the neckline.

Mr. Kozaki accomplished the "Roman Holiday in Palm Beach" theme with style and flair. According to Cotton Incorporated's *StyleFile* report, "His talent is quickly being recognized in the market."

Each advertisement carries a one-word tagline intended to evoke a property of cotton, along with a factoid about the fiber's market share. An advertisement showing a female figure bears the word "Casual" and states that the sales of women's business casual clothing have increased by 25 percent during the past five years.

Cottonworks®

As a recognized authority on design, color, and fabric, Cotton Incorporated is an influential research and marketing company and is funded by the U.S. growers of upland cotton and importers of cotton and cotton textile products. Cotton Incorporated has its headquarters in Cary, North Carolina, with offices in Los Angeles, Dallas, Shanghai, Mexico City, Singapore, and Osaka. It maintains a consumer marketing headquarters in New York City.

Fabric Library

A foremost trend presenter, the Cottonworks Fabric Library houses an impressive permanent fabric library that provides a one-stop shopping venue where manufacturers, designers, and retailers can come to source cotton and cotton-rich fabrics from major mills.

Cotton and cotton blend fabric swatches from more than 350 mills, knitters, and converters are mounted on hinged display panels and categorized by fabric type, such as stripes, gingham checks, textures, polka dots, and sheers, to name a few. Each fabric is labeled with a company name, style number, and fiber content. The library is updated seasonally. Fabrics are received on a daily basis, hung on the panels, and kept current.

The fabric library's access to textile mill resources makes the job easier for trend researchers. They can edit their sourcing search for the newest and most trendy natural fabrics, available in the marketplace, without having to shop dozens of mill lines. The Cottonworks Fabric Library also provides a directory, *Cotton: Where to Find It,* listing all the mills, knitters. and converters that are showcased in the library. The same information is offered on its Web site, www.cottoninc.com.

Multimedia Show

In addition to the resource library, The Cottonworks Fabric Library's fashion forecasting fabric presentations are given twice a year, in the spring and fall. This creative presentation, given twelve months ahead of the selling season, highlights the mills, knitters, and converters that are showcased in the library. The newest fabrics from the mills are also put into the trends of the season.

An audiovisual presentation of the seasonal color, fabric, and trend/silhouette direction provides designers, manufacturers, and retailers with the Cottonworks Fabric Library's latest developments. Garments on display that have been purchased from around the world emphasize silhouette direction.

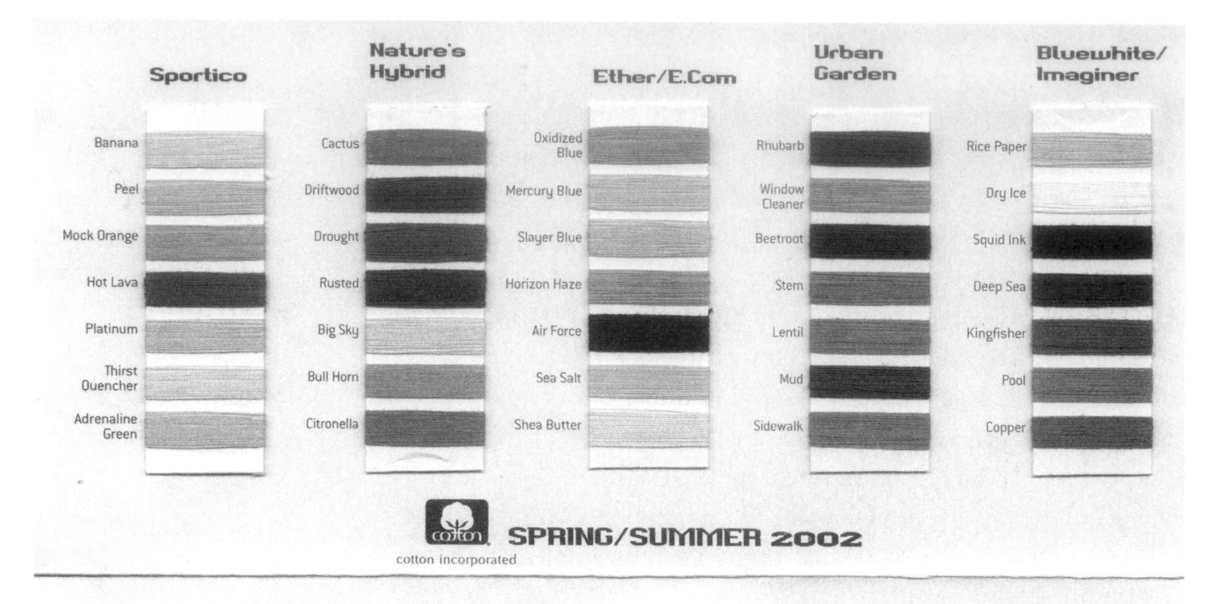

Cary
World Headquarters
6399 Weston Parkway
Cary, North Carolina 27513
Tel: 919.678.2220
Fax: 919.678.2230

New York
Consumer Marketing Headquarters
488 Madison Avenue
New York, New York 10022
Tel: 212.413.8300
Fax: 212.413.8377

Los Angeles
110 East 9th Street, Suite A-703
Los Angeles, California 90079
Tel: 213.627.3561
Fax: 213.627.3270

Dallas
Heritage Square Tower II
5001 LBJ Freeway, Suite 325
Dallas, Texas 75244
Tel: 972.726.6690
Fax: 972.726.6115

Basel
Bäumleingasse, 22
CH-4051 Basel, Switzerland
Tel: 011.41.61.206.8787
Fax: 011.41.61.206.8780

Osaka
Osaka Kokusai Building, 27th Floor
3-13. Azuchi-Machi 2-Chome
Chou-Ku, Osaka, 541-0052 Japan
Tel: 011.81.6.6266.0707
Fax: 011.81.6.6266.0710

Singapore
250 North Bridge Road,
36-02 Raffles City Tower
Singapore 179101
Tel: 011.65.337.2265
Fax: 011.65.337.3572

Mexico City
Av. Insurgentes Sur 1605-9-C
Col. San José Insurgentes
Del. Benito Juarez, 03900
Mexico, D.F. Mexico
Tel: 011.52.5.663.40.20
Fax: 011.52.5.663.40.23

Shanghai
Shanghai Overseas Chinese Mansion
Room 1405/1406
129 Yan 'an Xi Lu
Shanghai, 200040 China
Tel: 011.86.21.6249.4551
Fax: 011.86.21.6249.4553

WEBSITE: HTTP://WWW.COTTONINC.COM

This page and opposite page: *The Spring/Summer 2002 Cotton, Inc. color card includes five themes: Sportico, Nature's Hybrid, Ether/E.com, Urban Garden, and Bluewhite/Imaginer (above). The 2005 color card presents the themes Homegrown, Read Between the Lines, Heavy Metal, Peak Performance, and Fancy Pants. Note each theme with its coordinating image and fabric renderings (opposite). (See the color insert.)*

Colorful and theme-oriented trend books and color cards are a major part of the creative presentation while their *Style-File* newsletter keeps the industry up to date on cotton fabric and fashion information. Home fashion presentations are given once a year and also include a trend book and color card.

Five color and fabric groups for Spring/Summer 2002 included the themes Sportico, Nature's Hybrid, Ether/E.com, Urban Garden, and Bluewhite/Imaginer. Each theme is meant as a springboard to design ideas in cotton or cotton blend fabrics.

"The Urban Garden" color card explains that the palette is all about making peace with the conflicting elements of the urban environment. "Think of tending a rooftop garden with skyscrapers as a backdrop or practicing yoga to the sound of firetrucks rushing by. City-living neutrals and concrete grays collide with rave culture Brights in rhubarb pink and window cleaner blue." The themes for Spring/Summer 2005 are Homegrown, Read Between the Lines, Heavy Metal, Peak Performance, and Fancy Pants. The look is crisp and sculpted with linear patterns and seasonless fabrics.

Attendees

Presentations are given in small groups or in one-on-one meetings. Creative presentations therefore act as a catalyst for designers, colorists, stylists, design teams, product developers, manufacturers, and retailers from across the country, inspiring them with the latest color, fabric, and silhouette directions.

"The link with nature is increasingly important," says Kathryn Gordy Novakovic, Cotton Incorporated's director of the Cottonworks Fabric Library. "There's a renewed desire for natural fabrics that suggest their raw, unprocessed state."

Predictions/Presentation

The season's presentations are a culmination of extensive research conducted in Bali, Cannes, Cologne, Milan, London, Tokyo, Los Angeles, and New York. The staff also attends top industry trade and fashion shows such as Prêt-à-Porter, Heimtex, Première Vision, and IFFE. At some trade shows, Cotton Incorporated may also take a sales booth in which its color and trend products are displayed or a creative trend presentation is given for the trade show attendees.

While Cotton Incorporated has a strong presence in trend forecasting for the apparel trade, its creative fashion presentations for the home furnishings industry are equally as important and creative.

No Place Like Home 2003

"Home is turned upside down with new colors and dynamic trends, 2003 is a wide-screen wonderland celebrating every color of the rainbow and a bewitching selection of textures and touches," according to Elizabeth Hough, senior director of fashion marketing home fabrics.

Creative themes include Homespun, Natural Intelligence, Geometrics Take Heart, and Courageous Behavior, which are presented in two versions. Creative presentation boards display the themes with concept fabrics and related images. A trend and color card book also illustrates the trend message. The Homespun theme, for example, starts with the basics—quilting, gingham, lace, and fabric with embroidery, trims, and puckered textures. "We look to technology to help us . . . find beauty in meshing laser ideas with homespun basics," says the report.

Color ranges, such as Kansas, Twister, Journey, Technicolor, and Lollipop focus on colors that take some very unexpected twists and turns in 2003—from yellow corn to ruby red to emerald green. It is a veritable rainbow of hues and directions.

Below right and left: *The cover for Cotton Inc.'s 2003 presentation, entitled "No Place Like Home," and an invitation to the presentation. The cover reflects the themes of home, technology, and colors of the rainbow.*

Cotton Incorporated invites you
to reserve your place at one of the following

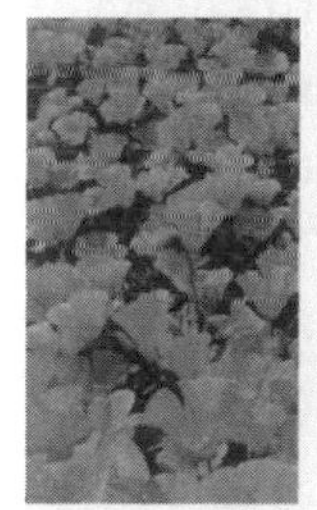

There's No Place Like Home 2003...

Color & Trend Presentations
Hosted by Liz Hough &
Gabrielle Obermeier

April 18th, 19th, 20th, 23rd & 24th
9:00 a.m. 11:00 a.m.

Presentations begin promptly @
488 Madison Avenue
(between 51st & 52nd street)
New York, New York
20th Floor

Call us @ 212.413.8344

Color and fabric direction for home furnishings very closely parallel the trends that are happening in the fashion market. Industry planners attend these presentations as a rich resource of design possibilities.

Masters of Linen

The only professional international association that brings together agricultural processors and industrial processors is the Confederation Européenne du Lin (European Linen Confederation). The confederation formed a promotion unit called "Masters of Linen" with the support of the European Community.

Forming a strong alliance, more than ten thousand linen growers in France, Belgium, and the Netherlands; twenty-two spinners in Italy, France, Northern Ireland, Belgium, Austria, and Germany; and ninety-six weavers located throughout Western Europe have pooled their talents and skills. At all stages of production, members settle for nothing less than excellence demonstrating the Masters of Linen tradition of quality.

To further augment their promotion program hangtag identification and warranty labels are available at no charge to garment and household linen manufacturers, designers, and distributors of Masters of Linen products.

Back to Nature

Creativity and innovation, a return to natural simplicity, and a departure from excessive decoration—these were the key trends presented to the fashion and home products industry guests in a Masters of Linen fashion forecast function at the Fashion Institute of Technology in New York City.

Mannequins modeled a half-dozen or more new garment designs in linen and linen blends, and racks were filled with new linen swatches. Ornella Bignami, a leading European fashion analyst, provided commentary at the event.

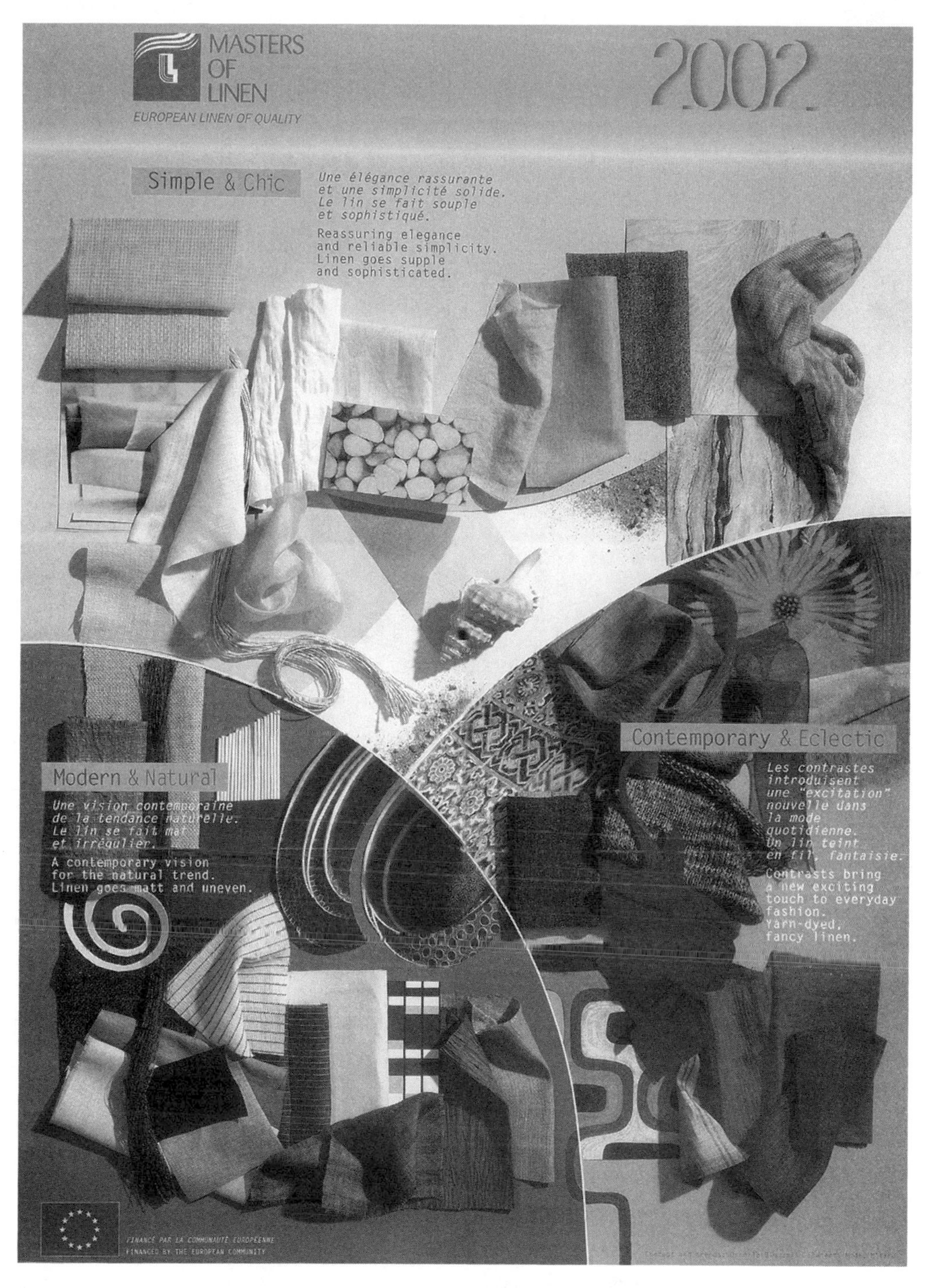

Masters of Linen promotes the European Linen Confederation. Its 2002 themes were Simple & Chic, Modern & Natural, and Contemporary & Eclectic. The text, presented in French and English, reveals that Summer 2002 is dedicated to creativity and innovation, but without embellishment. The trend is versatile and practical fashions that will be comfortable and stylish.

"The buzzwords for linen fabrics are comfort, delicacy, and style—style that is instantly recognizable for its inherent refinery and originality," said Ms. Bignami, who presented the fabric and color trends for 2002. Ms. Bignami pointed to the wide variety of effects that can now be achieved with different combinations of fibers, including textures and finishing techniques. She emphasized that linen is no longer confined to apparel destined to be worn only during the warmer parts of the year, but also for clothing year round in the cooler and colder months.

The color palette incorporated harmonious shades in a natural theme that Masters of Linen incorporated into three major linen trends: Simple & Chic, Modern & Natural, and Contemporary & Eclectic.

1. Simple & Chic: Fabrics in this grouping presented easy-care properties, stain resistance, washability, and quick drying to meet the demands of today's consumer.
2. Modern & Natural: Here, linen surfaces provided tactile sensations: straw, raffia, and paper effects, while stripes and checks draw inspiration from wood grain, rattan textures, and geometric carpet designs.
3. Contemporary & Eclectic: Linen fabrics in this trend explore ethnic or exotic fantasies as well as images of unspoiled nature.

Industry guests, manufacturers, and designers attending the creative fashion presentation also received a Masters of Linen members and U.S. representatives resource list.

Club Creation

Masters of Linen has also launched a progressive new program that brings young European designers together with licensed weavers and knitwear specialists to develop and encourage textile innovation with linen. Called Club Creation, the program allows freedom of expression that will attract rising stars as well as venerable talent to create designs that combine creativity and technology in one of the world's oldest fibers. Participating designers included Christian Le Drezen (France), Anna Ruohonen (Finland), Sharon Wauchob (United Kingdom), Innes Valentinitsch (Austria/Italy), Marithe + François Girbaud (France), Christian Tournafol (France), and Agatha Ruize de la Prade (Spain). These designers were able to realize their design concepts by working with specialists in spinning, weaving, textile design, finishing, coating, and printing.

THE TEXTILE PRODUCERS

Textile mills also share in the commitment to market their fabric collections in a creative fashion presentation venue. Themes, color, silhouette trend boards, and concept garments are all part of the visual package to promote a mill's new fabric developments, which are market driven for different segments of the manufacturing sector. To stimulate business and promote their lines, the mills continue to experiment with new technologies and incorporate performance stretch or innovative fibers into wovens or knits to create new fabrications each season.

Creative board presentations at the mill level are given for its customers—the designer/manufacturers and the garment producers of ready-to-wear apparel. A creative mill presentation takes place after the fiber companies have made their presentations. The timing for textile mill presentations is approximately one year ahead of the next year's selling season.

Here is an example of the schedule for textile mills shows:

July 2002 for Fall 2003

July 2003 for Fall 2004

January 2002 for Spring 2003

January 2003 for Spring 2004

Mill Presentations

Mill presentations are usually held at the showroom in a textile firm's offices. A fashion director, merchandiser, salesperson, or a stylist may give the actual presentation. These professionals work in tandem with other creative individuals within the textile mill to put together a comprehensive overview of the mill's original textile designs and color ranges.

Research of trends emerging in the worldwide textile centers is a major part of the fashion director's bank of inspiration. The director may also attend textile trade shows, such as Première Vision, Ideacomo, or Texitalia, to glean advance trend information. Subscribing to a fashion forecast service will augment the mill's research, as will observational research of what is selling in the international boutiques and what people are wearing on the streets.

In mill presentations, trend boards feature new color stories. Fabrications are identified by an overall theme, with additional related theme boards. The presentation may be given on a one-on-one basis or to small groups of individuals from a designer or manufacturer firm's design or product development team.

Men's Wear Forecasting

Trend boards with fabrications and inspirational images have themes with different messages to stimulate interest in the mill's new fabric collection. In the trend room, prototype concept garments in the mill's new fabrications feature the latest styles from casual to outdoors to tailored apparel. At this creative presentation, designers and manufacturers can get a feeling of the mill's diverse textile offerings and how they will look in silhouettes for the Spring or Fall season.

Men's Wear Presentations

The schedule for presenting fabrics that will be made into men's wear garments and eventually arrive for retail selling for Spring

2003 starts about one year before the actual selling period in the stores. The time line for a mill's presentation of men's wear fabrics is as follows:

January 2003 for Spring 2004: The designers and manufacturers visit the trend/color/concept garment workshop to get ideas and a feeling of what is innovative and will meet customer demand for comfort and easy fit. Early fabric presentations are very helpful so that designers and manufacturers can plan their new garment collections.

March–April 2003: During these two months, manufacturers place color and sample fabric yardage orders. The manufacturers will use the sample yardage to make up one-of-a-kind sample garments, such as suits, separates, or trousers.

May–June 2003: Manufacturers then show the retailers their collection of men's wear sample garments. Men's wear manufacturers work closer to a season, so at this point, the manufacturers take orders from the retailers, thereby preselling the garment collection. Some manufacturers wait until they have enough units of suits, jackets, or trousers presold before booking textile production.

June–November 2003: This is the period in which the mill fulfills textile production orders, which have been booked by the men's wear manufacturers.

June–November 2003: Depending on the manufacturer, garment production takes place during these months.

December 2003–March 2004: The garments are shipped to the retail stores for Spring 2004 retail selling to customers.

Darlington Fabrics: Critical Color Waves

A global leader in warp-knit elastic fabrics, Darlington Fabrics has a strong commitment to export excellence. Its market is strong worldwide and includes the Caribbean basin manufacturers.

When it comes to color, Darlington casts a critical eye on dye lots, which must exactly match product end uses. Darlington pays considerable attention to color, so that every garment produced has exact matching color standards.

Color Standards

Darlington's color standards are especially important to intimate apparel manufacturers. As a case in point, Darlington can help a stretch bra manufacturer ensure that the garments produced will be color specific to match the foundation garments made by another manufacturer. Darlington will also check that the dye lots match all other fittings within the garment, such as straps, hook and eye closures, and stretch inserts. At Darlington, every fabric order placed by a manufacturer is market specific and dyed to order.

The Color Consultant

Color is such a major consideration that Darlington's color management consultant, Phyllis Kay, is the consummate color expert. She develops color ranges and creates an overall theme name, with subthemes, for Darlington's different fabric end use color cards. She also creatively names each color in a color range.

Ms. Kay is an outside fashion consultant professional who is hired by the firm to establish its color stories each season. Her clients value her expertise because the accuracy of color decisions can dramatically reflect on the success of the firm's fabric collections each season.

A Swimwear Odyssey

Darlington's Swimwear 2001 color card, called Color Odyssey, is all about creativity and fabric end use. It presents color

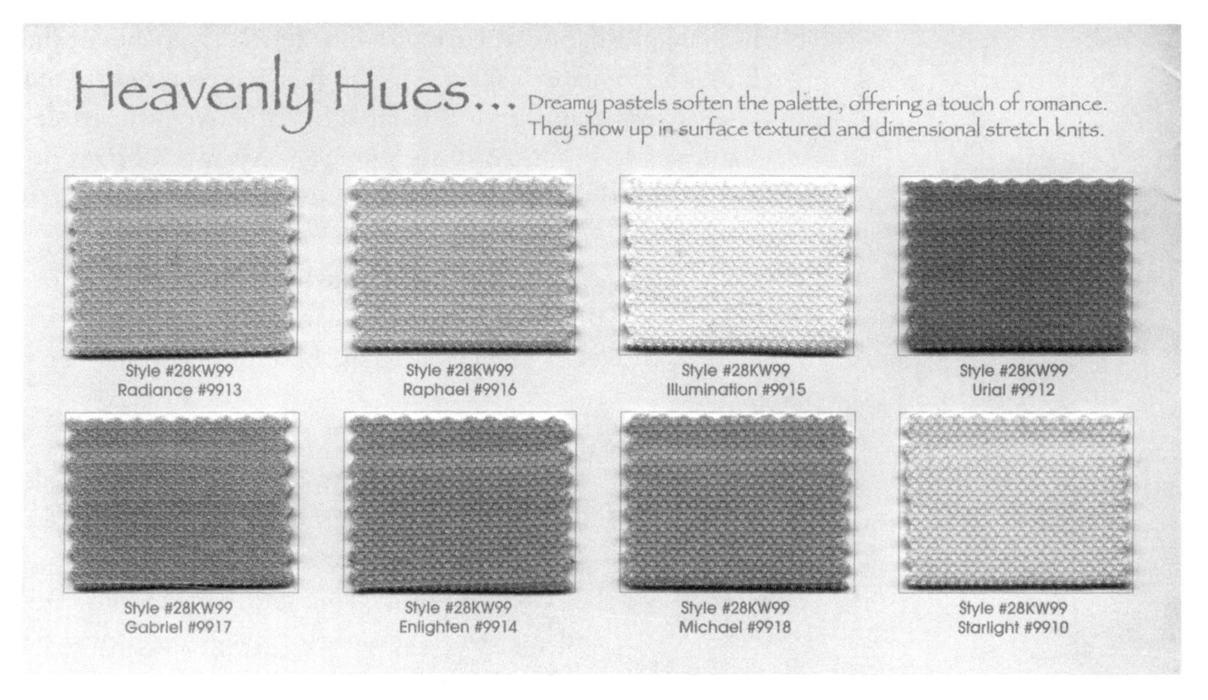

Darlington's swimwear 2001 color card for "Heavenly Hues"

ranges and fabrications categorized into creative themes in the firm's different swimwear fabrications. Each color on the color card is given a creative name and style number, as follows.

> Heavenly Hues: Dreamy pastels soften the palette, offering a touch of romance. They show up in surface-textured and dimensional stretch knits. Included in this range are color names such as "Enlighten," for a soft lavender, "Starlight" for a sunny yellow, and "Radiance" for pink.
>
> Cool Envy: Fresh, edgy colors in coordinating mesh and raised rib stretch knits destined for an array of swimwear designs, including tankinis and bandeau styles. Coordinating fabric swatches on the card include a light turquoise called "Reserved," a decidedly acid green called "Greedy," and a deep green dubbed "Selfish."

Bohemian Rhapsody: Exotic shades reflect the riches of the East, shown here in sportswear-influenced textured stretch knit. These colors give a fresh spin to active-inspired designs, such as Sanskrit, a deep purple; Krishna, a bright orange; and Maharaji, a brilliant blue.

Liquid Sun: A strong visual of warm-cast shades with orange tones, "the new pink" this year. Color is meant to inspire with names like Lava, Melt, Blaze, and Erupt.

The Forecast Room

In a forecast room rimmed with creative presentation boards featuring images and fabrics, Darlington sets the stage for its customer consultations on color direction. Fabric and silhouette trends are shown before the Spring and Fall seasons. Depending on the end use, Darlington also makes up prototype garments to illustrate silhouette trend ideas for intimate apparel or swimwear designers. The presentations may be given on a one-on-one basis or in groups with design teams or private label developers.

A Global Market

The firm has major color and fabric programs right through the layers of distribution from the top designers to manufacturers and the mass merchant private label garments. Susan Sternberg, Darlington's director of marketing, has an impressive travel schedule. She presents Darlington's American point of view in creative presentations with color cards, trend boards, and prototype garments to manufacturers in the global marketplace.

It is all part of customer satisfaction. Ms. Sternberg is the merchandising pulse of the firm's "on target" collections that meet the heightened demands by designers and manufacturers worldwide. Trade fairs are also on her agenda, such as the Intima/Intimatex, which showcases intimate apparel collections from North American, South American, and European designers and manufacturers. Industry experts lead a comprehensive seminar program, while couture and ready-to-wear fashion shows highlight exhibitor collections.

Fortune Fabrics

This company's goal is to provide a one-stop-shopping experience for its customers, who purchase high quantities of fabric for major jacket and pant coordinate programs for the moderate market. "We present our fabric ranges by creating visual boards that not only highlight the colors and trends of the season, but also feature decorative elements or images that emulate that trend," notes Wendy Bunin, vice president. "It's an added value for our customer."

She ought to know because Ms. Bunin, a former designer and merchandiser, realized the frustration a designer had when

Wendy Bunin is surrounded by fabric, fabric, fabric!

sourcing fabric from different suppliers. "The problem was lack of color coordination. At Fortune, color coordination is the major selling advantage, because the firm's diverse fabric ranges of updated fabrics are coordinated in cohesive color stories.

Color Research

"We subscribe to several key color services," notes Ms. Bunin. "However, no one color service can be tailor made to your firm's needs. We take the inspiration from all of them as a whole and develop our own color story for our specific target markets."

The firm also relies upon customer feedback as a guide to color direction and develops different color palettes and fabric ranges that are destination specific to appeal to customers in warm or cool climates. Fabric ranges may also be color specific for a particular ethnicity. "The Bible Belt, for one, is an example," says Ms. Bunin. "Manufacturers sourcing fabric

This page and opposite page: *Creative boards for the "Trend Equestrian" and "Trend Refinement" themes.*

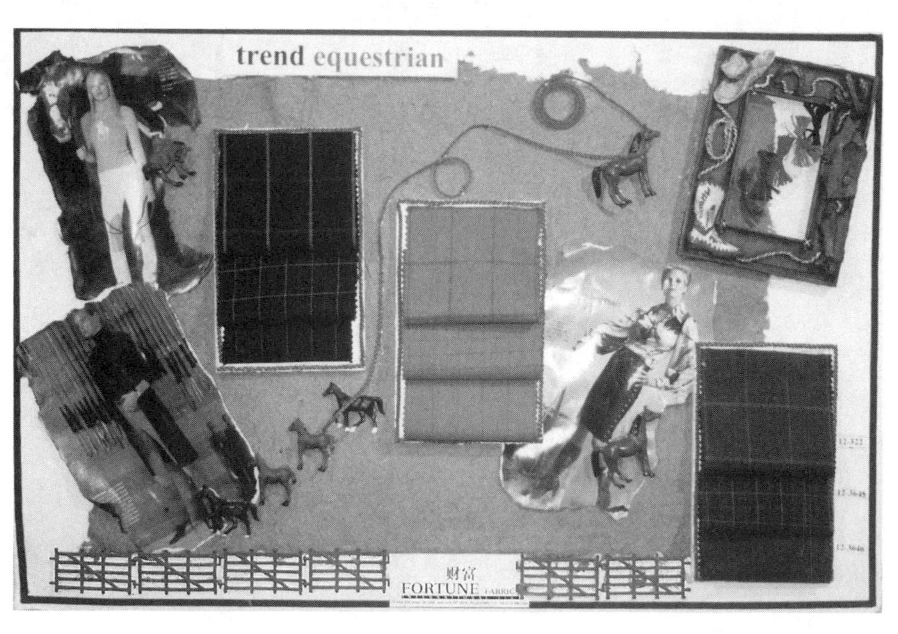

here make color choices that are highly selective for that Southern customer base."

Trend Boards

"Everything generates from the presentation boards—from creating a concept to the final product," says Ms. Bunin. "Every market week, the firm presents creative presentation boards as a stimulus to fabric sales presentations. One or two core fabrics drive the fabric groups of patterns and fancies in the trend and color waves of the season."

Trend Equestrian, for example, showcases linear checks and plaids and has immediate theme impact with miniature plastic horses as decorative elements, a picture frame with cowboy hat and boots, and images that convey an equestrian mood. Trend Sophistication is a black, new camel, and brown color story with fancies and patterns that pivot around the firm's core fabrics, such as gabardines or stretch twills. The Trend

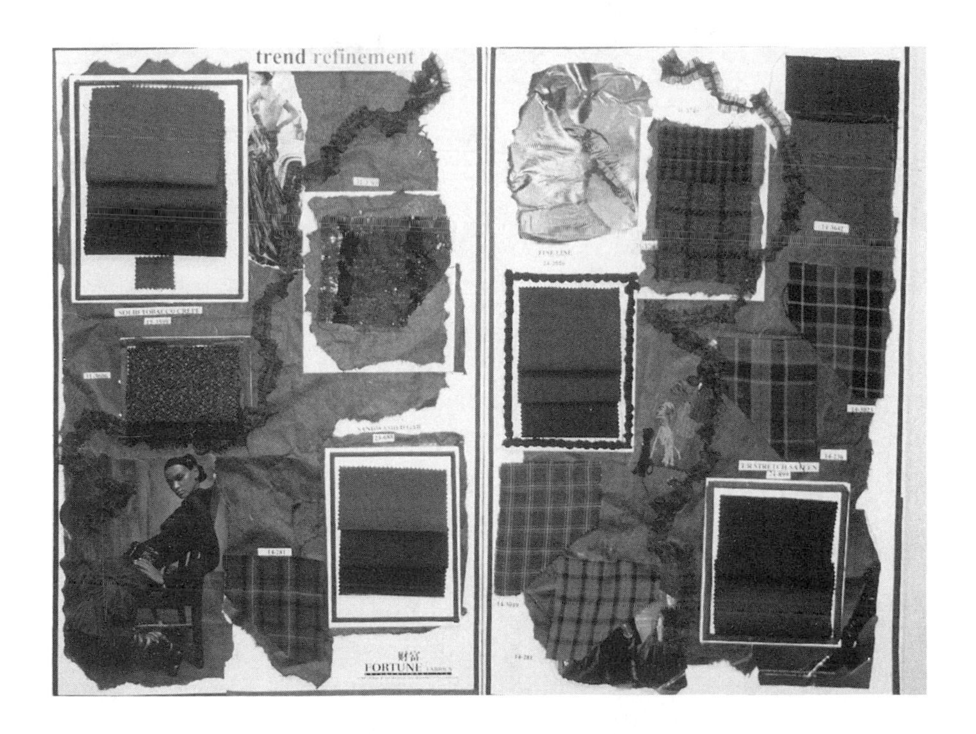

Refinement board, influenced by Yves Saint Laurent, evokes images of elegance with dark gothic colors of emerald, amethyst, and black. The firm also showcases prototype garments in tandem with the boards to illustrate the color coordinates and trends of the season. "Creative board presentations also stimulate the sell through of color-coordinated separates at the retail level," says Ms. Bunin. "When the customer walks into a store, the impact of color-coordinated groups draws customer attention. It clarifies the trend and makes it easier for the customer to color-coordinate a look."

Standtex USA

Creative boards, designed by themes of the season, are the visual marketing tool that augments the sell through of the fabric collections at Standtex USA. "Boards give our customers a good impression that we are current and follow the trends," says Joy Chen, general manager. "The apparel manufacturers have confidence that we are on top of what's new, and they can make intelligent fabric selections from hand loom samples."

Four Seasons

Research and development goes into creative board presentations for four seasons: Spring/Summer, holiday, transition, and Fall/Winter. The Standtex creative team hones its skills and develops trend input based on what is presented at major trade shows, such as Magic or the International Fashion Fabric Exhibition.

Theme names on the boards and photographic images evoke different fabric stories. The Fluffy board represents lofty, winter fabrics, Futuristic plays up nylon blends and polyester fabrics, while Cosy Cosy defines warm winter fabrics.

When Standtex gets a fabric order from a manufacturer, a minimum yardage order is required to go into production. The amount can range from 3,000 to 6,000 yards, depending on whether the fabric is piece dyed or yarn dyed. Yarn dyes need longer lead time, because it takes four to six weeks to weave the greige goods, followed by two weeks for specification dyeing. As a quick response fabric house, depending on the availability of the raw materials, the Standtex Taipei factory can ship the goods to the manufacturer in two weeks. Then it is back to the creative boards and a new season of trends is created as the sell through to apparel producers.

THE MANUFACTURING LEVEL

The dynamics of creative fashion presentations is an important marketing tool that apparel manufacturers use to showcase and present the "sell message" of new seasonal collections. In the past, design studios used to draw flat sketches of the new silhouettes and then add fabrics and colors. These were cut and mounted on boards with paste. This time-consuming process has been eliminated by technological advances and computer-aided design (CAD).

Computer-Aided Design (CAD)

Today the computer accelerates the process of generating illustrations for board presentations, which are used by manufacturers to represent their diverse ready-to-wear coordinate collections. The boards, which serve as a visual marketing tool, are used during the Spring/Summer, Fall/Winter, Transition, and Holiday market weeks.

Computer renderings of garment silhouettes make it possible to produce boards that accurately illustrate complete fabric and color ranges by solids and patterns. As a selling tool, the boards augment the manufacturer's presentation to its retail customers. While the boards illustrate and educate, they also visually impact the firm's presentation of the actual garments, which are shown in conjunction with the boards

Creative board presentations at the manufacturing level are therefore considered a necessary visual aid to merchandise a line. In addition, color printouts of the firm's boards are reproduced in smaller versions that buyers may take with them as a pictorial reference and to verify their purchases.

Sag Harbor

Sag Harbor's missy collection of moderately priced coordinated separates is driven by a high-volume print business that is merchandised to retailers on an exclusive basis. "We consider boards a very important element to augment the sell through to our retail customers," notes Marina Papavasiliou, design director. "A technical designer will produce silhouette sketches and the computer designer puts in the colors and prints. It's collaboration and team work to reach our goal to present the line in a creative and visual way."

Sag Harbor's creative computer-generated boards feature highly diversified solids and prints that are merchandised in groups. Each group portrays tops and bottoms in comprehensive color ranges and diverse patterns.

Before merchandising a new seasonal collection to retailers, the firm first shows the new designs to the salespeople. "We get feedback from the sales force that's critical to the final decision as to what goes into the line," adds Ms. Papavasiliou. "If shirtings are trend, then the designer might produce a board featuring maybe four shirt versions. The sales force, on viewing the board presentation, may strongly indicate that three bodies, one solid and two prints, would be more saleable. With their hands-on experience, the sales force is invaluable to merchandising the final components of a line."

Inspiration

The creative team also takes into consideration input from textile suppliers. These are insiders on the trade level who can indicate fabric selling trends. "We listen and evaluate each piece of information as it might apply to our collections. Influences can come from anywhere, we are open to new ideas," says Ms. Papavasiliou.

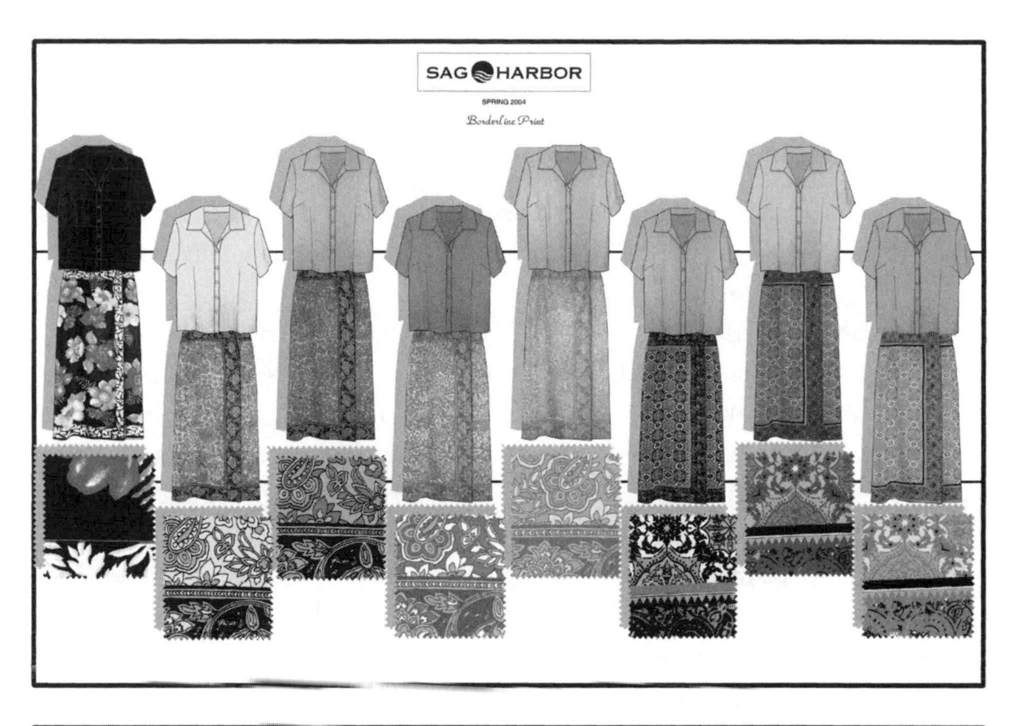

Sag Harbor's Spring 2004 transition collection for women's wear.

The creative team also shops better lines at retail, attends trade shows, such as the International Fashion Fabric Exhibition, and views the trend direction slide show given by Doneger Creative Services on Spring/Summer, Fall/Winter, and St. Tropez Summer. This research enables the team to zero in on the right styles, patterns, and colors for Sag Harbor's target customer.

Color inspiration is key to each season. Being on track with new color developments impacts the successful sell of the Sag Harbor collections at retail. To this end, the creative team hones in on color forecast presentations from Huepoint, Here and There, and Design Options, to name a few, and the team members also check the record as to what colors sold best in previous seasons.

"In putting together a coordinated collection the design team keeps abreast of the psychographics of consumer preferences," notes Ms. Papavasiliou. "Sag Harbor's creative board presentations are a valuable selling tool, designed to provide visual impact and to reinforce the sell of the actual garment during market week."

Alfred Dunner

Alfred Dunner, a family-owned business that has produced moderately priced ladies coordinate sportswear for more than fifty years, is a quiet giant among apparel manufacturers. Without advertising, but with a steadfast reputation, the Alfred Dunner company has moved forward with visual marketing tools to sell its collections.

"Creating the lines and story boards for the firm's four divisions—Misses, Petites, Women's, and Women's Petites—is a synergistic process of team work," says Ira Rubin. The head designer of each division, the president, the national sales manager, and the import administrator all participate in deciding which direction a coordinate group should take in career, jackets, or casual wear. "We examine what's been successful in the

Alfred Dunner's St. Andrews collection is a coordinated presentation of color, fabric, and style in trend boards and actual garments that make it simple for the retailer to visualize the merchandise mix.

past and what we will go ahead with for the future. If it's florals, geometrics, or butterflies, we are on trend each season with the latest motifs, fabrics, and colors. We also look to see how the garments performed at retail and how they sold at wholesale. This research is an important determining factor for developing styles for the new season."

The design staff's commitment to creating new styles is based on detailed research using color and forecast services, shopping the stores, and seeing what is selling in the marketplace. They evaluate the flow of product and seasonal trends before designing a line.

The Theme Boards

The firm's story boards feature coordinate ranges with such fetching theme titles as Dover Cliffs, a pearl gray, powder blue, and blush moleskin group; St. Andrews, a black, red, off white, and check Microfiber group; Sheridan Square, an indigo and lilac peachskin group; and Columbus Circle, a seasonless polyester black, powder blue, and novelty group.

Each storyboard is a visual springboard to illustrating the looks in each coordinate garment group. The boards are shown in conjunction with the presentation of the actual garments to reinforce the color and fabric stories. The firm also makes 8½" × 11" color reference copies of the boards for its sales staff and also for its retail customers.

As an added service, Alfred Dunner also provides its retail clients with a selling report. This report serves as a guide to show the retailer what the Alfred Dunner merchandisers suggested the retailer buy in each group, how the retailer bought the group, and how it actually sold.

In general, there is a minimum order to make a cutting ticket for production. "It's different for each style—an item may be dropped from a particular group one season, but brought back in the future," says Mr. Rubin.

Trade Terminology

Club Creation
Color card
Color coordination
Color palette
Color specific
Computer-aided design (CAD)
Computer-generated board
Concept garments
Core fabrics
Creative themes
Dissemination of information
Dyed to order
Dye lots
Elastic fabrics
Fabric library
Fashion research
Feedback
Filament

Garment silhouette
Generic
Global studio
Hangtag identification
Innovative fibers
Intimate apparel
Knitwear specialists
Market share
Market specific
Marketing tool
Merchandiser
Natural fiber
New talent showcases
No-charge presentations
Observational research
Performance stretch
Prognosticators
Promotion techniques
Public awareness
Sales force
Selling report
Silent sell
Synthetics
Theme-oriented trend books
Trend expert
Visual springboard
Weavers
Wovens

READING 6-1 The Great Fabric Debate

DANIELA GILBERT

NEW YORK—It's the proverbial chicken or egg theory—fashion style. The question comes up time and time again: What came first, the fabric or the design? Depending on who you ask, it can be either.

Catherine Malandrino describes her collections as "works in constant progress," adding, "each has a similar feeling with a different angle." Consequently, her trips to Première Vision—the biannual European fabric fair in Paris—give her the chance to both fill in her seasonal theme with the right fabric as well as bump into a few surprises.

The feeling for [one] sketch was a combination of the inspiration she felt early on for her Spring collection and her discovery of an interesting fabric at Swiss textile firm Jakob Schlaepfer, a very creative mill, according to Malandrino. "I love the irregular knitting techniques used in this fabric," she said of the mill's black and brown openwork fabric. "It's net-like, but not a net, and fit in perfectly with the idea I had for an extra-feminine and very sophisticated negligee."

Although Peter Som says he already has an idea of what he wants when he goes to the fair, "I'll then see things that are so amazing that they'll inspire a piece." Sometimes, he added, "I want the fabric to speak for itself." For the sketch of [an] anorak and slim pants, for instance, Som said the look started with the fabric.

"What I want for spring are clean shapes that convey lightness," he said. He also wants some of the pieces to have a sportif feeling, albeit with a more finished, elegant fabric. When he spotted the nylon taffeta he used here at the Italian mill Clerici Tessuto, Som said it fit the bill perfectly. "Taffeta is traditionally an evening fabric so the sophisticated connotation was there, but the nylon gave it a utilitarian edge that was less precious, which is what I wanted."

For James Coviello, inspiration for [one] dress came from an embroidered tablecloth he found in a vintage store. "I wanted a fabric for this dress that was both lightweight and casual, as well as being a great price, since I was going to be sending it to Peru to be embroidered," he stated.

Irish mill Ulster Weavers' linen jacquard was perfect, he noted. "The quality was amazing for the price, and it really matched the idea I had back when I found the tablecloth—pretty and feminine, but casual. The dress is going to wrinkle and be worn in a very casual way, yet there is still a very proper feeling about it."

"I always go to Première Vision with something in mind," offered Tracy Reese, who shops the fair for fabrics for her signature collection and the lower-priced Plenty. "But then I'll see things that will excite me." The highlight of Reese's Spring sketch is the vest. "It took me four years to find a synthetic leather for the Plenty line—we can't afford real leather for that line—and I was so excited that someone finally made it." Hers is by Sinpel Srl, based in Italy. For the long tunic, Reese wanted a drapey feel, so she chose a paisley print from Komar, based in France, that she would put on a silk ground in place of the rayon one offered by the mill. For the pants, "I wanted something a bit firmer than silk," she said. Although offered on a stretch cotton, Reese would opt to use a cotton voile instead.

"I try to internalize it, I ask myself, 'How would I want it to feel?' " she explained. "Comfort continues to be important and I want what I do to translate into something that's wearable."

For other designers, however, the idea of designing based on a fabric introduces the threat of uniformity—what if another designer chooses the exact same material? "That's something I definitely don't want," says Michael Soheil. "For me, fabric doesn't lead design, it's simply a canvas. And Première Vision serves as a base. I change, personalize or manipulate the selections I pick. I never use the fabric as is."

Such was the case with a blended nylon tulle he spotted some seasons back. "It was very drapey," he said. "And that's hard to find, especially when it's a heavier weight like this one was." He fashioned the tulle into a top, adding salmon-colored ostrich feathers in the folds of the tulle.

For his sketch, Soheil used two very lightweight, airy fabrics, each with a distinct texture, that were juxtaposed against each other. "The whole idea behind the design was to mix silhouettes, and the two fabrics I chose were perfect for that," he said.

While one-half of the skirt's shape is fluid—which was complemented by the lighter, rayon fabric—the other is more fitted, thanks to the heavier, more textured cotton blend.

"I like the difference of the smoother fabric against the rougher one with slashes," he said. "It's two odd combinations that come together nicely."

Benjamin Cho, meanwhile, chose the simplicity of a white cotton and linen blend to bring his idea for [one] dress alive. "I'm not really pattern-oriented," he pointed out. "For me, decoration is more texture-based. I like to create different textures using string, ribbon, gathers or other techniques."

While fabric may not always be the fuel that fires an idea, designers are constantly on the lookout for materials to use in new and very creative ways.

Source: *Women's Wear Daily*, June 18, 2002, pp. 10-11. Courtesy of Fairchild Publications, Inc.

READING 6-2 | Celanese's Color Spin on Spring 2004

NEW YORK—Celanese acetate predicts a "nostalgic and pretty" spring 2004, according to James Siewert, manager of trend direction, in his recent Directives presentation.

"The season ahead is comprised of intense color elements," he said. "Vibrant shades are key factors, as are defined neutrals and saturated pales."

The presentation highlighted six color trends as well as four fabric trends for the season. The color trends were Mineral, Water, Fire, Air, Earth and Flora.

Mineral featured elegant and refined colors that mix base shades and tinted accents. The palette included both a light and dark gray, as well as a rose and a medium lavender color as accents in addition to a mocha brown. Black and white were key additives to the palette, Stewart said.

"While traditional tailored designs will use these colors as a base," he said, "more sportive separates will utilize them in pattern play."

Soothing shades made up the Water palette. The grouping is a series of blues and includes navy, baby blue and light turquoise. "While a tonal play is the first visual here, each color option can be worked across the board as accent or base color," said Siewert.

Fire, a group of warm-based reds, included brick, pink and plum reds. "A key factor for the season is a continued interest in the berry, burgundy and coral shades," he continued. "Here, too, a tonal play is an important option as well as one of contrast. Both the brick and blackened plum allow for an elegant base that can define both a contemporary or a classic mood."

The colors in the Air grouping were pale and diluted. It included a flesh pink, light yellow, blue, green and a washed camel. "These pastel-based colors offer a light visual look for topweights in knits and wovens," said Siewert. "While warm based, the colors allow for a play against the cool water colors and become a significant accent with the grays and mocha brown from the Mineral group."

The colors in the Earth group were midtone and transitional. They included yellowed khaki, as well as pea green, medium-toned purple, olive green and bright orange. "Each option here can be worked with a more significant bright accent," he added.

The brightest of all the palettes, Flora included saturated tones of red, blue, orange, green and medium brown. "The visual strength of each of these colors allows for base use in the most sportive designs, as well as tools for prints and luxurious luster jewel tones for satin," said Siewert.

Siewert's fabric trends fell into three groups: Eloquent, Elementary and Evocative.

Eloquent included fluid fabrics, in both knits and wovens, that featured supple textures, such as sculpted surfaces and metallic-shot patterns. "Beyond the traditional focus on after-five designs are more contemporary uses that will play these fabrics against simple, plain weaves or, in the most contemporary markets, as a foil to denim," he said.

Elementary featured lightweight and fluid looks that allow for cross-market categories. "The look of texture is an important factor through the weave or, as a fancy, adding an element of dimension without adding weight," Siewert said. "Subtle effects are newest, utilizing bright colors as the focal point or simple pattern work."

Finally, Evocative was a return to elegant weaves. The overall effect, said Siewert, was that of a fluid, lustrous surface that allows for more couture-like designs. Another important component of the grouping was bias cuts, dressmaker tailoring, embossing and through-the-weave surface treatments that add a visual look. "While overall, the more tailored markets will use this group for an elegant story," Siewert concluded, "contemporary markets will utilize them with more casual fabrics as contrasts to sportive separates."

Source: *Women's Wear Daily*, June 24, 2003, p. 9. Courtesy of Fairchild Publications, Inc.

READING 6-3 | Cotton's Real World for Fall 2004

NEW YORK—Cotton Incorporated's forecast for the fall 2004 season is based on a blend of realism and positiveness.

"Overall, the color palette for this season balances both these things in a blend of brights, darks and naturals for a cohesive look," said Kathryn Novakovic, director of fashion marketing. "Dark and murky shades such as navies, grays, browns and faded blacks continue, punched up with brighter shades of red, purple and green, while softer neutrals provide the perfect backdrop for these stronger colors."

The five color groups in the forecast were: Night Bright, Flea Market, Trail Mix, Enchanted Forest and White Out.

The colors for Night Bright, which Novakovic said would be suited for the activewear market, take their inspiration from the sea. Heavily influenced by greens, blues and browns, the palette includes Lime Light, Deepest Midnight and Silt Shimmer—a sandy shade suitable for sateen and velvet looks.

Flea Market included colors inspired by Seventies rock 'n' roll, as well as patchwork. "The look is very mismatched here," said Novakovic. The colors, including Butterscotch, Pool Table and Lava Orange, evoked lollipops, circuses and comic books.

The colors in the Trail Mix group were earthy and natural, dominated by greens and browns. "It's inspired by the colors of natural grains and seeds with a surprising jolt of color from wildflowers," she added. "It's both clean and natural, a very basic approach to color." The group included tones such as Poppy Seed, Chamomile, Lentil and Wild Flower.

For the Enchanted Forest, the palette was romantic and exotic, including hues called Kyoto Plum, Genie Green and Smoked Blue. "Think flying carpets, magic genies, golden palaces and opulent costumes," she said. "The colors are perfect for sateen and chintz looks, as well as polished cottons."

The first snow of winter was the inspiration for White Out. The soft palette included Winter Shadow, Glacier Blue and Lichen. "Here, the whites play together in heathered yarns and white-on-white prints," she continued. "Great fabrics in this group would include soft cottons blended with angora, cashmere or wool."

In fabrics, said Novakovic, "surface interest enhances and enriches color while adding dimension and depth. Texture remains extremely important in denim, knits, corduroy and weaves. Prints are self-assured and feature clean graphics, bold stripes, Art Nouveau florals and influences from Pop Art and Impressionism."

She named her five fabric trends On Track, Hipster How-To, Tip-Top Precision, Classic Construction and Print Personalities.

On Track reflected the athletic influence on knitwear, with fabrics that featured technological innovation, activewear design influences and comfort qualities. The group included double-sided fleece, denim influences on knitwear, indigo overdyes, bleaching effects, wax-look coatings and soft, plush knits inspired by the terry tracksuit craze. "The grouping is very technical," Novakovic said. "An example is an antimicrobial cotton and nylon blend."

Denim and corduroy were the focus of Hipster How-To. The group relied on surface-interest features, such as slubs, to create abstract lines and unevenness and used flocking to give a faux suede look. The group also featured bicolor cords with combinations of wide and thin wales.

Shirting fabrics were the focus of Tip-Top Precision. "The look is refined and distinctive and includes multiple textures and weaves," said Novakovic. The group featured overdyes in hazy hues, two-tone pinstripes and flannels brushed on both sides, home-inspired jacquards, plaid and floral prints. Tip-Top also featured cotton and metal combinations that looked like linen and leather-like polyurethane coatings.

The theme of Classic Construction, created specifically for bottomweights, was compactly structured looks with lots of surface interest. The group used textured jacquards, felting techniques, double-faced fabrics, micro sanding effects and peach touch surfaces to add substance and depth to the fabrics. "It's another example of bringing home looks into apparel with the tapestry jacquards," said Novakovic.

The prints in Print Personalities included home-influenced printed velvets, Japanese-inspired bold and graphic looks, Mod and Art Deco prints from the Sixties and artistic looks that included craft-inspired geometrics.

Source: *Women's Wear Daily*, July 8, 2003, p. 17. Courtesy of Fairchild Publications, Inc.

7

The Retail Challenge

Retailers today face many challenges. Why? Because retailing is affected, in a major way, by people's developing tastes, by changes in their buying habits, and by the country's economic conditions. We are dealing with psychographics and the changing mood of the consumer. It is important, therefore, to reassess what is important to them.

Today's customer is a cross-shopper, who frequents not only traditional department stores, but also many other retail venues, including discount stores, outlets, and the Internet. Wooing the consumer, therefore, has a more competitive edge today, because fashion has made the consumer smart enough to expect quality and to demand it at affordable prices. Lifestyle also has dictated these changes. and the consumer's decisions reflect her or his value-oriented personality. Further, customer profiles reveal that today's consumer is more independent and shops whenever it is convenient and wherever a bargain may be found. Loyalty to a particular retailer has diminished. As a result, the entire industry is vying for market share in the retail sales pie. The competition for customers, however, takes priority and is the prime reason why retailers are sharpening their special event and fashion office activities to attract shoppers into the store.

As the retail community has become more complex and diversified, the retail doors competing for business include:

- Catalogs
- Category killers
- Chains
- Department stores
- Designer boutiques
- Discount stores
- Electronic retailers
- Factory outlets
- Flea markets
- Franchises
- Hypermarkets
- Mail order catalog companies
- Mass merchandisers
- Mom and pop stores
- Off-price stores
- Online retailers
- Shopping centers/malls
- Specialty chains
- Specialty stores
- Superstores
- Thrift shops
- Warehouse clubs

THE DEPARTMENT STORE

In view of the diversified retail mix, traditional retail department stores are striving to find new ways to maintain loyal customers and attract new customers to the store. To this end, stores are trying to become more interesting and more exciting places to be. Retailers are turning stores into exciting showplaces that include entertainment with merchandise promotions. Although the consumer is now a much smarter shopper, she is likelier to spend money if the presentation is new, educational, and entertaining. Retailers, therefore, are challenged to be flexible enough to satisfy diverse customer profiles. To achieve this goal, top management is very supportive of the fashion office.

THE FASHION OFFICE

The fashion office plays a key role in the retail department store's organization and, as such, is a major player in determining the right merchandise for each season. The dissemination of forecast information on color, fabric, and silhouette is a major element that will identify the store's merchandise assortments. Creative trend presentations are presented to the general merchandise managers, the divisional merchandise managers, and the merchants (the buyers) in advance of a season, as dictated by the guidelines for each division's segment of the market. In addition, the fashion office forecast directives serve as influential communications that affect the store's promotions, public relations, advertisements, catalogs, and window and in-store displays.

THE FASHION DIRECTOR

The senior fashion director is a key member of a store's executive team. As such, the job description has changed to reflect greater responsibilities that even include supervising sizable staffs and managing the fashion department budget. Recognizing the important status of the fashion director, many corporate organizational charts list that position as "senior vice president/fashion direction," "senior vice president/fashion merchandising," or "senior vice president, director of fashion and product development."

Some fashion directors were once store buyers and that is invaluable, because a good fashion director has to sell ideas and concepts and understand what it is to take markdowns. The vice president title is not only prestigious, but it also puts the fashion director on the same level as the merchandise managers and other business executives running the store.

Disseminating Ideas

However, the senior fashion director never dictates policy; rather, the director disseminates information, not only to the line and staff, but also to the rest of the store's employees. Applying the art of gentle persuasion, the fashion office has to get the merchants excited and motivated to endorse new ideas. For example, although advertising must reflect the fashion image of the store, the bottom line reflects the merchant's point of view. The fashion director, therefore, must exhibit a certain degree of flexibility in making final decisions.

Forecasting and Market Research

The fashion director's primary responsibility to the merchants in the store is to stay tuned to world fashion developments and to forecast trends. The fashion director hones her skills by investigating different market segments. She identifies and communicates major trends, prepares color/fabric and fashion forecast reports, conducts trend seminars, and shops the market scouting for new resources, hot items, and new designers. The fashion director is primarily a consummate market researcher who pursues leads through the following activities:

1. Attending creative fashion presentations at
   - A. Fashion forecast services
   - B. Fiber producers
   - C. Fiber promotion companies
   - D. Leather firms
   - E. Textile producers
   - F. Trade shows
2. Covering the seasonal market week shows (Spring/Summer and Fall/Winter)
   - A. New York 7th on Sixth
   - B. Merchandise marts: Atlanta, Chicago, Dallas, and Los Angeles
   - C. Paris haute couture shows
   - D. Prêt-à-porter shows in London, Paris, and Milan

3. Comparison and window shopping
   A. New York stores
   B. Major U.S. city stores
   C. European fashion capitals

Her major areas of market research are:

1. Accessories
2. Children's wear
3. Cosmetics
4. Domestics
5. Gift market
6. Home furnishings
7. Intimate apparel
8. Men's wear
9. Toy market
10. Women's apparel

In addition, the fashion director assumes the following responsibilities:

1. Planning and scheduling window displays
2. Working with the advertising department
3. Consulting with the public relations department
4. Advising the catalog department
5. Consulting with the visual merchandise team

Staying Tuned to World Events

As the prognosticator of trends, the fashion director must stay tuned to what is going on worldwide. This includes a broad arena of activities and keeps the fashion director on a sometimes-whirlwind schedule. From keeping up with the latest fashion newspapers and magazines to theater, movies, art exhibitions, and clubs to knowing the newest "in" restaurants covers just some of the areas in which fashion trends and ideas originate. Observational research includes observing street fashions, visiting avant-garde designers, and finding nontraditional areas of fashion at thrift shops or flea markets.

To be "au courant," the fashion director also joins professional organizations, such as the Fashion Group International, and subscribes to the Fashion Calendar, a comprehensive publication listing all fashion events in the United States and abroad.

Although the senior fashion director may lead an exciting and social lifestyle, it is all business-related. By associating with the top designers and fashion industry intelligentsia, the fashion director is also seen and often photographed at fashion industry related openings, parties, and charity events. The fashion director may also be a keynote speaker at such happenings or receive an award herself or on behalf of the store she represents. The resulting publicity in trade or consumer newspapers or magazines contributes to recognizing the store as a major player in the business of retailing.

Arbiter of Taste

As the arbiter of taste for the store and as a member of the top management, the senior fashion director associates closely with the store's corporate officers, from the CEO to the president, keeping an eye on business and assuring the dissemination of trend information throughout the store.

The senior fashion director takes the store's vision and makes it happen in a team effort with the store's merchants to assure that what they buy represents the best of current trends while remaining appropriate to the image of the store. The director and staff work with the store's merchants so that the store's purchases reflect their taste level. In the same capacity, the fashion office interacts with the product development buyers on private label merchandise.

The senior fashion director and the special events coordinator may also be instrumental in the staging of timely and sometimes provocative special events that entertain, encourage customer participation, and drive customers into the store.

DIVISIONAL FASHION DIRECTORS: MARKET SPECIFIC

The fashion director's staff consists of divisional fashion directors, who are responsible for a specific classification of merchandise, such as coats and suits or sportswear/separates. The divisional fashion coordinator therefore provides directives that guide and advise specific merchants.

These divisional fashion directors disseminate trend information, which is market specific to a segment of the industry. They work in a synergistic relationship with the buyers by shopping the market, reviewing lines, and participating in the development of the store's private label programs. The divisional fashion directors, like the senior fashion director, hone their skills, but in a specific classification of merchandise. In the course of doing market research they become informed professionals whose trend directives are respected and activated at retail. For example, if the divisional fashion director/coordinator's responsibility is the men's wear market, then all aspects of that industry from market knowledge of vendors to domestic and international color/fabric and fashion trends, trade shows, and industry events come under the market research umbrella.

THE FASHION ACTIVITIES

While the fashion director is involved with the store's overall fashion image, there is a synergistic relationship with the fashion office staff. Meetings are held regularly to establish new promotions, schedule designer personal appearances and trunk shows, discuss window displays and catalog deadlines, and follow through on upcoming events. The fashion office keeps track of current and future happenings by placing them on a giant size calendar for easy referral day-by-day and month-by-month. The scope of work is quite diversified and includes the dissemination of trend information or working with different departments on the following:

- Branch stores
- Buyer communications
- Color card/fashion trend reports
- Designer personal appearances
- Fashion advertising
- Fashion shows
- Market research
- Product development
- Promotions and special events
- Public relations
- Sales training
- Seasonal trend seminars
- Styling for catalog
- Theme shops
- Trunk shows
- Visual merchandising for interiors
- Window displays

The calendar of events will also include informal modeling schedules, as well as major seasonal fashion show launches of Spring/Summer, Fall/Winter, and holiday merchandise. In this case, the store's organizational chart will include a slot for a model coordinator.

The activities of a flagship store's fashion office also serve as a guideline for branch stores. The fashion office recognizes trends and signals them to store branches through written reports and videotape presentations. However, each store is community specific and tailors its fashion programs with its target customers in mind.

THE STORE'S IMAGE

A store's image is a concept, an intellectual creative impression about a retailer. It is a distinguishing identity that is projected by the quality of a store's fashion merchandise, the price points, the promotions, and the visual ambiance of the store and its windows. A symbolic logo or the way the store's name appears on packaging, shopping bags, and advertising can also convey image.

High fashion retailer Bergdorf Goodman freshened its image from one of the conservative grand dames of retailing to one that is on the cutting edge of fashion merchandising. The goal was achieved by introducing new young designers to reach out to affluent young customers, while the store maintained its loyal customer base with couture and European fashion designer merchandise. The store's window displays do not merely show fashion in seasonal themes. Instead, the prestigious image of the store is further augmented by the work of highly creative artists who evoke dramatic stories in displays that captivate shoppers and draw them into the store. As a case in point, a window retrospective on the style of Jackie Kennedy was timed to tie into an exhibition at the Metropolitan Museum of Art.

The historic landmark area of Ladies Mile, so named for the historic stores once located on Sixth Avenue between 14th Street and 23rd Street in New York City, now houses a new generation of retailers. Old Navy, for one, projects an image of self-service.

The image of a store permeates through the chain of command from top management to buyer level. The fashion office acts as a sort of "keeper of the image," making sure that the image is conveyed throughout the store and in design elements that customers can recognize.

LORD & TAYLOR

For more than fifty years, the long-stemmed American Beauty rose has been the design symbol for Lord & Taylor. It celebrates the enduring quality and beauty that characterize the store and is a consistent theme in packaging and advertising.

The history of the rose image is quite interesting. Shortly after Dorothy Shaver became president of Lord & Taylor in 1945, she requested an enduring design symbol that would signify beauty and quality. From all the designs submitted, she chose the long-stemmed budding American Beauty rose. Eleanor Roosevelt was reported to have admired the rose design on Lord & Taylor wrapping paper and sent a letter to the store saying it was the prettiest rose she had ever seen. Incidentally, Dorothy Shaver was the first woman president of a major retail operation and as president, she was also the first to actively support and encourage American designers.

Establishing unique customer services can also convey an image. Considered the "Signature of American Style," Lord & Taylor begins each day by playing the "Star Spangled Banner," a tradition which started in 1980 to express support of our country during the Iranian hostage crisis and has continued ever since. The store's tradition of inviting customers in and serving coffee a half-hour before the store opens actually dates back to the 1940s and continues today. Image is what it is all about, so Lord & Taylor uses china, not Styrofoam cups. Other firsts, which increase image awareness, are Lord & Taylor's innovative Christmas windows filled with traditional holiday stories instead of merchandise.

MACY'S

One of the most recognizable nationwide image promotions is Macy's annual Thanksgiving Day parade, which is widely attended and televised. The store's annual spectacular flower show also draws huge crowds. As an added customer service, knowledgeable lecturers on scheduled mini tours give customers pertinent information about the exotic and traditional flowers and foliage on display.

INDUSTRY PROFILE 7-1 | Lavelle Olexa

Artist Richard Estes greeting customers at Lord & Taylor.

"If the Guggenheim can do Armani, then Lord & Taylor can present art," says Lavelle Olexa, Lord & Taylor's senior vice president of fashion merchandising. "The merchants do what they do best, the buying and selling of merchandise, and one of the fashion office's key roles in the organization is to open the store to new horizons. I bring an idea to the organization and clear the path for all creative levels to execute the vision of the store."

With the support of the 175-year-old chain's new president Jane Elfers, the aim was to modernize Lord & Taylor's look, from advertisements to catalogs and the famed Fifth Avenue windows. "The right merchandise is key," notes Ms. Olexa. "However, we wanted to offer something cultural or educational, and provide added value to the customer. To this end, in order to make Lord & Taylor a more interesting place to shop, the store took a cultural approach and began to feature famous artists' works in its windows. Lunchtime events became part of Lord & Taylor's new strategy to become a cultural destination, and at the same time maintain its reputation as a destination for clothing. The aim is to ring up more sales in the process."

As a case in point, when Lord & Taylor showcased Larry Rivers, one of America's most renowned and enduring figurative

Lavelle Olexa has used artists and their work to modernize Lord & Taylor's windows, add a cultural dimension to the shopping experience, and, in the process, increase sales.

artists, the promotion represented a coup in the chain's drive to raise its profile. "There's no question stores have to find ways to attract new customers," says Ms. Olexa. "Three hundred people came and stood patiently and quietly to meet the artist and view a series of twenty-four paintings and drawings by Rivers called Fashion Show Monte Carlo. People came to see Mr. Rivers' whimsical depictions of shoes, belts, and runway models displayed in the windows. Bringing art exhibits to the store builds the store's image."

In another event, approximately five hundred people mobbed the tenth floor to meet artist Richard Estes, renowned for his New York City street scenes, and to get an autographed poster of one of his paintings. While waiting patiently, the fans were entertained by the John Pizzarelli jazz trio.

"It doesn't have to be just art," notes Ms. Olexa. "In another special event series, we present women's health programs, called Wellness Wednesdays, which focus on women's physical and spiritual well-being. It is part of Lord & Taylor's continuing commitment to women's health issues. At a typical Wednesday lecture, the National Osteoporosis Foundation presented Dr. Ethel Siris, Department of Medicine, College of Physicians and Surgeons, Columbia University, who discussed new advances in the diagnosis and treatment of osteoporosis."

Ms. Olexa points out that as fashion director she has to be tuned into diverse areas of research. For example, when she attended a book fair in Chicago, she realized that there was an incredible interest in children's books and this led to establishing Claire's Corner. As part of the "Tell Me A Story!" program, the children's Saturday reading corner features celebrity readings by authors and such stars as Julie Andrews. "I find it personally interesting to seek out these different avenues for store promotion," says Ms. Olexa.

She concedes that over the course of the years the role of the fashion office has changed. However, most importantly, the fashion office plays an important role in establishing the direction and image of the store and supports the president's vision. "It's important to understand the direction, and support the changes in the chain's diverse retail stores. I attend all the new store openings. However, each store is defined by need. The fashion office filters out information to the merchandise managers and merchants in the branch stores.

As a consummate fashion researcher, Ms. Olexa travels two to three times a year with the vice president of fashion merchandising and visual merchandising staff to

This page and following page: *Four Lord & Taylor windows in the "Accent on Accessories" theme range from scarves and handbags to millinery and shoes.*

WESTERN
ACCENT ON
accessories
NATURAL
ACCENT ON
accessories

Lord & Taylor windows showcasing the work of artist Larry Rivers brought customers into the store to meet the artist and view an exhibit of his paintings and drawings. Such promotions enhance the company's image, while giving people another reason to enter the store.

attend the prêt-à-porter runway shows in London, Paris, and Milan, and textile trade shows, such as Première Vision. On a visit to St. Tropez, the popular seaside village in the south of France noted for its celebrities and people watching and trendy boutiques, they look for emerging trends and interpret their influence on upcoming fashions.

"Information gets filtered out to the merchants. Communication is key," notes Ms. Olexa. "The fashion office creates a flow, a dissemination of information throughout the entire store to define the look, color, and fabric points of view. We all work synergistically, and pull all the elements together to lead in the same focused direction. As a result, brainstorming meetings are a typical part of the agenda of the fashion office calendar."

In a program to keep merchants, management, and private label merchandisers informed and on target, Lord & Taylor also identifies themes and tracks color, fabric, print, and pattern in seasonal books that establish the retailer's point of view. In a Fall booklet, the themes creatively introduced several color ranges: Balance, incandescent pales; Spirit, lively brights; Strength, saturated darks; Harmony, autumnal combinations; and Wisdom, fall's new neutral tones.

Ms. Olexa began her career at Neiman Marcus, in Dallas, when Stanley Marcus was running the store. "That made a difference," she notes. "Shopping was glamorous, fun, and educational. I joined Lord & Taylor in 1989 and it's been a stimulating and rewarding association."

DISCOUNT STORES

Discount stores also upgrade their images to accommodate evolving customer lifestyle preferences. JC Penney, for one, used the theme, "There's a change in Penney's, because there's change in you," to emphasize the fact that while it was still addressing the needs and wants of its loyal customer base, its new image was implemented to appeal to the new, younger shoppers. The chain accomplished this image upgrade by bringing in brand-name designers, modernizing its stores, and projecting this new image in advertising.

BLOOMINGDALE'S: A HIGH-KICKING MOVIE TIE-IN

Promotions tied into a movie not only associate a department store with Hollywood glamour, but have proved to be a highly effective technique for captivating the crowds, drawing people into the store, and stimulating business.

Thousands came to see Nicole Kidman, star of 20th Century Fox's *Moulin Rouge,* and blocked traffic on Lexington Avenue in front of Bloomingdale's. When the windows were unveiled, out raced the cancan dancers, kicking high and throwing up their petticoats, just as they do at the Moulin Rouge in Paris. On the store's third floor, the Moulin Rouge shop featured tempting black lace bustiers, red taffeta and black evening and cocktail dresses, sexy lingerie, and cool tees. The movie inspired many accessory trends, such as beaded lace necklaces, fancy cancan hair ornaments, hats, and even makeup from Christian Dior. As the crowd surged into the store for the opening reception, the Moulin Rouge shop was the site of overwhelming customer activity.

At the forefront of developing this explosive movie tie-in promotion was Kalman Ruttenstein, senior vice president of fashion direction of Bloomingdale's flagship store in New York City and its twenty-three branch stores.

"I immersed myself in the theme and even went to the Moulin Rouge in Paris. I studied everything about the era and

Retail outlets use a variety of promotions to attract customers. Bloomingdale's display based on the movie Moulin Rouge *brought cancan dancers to New York's chic Lexington Avenue.*

especially the clothing. Further inspiring the movie tie-in, I had noticed a lot of the Paris couture and prêt-à-porter clothes were basically corsets and bustiers with turn of the century styling." The timing was right, and the Bloomingdale's tie-in with the *Moulin Rouge* movie caused a sensation. "We decided to do a shop with clothes that reflected the mood and invited designers to see some clips in a screening room in California. Everyone loved it and was inspired. We edited and rejected and again edited the fashions for the Moulin Rouge shop and had six weeks of incredible selling."

When Mr. Ruttenstein is not planning the next major promotion, depending on what major event is happening in the store, he has daily impromptu meetings. The Bloomingdale's fashion office has twelve staff members including six divisional fashion coordinators:

1. Fashion coordinator: men's wear/children's wear
   Assistant fashion coordinator
2. Fashion coordinator: designer and bridge
   assistant fashion coordinator
3. Fashion coordinator: contemporary
4. Fashion coordinator: dresses, coats/suits, swimwear and intimate apparel. This market specific coordinator not only disseminates information on color, fabric, and fashion trends, but also attends and writes reports on Première Vision, the textile trade show held in Paris.
5. Fashion coordinator: special sizes, Sutton, and moderate missy lines. This coordinator travels and works hand in hand with the merchandise manager on sweater programs and private label merchandise.
6. Fashion coordinator: fashion accessories, handbags, and shoes. Assistant fashion coordinator.

The Fashion Books

The fashion office's seasonal Trend Direction Reports are based on the prêt-à-porter shows held in Europe in March for the

Fall/Winter and in October for the Spring/Summer. Setting the pace in fashion direction, the title of Bloomingdale's Designer Campaign was "A New Standard," in which high fashion designers, color standards, ready-to-wear top picks, and accessories were clearly defined in pictorial layouts and written reports. These Trend Direction Reports are sent to everyone in the store from the executives right down to the merchants and the staff of the store to totally immerse them in the fashion direction and colors.

Under Mr. Ruttenstein's direction the look of the windows, advertisements, and floor displays is also influenced by the fashion office's input. Mr. Ruttenstein and his staff determine the content and designer to be featured in window displays. The staff pulls the merchandise from the fashion departments not only for the windows, but also for the interior displays.

At "style out" sessions, all the merchandise that is under consideration for the pages of Bloomingdale's consumer driven fashion books is brought into the fashion office. The fashion books include publications featuring seasonal merchandise, the Sutton Studio collection, men's wear, swimwear features, and Christmas merchandise. At these sessions, Mr. Ruttenstein, his staff, and an in-house stylist are hands-on decision makers. They review the merchandise and determine what is actually going into the pages of the fashion books. These professionals also have input in Bloomingdale's catalog store publications.

"The fashion office is the facilitator of trends. We give advice, the buyers make the final decision," notes Mr. Ruttenstein. "We are primarily the conscience of the store and create the image of the store."

DILLARD'S SOUTHERN MENTALITY

Fashion direction and color are key to Dillard's, the Little Rock, Arkansas-based department store's private brand merchandise. "In the New York office, we have 100 percent private brand concentration," notes Elaine Flowers, trend director of the New York fashion development office. "Although Dillard's is geographic specific and mostly Southern driven, our point of view reflects a seasonless approach to merchandising product."

Ms. Flowers points out that the one big difference at Dillard's is color. The Southern customer responds to color, so when Ms. Flowers develops the color trends she considers the fact that color has to pop on the floor. "If the trend is a brown palette, we don't want to make it as somber, but feminize rich brown with accents of sunset colors like cayenne and sienna," notes Ms. Flowers. "With this approach we are still on trend with a Southern mentality."

From wardrobe basics to the latest fashion-forward collections to home furnishings, Dillard's private brands each stand for their own identity. The product development office works color and trends to provide each brand's design team with inspiration and direction.

Ms. Flowers "Europe at Retail Report" covers trend direction based on fashion and trade shows, street scenes, and retail in Milan, Paris, and London. It covers color, fabric, print, and pattern and provides overall key ideas and influential fashion items in both written and illustrated format for design interpretation. The report goes to the entire production team, as well as the store groups from president to buyer level.

"Fashion is an instantaneous commodity," says Ms. Flowers. "We evaluate the trends. If it is appropriate we jump in or wait to test the waters." She points out that some trends may take a while to kick in and may work only for one of Dillard's labels.

Béchamel, for example, is an important key brand fashioned for the mature woman who loves print, pattern, and embellishment, particularly conversational driven appliqués and re-embroidery motifs, such as a border of flowers or whimsical cats. "If florals are important, we consider the label's point of view and determine if it should be simplistic, high coverage or spaced florals," says Ms. Flowers. "We can take one idea like splash and splatter prints and interpret it on several levels. We move fast on trend ideas in order to get them into the stores. Black and white was phenomenal and worked through all themes including the Preston & York brand for the career consumer."

As trend director Ms. Flowers must consider all Dillard's brand profiles. She puts together fashion silhouette and accessories trend boards that will influence design decisions for all the brands and includes fashion specific ideas for the younger customer. "Copper Key is our junior brand for separates. It's our edgiest in a conservative way."

The written report for children's wear may represent some of the same trend ideas as ready to wear but is interpreted with a children's wear outlook. Color may be sophisticated in ready to wear but will be packaged more understandably for the children's market. Color must be brighter for children.

Dillard's sees growth in individualizing and making their mark exclusively with proprietary labels. Currently the retailer is expanding its private-brand-merchandising program.

SEARS, ROEBUCK, AND CO.: MASS MERCHANT POINT OF VIEW

A fashion director at a major chain establishes the fashion trends customers will see when they walk through the door. Take Fran Yoshioka, fashion and design director, private brand development, for ready-to-wear at Sears, Roebuck and Co. She analyzes and edits trend information with the Sears point of view not only for the design teams, but also for the merchants.

How does she do it? Ms. Yoshioka attends the seasonal fashion presentations given by both American and European forecast and color services. She shops Europe's fashion stores and attends fashion and trade shows, such as Première Vision.

With a keen eye trained by years of experience, she analyzes what is new, what items are hot, and what will be the fashion themes that will permeate the missy merchandise assortments at Sears.

As fashion and design director, Ms. Yoshioka interacts with many different people on both the creative and merchant levels. Her position combines the skills of an administrator, communicator, diplomat, financial budget supervisor, and people manager.

Although she recognizes that technology is important in regard to students' education, she equally values an effective oral and creative presentation and advises, "You must be able to articulate what your eye sees." That's what Ms. Yoshioka does best. Working with the private brand teams, she incorporates the trends into creative presentation boards with color, fabric, and silhouette detail, so the designers and merchants understand where the trend is coming from and how to interpret it. "Color is the first step in the success of a line," notes Ms. Yoshioka. "I often show them the previous season's boards so they can see what is different and what will look new to the customer."

Her relationship with the ready-to-wear design teams is not just as a forecaster, but as a mentor to inspire them and to keep the paths of creativity open for them. She must understand the demographics and psychographics of each of Sears' brands and how to turn great trend and design ideas into saleable apparel the customer will understand.

Trend Follow Up

Seasonal slide presentations, another important fashion director's tool, illustrate important items and fashion/color/fabric trends aimed at guiding merchants in their buying decisions. The merchants also receive a seasonal trend book, which is a visual representation of the slides. It shows the big trend ideas for the season and identifies key items the customer must have.

Ms. Yoshioka advises that one of the most important attributes a fashion director must have is the ability to give a compelling and convincing presentation. She or he must be able to stand up in front of a group of people and excite them. Effective communication begins with speaking with skillful analysis, specific articulation, and an enthusiasm to show design teams, merchants, and management how to adapt new ideas for the sell through of fashion.

SAKS: AN EXAMPLE OF A CHARITY EVENT

Retailers also engage in civic-minded events that bring focus to a store's charitable initiatives. It is all part of community relationships that showcase a store's concern for its prime customer base, which is a woman. Charitable events are not only good fund raising vehicles—they draw customers into the store.

In 1999, Saks Fifth Avenue initiated its shopping weekend in support of breast cancer research. Since then, the company has donated more than $9 million to organizations throughout the United States. Then, in April 2003, Saks announced its latest initiative, the "Key to the Cure," founded in partnership with the Entertainment Industry Foundation and its Women's Cancer Research Fund. This initiative is an expansion of the original program to include all reproductive cancers. Actress Nicole Kidman, on behalf of the David Geffen School of Medicine at the University of California, Los Angeles, and as the first chair of the Women's Health Fund at UCLA, agreed to become the first model for the "Key to the Cure." Money raised through the program will benefit more than sixty charitable programs.

According to Christina Johnson, president and CEO of Saks Fifth Avenue Enterprises, because "the majority of our customers and associates are women, we think that there's no

Special thanks to Nicole Kidman, Saks Fifth Avenue's Key to the Cure 2003 ambassador and chair of the Women's Health Fund at UCLA, a beneficiary of the Entertainment Industry Foundation's Women's Cancer Research Fund. The 2003 limited edition Danskin T-shirt was designed by Stella McCartney, exclusively for Saks Fifth Avenue's Key to the Cure.

better way to give back to the community we serve by raising not only awareness but also significant funds to help combat breast and other reproductive cancers."

This new charitable venture began in September, with a nationwide shopping weekend at Saks stores. A percentage of all sales was donated to local and national breast and women's reproductive cancer research centers. Ms. Kidman appeared in national service announcements wearing the initiative's Danskin T-shirt, designed by Stella McCartney. The announcement appeared in major fashion and lifestyle magazines.

In addition, Mercedes-Benz, as a national sponsor of the event, expects to donate a substantial amount through the sales of a limited number of special edition Cabriolets, which were designed exclusively in support of the "Key to the Cure."

Charity events are an example of learning a lot more about a retailer's customers and addressing issues that are key to their lifestyle. Successful charity events are part entertainment, part merchandising. They garner publicity, increase sales, and draw in the customers.

RETAIL ORGANIZATIONS

This is a challenging time for retailers because of the state of the world economy. These issues are addressed at the National Retail Federation's (NRF) Annual Convention and Expo, which is held in January at the Jacob Javits Convention Center in New York City. More than fifteen thousand retail peers and business partners attend the convention.

For four days the NRF Expo seminars cover a wide range of retail-related topics, including global brand positioning, multichannel marketing, change in management strategies, and the latest financial paths that will lead to profitability. It is the biggest all-retail industry gathering in the world and features industry speakers, educators, and more than three hundred exhibitors representing new technology, store promotion, and even shopping bag design.

As the world's largest retail association, NRF's mission is to conduct programs and services in research, education, training and technology, and government affairs to protect and advance the interests of the retail industry. NRF's membership includes the leading department, specialty, independent, discount, and mass merchandise stores in the United States and fifty nations around the world. NRF also publishes *Stores* magazine.

Trade Terminology

Arbiter of taste
Calendar of events
Charity event
Cultural destination
Divisional fashion director
Fashion calendar
Fashion office
Market researcher
Market shares
President's vision
Prognosticator
Retail doors
Retail report
Special event
Store image
Store merchants
Stores magazine
Style out

READING 7-1 | Direction: The International Textile Design Show

DIRECTION, The International Textile Design Show, is the most comprehensive textile design event in New York City. It showcases prints, knits and novelty textile designs, CAD technology, color and trend forecasts, international publications, innovative fibers, yarns and trims, as well as digital production resources for unique and short runs. DIRECTION is considered a goldmine of inspiration for its exhibitor base, SURFACE Seminar Series, quick-read trend displays and trend reports.

FALL 2004 PRINT TRENDS

DECO—Art Deco artfully echoes in leaves, petals and geometrics.

OCULAR—An opposition of color and optical illusion clash and merge for eye-popping effects.

TAPESTRY—Elegant tapestries and fancy fabrics borrowed from interiors appear weathered, time-worn.

PAISLEY—Smoldering hues and ombré vibrations intensify time-honored and contemporary ornamentals.

ROMANCE—Pretty, charming floral impressions gently mix, meld and layer.

LINE—From orderly to leisurely to curvilinear, linear looks have feminine appeal.

FALL 2004 CHILDREN'S PRINT TRENDS

FLOWER POWER
Hip, mod swirls, paisleys and flowers are fun, funky and fabulous.
COUNTRY FLORAL
Vintage flowers crafted with gingham, embroidery and lace are sweet and naïve.
BEST BUDDIES
From cat and mouse to man's best friend, charming creatures are irresistible.
BEAR ESSENTIALS
Cute, cuddly teddy bears innocently mix with stripes, hearts, flowers and leaves.
ALL STARS
Championships, competitions and contests—it's a ball and numbers game.
X-TREME
From mountain bikes to skate and snowboards the fun is in the challenge.
ON THE ROAD
Swift and speedy, racing wheels are a winner on and off the beaten track.

SUMMER 2004 PRINT TRENDS

BLUE—Indigo and blues in florals, paisleys, knits and more. New takes on denim too.
ASIA—Chinese and Japanese influences with florals and kimono prints.
SARONG—Indonesia and South East Asia inspire batik-style florals.
SILHOUETTE—Simple, bold silhouetted and shadow motifs are often bi-colored.
TROPICAL—Exotic island florals for the height of summer.
VACATION—Scenics, beach and underwater. Verbiage tees and sport motifs with tropical flair.
PAISLEY—Light, airy and decorative interpretations for summer.
TRIBE—Primitive looks incorporate texture, symbols and tropical motifs in a tropical mood.
ROMANCE—Small dainty florals have vintage appeal.
POP-Y—Palm Beach, Scandinavian modern, 60's and 70's florals.
STRIPE—Plaids and stripes from simple to crazy—on their own or topped with dots or flowers.

SPRING 2004 PRINT TRENDS

For Spring 2004 all kinds of floral prints take the lead including spring-like, Asian influenced, Scandinavian modern interpretations, feminine dainty variations and tropical blooms. Tropical influences about with flora as well as balmy palm frond prints and island primitive looks to beach vacation themes. Graphic prints are bold with an emphasis on stripes and polka dots, often clashing together. An obsession with the past continues where ethnic paisleys are reworked, the 50's, 60's and 70's become inspiration for conversationals and florals, art deco and art nouveau make a statement and novelties are inspired by vintage textiles from Victorian florals to elegant and aged tapestries and brocades reinterpreted into prints.
SPRING BLOOMS—Fresh, lively, bold.
Spring flowers in full bloom are larger-than-life.
TROPICAL BLOOMS—Hot, fragrant, alive.
Tropical flora and island scenes are in living color.
ASIAN BLOOMS—Beautiful, delicate, lustrous.
Asian influences abound and move gently into art nouveau.
BALMY—Palms, fronds, shade.
Shady and breezy islands foliage inspires rich tropical prints.
PRIMITIVE—Natural, textured, symbolic.
Bamboo, foliage and fruits are exotic on organic or rustic grounds.
GRAPHIC—Wild, crazy, intense.
Fun, youthful graphics include all kinds of crazy polka dots.
ORNAMENTAL—Decorative, paisley, novelty.
Soft ornamentals take ethnic into the feminine realm.
RETRO—Fun, funky, hip.
Decades past inspire florals and funky conversationals.
VINTAGE—Romantic, feminine, fancy.
Elegant jacquards worn by time recall a decorative past.

Source: Direction Show trend report, 2004. Courtesy of Direction Show.

READING 7-2 | Spotting the Trends

One of an elite corps of fashion forecasters, David Wolfe, 60, travels the globe sizing up the sartorial zeitgeist. "The industry depends on world economics, politics, quotas and duties—things most designers don't concern themselves with," he says. A former fashion illustrator, Wolfe, who grew up in Ashtabula, Ohio, and began forecasting in London in the 1970s, is creative director for the Doneger Group, the world's largest fashion-merchandising consulting firm. His more than 500 clients include retailers like Nordstrom and Wal-Mart, as well as designers, cosmetics companies, financial firms and rock-star stylists. Working 18 months ahead of each season, Wolfe predicts what styles and colors will catch on. "The trick part is the timing," he says. "Everybody knows skirts are going to get shorter and longer. They can't do anything else. But how quickly is it going to happen?" Wolfe, who lives in New Preston, Conn., with his partner, writer Steve Roos, was interviewed at his Manhattan office by PEOPLE writer-reporter Toby Kahn.

Q. Where do you look for trends?
A. Everywhere. I go to the theater, the movies. I read. The most important thing is to travel and watch people—not just models on the runway. I go to the French Riviera every summer to get a feel of what's a heartbeat ahead. Saint-Tropez is the mecca for fashion believers. You get a lead on whether they still want cleavage or if the bare back is next.

Q. What did you see there last summer that will trickle down to the rest of us in the next few months?
A. Prints galore. Preteens to little old ladies in garish, loud prints. It made me suspect prints were going to have a longer shelf life than predicted.

Q. What's the big look for this spring?
A. The No. 1 trend is going to be a Latin, south-of-the-border interpretation of femininity. Next fall's movie about Mexican artist Frida Kahlo is going to focus attention on traditional Latin looks: off-the-shoulder blouses, bright embroidery, full skirts—a colorful, sexy look. Our fascination is a result of the explosion of Hispanic culture in America.

Q. What else is in store for us?
A. It's going to be the most feminine, romantic spring we've had for years: lace blouses, lace-trimmed dresses and accessories, all kinds of embroidered tulle and eyelet.

Q. How will the clothes fit?
A. We are finally seeing signs that things are loosening up. That's great for everybody over the age of 14. God bless Britney Spears, but she has a lot of fashion disasters to answer for, like midriffs we don't want to see on display. We've had tight for so long, it's time for a change.

Q. How did Sept. 11 affect fashion?
A. At first people were afraid to shop. They've become less frivolous and have changed their priorities. They'll be looking for more quality and a longer life span for their clothes. Classics will be more important.

Q. How does psychology play into forecasting?
A. I always look for the psychology underneath everything. That's how you figure out what's going to be successful. Because of 9-11, designers were anxious to erase the negativity and fear. These new clothes for spring are optimistic and young and pretty.

Q. Does that mean that another color is replacing basic black?
A. This long black cycle started in the late '70s with London punk and was picked up in the '80s by the Japanese designers. Electronic gadgets were black. People wanted black cars. Now black just looks too depressing and sinister. For spring, everything that was black is now white. Entire runway shows were all white.

Q. Why did so many designers come up with the peasant look at the same time this season?
A. Again, it sprang from the emerging Latin influence. Tom Ford's gypsy blouse from the Yves Saint Laurent collection was an important item from last season. It's everywhere now. We were looking for a new erogenous zone besides the midriff. The shoulder seemed right.

Q. Which stars are trendsetters?
A. Gwyneth Paltrow—not for a particular trend but for being a dedicated fashion follower. Britney Spears hasn't lost her grip on the nubile adolescent market. Julia Roberts is hit-and-miss. She'd be a stronger fashion influence if she'd lock into one look.

Q. How long does a trend last?
A. Two seasons is probably the max. An example is the Louis Vuitton graffiti bag by Stephen Sprouse that came out last spring. If you bought it from Louis Vuitton, it's over. But if you're on the next loop of the cycle, there are interpretations from Guess? and Tommy Hilfiger selling right now. The trend is lasting, just filtering its way through different segments of the market.

Q. What clothes are worth keeping?
A. Classics keep coming around. If you own a great pair of gray flannel Saint Laurent pants from 1976, they've been in fashion about five times since then. A great white oxford shirt. A Chanel suit. Oversize sweaters. They are going to be very important for fall 2003.

Source: *People*, March 6, 2002, pp. 71-72. As told to Toby Kahn/People Weekly © 2002 Time Inc.

READING 7-3 | Fashion Oracle BY DAVID MOIN

The fashion director of the luxury-filled Neiman Marcus chain would be expected to have a certain amount of flamboyance—and Joan Kaner has just the right touch of it. It comes from her bold streaks of white hair, and the chicly understated clothes and big necklaces she wears to fly the Neiman's flag.

But what really drives Kaner, the New York-based senior vice president and fashion director of Neiman's, is her down-to-earth perspective, pragmatism and balance between family and work that are rare for someone immersed in the fashion world. Then there's her Old World charm and unaffected disposition. During an interview, for example, she never effused about things being "fabulous," like so many of her peers.

Kaner believes in "slow romancing" designers and promoting styles that are timeless, "not obvious." Nor does she get caught up in the frenzy of fashion week and rush to judgment. For Kaner, fashion is a job, a business, not a front row seat.

"I've always said that I take my work seriously—not myself," Kaner said. "A job is a job. But I enjoy it obviously. I love fashion. I have always loved fashion. My earliest childhood memories are looking at *Vogue* magazine.

"If you do this long enough, the thing that really sticks in your mind's eye are the things that really matter. There comes a point in almost every show, or in the best of shows, when you suddenly get the message loud and clear. It's almost like a bell goes off and you say 'Wow!' It can be a certain item, or a certain passage that comes down the runway, and for me that's the message."

Her directions and advice to buyers on new designers and important looks for the upcoming season come after she's had time to digest the spectacle of the runway shows, and some time for herself—those rare moments when she's not in the market. "I take notes, but they're like a security blanket," she said. "Often, I truly don't look at them. To me, the best thing is going through my slides. If I still love [a collection] when I see it the second time around—without the music, without the hoopla—then I know it's right."

She also has a life outside fashion. She was married at 19, had her first child at 23 and has four grandchildren. "I've always had a husband and children to go home to. I did what I had to do within the industry, but that wasn't what drove me or pushed me. I think [family] has given me a marvelous balance."

Fashion directors are a dying breed in retailing because most stores' buying decisions are often ruled more by matrix systems and margin agreements than old-fashioned fashion instincts. In the post 9/11 era of inventory reduction, many stores have cut back designer offerings and are less willing to take risks on new designers. Also, in some cases, fashion directors have taken on other responsibilities in the store organization, diluting their fashion authority.

However, with Neiman Marcus on a mission to build up luxury offerings and exclusive items and solidify designer partnerships, Kaner's role seems as relevant as ever. She's sometimes the first to discover talent and she reports directly to Burt Tansky, the company's chief executive officer. "I have absolutely not changed how I operate," Kaner stated. "One thing we've never done is compromise. Neiman's may have cut back, which was economically feasible, but we have not compromised the quality or the style of our offerings.

"Our buying and selling is sharper, and that has proven to be really beneficial," she added. "We have not done the promoting a lot of our competitors have done. Usually, we are the last to take markdowns. We ended the year successfully, because we bought less and sold more at regular price."

One thing has changed. "I used to travel to more stores, but we are constantly in the market one way or the other, in showrooms, at trade shows, with the Europeans who come with early parts of their collections. I go to Europe four times a year, twice for the couture, twice for the ready-to-wear collections. The market goes on endlessly."

Sifting through the morass can sometimes be rewarding, as Kaner remembers how Neiman's started selling Chado by Ralph Rucci. It was seven years ago, when Rucci was attempting a comeback after being out of business for a long time, and was working out of a little showroom that he shared at 530 Seventh Avenue in Manhattan's garment district.

"I was very taken with the make and quality of the clothes, and at that level, which we call couture, not to be confused with haute couture, I felt he was doing something that was missing in the marketplace," Kaner recalled. "He was dressing a woman, not girls. He didn't run after the waifs or try to be trendy.

"The next step was putting a small collection in several stores. Then he started to do trunk shows for us, at the downtown store in Dallas," she said. The Beverly Hills branch also bought some Rucci goods.

At a Chado trunk show at Neiman's in Los Angeles a few seasons ago, the unimaginable happened. James Galanos showed up. It's rare in the ego-intensive competitive rag trade when one designer acknowledges another, and for Galanos to be there was a huge compliment to Rucci, considering Galanos' couturier reputation and exacting standards for quality.

Kaner remembered that Galanos came in and told Rucci, "I heard about your clothes from several of my customers. I just had to come in and look." They became friends later, and when Galanos comes to New York, he stops in to see him.

Chado by Ralph Rucci is currently sold in about a dozen Neiman's locations. "It's a very big business, and a lot of it is special order, because he is willing to customize for customers," Kaner said. "I don't know if it will be in 30 stores, but he has the opportunity to grow, and grow in each of the stores.

"The point is you have to romance it, you have to get behind it, and have to explain why it is what it is. You don't just buy it and put it on the floor, and expect the customer to walk by and say 'what is that?' We like to grow a business slowly, especially if you are dealing with new young designers. Very often, you can overwhelm them. Miguel Adrover became too big, too quickly and no one was able to handle it. It's prudent to start slowly, on everyone's part."

Because Neiman's takes it slowly with new designers, Kaner said she's able to get most of her recommendations acted upon. Asked if there are any new Calvin Kleins or Oscar de la Rentas emerging, she replied, "This season in particular, Zac Posen has proven that he is not a one-shot wonder. There are a few young people that we have our eye on, that we think can grow into important designers for us. I do wish that the CFDA would give more financial support to those people, so they can do a show."

Sometimes even with corporate backing, things can go awry. "It's usually not black and white," Kaner said, though, "there are some people who feel very constrained. We saw that with Isaac Mizrahi. I certainly hope he comes back. He had a wonderful sense of design and color and fun. He could add a lot to the mix."

Rather than corporate controls, Kaner said, "what worries me more is that designers for a long time have given way to stylists and editors. That's a detriment to the business. Everybody jumps on the bandwagon. They all want to be in the magazines and they all want the fashion editors to cover the collections. For a long time, we were locked in the vice of everybody doing the same looks because of a few people in the industry who more or less were dictating what they wanted to see on the runways. I remember doing a presentation and unless the name was on the back of the slide, I couldn't tell if it was designer A or designer B. It all looked alike, and again I think it was the dictates of what the editors were wanting to see.

"You have to give designers full rein. If they are good, they are going to do their thing, not yours. And you have to decide if it is right or wrong and make your decision based on that. Designers are to blame for allowing themselves to be caught up in that game. I knew a designer who didn't do black, because a certain editor didn't want to see black on the runway, and I said, 'You know, you are working and living in New York City.' "

However, Kaner added that in the last couple of seasons, designers apparently regained control. "It's a good change. We need variety. We need individual statements by designers."

Much of the spring ready-to-wear collections looked very saleable, she said.

"We've just come off all the peasant looks and ethnic looks, so there's been kind of a swing the other way. It's cleaned up and more sensual." And in a sense, in the spirit of Ralph Rucci. "The [woman] replaces the waif, the clothes are more sophisticated, polished, more pulled together and all that smacks of good business, because that's who our lady is. We're seeing more reality on the runways, and certainly in the American collections you see more reality than you do in Europe. . . . There are lots of dresses and slim skirts I feel very strongly about."

This past year, "What's been working for us has really been two things, and almost a juxtaposition of each other: Akris and Chado have been very successful. The customer who buys Akris and Chado buys high quality, a certain kind of simple elegance and they're not necessarily trendy. When you buy clothes of that type, you are buying something that has longevity."

At the other end of the spectrum, Neiman's is also selling "feel good" clothes, like Roberto Cavalli, Blumarine, Dolce & Gabbana, and [Moschino's] Cheap & Chic. "It can be anything from peasant looks to little flapper beaded dresses, but they are fun kind[s] of clothes," Kaner said.

Amid the fashion changes and economic changes, Kaner believes the constant at Neiman Marcus is its ability to maintain focus. While other stores lose focus, for Neiman's, she said, "I don't think it's that hard, when you have solid, experienced merchants." She noted that the general merchandise managers have been at Neiman's for many years, she's worked at the store for 13 years, with Tansky at the helm for eight years, all helping to keep the company on course. Prior to Neiman's, Kaner worked at Macy's and Bergdorf Goodman, a division of the Neiman Marcus Group. She also worked at Henri Bendel.

"There is a consistency, a viewpoint," Kaner explained. "We try to understand who our customer is and I think we do. The one constant is we are addressing a monied customer. She is affluent. If she is not married to someone who is the head of a company, she is running a business. She is social and very active in charity. She has clothes to wear to all the functions. She travels with her husband, or she is [a] businesswoman who travels. She is well dressed and she has the money to spend on the clothing. That's all a generality at the highest end, the couture end.

"Then it filters down and you have the contemporary customer. Our contemporary business in the last five years has grown tremendously and that's where we really address the more avant-garde. That's a business that's more item-driven. It's Seven jeans, D&G, Just Cavalli, Theory. It's relaxed, but it's more trendy.

"Through the slowdown last year, contemporary has been extraordinary. I think today contemporary is what juniors used to be years ago. It's the customer who is really looking for fast fashion. She wants gratification instantly."

Source: *Women's Wear Daily,* October 15, 2002, p. 26b. Courtesy of Fairchild Publications, Inc.

8

The Fashion Show Circuit: New York / London / Paris / Milan

What will be next year's biggest fashion trends? Which shows will get press coverage? Who will be recognized as the season's top designers? Which emerging star will capture the limelight? These questions are on the minds of retailers, the fashion press, and fashionistas who twice yearly attend the ready-to-wear shows in the fashion capitals of the world.

These fashion professionals have developed an eye for editing the collections and evaluating the trends. They have to be there to discover the innovators, the new emerging designer talent. Even if it is an outrageous, theatrically staged show, they will recognize what looks are adaptable, what is going to make it as the key silhouette or the item of the season.

THE CATWALKS

As the pinnacle of international fashion show events, four cities have emerged as major fashion capitals: New York, London, Paris, and Milan. In these cities, international catwalk shows are viewed by the press, the retailers, and trade guests.

In June, fashion forecasters, trend setters, and retailers may also venture to St. Tropez, the chic resort in the south of France, where French visitors are usually ahead of the curve when it comes to fresh new ways of dressing. The trendy French vacationers provide inspiration for hot new looks that are likely to jump start the direction in colors and fashion items for the following summer in the United States.

THE SCHEDULE OF SHOWS

Buyers and the fashion press travel to London, Paris, and Milan, the foreign fashion capitals, in March for the Fall Prêt-à-Porter, ready-to-wear collections, which are also referred to as the "Prêt." These fashion professionals make the same ritual visit to the fashion capitals in late September or early October to see the catwalks, which showcase the Spring collections for the following year. There has been considerable debate about which country will show first. In the past, Paris was the first run of "Prêt" shows scheduled on the Fashion Calendar. However, recently the schedule was changed so that New York City became the headliner on the schedule of shows.

There is a heady mix of excitement at show time with press and retailers juggling their schedules to attend as many shows as possible. Spring/Summer collections are shown in October 2004 for Spring 2005. Fall/Winter Collections are shown in March 2005 for Fall 2005.

FASHION MARCHES ON

In Paris, the Chambre Syndicale de Prêt-à-Porter, a branch of the Fédération Française de la Couture, is an association that represents the ready-to-wear collections of the couture designers, as well as the other French Prêt-à-Porter designers. Although the Haute Couture is the apex of French fashion, the Prêt-à-Porter is the moneymaker for the couture houses.

Refusing to buckle in the face of the terrorist attack on New York in September 2001, the shows in Europe went forward as scheduled. However, many events and parties were considered inappropriate and were canceled.

Didier Grumbach, president of the Fédération Française de la Couture du Prêt-à-Porter des Couturiers et des Créateurs de Mode, confirmed that none of its members had requested a delay in the show schedule. Although security was stronger than ever, the French spirit was undaunted and the Prêt shows captured the international spotlight.

EAST MEETS WILD WEST

"It takes a great mix to create a fab party and that is exactly what John Galliano delivered in his Spring collection for Christian Dior." That is how *Women's Wear Daily* described Galliano, whose runway is always more about a raucous fashion party than window dressing for real life. "Street Chic" is what Galliano dubbed his Prêt collection. There were cowboys, cowgirls, Elvis impersonators, and everything from Viva Las Vegas swimsuits to jeweled denim pants and jeweled chiffon dresses. The press adores this kind of showmanship; it gives them something to write about. The buyers will visit the designer's salon to place orders and view tamer garment versions.

THE MEDIA EVENT

Fashion shows are the ultimate media event, a mere twenty- to thirty-minute window of opportunity to showcase a designer's collection. Fashion shows are like Broadway productions; they represent the pinnacle in Fashion Theater! It is the one venue in which each designer is judged by a coterie of retailers and the press, judgment that can have serious consequences that will affect their business. In addition, there are no tryouts out of town and, in most cases, no time even for a rehearsal. The models, music, and show must come together with precision timing.

So why do well-known designers and newcomers subject themselves to such scrutiny? For one thing, designers need a showcase—one that will promote their image and result in publicity. Sales do not directly result from the show, but the fashion catwalk will influence buying decisions. After the show, buyers and retail merchants usually go to the designer's showroom to review the collection and place orders.

Seating Priorities

The strategy of seating is a crucial issue. The designer's production team organizes the seating plan so that key buyers, the designer's important customers, celebrities, and members of the press will be properly looked after and seated in the front rows. For the designer, a headliner guest is a huge bonus, because publicity about the show is the desired result. When a movie star or entertainment personality arrives, the *paparazzi* rush to snap photos that will appear later in newspapers and magazines worldwide.

7TH ON SIXTH

7th on Sixth, held in Bryant Park in New York City, the traditional fashion week locale, identifies with the quintessence in fashion show presentations. Along with the important retailers and fashion editors, the chic guests sit hip-to-hip before the catwalks, all keen observers of the activities of the roster of diverse designers from around the world.

In the spring and fall, during the seven-day week, New York City becomes the mecca of fashion activity, with events, openings, parties, and receptions. Typically, more than one hundred shows are on the New York calendar, with as many as fifty held in huge white tents in Bryant Park. It is an exhilarating mix of buyers, press, and fashionistas all vying to take part in the event of the season.

Sponsorship

Design talent is not limited to the runways. In 2001, New York's fashion week became known as the Mercedes-Benz Fashion Week because the luxury car company was now the title sponsor. Other returning sponsors in the past include Evian, Target, Style Channel, *Harper's Bazaar, The New York Times*, and Style.com.

The involvement of Mercedes-Benz is part of the carmaker's global campaign to identify its brand with fashion.

During fashion week, Mercedes-Benz unveiled its latest automobiles which embody key fashion elements such as lifestyle, cutting-edge design, and youthfulness.

In January 2004, Olympus, a major manufacturer of cameras, became the title sponsor of fashion week. The 2004 show included several designers who were showing for the first time, including Zac Posen and Jeffrey Chow, as well as well-known designers who were returning after recent absences, including Nautica, Cynthia Rowley, and Marc Bouwer.

International Management Group

Management of 7th on Sixth has spun off from the CFDA, Council of Fashion Designers of America to IMG (International Management Group), the sports licensing, talent, model management, and event-producing conglomerate. CFDA will continue as an industry trade organization. Going forward, IMG will produce the fashion shows.

7th on Sixth has redesigned its venues to include two spaces in Bryant Park rather than four, each with four shows daily. The "Theater," a smaller version of the former "Tent," seats 700 guests and rents for $34,000. The "Gallery" seats 424 people and rents for $40,000.

In addition to important American designers, such as Tommy Hilfiger, Michael Kors, Oscar de la Renta, Anne Klein, Bill Blass, and Jeremy Scott, London designer Matthew Williamson and Nicolas Ghesquiere for Balenciaga showed their collections. Other designers included Perry Ellis, BCBG Max Azria, Boss Hugo Boss, Cynthia Rowley, and Douglas Hannant.

Fashion Week Soho

Three additional spaces for fashion shows were available in the Puck Building in Soho on Houston Street, where Rand M. Productions produced eighteen shows for smaller companies. These venues are known as Mercedes-Benz Fashion Week Soho, and the cost ranges from $11,000 to $17,000, seating 180 to 450 people. Companies showing in Soho included Donald Deal, Zang Toi, Girls Rule!, Nanette Lapore, the European Designers Collective, and the Nijole Group.

Party Time

A fashionista cannot get to everything, but key events draw the fashion intelligentsia to the doors of special events. A typical scenario during Fashion Week 2001: At the Donna Karan flagship store on Madison Avenue, excitement mounts as the crowd presses to the entrance. Nearby, Tom Ford is christening his new YSL Rive Gauche store and in Soho, the opening of the Armani Casa store is studded with celebrities and wannabes.

Spectacular sites also host designer shows that require an incredible expenditure to produce. Downtown, the crowd has been in its place for an hour, waiting the start of the Marc Jacobs show held in one of the huge white tents in Hudson River Park on the West Side Highway. Well worth the wait, the show gets rave reviews, and later the guests celebrate at the party launch of Jacobs' fragrance.

Back in Bryant Park, under the white tents, 7th on Sixth is the epicenter where fashion week kicks off with men's and women's wear designers presenting their views for the season in runway presentations.

Although show budgets are not available, industry estimates project that a show staged in one of the tents in Bryant Park can run, for example, between $250,000 and $400,000. The expenditure includes the rental of the tent, the pricey models, particularly if a super model is engaged, the staging, the original music, and the special lighting or sound effects.

A Champagne Sponsorship

Providing a creative forum for gifted young designer talent is another way that fresh ideas and viewpoints in fashion are introduced, in a group show at 7th on Sixth. The Fall 2001 Moët & Chandon Designer Debut show marked the fifth season that Moët & Chandon showcased up-and-coming designers. Selected by a committee of fashion editors and store buyers, three of fashion's most talked-about young designer shows were Christine Ganeaux, Elisa Jimenez, and Seth Shapiro.

Downtown favorite Christine Ganeaux offered a sophisticated twist on iconic masculine and military dressing. Her pin-

Among the young designers introduced by Moët & Chandon, three reflect the diversity of today's fashions. **Above:** *Christine Ganeaux's "Easy Rider" three-piece grey wool cashmere suit* **(above left)**, *and her "Coat of Armor," a laced cotton duster over a hand-knit turtleneck with a striped trouser* **(above right)**. **Opposite page, top:** *In contrast to Ganeaux's military look, Elisa Jimenez created softer images with "Air Supply," a stretch jersey dress with side cutouts* **(top left)**, *and "Fallen Angel," a two-piece ensemble in gold* **(top right)**. **Opposite page, bottom:** *Seth Shapiro's more whimsical creations included "Stars and Stripes," with a silk Edwardian-style blouse and layered skirt* **(bottom left)**, *and "Blanket Statement," a wool plaid poncho with slim-cut pants* **(bottom right)**.

stripe three-piece suit with cropped vest and signature low-slung slim cut pants struck a chord of hard-edged elegance. By contrast, Elisa Jimenez' mythology-inspired collection featured a knotted stretch jersey minidress with "wings" of spun tulle. Inspired by a famous scene from *Gone with the Wind,* Seth Shapiro's deconstructed period looks included a cascade of contrasting ruffles topped by a striped Edwardian-style blouse.

In addition to its involvement with New York's 7th on Sixth as "The Official Champagne of Fashion Week," Moët & Chandon participates in London Fashion Week, Milan Fashion Week, the Moët Fashion Awards in Argentina, Promenade Moët in Brazil, and the Fashion Editors Club in Japan.

Qualifying the Press

Editors, the press, photographers, and camera crews who wish to attend the Mercedes-Benz Fashion Week shows must qualify with the 7th on Sixth press relations office. An application that validates the frequency of publication and circulation is submitted with a nominal registration fee. Once an individual qualifies, he or she is sent a show calendar, a list of shows, and each designer's public relations contact.

7th on Sixth does not send or distribute invitations. Before show time, designers receive the list of press people. The designers and their public relations firms then issue invitations to buyers, retailers, and industry guests. If you receive an invitation, the public relations firm expects you to call to confirm. Seating is assigned, with priority and front-row seating reserved for the designer's top retail accounts, as well as celebrities or special guests. If seats are fully booked, you may be put on the designer's stand-by list.

Of the Mercedes-Benz Fashion Week shows that went on as scheduled, a spectacular lingerie show stands out, with its first time appearance at fashion week.

INDUSTRY PROFILE 8-1 | Bill Cunningham BY LISA LOCKWOOD

NEW YORK—"I prefer to be invisible." That's been the motto of Bill Cunningham, fashion photographer of The New York Times, throughout his 35-year career at the paper. This Sunday, though, The Times is shining the spotlight on Cunningham with a 20-page special section devoted to his work and the way in which he has chronicled fashion for the past four decades.

In the section, Guy Trebay, William Norwich, Cathy Horyn, Michael Kimmelman and Harold Koda, chief curator of the Costume Institute of the Metropolitan Museum of Art, weigh in on Cunningham's influence on fashion and, specifically, street style.

With his three-pronged attack, Cunningham's modus operandi has always been to photograph the runway shows, street fashion, and women at parties to get a full picture of what people are wearing.

"I realized that you didn't know anything unless you photographed the shows and the street, to see how people interpreted what designers hoped they would buy. I realized that the street was the missing ingredient," writes Cunningham in one of the section's features, called "Bill on Bill."

In a telephone interview with *WWD* Thursday, Cunningham described what life is like as New York's roving fashion photographer and which decade proved to be the most fun.

Currently, Cunningham senses something is bubbling on the street. "Right now is particularly exciting; there's a transition into something new. I don't have a crystal ball, but there's a change underfoot. It's terrific and it's the opposite of what you expect. It's confirmed at night." He declined to divulge the actual looks he was describing for fear of giving away an upcoming layout.

"It's all a challenge now because everyone's so understated," he added. "The Fifties were very understated too. The peak period was the Sixties. The whole youth revolution. You had the Flower Children and the Hippies and the Upper East Siders trying to get into Courrèges and Cardin. Courrèges was the revolution. I thought it was something I never saw in my life. It was different. When I saw Courrèges, I thought he invented the third sex. If he pulled a tunic that covered the hip and the butt, women could do it without looking strange. It wasn't the little white boots. He had the proportions of Balenciaga. He was a hot house of 21st century glamour and put it on a spaceship."

However, Courrèges is what cost Cunningham one of his earlier jobs as a fashion columnist at *WWD*. After a successful run as a hat designer, Cunningham was recruited by John Fairchild, editor in chief of *WWD* at the time, to write a fashion column.

In Sunday's article in the Times, Cunningham explains that Fairchild told him to "write whatever you see." So Cunningham raved about Courrèges. "But John killed my story. He said, 'No, no, Saint Laurent is the one.' And that was it for me. When they wouldn't publish the Courrèges article the way I saw it, I left. They wanted all the attention on Saint Laurent, who made good clothes. But I thought the revolution was Courrèges. Of course, in the end, Saint Laurent was the longer-running show. So Fairchild was right in that sense."

In the past, Cunningham traveled to Milan, London and Paris but he now focuses all his attention on New York and Paris. He's never been to the Far East. "It's too late now. I should have gone to Tokyo 10 years ago, but I used to see the Tokyo kids in London at Vivienne Westwood's shows," he said.

Interestingly, Cunningham is an employee of The Times, but pays all his own expenses, including hotel and airfare. "It gives me my freedom. This way I can go wherever I want and shoot whatever I want. I travel where I think the news is," he said.

For the first 25 years, Cunningham was a Times freelancer, but after a truck hit him on his bicycle about 10 years ago, he joined the company so he could have health benefits. Despite his status as a freelancer, he never sold his pictures elsewhere. He said he prefers to have total control, writing all the copy himself for his photo essays "On the Street."

"You must protect the people you photograph," said Cunningham. "Early on, I had a bad run-in. A big magazine asked for a particular layout. I did it, and the copy [they wrote] was insulting. One of the people [photographed in the layout] wanted to sue me, and I don't blame them. I've never sold a picture since."

Nor is he interested in publishing a book of his photographs—many of which have never seen the printed page. "I don't have an interest in that. I want to stay on the street. I'm too busy filling the space at The Times," he said.

Over the years, Anna Piaggi, a fashion editor, and Anna Wintour, editor in chief of Vogue, have been key subjects.

"I think she [Piaggi] is like a work of art. She's so inventive. The way she puts herself together. I first saw her at a Chloë show and she was in a tailored black suit, without a hat. It was the Sixties, and she had on a pin with plastic grapes like a corsage. The next time she was outside YSL's first or second show in Paris, and she was wearing pj's from the 1930s with a tank top, and holding a sun parasol. She mixes everything up, the old and the new," he said.

Cunningham first discovered Wintour at the couture shows, when she was an assistant to one of the editors at Harpers & Queen. "It was very uptight at the couture show. Here was this wonderful, delightful young person in all these London clothes.

"She's a very classic dresser, but in the Sixties she reflected the mod-and-swinging London, with bell bottoms and long scarves. Nowadays, the simplicity is the key and her dressing marvelously fits her body. It looks like custom-made, but it's not. The proportions, the colors and the fit of it, and her legs. She's very interesting for a lot of women. There's a certain balance between fashion and reality."

Nowadays, there are women who consistently catch his eye, such as Isabel Dupré, style director of Elle. "She's terrific. The way she puts it all together. She'll wear a top from Stella [McCartney] with her own jeans. It's the mix, without being eccentric," he said.

Despite being at all the key fashion shows and covering practically every black-tie charity event in the city, Cunningham said he doesn't really have much interaction with designers. "I try to keep a distance [from fashion designers] so no one influences me. They think, 'He's dangerous because he doesn't play the game.' I let the street speak to me," he said.

Cunningham doesn't particularly enjoy photographing well-known people, although his photograph of the reclusive Greta Garbo landed him his first half page in The Times in 1978.

At 73, Cunningham hasn't lost his enthusiasm for the job, nor has he any intentions of retiring. He travels all over the city by bike, photographing in SoHo, the East Village, the Meatpacking District, Chelsea, the West Side, Madison Avenue and, of course, 57th Street. He still covers parties until the wee hours, then hops on his bicycle to travel home. He doesn't use a helmet, but wears a reflective vest. "I think every reporter should have a bicycle," he said.

Asked if he wears tuxedos to black-tie events, he said, "I dress to be invisible."

However, he does worry that all this publicity in The Times might cramp his style. "The only thing about this section is it kind of tears it down a bit. I'll have to go to Arthur Avenue in the Bronx."

***Women's Wear Daily*, October 25, 2002**

TULLES OF SEDUCTION

In an area often overshadowed by ready-to-wear lines, intimate apparel took center stage in the "Tulles of Seduction," fashion show at the Pavilion in the park. Although scheduled early on a Sunday morning, the time slot did not deter the 700 attendees who crammed the huge tent. It was sponsored by the Intimate Apparel Council; a division of the American Apparel & Footwear Association. Acting as cosponsor was Cellisis Skin Care, maker of proprietary products reputed to reverse skin aging.

In one dynamic forum, the show was presented on a semicircular stage featuring thirty models showcasing the most striking and compelling designs in the intimate apparel industry. Among the well-known designers whose fashions paraded down the runway were Natori, Eileen West, Carole Hockman Designs, Hanky Panky, Flora Nikrooz, Stan Herman, Oscar de la Renta, Ralph Lauren, Jockey, and Movie Star. Although men's undergarments and sleepwear were far from neglected in the extensive presentation, the main emphasis was, of course, on women's fashions.

The Intimate Apparel Council had a vision to put together three different trends, starting with bras, thongs, and bikinis and then moving on to robes, pajamas, and daywear. Themes included "Simplicity" and "Sculptural" silhouettes that included foundations and sleepwear. "Seduction" represented the

The "Seduction" theme is luxuriously represented in this example from the Spring 2002 7th on Sixth.

most enticing trend, with diaphanous designs in lush, cosmetic tints of coral, pink, and peach in breathtaking lingerie concept garments. Heightening the seductiveness were materials as sheer fabrics, the lavish use of lace, and such embellishments as sequins, beading, and glitter. Among the unusual combinations were materials including a leather and jersey bustier with a tulle skirt and a leather bustier worn with hot pants and a lace duster.

Sephora: Bringing Backstage Forward

Ask a fashion insider where the hottest spot is at New York's Fashion Week, and you are likely to hear "backstage." So many people want to be backstage at the fashion shows to get a sneak peak of the next season's hottest trends, that Sephora decided to create an unusual twist on the catwalk show formula by bringing the behind-the-scenes action to the front of the house. Editors and industry guests were invited to speak to the makeup artists and designers in an all-access, all-beauty show without the catwalk.

Sephora cleared away the traditional runway and seating and created a virtual facsimile of the backstage environment in the Pavilion tent. Each makeup artist had a front of the house makeup station and three models. Beauty editors and television cameras crowded close to catch the action as the ten brand makeup artists revealed the new looks. Addressing trends in a meaningful way S. J. Teasdale did Christian Dior's look with a sheer wash of pretty pastels for spring, while Jeanine Lobell for Stila did smoky eyes in greens and browns with dark berry Stila lip glaze. Editors left with black tote bags stuffed with products from participating brands. Sephora was a sponsor of the Mercedes-Benz Fashion Week from Fall 2000 to Fall 2001.

Asian-Inspired Hong Kong Collections

Mystery, allure, and elegance marked the Spring/Summer 2002 Hong Kong collections presented in Bryant Park. The dramatic show commenced with Chinese drummers welcoming more than six hundred fashion buyers and editors to a scarlet runway. Sponsored by the Hong Kong Trade Development Council (HKTDC), the show kicked off with Flora Cheong-Leen's bright camisoles and bolero-inspired blouses matched with chiffon pants and velvet bell-bottoms. Cecilia Yau presented asymmetrically cut, pleated silk skirts with lace insets, while Shanghai Tang captured attention with hand-painted blouses and sheer organza jackets.

This was the second year that HKTDC organized a delegation of designers and brands to the New York Fashion Week. This year's promotion represented HKTDC's ongoing efforts to highlight Hong Kong's design excellence and capability in the world's fashion arena.

Off-Site Venues

Venues other than the fashion week tents bring guests to unusual sites that enhance collections. Take French-born designer Catherine Malandrino, for example. She had Harlem on her mind, and that is where she showed her collection—at the legendary Apollo Theatre on 125th Street to the sounds of a jazz/gospel ensemble. Many of the looks had the flavor of the 1920s, right in the heart of Art Deco and the Harlem Renaissance era.

Fashion Week Goes On

A dozen or more designers, unable to present their new collections before Fashion Week was canceled, quickly rescheduled holding showroom presentations and events at local hotels.

If Broadway shows need an angel, why not fashion shows? For one thing, Anand Jon must believe in "angels," because he got a second chance to showcase his collection thanks to an angel in fashion—the grandmaster of fashion himself, Giorgio Armani.

The show originally scheduled for September 11, a few hours after the terrorist attacks on the World Trade Center, was canceled causing tremendous losses and leaving empty front row seats usually reserved for celebrity clients. Celebrities included Gloria Estefan, Mya, Nadja Swarovski, Alanis Morisette, Mary J. Blige—Park Avenue princesses and real-life princesses who frequent Anand Jon's collections.

A month later, the legendary designer Giorgio Armani sponsored the Anand Jon show at the Armani showroom. The overflow crowd of fashionistas, including society's who's who and celebrities, left many famous personalities and guests stranded outside the showroom.

Well worth the wait, Anand Jon's clothes were classy, sexy, and imbued with a sense of personal freedom. Stars such as Amanda Hearst, Hearst Publication heiress, Marissa Bregman, daughter of movie producer Martin Bregman, and singer Samantha Cole all strutted in lavish creations giving the runway an extra celebrity persona on and off the catwalk.

Patriotic Focus

Tommy Hilfiger's show, held for the press in the firm's showrooms, was the most patriotic. It was a celebration of pure American sportswear. Talking about the collection Tommy Hilfiger said, "I have always looked to American traditions for inspiration in my work. Individuality, athleticism, and of course,

Anand Jon's show may have been delayed by 9/11, but the impact was still great. Jon's elegant and sensual fashions were presented to a high-profile audience by high-profile models, including Amanda Hearst (left). At the finale of the show, Jon was escorted down the runway by Hearst on his left and Marissa Bregman on his right, both in feminine and alluring gowns.

red, white, and blue are integral to my designs. For spring, I've tried to provide effortless pieces that allow the American woman to express her own casual but chic sense of style."

The Spring/Summer 2002 women's collection highlighted the versatility of classic American sportswear. The collection defined a purely American chic with lean and easy silhouettes. Sportswear that revels in its athletic roots featured clean, street-smart clothes with a classic preppy pedigree. Vintage-inspired tracksuits were rendered modern with lean lines while travel clothes for a mobile life featured construction pieces in the

Tommy Hilfiger's tribute to all things American is clearly evident in his sportswear, jewelry, and intimate apparel. The lines are clean, the patterns patriotic.

men's wear tradition. Tommy gave the Safari jacket an urban twist with fitted proportions and pinpoint detailing.

The Show Finale

At the end of each show, the designer has an individual way to acknowledge the fans. The designer's finale bow may be as entertaining as the show. As convention dictates the designer is expected to make some kind of appearance. In a show of bravado, a designer usually parades down the runway surrounded by the runway models. On the other hand, designers who are shy may merely pop out at the end of the show, take a bow, and quickly disappear. Temperamental designers let the finale applause go on far too long. When they eventually do appear, it is as if they were pushed onto the stage in a last minute show of acknowledgment. It is all part of the fashion show ritual. Fans rush up and airborne kisses alight on the designer in the frenzy of the show's finale.

INTERNATIONAL FASHION WEEKS

Although New York City is considered the capital of fashion, other cities throughout the world sponsor Fashion Week runway shows to present designer ready-to-wear collections.

British Style

Since "Swinging London" became the capital of cool in the 1960s with youth-inspired fashions by Mary Quant and Zandra Rhodes, British fashion has been riding the crest of a wave on the international fashion circuit. Although British Couture is nonexistent, ready-to-wear more than makes up for it with the London designer collections.

In terms of creativity, British designers are now recognized around the world as global leaders. Their collections have proved that British fashion provides that increasing mix of originality and marketable ideas. Today, London Fashion Week continues to grow as an effective platform for British design

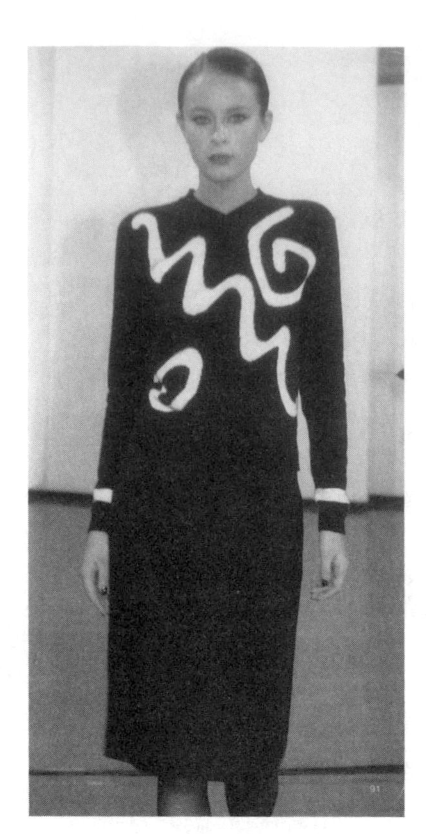

Although British designers are known largely for their ready-to-wear collections, some do create innovative couture fashions. (Left) Julien Macdonald's luxurious designs include eye-popping diamanté and beading. (Center) Jean Muir's collection shows sleek, modern lines that are softened by stitching, punching, and delicate beading. Fabrics include cashmere, suede, nappa leather, silk, and tweed. (Right) Paul Costelloe's line continues to expand. It now includes shoes and a china range for Wedgwood.

talent. With its reputation for innovative design, some of Britain's most gifted talents in the past have been lured to Paris: John Galliano for Dior, Stella McCarthy tapped to revamp Chloë. Julien Macdonald, a Rover British Fashion Awards Glamour designer of the year and new king of the Paris throne of Givenchy, breathes glitz and showmanship into the collection.

London Fashion Week

The unique spirit of London Fashion Week, sponsored by Vidal Sassoon, kicks off the European catwalk calendar, with six days of inimitable style set in and around central London. This hotbed of creativity spans established designer names to undiscovered talents.

At a time when Jean Muir originals are enthralling a new generation that sees them as precious vintage prizes, the design team of her label is continually developing her understated sophisticated collection for a contemporary lifestyle.

Paul Costelloe's easy, high-quality, classic-with-a-twist clothes starring linens and tweeds from his native Ireland included core items for his Dressage range, costing 25 percent less, making his label more accessible.

The British Fashion Council

The British Fashion Council (BFC), which organizes London Fashion Week, was created in 1983 to stimulate and promote British fashion. The BFC also runs the annual Rover British Fashion Awards, which promote the whole of the United Kingdom's fashion industry.

The tented complex on the grounds of the Natural History Museum is the heart of London Fashion Week. Many of the shows are held either at the British Fashion Council's west lawn tent or at a second BFC show venue, Porchester Hall. London Fashion Week has grown from fifteen catwalk shows in 1994 to more than fifty in 2001.

The London Designers' Exhibition remains Europe's largest selling exhibition for designer fashions, featuring ready-to-wear and accessories from more than 150 designer exhibitors, including collections from a new wave of fresh talent, all of whom have been vetted by a distinguished panel of buyers and press.

New names at the exhibition include Buddhist Punk, a very different T-shirt collection that takes its inspiration from its contradictory title; Emma Bernhardt, an ex-*Elle* décor stylist turned designer, who has made the transition from home to fashion accessories with great wit and originality. Maggie May

London's Maggie Bell designer, a Notting Hill spirit, has made her name as an original exponent of customized recycled denim, leather, and cashmere.

London Fashion Week continues to attract top press from around the world. The number of journalists covering the event has risen from 250 to 800. The number of overseas buyers rose to more than 1,100, and serious business is done. The success of London Fashion Week has also made a significant contribution to the retail scene in London. Media coverage, both in the U.K. and abroad, included some 200 photographers and television crews.

The British clothing and textile industry is the thirteenth largest U.K. exporter and employs more than 250,000 people.

VIVA ITALIAN FASHION

The Italians have built an international reputation for uncompromising luxury products and timeless elegance that is synonymous with beautiful leather goods, high-quality textiles, fine craftsmanship, and state-of-the-art production facilities.

Although Milan is Italy's fashion capital for Moda Pronta (ready-to-wear), when it comes to accessories and men's fashion, Florence, the Renaissance city, is equally important and showcases the Pitti Imagine Uomo, tailored men's clothing, as well as Pitti Filati, the yarn exhibition.

Like France, Italy's fashion industry is export driven and is promoted by the National Chamber of Fashion. The worldwide presence of Italian textiles is featured at Moda In, Italy's leading international exhibition dedicated to clothing fabrics and accessories. Designer recognition is presented at Milan Collezioni Donna and MOMI-Modamilano (women's ready-to-wear), both held at the Fiera Milano fairgrounds. Headliners of the Italian collections include Gucci, Prada, Dolce & Gabbana, Krizia, and Alberta Ferretti. At the MOMI fair,

Four of Alberta Ferretti's fashions from her Fall 2001/2002 runway show.

which may run concurrently with Modamilano, several new categories included a bridal section, a new high-end zone, and a lingerie and stocking area. Up-and-coming designers, like twenty-six-year-old Francesco Scognamiglio, who hopes to carry on in the tradition of other Neapolitan sartorial artisans, drew buyer attention with his stunning satin turquoise evening gown.

Twice yearly, the retailers and press travel to Milan to view the ready-to-wear collections. *Women's Wear Daily* reported: "As the Milan collections moved into high gear, Tom Ford gave his glossy Gucci woman a more relaxed look, while Miuccia Prada combined simplicity with decoration. Alberta Ferretti's Philosophy collection took a crafty turn with a flurry of lacy white laser cut dresses, skirts, and tops. Donnatella Versace went wildly colorful for Versus, while sexy looks were the order of the day in Mariccia Mandelli's Krizia collection."

Italian Trade Commission

With more than thirty collections, Made in Italy at the Fashion Coterie, held in New York City, is the most important showcase on the U.S. east coast for the best of Italian women's clothing and accessories collections.

The event is organized by Ente Moda Italia (EMI) and is supported by the Italian Trade Commission (ITC), the New York-based Italian government agency entrusted with building understanding among American buyers and journalists about what makes Italian products and lifestyle unique and compelling. In addition, ITC has launched a new marketing campaign, "Italia: Life in 'I' Style," to promote three key areas of Italian production: fashion *(Moda),* home design *(Abitare),* and film *(Filmare).* ITC also organizes many Italian pavilions within major trade shows including Magic, I-Texstyle, JA, and Natpe to increase the visibility and availability of Italian products to American buyers.

CANADIAN FASHIONS

Montreal Fashions on Ice: A Cool Runway

The Quebec designers are also vying for their share of the fashion spotlight. A uniquely engaging fashion show is the best description of Montreal Fashions on Ice Show, produced every year by the Quebec Government House in New York at the rink at Rockefeller Center from 1996 to 2001. "It was a daring concept," is the way Denise Bigo, the show's originator and producer, describes it. "As the Commercial Attaché responsible for promoting Quebec's fashion industry, I was looking for a way to leverage the work that I and each of the individual companies were doing. One day, the idea came to me: I would showcase Montreal's top winter fashion collections via ice dancing on the ice rink at Rockefeller [Center]. The Ice Theatre of New York would choreograph the show to the enchanting music of Quebec's Cirque du Soleil. Quebec's actor Jean Leclerc would host the evening."

Each year the show featured eight to ten Montreal designers. As the medallist skaters of the Ice Theatre of New York glided across the silvery rink, each garment came to life. Collections included evening dresses by the Algo Dress Group, winter coats by Hilary Radley, leather coats with oversized collars from Jean François Morisette Design, sporty leathers for men and women by Oscar Leopold, jewelry by K'len Art, cashmere jackets by Louben, young men's snowboarder-style jackets from Magique Society, children's outerwear from Le Grenier des Frimousses, and an extravaganza created just for the show by Tristan and America.

The press and buyers watched the show through the glass wall that separates the rink from the Rockefeller Center Café.

The results were equally spectacular. Each year, every television affiliate in New York reported on the Montreal Fashions on Ice Show, as well as several broadcast clips throughout the United States. In addition, the Associated Press and trade

This page and opposite page: *The Montreal Fashions on Ice Show was an innovative idea that showcased winter fashions on ice dancers performing on the rink at Rockefeller Center in New York City. The show, which took full advantage of the growing popularity of ice dancing, received international press coverage and was immensely popular.*

publications covered the event. As a result, it was featured in some ninety newspapers, magazines, and other publications.

Montreal Fashion Week

Montreal Fashion Week, a twice yearly event, was established by the Montreal Fashion Network to not only increase the visibility and renown of the Quebec apparel industry, but also to position Montreal as one of the world's fashion capitals. The goal was to push the province's $3 billion apparel industry into the U.S. market.

"Montreal Fashion Week allows buyers and media to view new collections of some of Montreal's most talented designers in just a few days," says Alan Herscovici, president of Montreal Fashion Network, the industry group coordinating this promotional initiative.

The first edition of Montreal Fashion Week, launched in September 2001, showcased the Spring/Summer 2002 collections. The various activities on Montreal Fashion Week calendar allowed fashion professionals to discover key Montreal designers and ready-to-wear labels, including Michel Desjardins, Claudette Floyd, and Marisa Minicucci. The five-day event attracted buyers and the media to various sites around the city.

Montreal is home to 850 clothing designers and manufacturers. A third of its production is export, and 95 percent of that comes to the United States.

HONG KONG FASHION WEEK

On the international show circuit, Hong Kong Fashion Week, sponsored by the Hong Kong Trade Development Council, reinforces Hong Kong's design diversity and production capability to offer buyers a wide choice of designer collections.

Showcasing the products of prominent designers and fashion houses from Hong Kong and across Asia, the fair's opening was the Hong Kong Extravaganza entitled "Fly Now," an air travel theme fashion show sponsored by Cathay Pacific Airways.

In the first take, "Travel Ease," a jet cabin becomes the key theme as better-end sportswear ranges from Bonita Cheung, Benjamin Pun, Charcoal, and Rowena U show the world that flying can be a superlative style experience. The airline theme extended into the second scene, "Voyager Chic," with active and decorative summer ensembles from Ruby Li, Joanna Chu-Liao, and Grace Choi. Still flying high, Hong Kong designers put together a high-altitude story to wear first class with lighthearted couture styles from Tony Chow, Virginia Lau, and Shanghai Tan.

The catwalk shows cover clothing of various categories and price ranges. In addition, the Asia Pacific Designers Shows presented design talents from Japan, Korea, Singapore, Malaysia, Taiwan, and Hong Kong. The show gave attending buyers a comprehensive idea of what was offered in the fairgrounds.

MADRID FASHION WEEK

The Madrid Fashion Week, spearheaded by Semana Internacional de la Moda de Madrid (SIMM), is the second largest ready-to-wear fair in Europe after Germany's IGEDO, with 827 exhibitors at the Juan Carlos I fairgrounds. Director Pola Iglesias ticked off the facts: attendance in 2002 reached 28,200, including major buying groups from Portugal, Mexico, Brazil, and Russia.

SIMM is a clear reflection of the maturity of the ladies' fashion sector in Spain, a section that is recognized for its highly fashionable creations, quality, and competitive prices in the international market. In addition to presenting all types of ladies' fashion (avant-garde design, foreign clothes manufacturing, eveningwear, fur and leather, and youth fashion trends) in its various pavilions, SIMM also uses numerous catwalk parades to present new trends.

The fair includes Imagenmoda, the international women's fashion fair; Cien X Cien, jeans, streetwear, and sportswear; Intima-Moda-Bano, swimwear, corsetry, lingerie, and hosiery; Iberpiel/Peleteria, the international fur and leathers.

Boutique Europa is the design and quality sector, and Espacio Cibeles is reserved for all designers who put on shows in the Cibeles fashion show and to a selection of other firms.

TRENDY ANTWERP

Antwerp fizzes with fashion, and the effect reaches far beyond its borders. Today, Belgian designers are considered to be at the absolute cutting edge of the international fashion world.

Belgian talent has been brought to full blossom by the professionalism of Belgium's two most important fashion schools. In Brussels, La Cambre trains students in the various skills associated with fashion. The fashion department of the Academy of Antwerp has a longer history, and its end-of-the-year fashion show is one of the "not-to-be-missed" events of the fashion season. The strength of both schools lies in the fact that they are behind the promotion of creative and artistic Belgian talent. An umbrella organization, the Flanders Fashion Institute (FFI), also helps promote and support Belgian fashion and its designers and is responsible for the Fashion Promenade and Mode 2001 Landed-Geland together with Antwerpen Open.

Small Country, Big in Fashion

Until the 1960s, Belgian fashion was synonymous with made-to-measure and couture, and Paris was faithfully followed just as in the rest of the world.

In the late 1960s, when the first students had not yet graduated from the fashion department of the Royal Academy of Fine Arts, the Antwerp designer Ann Saelens was a lone pop culture icon.

The ball really started rolling in the late 1980s, with the appearance of the now mythical "Antwerp Six," all former students of this fashion department. Walter Van Beirendonck graduated in 1980 together with Martin Margiela, who almost immediately left for Paris. Ann Demeulemeester, Marina Yee, Dirk Van Saene, and Dries Dan Noten graduated in 1981, followed by Dirk Bikkembergs in 1982.

In 1986, "The Six" went to London, where they presented their collection. After that, they went their separate ways; each became famous on their own. We now see an army of celebrated young designers following on their own, including Raf Simons, Veronique Branquinho, Bernhard Willhelm, Angelo Figus, Lieve Van Gorp, Patrick Van Ommeslaeghem and An Vandevorst. Their clothing is sold all around the world and is pictured in today's most authoritative fashion magazines.

As of 2002, Antwerp has a fashion headquarters, the ModeNatie, which will house the Flanders Fashion Institute, the new Mode Museum (MoMu), and the fashion department of the Royal Academy of Fine Arts.

REGIONAL APPAREL MARTS

Regional apparel marts across the country are important wholesale centers for men's, women's, and children's apparel. Although there are apparel and home furnishings market centers in almost every major city, the four major venues are Dallas, Atlanta, Chicago, and Los Angeles. These wholesale centers are vital sources for regional designers and manufacturers to showcase their collections. They also provide merchants and retailers with buying options outside the New York City market. With escalating costs on business travel, time restraints, and airline security of major concern, retailers are spending more time at the regional apparel marts.

Dallas Market Center

The world's largest wholesale merchandise mart, the Dallas Market Center, conducts more than fifty markets annually. These markets are attended by more than 150,000 retail buyers. Founded in 1957 by real estate developer Trammell Crow, the Dallas Market Center was the first permanent facility to unite regional wholesalers under one roof. Today, the mart attracts specialty and department store buyers from all fifty states and eighty-four countries. The Dallas Market Center is comprised of six buildings comprising 6.9 million square feet, making it the largest wholesale mart in the world. The buildings contain more than 2,200 permanent showrooms and 460,000 square feet of temporary show space. Fashion show and special event sites include the Great Hall, the West Atrium, and the Fashion Theatre.

The International Apparel Mart is the largest building of its kind in the world, with 1.8 million square feet. It opened in 1964 and has been expanded several times. More than 12,000 apparel lines are showcased, including women's designer, missy, junior, contemporary, intimate apparel, bridal, accessories, footwear, activewear, outerwear, plus sizes, petites, maternity, special occasion dresses, men's wear, children's wear, and western wear.

AmericasMart—Atlanta

AmericasMart—Atlanta is a leading national wholesale buying venue, easily accessible by the more than 125,000 specialty store retailers, primarily from the Southeastern and Midwestern states, who attend annually.

The apparel and accessories industries are housed on nine floors of the Apparel Mart located on the AmericasMart campus. The floors are organized by product to ensure easy accessibility. The campus currently houses more than 500 permanent showrooms and contains approximately 10,000 of the nation's leading men's, women's, and children's apparel and accessories lines, representing all merchandise categories and all price points. Each market serves a different selling season and highlights specific merchandise categories.

The Fashion Office

The Fashion Office is a full-service facility that provides showroom owners with integral trend information and fashion direction each season. Kaye Davis, the fashion director, conducts two trend seminars a year in the spring and fall.

The Fashion Office also produces more than twenty-five apparel and accessories runway shows to aid retailers as well as showroom owners in disseminating information about the coming trends.

Fashion Show Production

Kaye Davis says, "There are five women's and children's markets and four men's markets per year, and I produce fashion shows in all product categories for these markets. In general, this is the schedule. However, other shows can be added throughout the year. I use both model agencies and freelance models. Approximately four times a year, I have models audition so I can see new talent; agencies send models to me frequently when they have someone new. I produce the shows in the atrium of the mart."

The AmericasMart consists of fifteen floors and the atrium is open to fourteen of those floors. The breathtaking atrium provides capacity seating for approximately one thousand guests. Standing room capacity, including spectator viewing from open-ended balconies up to the fourteenth floor, substantially increases the audience.

Shows are also produced in the Fashion Theatre on the fifteenth floor, a room that accommodates approximately six hundred people in theater-style seating. Professional dancers are used instead of models in the shows featuring gift products that are held twice yearly.

The DIVA Fashion Awards

In addition, the Fashion Office also produces The AmericasMart DIVA (Design, Impact, Vision, Atlanta) Fashion Awards, which are an annual high-profile event. Held each October in a hotel ballroom, the DIVAs spotlight outstanding retailers, designers, and fashion journalists who help shape and define the current apparel industry. The DIVAs is one of the hottest tickets in town.

Men's wear is highlighted in two shows, which are held in Atlanta nightclubs.

The Future of Fashion™ Magazine

AmericasMart—Apparel publishes nine four-color "magazine-style" direct mail pieces annually that are sent to more than 40,000 national retailers before each market. AmericasMart's *The Future of Fashion* magazine has become an essential tool that both buyers and exhibitors may use to learn about important trend information, future market dates, upcoming events, and floor directories.

The Chicago Apparel Center

With the Mart Fashion Productions ideal location in the Chicago Apparel Center and its full-service creative components, the Mart Fashion Productions has become an unparalleled resource. Fashion shows take retailers inside the world of fashion and unveil all the hottest trends and styles.

Chicago's Stylemax, sponsored by Merchandise Mart Properties at its debut in 2000, was a major headliner. Instead of the usual showroom format, Stylemax was a large-scale trade show, with special booths set up to attract additional buyers and facilitate shopping.

Capturing rave reviews, the packed house at the fashion show held in the Merchandise Mart lobby created a dramatic venue, which drew many New York lines that normally do not show in Chicago.

Fashion Show Production

Under the direction of fashion director Susan Glick, Mart Fashion Productions covers all the details from concept and plan-

Mart Fashion Productions offers its clients a wide range of services at the Chicago Apparel Center.

ning to full-scale production. Shows, events, and displays are tailored to fit each client's needs and budget, while remaining entertaining and informative.

Mart Fashion Productions is a division of Mart Services, LLC, Merchandise Mart Properties, Inc. (MMPI). MMPI is both a property manager and trade show producer, hosting dozens of trade shows and more than three hundred conferences, seminars, and special events throughout the year for apparel and accessories, gift and home accessories, residential furnishings, casual furnishings, and commercial furnishings.

California Mart

At the California Mart, fashion show production goes into high gear twice a year during the busy Spring and Fall markets. The shows are under the Mart's direction.

Tenants at the California Mart are invited to participate in seasonal shows. A press release, including time, season, and date, is sent to all the "trade" fashion press. According to Karen Mamont, marketing/public relations director, Mart tenants bring fashion clothing to the fashion office for the fashion team to jury. Ms. Mamont says, "If the merchandise fits into what we are showing, then we put it into the show. We hire/contract models, dressers, people to 'pull' clothing and accessories, DJs, lighting, sound, video, and photographers for each show. They work with our fashion office. We only use professional models from the Los Angeles modeling agencies."

Ms. Mamont adds, "If you don't use professional models, your show doesn't look savvy! However, if you are showing hip-hop or street clothing, it is fun to put in a few personalities, such as a DJ, celebrities of the genre, or showroom reps who understand the line and know how to wear the look and live the lifestyle."

The California Mart, "Connecting the World with Style," is open fifty-three weeks a year. That is unique to marts. New York, for example, does not have a building where manufacturer and designer firms are centrally located.

Trade Terminology

American chic
Bryant Park
Chambre Syndicale de Prêt-à-Porter

Fashion angel
Fashionista
Fashion capitals
Fédération Française de la Couture
Hong Kong Fashion Week
IMG (International Management Group)
Intimate Apparel Council
London Fashion Week
Mercedes-Benz Fashion Week
Moda Pronta
Montreal Fashion Week
Prêt Shows
St. Tropez

READING 8-1 | Mixing the Naughty and Nice BY KARYN MONGET

PARIS—The Salon International de la Lingerie took on a two-sided personality last month: a bold and saucy mix of Silkette-inspired looks from the motion picture "Moulin Rouge," mixed with a fantasy lineup of ethereal sheers and gossamer metallics worthy of "A Midsummer Night's Dream."

Always a prolific presentation of directional concepts, the Brand Fashion Show featured 300 silhouettes and 90 brands in an opera setting replete with red curtains, a romantic rose-and-gray-tinted background and a soundtrack of the late opera diva Maria Callas.

Opening with the cabaret spirit of the glory days of Montmartre and La Belle Époque, key brands included Lejaby, Argentovivo, Féraud, Huit, Passionatta, Mey, Barbara, Chiarugi and Gossard. Among the top ideas were:

- Corsets, Merry Widows, garter belts and the all-important thong in cherry, lacquer red and burgandy combined with black.
- Triangular embroideries, embroidered florals, velvet knots and lace ribbons, tattoo and ombré effects, and Toulouse-Lautrec-inspired rose prints.
- A boundless number of supersexy Chantilly lace numbers.

The second major theme showcased a roundup of bustiers, bras and high-rise panties in liquid-looking metallics of copper, gold, pewter and silver, along with shimmery mother-of-pearl finishes and sparkle treatments, often embellished with butterflies and birds of prey motifs. Special effects here included stretch tulle layered over Tactel microfiber knit and a Lycra spandex stretch voile paired with shiny Leavers lace.

Among the brands portraying this theme were Chantelle, Bolero, Ravage, Aubade, First and Lejaby.

The fair also presented visitors with a variety of colorful distractions called "Non-Stop Fashion Info," which included:

- The Ultra Lingerie Forum, a display of 67 brands on forms created by Carlin International.
- An exhibit of vintage corsets ranging from circa 1800 to present day, from Parisian boutique Les Nuits de Satin.
- The Atelier Lingerie, a concept shop created by Concepts Paris that explored merchandising ideas around a theme entitled, "The Temptation of Modern Lingerie." The theme, as described by director Jos Berry, highlighted "the increasing role of lingerie as a universal fashion product and the emotional dimension which is hidden behind each brand."

Two areas at the Atelier illustrated the theme "Discovery," which examined seduction and sex appeal with brands such as Mixona's African, Indian and Japanese-inspired pajamas; luxury at-homewear by Marie-Claude Fremau; junior lingerie by Christian Cane, and novelty panties by Spatz.

The second area, which Berry described as "commercial," focused on 11 brands: Calvin Klein, Verde Veronica, Argentovivo, Marie-Jo, Chiarugi, Aubade, Chantelle, Barbara, Simone Perele, Lise Charmel and Princesse Tam Tam.

Key merchandising ideas included a softly illuminated wall to display bras; a surreal wrought-iron tree with fabric and lace leaves that featured a soothing soundtrack of singing song birds, and clear, ultramodern mannequin fixtures lining the walls, which highlighted the delicate detailing of sheers and laces.

Source: *Women's Wear Daily*, February 11, 2002, p. 6. Courtesy of Fairchild Publications, Inc.

9

The French Connection

As Ambassadors of French tradition and quality, the prestige of the Haute Couture enhances the reputation of Paris as the center of fashion. The handwork specific to the Haute Couture is known as "pearly" and constitutes a laboratory of ideas and techniques in which creativity is freely expressed. The Haute Couture, whose international fame goes back to its origins, plays a major part in making Paris the fashion capital of the world.

The couture also influences the success of other commercial products for export to international markets. Further fueling the export of French products, the French government supports couture activities by financial endorsement of couture shows and channeling publicity worldwide. The Fédération Française de la Couture represents two levels of fashion enterprise: The Haute Couture and Prêt-à-Porter, the ready-to-wear collections.

THE HAUTE COUTURE TODAY

The Chambre Syndicale de la Couture Parisienne consists of the Haute Couture houses, which are companies that create original models, made-to-measure for their clients. Law protects the terms "Haute Couture" and "Couture Creation," and only companies which appear on a list established by a commission at the Ministry of Industry are allowed to use these terms.

According to the Fédération, the Haute Couture has 2000 private clients throughout the world. The Spring/Summer couture shows are held in January, and the Fall/Winter shows are held in July. These shows are held in couture houses, mansions in tony residential neighborhoods, and are by invitation only to private clients and the press. The designs presented are either repeated by the couture house to the measurement of a specific client or sold as paper or linen patterns to French or foreign buyers authorized to produce them.

WORLD ACCLAIM

The Haute Couture is a research laboratory that attracts more than 1,000 French and foreign journalists. Its exceptional power is illustrated in more than 1,500 editorial pages and 150 television and radio programs that are broadcast worldwide. The Haute Couture story is exceptional not only because of its creative aspect and the quality of its products, but also because of its induced effects, such as licensing and the Prêt-à-Porter lines.

Often compared to a train engine towing many carriages filled with a range of different products, the Haute Couture is indeed the motor of many activities, such as textile, ready-to-wear, furs, underwear, accessories (jewelry, leather work, and scarves), and perfumes. These product lines provide the couture house with high-profit margins. Perfume for example fuels the coffers of the couture. It is an affordable product that most women who are not couture customers can purchase.

Today, the Haute Couture is composed of twelve fashion houses: Pierre Balmain, Chanel, Christian Dior, Christian Lacroix, Emanuel Ungaro, Feraud, Givenchy, Hanae Mori, Jean-Paul Gaultier, Scherrer, Torrente, and Yves Saint Laurent. The Chambre Syndicale included ten "members invités" in the Fall/Winter 2001/2002 schedule of shows: Adeline André, Carlo Ponti, Dominique Sirop, Franck Sorbier, Fred Sathal, Frederic Molenac, Ji Haye, Maurizio Galante, Morteza Pashaï, and Seredin & Vasilieu. The two corresponding members are Valentino and Gianni Versace.

INDUSTRY PROFILE 9-1 | Charles Frederick Worth

Charles Frederick Worth and one of his sketches.

The life of Charles Frederick Worth, the greatest couturier, is the remarkable story of an Englishman from Lincolnshire who conquered the world of French fashion. As a young man, Worth spent his life among dress materials in London, but his prospects as a salesman in Swan and Edgar's were limited. Lured by the luxurious level of trade and fascinating pleasures he envisioned working abroad, Worth dreamed of going to Paris, the capital of France, which tugged at his youthful desires for adventure and advancement in his career.

This was a bold decision because he did not speak a word of the French language and lacked capital, friends, or connections. With a small sum of money lent to him by a relative, he left London in 1845. Going to Paris at the age of twenty, Worth had no assets other than an apprentice's training, but he did have youth, energy, optimism, and a complete knowledge of his trade. After a year or so Worth obtained work in one of the most fashionable shops of the day, Gagelin and Opigez of 93, rue de Richelieu. His new employers sold cashmere shawls and ready-made clothing, and were particularly known for their fine materials.

Worth was in the center of high fashion and leading dressmakers of the day came to Gagelin for their fabrics. Seizing on the opportunity to create new fashions, Worth drew on the history of costume to create lavish, expensive gowns for his wife, Marie, who also worked at the store. When she began wearing the dresses, made in Gagelin's materials, these designs attracted interest from customers. Worth varied the cut of sleeves and bodices, and persuaded his customers to wear new materials, colors, and ingenious trimmings. Eventually, even the court dressmakers and seamstresses consulted with Worth about materials and naturally they bought the finest that Gagelin offered. Business soared. Gagelin allowed Worth to organize a large department devoted entirely to fine dressmaking and he soon began to influence the fashion world. Worth made a fortune for this firm, but he had not done well for himself.

In 1858, he decided to take the risk and open a business of his own. However, Worth needed financing and capital investment came through Otto Bobergh, and they opened Worth et Bobergh, a high-class house at 7, rue de la Paix. Worth was the undisputed creative genius behind the House of Worth. He became one of the great self-made Victorians and before the age of forty, he had made himself the arbiter of Parisian dress.

Worth understood the importance of gaining patronage of the famous and infamous from Princess Pauline de Metternich to Queen Victoria and to notorious courtesans, who were style setters of the day. Most significantly, during the court of Napoleon III, who stimulated the luxury business, Worth's most valuable client, Empress Eugénie, patronized his creations and so did the ladies of the court and foreign nobility. As dress designer *par excellence*, Worth garnered the exalted reputation as Couturier to the Empress Eugénie. Under that patronage, the House of Worth created lavish, expensive gowns that raised dressmaking to a new level, called Haute Couture.

As Empress Eugénie drove about Paris in her open barouche, she passed along the streets like a vision in an imperfect world. She owed much to Worth, for his art and the infinite trouble he took on her behalf. Even with the disadvantages of middle age, she kept up her reputation as the most beautiful woman in Europe.

The House of Worth became the longest running fashion dynasty. After years of financial success at the House of Worth, Otto Bobergh retired in 1870. Worth, on the other hand, enjoyed his work far too much to think of retiring.

Worth's designs dominated women's fashion for almost a century. He was the first designer to use live models to parade his creations and to select models who resembled his patrons. Like designers today, Worth's association with leading female figures in the royal courts and international society gave him the patronage and notoriety that fueled his undisputed reputation as the czar of fashion. The boy from Lincolnshire had beat the French in their own acknowledged sphere.

After Worth's retirement, his sons Jean and Gaston continued the business and were responsible for organizing the couture, which expanded into the Chambre Syndicale de la Couture Parisienne. The House of Worth was sold in the mid-1950s, although a perfume with its name is still sold.

Reference

Saunders, E. 1955. *The Age of Worth: Couturier to the Empress Eugénie*. Indianapolis: Indiana University Press.

HAUTE COUTURE CRITERIA

To use the terms "Haute Couture" or "Couture Creation," a company must meet a few criteria. As of 1993, the criteria were set as follows:

- The existing couture fashion houses must employ at least twenty people in their workshops, called ateliers. At Ungaro, for example, workers wear white laboratory coats to give the impression of scientific work. Hence, Paris is often referred to as the "Laboratory of Fashion." Separate ateliers specialize in dresses, suits, or ball gowns, each headed by a manager.
- The couture house must present at least fifty designs, day and evening garments, to the press in Paris during the Spring/Summer and Fall/Winter seasons.
- The collection must be presented to potential private clients in the respective couture houses in a determined location.

Emerging talents are also given an opportunity to showcase their collections over a trial period of two years. For newly created houses, during a transitional period of two years, the requirements are as follows:

- They must employ a minimum of ten people in their workshops instead of twenty.
- They must present a collection of at least twenty-five designs to the press instead of fifty.

PRÊT-À-PORTER COLLECTIONS

Aware of the importance of Haute Couture with regard to their fame, the couturiers have been able to maintain their status at the top while they diversified their activities to include accessories and Prêt-à-Porter, ready-to-wear collections.

fédération française de la couture du prêt à porter des couturiers et des créateurs de mode

calendrier des collections haute couture printemps-été 2004

du 19 au 22 janvier 2004

www.modeaparis.com

haute couture
calendrier définitif

lundi 19 janvier			
	TORRENTE	11h00	Palais Brongniart, Place de la Bourse -Paris 2e
	GRIMALDI GIARDINA*	12h30	Salle Wagram - 39 avenue de Wagram - Paris 17e
	CHRISTIAN DIOR	14h30	Polo de Paris - Route des Moulins - Bois de Boulogne - Paris 16e
	ADELINE ANDRÉ*	18h00	Union Centrale des Arts Décoratifs - 103 rue de Rivoli - Paris 1er
	MAURIZIO GALANTE *	19h00	Fondation Cartier - 261 boulevard Raspail - Paris 14e
	VERSACE**	20h30	Hôtel Ritz - Place Vendôme - Paris 1er
mardi 20 janvier			
	CHANEL	10h30	Hôtel de Bourbon Condé, 41 boulevard des Invalides- Paris 7e
	CHANEL	12h30	Hôtel de Bourbon Condé, 41 boulevard des Invalides- Paris 7e
	DOMINIQUE SIROP	15h00	Hôtel Meurice - 228 rue de Rivoli - Paris 1er
	CHRISTIAN LACROIX	17h00	École Nationale Supérieure des Beaux-Arts - 14 rue Bonaparte - Paris 6e
	JI HAYE*	18h00	Four Seasons-George V, 31 avenue George V- Paris 8e
	GIVENCHY	19h00	3, avenue George V - Paris 8e
	GIVENCHY	20H30	3, avenue George V - Paris 8e
mercredi 21 janvier			
	FRANCK SORBIER*	10h00	Théatre Marigny - Carré Marigny - Paris 8e
	EMANUEL UNGARO	11h00	2, avenue Montaigne -Paris 8e
	EMANUEL UNGARO	12h30	2, avenue Montaigne -Paris 8e
	HANAE MORI	14h00	Hôtel Bristol - 112 rue du Faubourg Saint-Honoré - Paris 8e
	JEAN-LOUIS SCHERRER	15h30	Pavillon Ledoyen - Carré des Champs Elysées - Paris 8e
	VALENTINO**	17h00	École Nationale Supérieure des Beaux-Arts - 14 rue Bonaparte - Paris 6e
	JEAN-PAUL GAULTIER	19h00	Palais de la Porte Dorée, 293 avenue Daumesnil- Paris 12e
jeudi 22 janvier			
	RALPH RUCCI*	11h00	56 avenue Foch - Paris 16e
	DUPRESANTABARBARA*	14H00	L'Atelier Richelieu- 60, rue de Richelieu- Paris 2e
	ELIE SAAB*	15h00	Palais Brongniart - Place de la Bourse - Paris 2e

* membres invités

** membres correspondants

Haute Couture fashion events are by invitation only.

The Fédération Française de la Couture du Prêt-à-Porter des Couturiers et des Créateurs de Mode is composed of couture houses and fashion designers who produce ready-to-wear collections. In this case, the title "Créateurs" distinguishes designers who solely produce ready-to-wear Prêt collections from the Haute Couture designers who in addition to their couture collections are also engaged in producing ready-to-wear Prêt collections. A third branch of the Fédération, the Chambre Syndicale de la Mode Masculine is composed of couture houses and fashion designers of men's ready-to-wear apparel.

Therefore, Haute Couture designers who also create ready-to-wear collections are joined by fashion designers whose only activity is ready-to-wear, but whose image is close to that of the couturiers.

Among the fifty designers presenting ready-to-wear collections are Balenciaga, Courrèges, Francesco Smalto, Hermes, Jean Charles de Castelbajac, Lolita Lempicka, Louis Vuitton, Nina Ricci, Pierre Cardin, Sonja Rykiel, and Thierry Mugler.

THE PRÊT-À-PORTER SHOWS

The Fédération groups all the ready-to-wear Prêt shows together in one place to present the fashion designer's collections and facilitate the work of the French and foreign journalists. These group shows not only promote the ready-to-wear industry, but the overall commercial products of French fashion designers and couturiers.

Since 1994, shows have taken place in the rooms of the Carrousel du Louvre, which is especially equipped for the occasion. The Fédération has also had at its disposal a number of unique and prestigious places in the heart of Paris, such as the Jardin des Tuileries and the restored Cour Carrée and Cour Napoleon in the Louvre Museum.

THE PRICE OF PARISIAN CHIC

Haute Couture clothing is incredibly expensive, from a daytime dress costing $5,000 to an evening gown priced to begin at $50,000. A truly magnificent, jeweled ball gown may range upward to $100,000. More elaborate productions are what dreams are envisioned and may cost a fortune. Why so costly? Couture garments require hours of labor, intensive handwork, expensive fabrics, custom buttons, and signature handcrafted details that could only be made by the talented and skilled dressmakers employed by the couturiers.

SIDEBAR 9-1 | Toujours Couture

The origin of haute couture is synonymous with the period dubbed the Age of Worth. Charles Frederick Worth conquered the fashion world, which for centuries had belonged to French designers alone, and established the House of Worth in 1858. As couturier to Empress Eugénie, he became the arbiter of Parisian dress.

Worth's reputation and influence on the social scene was enormous and it spread to many levels of society as well as other countries. It was a time of unprecedented luxury when Empress Eugénie and regal ladies of the royal courts, followed by women of wealth and foreign nobility, spread the word that a dress bearing the Worth label gave its owner an air of beauty and distinction. Dressmaking was an art form that produced exquisite one-of-a-kind garments made to the exact measurements of a client. Extensive fittings were arranged and a small fortune was soon spent.

Even today, women who can still afford haute couture echo the feeling that there is a special cache to wearing couture clothing. In the elegant salons of the couture houses, located along the tony Avenue Montaigne and the Faubourg Saint Honoré, private clients—society women, princesses, movie stars, and celebrities—come to Paris in January to see the Haute Couture shows, select garments for their spring wardrobes, and start the ritual of fittings. Really rich women do not even bother returning to Paris for fittings. The fitters from the big houses may travel on a client's private jet to personally serve and accommodate the client's schedule.

Timing is essential, as the garments will take several weeks to complete. While the skilled workers in the haute couture atelier (workrooms) make the garments exactly to a client's measurements, the haute couture customer may take off for St. Moritz or some other fashionable place to ski and return later to pick up her spring wardrobe. The same ritual takes place in late June/July when the couture customer returns to Paris to make her selections for her Fall wardrobe. However, this time her social agenda may take her to St. Tropez or Biarritz before returning to Paris.

With a mere two thousand wealthy and fashionable women in the world who can afford to buy couture, one may easily question: "Why does Haute Couture survive in the competitive arena of fashion?" The answer is complex, but one thing is certain—the influence of the couture shows is felt worldwide, and its entertainment value extends way beyond the thin, chic women who sit in the front rows.

HAUTE COUTURE VENTURES

Despite the hype that accompanies Haute Couture fashion shows, which generate enormous publicity worldwide, and private couture client business, a couture house does not thrive on these elements alone. To compete in the international marketplace, couture houses have expanded their empires into Prêt à-Porter, ready-to-wear collections, cosmetic and perfume lines, children's wear, accessories, and licensing agreements that fuel international profits. According to the Fédération, member houses earn approximately 70 percent of their turnover in exports, making fashion one of France's top export industries.

Ownership of couture houses has also changed, and that has better positioned conglomerates with a more aggressive competitive edge in the worldwide marketplace. The combination of couture, cosmetics, and scents was started in the 1980s by the luxury French group, LVMH Moët Hennessy Louis Vuitton SA, which owns Christian Dior, Givenchy, Christian Lacroix, Kenzo, and many other brands in the $8 billion company. Bernard Arnault, chief executive officer, has also collected retailers, such as the perfumer Clarins and the Sephora cosmetic stores. As another example, Italy's Salvatore Ferragamo SpA bought Emanuel Ungaro.

Although each designer brand operates with autonomy to maintain its image, conglomerates operate with greater power in the supply-and-production chain. As a result, they are able to aggressively capture market share through strengthening their global exports.

SHOW CALENDAR

The following is an example of a fall Prêt-à-Porter, ready-to-wear runway show calendar. It is current as of press time; attendees are encouraged to confirm times and locations.

Monday, March 1
3 p.m. Naco, Atelier Renault, 5 Avenue des Champs-Elysées, Paris 8th.
5 p.m. Enzuvan, Le Trianon, 80 Boulevard de Rochechouart, Paris 18th.
6 p.m. Undercover, La Cigale, 120 Boulevard de Rochechouart, Paris 18th.
7 p.m. Y'S, Musée d'Art Moderne, 11 Avenue du Président Wilson, Paris 16th.
7:30 p.m. ES, Palais de Tokyo, Tokyo Eat, 13 Avenue du Président Wilson, Paris 16th.
8:30 p.m. Fatima Lopes, Théâtre Marigny, Carré Marigny, Paris 8th.
9 p.m. Ohya, BETC EURO RSCG, 85/87 Rue du Faubourg Saint-Martin, Paris 10th.

Tuesday, March 2
9:30 a.m. Isabelle Ballu, Drugstore Publicis, 133 Avenue des Champs-Elysées, Paris 8th.
10:30 a.m. Isabel Marant, Musée de l'Homme, 17 Place du Trocadéro, Paris 16th.
11:30 a.m. Jean-Paul Knott, Le Carrousel du Louvre, Salle Gabriel.
12:30 p.m. Dice Kayek, Le Carrousel du Louvre, Salle Soufflot.
1:30 p.m. Bruno Pieters, Espace Pierre Cardin, 3 Avenue Gabriel, Paris 8th.
2:30 p.m. Sharon Wauchob, Espace Commines, 17 Rue Commines, Paris 3rd.
3:30 p.m. Gaspard Yurkievich, BETC EURO RSCG, 85/87 Rue du Faubourg Saint-Martin, Paris 10th.
4:30 p.m. Haider Ackermann, Musée de l'Homme, 17 Place du Trocadéro, Paris 16th.
5:30 p.m. Andrew Gn, Le Carrousel du Louvre, Salle Gabriel.
6:30 p.m. Lutz, BETC EURO RSCG, 85/87 Rue du Faubourg Saint-Marin, Paris 10th.
7:30 p.m. Bernhard Willhelm—59, Rue de la Charonne, Paris 11th.
8:30 p.m. Af Vandevorst, Salle Charly Parker, Grande Halle de la Villette, Paris 19th.

Many Haute Couture fashion houses have expanded into Prêt-à-Porter collections so that they can expand international sales.

THE DESIGNER TALENT

Today, many fashion houses retain the prestige of the original designer's name, but new designers are capturing rave reviews for their collections. John Galliano, the flamboyant Englishman known for incredibly creative collections, designs for Dior and his signature collection, and Karl Lagerfeld is synonymous with the edgy young styles of Chanel. Oscar de la Renta, the

American high-fashion designer, not only designs his American signature collection, but in the past he crossed over to Paris to design Balmain's couture collection.

DESIGN PROTECTION

While style piracy or knock-offs appear to be common in the American market, grand couturier and fashion designers are frequently victims of forgery (illegal copies of their creations, counterfeited labels, or illicit use of labels), which are detrimental to the entire fashion industry. To combat such practices, the Fédération works in close collaboration with the government and all related public services to fight against any kind of forgery in France, in the European Union (EU), and throughout the world.

THE COUTURE CATWALK

Couture shows are enormously expensive to produce. Budgets need to incorporate expenses for a posh venue, the catwalk show, engaging top models, especially designed accessories, the production of labor-intensive garments, with their extensive handwork, and public relations activities. The shows take place in a number of prestigious places located in the heart of Paris, including the Hotel Bristol, Consulat des Etats Unis, Carrousel du Louvre, Theatre des Champs-Elysées, and in the Union Centrale des Arts Décoratifs.

Press coverage of the Haute Couture shows is a major consideration that justifies the enormous investment in creating a collection and actually showcasing it on the catwalk. Some couturiers go to extreme measures to receive publicity with theatrical productions that create a certain magic and fantasy. You can imagine that the cost of such a production is enormous, but the publicity generated more than makes up for the expenditure. While hundreds of the international press converge on Paris for the shows, the Fédération supervises their press accreditation.

FÉDÉRATION FRANÇAISE ACTIVITIES

Organizing the Shows

Every season, the press relations department of the Fédération works out the Spring/Summer and Fall/Winter Haute Couture and ready-to-wear collection show schedules. After preliminary consultations with the different fashion houses participating in the shows, the press department establishes a show program that allows no overlapping, so that the press and buyers will be able to cover all of the various collections. The schedules are then sent to journalists, French and foreign buyers, and trading consultants.

The Privileged Press

The Fédération has established strict rules for press attendance. Private clients invited by the couture house also attend by invitation only. Therefore, every season, before the collections start, an application form and a regulation note are sent to the French and foreign newspapers and magazine editors who are officially recognized by the Chambre Syndicale de la Couture.

The editor must complete the form with information concerning his or her newspaper, such as origin, periodicity, and circulation figures. The editor also has to enclose the list of journalists and, if necessary, the photographers who will cover the shows. This list is given to the fashion designers so that they can send invitation cards to the journalists, ensuring that they will be well received at the fashion houses.

Trade Terminology

The French Connection
Ambassadors of fashion
Chambre Syndicale de la Couture Parisienne
Fédération Française de la Couture
Haute Couture
Laboratory of fashion

Licensing
Made to measure
One-of-a-kind
Parisian chic
Press coverage
Prêt
Prêt-à-Porter,
Private clients
Style piracy

READING 9-1 | Sun, Celebs and Luxury Shops BY KEVIN WEST

SAINT-TROPEZ—Some things never change in Saint-Tropez.

At three o'clock Saturday afternoon, it's lunchtime at the beachside restaurant, Le Club 55. Under the striped shadows of slatted sun shades, the "lucky few" settle into an easy meal of grilled fish washed down with *vin rosé.*

At one of the better tables—one with a view of the beach entrance—Paris-based businessman and socialite Cyril Karaoglan, who has spent most of his 30-some-odd summers in Saint-Tropez, glances up from the conversation.

"Oh, look who's here," he says smoothly.

Just then, the house paparazzo dashes past to snap the arrival of someone who passes for a celebrity in the off-peak month of June. Ivana Trump has just sallied in for lunch.

It's the eternal Tropezian moment. Ever since Brigitte Bardot walked barefoot through the port—trailing paparazzi like stray dogs—the legend of "St. Trop" has rested on its potent mix of sun and celebrity. If not a star here, one is by definition a stargazer. Even Karaoglan—who is himself received as a local crown prince thanks to his lifelong visits—and his lunch group brighten at the rumor that Richard Gere and Carey Lowell will be in Saint-Tropez for the weekend.

Plus ça change. . . .

But from another point of view, there is something new under the Mediterranean sun this summer. Christian Dior, Pucci and Boucheron all have opened boutiques on or near the principal shopping square, Place de la Garonne. New restaurants include the trendy pan-Asian Le Poete Ivre behind the port, and the expensive Bayader, poolside at the Byblos Hotel, with its fusion cuisine. And just outside of town, an exclusive new eco-luxury hotel, La Villa de Marie, offers a calm "ying" to the rah-rah "yang" of the flashier Saint-Tropez establishments. Built on six acres of piney hills overlooking the sea, the Villa murmurs "Nicole Kidman" as gently as the Byblos shouts out "P.Diddy."

All this new investment—particularly that from luxury goods groups LVMH Moët Hennessy Louis Vuitton (Dior and Pucci) and Gucci Group (Boucheron)—suggests that the character of Saint-Tropez has shifted subtly but noticeably in the past few years. Much like the Hamptons, Saint-Tropez has become a virtual weekend satellite community for the well-to-do from Paris, London and Switzerland. Just look at local decorating styles, suggests Karaoglan, who works in his family's insurance business and so casts a professional eye at the furnishings and artworks in local houses. A decade ago, most people favored a simple, summery style—so that, come September, the Villa could be shuttered and abandoned until the following summer. Now, more homeowners are installing art, collectibles and fine furniture—to say nothing of the necessary security systems and regular housekeepers—with an eye to making year-round visits.

"Before, it was just the summer season here," says Karaoglan. "Now, people come all year."

In his opinion, this summer's high-profile shop openings simply show that the luxury goods groups are at last catching up with the port's new, year-round realities. "To open a boutique in Saint-Tropez wasn't worth the trouble before," Karaoglan continues.

Down the strand at another sandy eatery, Le Palmier, Dior chief executive Sidney Toledano expands on the same argument.

"It's funny how these resort places are becoming more residential places," he muses, adding, "People come here more often. People need the full selection, full service. There used to be small multibrand stores. It is our clients who have brought us here."

Last summer, Dior opened its first resort store in Marbella, Spain. Encouraged by the "fantastic" results, says Toledano, the house has decided to expand its "resort network" with shops in Saint-Tropez, then Deauville and Courchevel in the future. Other sea-and-ski outposts have already opened in Aspen, Monte Carlo and Cannes.

The Saint-Tropez outlet, on a prominent corner of Rue Gambetta near the port, has 2,000 square feet of sales space on three floors for its ready-to-wear collection, accessories and fine jewelry. Open 11 months of the year, the store even will stock the Dior winter collection in July. To signal the boutique's strategic importance, LVMH chairman Bernard Arnault and his wife, Helene, attended the opening earlier this month. (By contrast Arnault let his children, Delphine and Antoine, host a party to open the Pucci boutique a week before.) And although designer John Galliano did not attend the opening, he can always check in on the shop later. Dior confirmed local rumors that the designer has rented a villa in the resort for the summer.

While the arrival of Dior, Pucci and Boucheron—joining the ranks of Hermès, Louis Vuitton, Tod's, Malo, Cartier and Kenzo—may signal a new shopping era for some visitors, not everyone is thrilled at the prospect of more big-city brands invading the port. (Chanel and Armani also are rumored to be scouting locations.)

At a dinner hosted by Dior after the store opening, Janie Samet, Le Figaro's fashion maven, lamented the days gone by, when *tout le monde* ducked into one or two local shops to snap up whatever summery little things were on the racks. Each year, a local trend—turquoise tops, for example—would sweep across the beach like a refreshing breeze.

"Now there is no more local fashion," she sighs. "It's all international marketing; it's the phenomenon of globalization."

Besides, as she points out, the whole concept of dressing up for Saint-Tropez kind of misses the point.

"In Saint-Tropez, there's not a style of dressing," she says, like a parochial school matron teaching the maxims of right behavior. "There's a style of undressing."

Source: *Women's Wear Daily*, July 2, 2003, p. 6. Courtesy of Fairchild Publications, Inc.

READING 9-2 Rethinking Couture Down to the Skin

BY CATHY HORYN

PARIS, July 11—In a season strong on statements but bereft of real emotion, Jean Paul Gaultier effectively closed the fall 2003 haute couture collections with a powerful show that attempted to take fashion into another dimension.

The concept, inspired by the Dutch designer Jurgen Bey, who works in witty and ironic transformations of everyday objects, was ambitious, and it pushed Mr. Gaultier and his workrooms to the limit. The show had its flaws, and it started more than an hour late because one of the key pieces, a corset that morphed into a nude embroidered bodysuit, had not arrived from the atelier. And when it did finally come, it took another 15 minutes to tighten the laces on the model.

But it was worth the wait. Couture is about the precise, often magical relationship between the body and a garment. And by creating a different bodysuit for each of his models, Mr. Gaultier was not only giving another dimension to the body—a second skin in lace, quilted patchwork, embroidered glove leather and even white python—he was also creating a new surface to merge and contrast with the clothes. The show, and the tension caused by the delay, seemed to take it out of the designer. His eyes were filled with tears as people poured backstage to congratulate him.

Mr. Gaultier's ways of imparting a sense of fashion as an organic, three-dimensional object were as varied as they were ingenious. A beautiful black velvet dress, with lavish ties at the shoulder, stood out in relief against the model's white python bodysuit, while a leather bodysuit embroidered with sweet flowers heightened the sensuality of an evening dress in feathered coral chiffon. In the end, the models came out wearing only their bodysuits and carrying things like umbrellas and boomboxes tightly covered in the same fabric. It was then that you realized how much work and thought Mr. Gaultier had put into this brilliant performance, enough to drive you crazy.

There were other behind-the-scenes dramas. On Thursday, as the couture shows ended, the house of Dior put to rest speculation that Hedi Slimane, its men's wear designer, was frustrated in his limited creative role, or might even go to Givenchy, which has been floundering under Julien Macdonald. But Sidney Toledano, the president of Dior, said that Mr. Slimane had renewed his contract and would be given more creative control with men's fragrances and cosmetics.

Meanwhile, on Wednesday, it was Oscar night at Valentino's bossy big show. Since a lot of journalists routinely describe Valentino's evening clothes as ripe for the red carpet, the designer decided to grandly turn the tables. Instead of his logo on the electronic backdrop, he projected the Oscar statuette—and, of course, the stars who wear his clothes. The models came out in turbans and shades and looked smug-elegant in crisp coats sashed with bows. The big effects were for night: a many-tiered pink gown edged in gold: a sexy ensemble that paired a transparent apron-tied top with a frilly skirt.

Afterward, about 70 guests, including Gwyneth Paltrow and her mother, Blythe Danner, drove out to Valentino's chateau in the country, where the long drive was lighted with candles. The backyard, too. Some yard.

During a fitting for his bride, who this season was played by Linda Evangelista, Karl Lagerfeld told several editors who had dropped by his Chanel studio that he had recently weighed the jewelry he had on—diamonds and chains by Chrome Hearts—and it had come to seven kilos, or about 15 pounds. He also mentioned that few of the established models were thin enough to wear his latest couture suits, which feature long drainpipe sleeves and narrow skirts gathered in folds above the knee, and that even Natalia Vodianova had to shed 10 pounds, presumably in baby fat.

Mr. Lagerfeld could be accused of being weight-obsessed. He could also be called the best couturier that France has at the moment, and not by default of Saint Laurent. He has made Chanel the standard-bearer of couture; if you want to see the real McCoy, he seemed to be saying with tweed skirts that appear to evaporate into speckled hems of sequins and sable, come to Chanel.

The ideas for his collections come to him in a dream, he often says, and he responds with a fury of sketching. This collection would have given Freud a run for his money, for it combined elements of good and evil (lace Juliet caps, Draculean collars), discipline and gluttony (precise tailoring, all-in-one leather pants and boots), and at times it went down like a heavy German meal.

There was a lot going on: allusions to armor in the saddle shoulders of jackets and the platelike layers of a gray organza dress, and references to current fashion, in wide leather belts and those crunched hemlines. Yet the clothes seemed trapped in the dream. And though his elongated shapes aimed to be modern, the collection lacked the mental lightness of the last few seasons.

Contradictions kept surfacing all week. Here was Emanuel Ungaro, drawing upon those eternal soul sisters in glamour, Ava Gardner and Marilyn Monroe, but in a fresh way, with sensuous suits and superlight wool jersey dresses followed by a spree of Léger-inspired embroideries. You could see that he was trying to restrain himself, to avoid the old tangle of prints and damsel drapery.

But what would the newspapers record the next day? Thoughtful Léger spirals? Or that he had Leah Wood and the sisters Theodora and Alexandra Richards, daughters of Ron Wood and Keith Richards, in his front row? Couture can scarcely afford to be seen as old, and for that reason the spotlight has shifted away from young socialites to even younger daughters of clients like Suzanne Saperstein, whose daughter, Alexis, also watched the Ungaro show and will have her debutante dress made by Givenchy. All designers need publicity, but for a craftsman like Mr. Ungaro, it put a strain on his credibility to be playing big daddy to the children of rock stars when he's selling subdued Avas.

The house of Scherrer is in another kind of bind. Few American editors have bothered to attend its shows in recent years, and after last season's striptease, you would understand why. The house's owner expressed eagerness to change, however, and on Wednesday, the designer Stephane Rolland unveiled a Scherrer collection that was indeed radically transformed—in the image of Saint Laurent. Clearly, to a house looking for approval and clients, Saint Laurent's broad shoulders and sassy tuxedos are the way to go. The clothes were much improved over last season, but that is not saying a lot. Having Saint Laurent's polish without his finesse still doesn't solve Scherrer's problem. It only avoids the much harder job of coming up with a genuine vision.

What is it with young designers and mumsy old clothes? Julien Macdonald staggers under the weight of Audrey Hepburn's legacy at Givenchy—and heavy it was. Everything had the trussed look of torturous chic, with blown-up collars, tight waists and skirts spreading stiffly in peplum ripples. You couldn't make out if Mr. Macdonald was being intentionally campy with his 1950's silhouettes or merely matronly.

Coming out of Ralph Rucci's terrific show on Thursday, the designer James Galanos said, "When you see this, a lot of other things look tired." And how. Mr. Rucci offered impeccable polish with a continual sense of surprise, marrying layers of chocolate chiffon to the brown alligator bodice of a dress; challenging Lesage to make a jacket in a basket weave of leather and suede and showing it with suede jeans; pintucking blouses to dramatic effect; and enlivening somber clothes with playful gestures like elbow-length sable mittens.

In three seasons at the Paris couture, Mr. Rucci has found clients, he has found press, and he has found himself. In New York, working independently on Seventh Avenue, it is doubtful he could have made such an enormous leap. But Paris has given him both lightness and the confidence to play.

Christian Lacroix also seemed light on his feet, blending elements of flamenco with Spanish court colors in a lucid and original take on modern dressing. Mr. Lacroix will do things his way, in a whirl of fabric and texture that, to some, might resemble the dog's dinner. But when he opened his show with frothy coats over spare minidresses in gauzy layers of lace and chiffon, he captured the essence of couture. The clothes evoked privacy, a sense of complicity with the wearer and that shudder of nude colors passing over bare flesh. Where does the body end and the dress begin? That is the question that engages Mr. Lacroix, Mr. Gaultier and every great couturier.

10

International Trade Shows

Market expansion is the top priority of businesses that exhibit and sell new yarns, fabrics, accessories, and ready-to-wear collections at the international textile and apparel trade shows, as well as at the fashion fairs held in the global marketplace. These shows provide a high-profile platform, twice a year, for exhibitors to showcase and sell their new products to world buyers and retailers.

TRADE SHOWS

Bringing buyers and sellers together in one comprehensive marketplace, the trade show is an environment that is highly conducive to business. In general, trade shows are held in major city convention centers and large exhibition halls that provide enormous space for hundreds of exhibitors to showcase their products.

Trade Show Organizers

Trade show organizers work to keep the interests of the international sector in the fashion forefront. The Igedo Company, for example, is a pioneer organizer for international trade and industry events. Exhibitors lease booths or pavilions from a firm engaged to organize the event. The trade show itself is usually scheduled as a three-day happening, often starting on Sunday and continuing during the week. Exhibiting is expensive, but exhibitors expect to derive substantial business from international buyers who will source fabrics and/or merchandise and place orders.

An exhibition is a place where new lines can also be discovered, and it provides the right atmosphere to conduct business with customers.

The shows also provide organizers with an enormous lure with which to attract attendance by professionals from diverse industries, retail fashion visitors, and journalists and photographers. Press reports in newspapers and magazines, plus many hours of television coverage on channels all over the world, further draw attention to the event.

Registration

Industry trade show visitors usually preregister to attend an exhibition, often via the Internet, although one can also register on-site. Attendees receive a free visitor's guide featuring useful information such as the list of exhibitors, with pavilion numbers and a layout plan of the exhibition halls. Buyers and visitors, who attend from worldwide fashion centers, are given special consideration to ensure their comfort and convenience. To this end, organizers set up VIP lounges with resting and office facilities for use by buyers.

The Show Focus

Trade show exhibitions in the United States or other international cities usually have a specific exhibitor focus on either fiber/fabric, fashion apparel, or accessories. The exhibitions are staged nearly one to one-and-a-half years prior to a selling season. Most exhibitions also feature creative presentations on trends in color/fabric/fashion, as well as catwalk shows that highlight the offerings of the exhibitors.

Who Attends

From a time management point of view, trade shows, where all the manufacturers are gathered in one location, are a win/win situation for both the exhibitors and buyers. The industry visitors, who otherwise might have to travel to a great number of international sectors to source new products or fash-

JUNE

1–3, Moda Prima (knitwear—formerly known as Esma), Milan Fairgrounds, Milan. Contact: Efima. Tel: (39) 02 6610 3555. Web site: www.fieramilano.it

2–4, Gulf Beauty 2003 (fragrance, cosmetics and body care), Dubai, United Arab Emirates. Contact: Justin Boutros. Tel: (971 4) 2824737. Fax: (971 4) 2825757. E-mail: channels www.channelsexhibitions.com.

6–9, Chibidue and Chibimart (jewelry and accessories), Milan Fairgrounds, Milan. Contact: Fiera Milano. Tel: (39) 02 485501. Web site: www.fieramilano.it

7–9, Hair Expo Australia, Sydney Convention and Exhibition Centre, Darling Harbour Sydney, NSW. Contact: Hair Expo Australia. Tel: 61-7-33717955. Web site: www.hairexpo.com.au

7–10, National Association of Chain Drug Stores Marketplace (cosmetics, skin care and toiletries), San Diego, California Contact: Bill Sittman. Tel: (703) 837 4161. Fax: (703) 549 6357. Web site: www.nacds.org.

7–12, Vincenza Oro 2 (jewelry) Vincenza Fairgrounds, Vincenza. Tel. (39) 0444 969111.

10–11, Luxe Pack Monaco (packaging), New York, New York. Contact: Annik Klein. Tel: (212) 925-2869. Fax: (212) 925-2507. Web site: www.luxepack.com

11–13, Salon Luxe, Santé, Beauté (fragrance and cosmetics), Paris, France. Contact: Ourihya Guerdane. Tel: (33-1) 41 40 41 40 Fax: (33-1) 42 70 96 83. Web site: www.golding.fr

17–19, Expofil (fibers and yarns), Paris Nord Villepinte Halle 1, France. Contact: Marie-Odile Verrier/Expofil SA. Tel: (33-1) 47 56 31 63. Fax: (33-1) 40 87 16 22. E-mail: expofil@expofil.com Web site: www.expofil.com

17–19, Heimtextil Japan Interior Lifestyle. International, Tokyo International Exhibition Center, Big Sight, Ariake, Tokyo, Japan. Contact: Messee Frankfurt. Tel: (49-69) 75 75 0. Fax: (49-69) 75 75 64 33. Web site: www.messefrankfurt.de

17–19, Fashion Shoe (footwear), Bologna Fairgrounds, Bologna. Contact: Bologna Fiera Tel: 051 282111. E-mail: fashionshoe

The Calendar of Events from a recent list of international trade shows.

ion apparel, find it more profitable to attend a trade show instead. It's a one-stop-shopping opportunity to place orders and glean advance fabric or trend information.

For the mill or apparel manufacturer exhibitor, the cost for exhibit space may be high, but it is well worth it. Exhibitors gain the opportunity to reach and sell not only to their established customer base, but to a vast audience of new buyers from countries worldwide.

Special Enticements

To entice exhibitor participation, organizers may offer special travel rates to participating exhibitors, construct a pavilion at the show to showcase their products, and provide other services such as translators, fax machines, comforters, and telephones. Free shuttle bus service may also be offered from the main entrance of the exhibition center to car parking areas. Some trade show organizers may also hold seminars on trade analysis and conduct special sessions that address the issue of international trade opportunities.

The proliferation of trade shows attests to the fact that fashion is big business and every country is competing for its share of the market. See the sample calendar listing of shows in this chapter.

CPD FABRICS, DÜSSELDORF

CPD (Collection Premiere Düsseldorf) Fabrics, held in Düsseldorf, Germany, is now considered the largest fashion fair in the world. It is held in 18 halls, showcases more than 7,000 exhibitors, and attracts more than 150,000 trade visitors from all over the world. The show kicks off the Fall round of fabric fairs and has now established itself as a fixture among both buyers and exhibitors from northern, central and eastern Europe, the Middle East, and Asia. According to CPD, exhibitors consider it the most profitable fashion fair.

This fair focuses on fabrics, accessories, and predictions for women's, men's, and children's wear, as well as on jeans and sportswear. The Igedo Company, which organizes the fair, also views itself as a partner and troubleshooter for its exhibitors. Igedo also acts as a service provider and middleperson in the tough, global competition of national and international fashion industries.

The excitement of the Collection Premiere Düsseldorf is palpable in these illustrations. From entrance to runway, the atmosphere is charged at this most profitable fashion fair that attracts exhibitors, trade visitors, and press from around the world.

The Igedo Company has helped many young unknown designers from various regions of the world gain recognition beyond their borders by presenting their fashions on the catwalk or by having Creative Haus Düsseldorf, of which Igedo is one of the key founding members, sponsor them.

Buyer Comforts

At Igedo, no efforts are spared to make the tiring visit to the fair as pleasant and efficient as possible for national and international buyers. The VIP Club, for example, is a welcome respite from the rigors of shopping the show and walking through the miles of exhibitor space.

Approximately four weeks before the start of the fair, a current list of exhibitors and a layout plan of the exhibit hall can be found at www.igedo.com. For first-time attendees, a welcome desk and visitor information system help visitors find their way around the fair.

Trend Presentations

The clothing manufacturers, designers, stylists, and buyers from large retail stores throughout the world use the August date of this fair to create a well-timed marketing and communication platform. This early date enables them to gain insight into an overview of the themes, colors, and fabric concepts for the coming 2004/2005 season. The "Latest Hits" for Spring/Summer 2004 were also presented.

A representative survey polling visitors at a previous event found that 88.8 percent rated seeking innovations and new trends among their most important reasons for attending. Almost half of that percentage had established appointments with regular suppliers at the fair.

Special Segments

CPD is the international fair for moderate to better-priced women's wear and includes niche categories such as "New

Classics" and "Plus Sizes." Special segments have also been established in designated hall areas that include the "Fashion Gallery," with a total of 180 collections, including high-quality accessories.

The "Creative Club" in the "Fashion Gallery" presents international labels and new designers. Here retailers benefit from the opportunities that these collections provide to represent the new direction of fashion. The Club also enables retailers to incorporate new designers in their merchandise collections.

The "Country and Weekend" segment features a large range of new country life fashion trends from international collections, while "Forum Accessories" presents innovative ideas for fashion jewelry, bags, belts, hats, and caps.

Trend Leader

CPD also touts itself as "The Fabric Show for Trend Leaders." As a major part of its support programs, CPD offers a "Future Directions" trend seminar on the coming fashion seasons given by the internationally renowned Studio Carlin International, Paris. The seminar featured an audiovisual presentation on the influence of lifestyle on fashion, consumer behavior, key fabric, yarn trends, and color trends, as well as pioneering silhouettes for women's and men's wear for the 2003/2004 Fall/Winter season. In addition, Studio Carlin projects ahead and provided an initial view into the 2004 Spring/Summer season.

The designer catwalk shows featuring well-known designers and international brands make a visit to the show a "must" for retailers who wish to keep abreast of the latest news in the industry.

MESSE FRANKFURT

Messe Frankfurt, a leading producer of more than one hundred international trade fairs each year, brings the world together in Miami, Florida, at Intima America, North America's first international intimate apparel trade fair. Exhibitors of intimate apparel and textiles present their newest collections under one roof at the Miami Beach Convention Center.

Apparel and textile buyers can take advantage of the show to purchase merchandise for the year, learn about technical innovations, and preview the hottest design trends in the market. The cutting-edge Lifestyle Trend Pavilion, for example, showcased color and trend presentations. Intima America, held in March and September, attracts more than 2,500 buyers from North America, South America, Central America, Europe, and Asia.

Messe Frankfurt also partners with Fashion Week of the Americas, to coproduce an entire apparel fashion week with top designers from the United States, Europe, and South America. Exhibitors can take part in the general fashion shows as a complement to their booth displays. The dazzling runway fashion shows include the latest creations by the hottest Latin American, European, and North American designers.

Industry experts on topics such as e-commerce and import/export strategies also give seminars.

PREMIÈRE VISION

Première Vision began in 1973, as a joint promotion effort on the part of fifteen weavers from Lyon, France. Today it has become the world's premier fabric show. Première Vision is spread out over acres of indoor space at the Parc d'Expositions, Paris-Nord, France. The show is considered a driving force behind creative design and attracts 45,000 visitors from more than 110 countries.

The Première Vision is the weaver's salon, created and run by weavers. Its mission is to promote its European weaver exhibitors and to facilitate their expansion worldwide. The Première Vision Salon is to the textile and clothing professionals what Paris is to fashion: a capital of trends where decisions about a whole season's colors and materials are given a year before they hit the streets.

Twice a year, in February and September, for four days, the Salon offers an environment where people come and see, touch, feel, and decide what will make up tomorrow's fashion. The Salon invites visitors to discover presentations of the seasons most creative and innovative fabrics from hundreds of European weavers. Exhibitor booths showcase a palette of fabrics that bring together the standard classics, as well as unusual, original, luxurious, and the most technologically advanced products.

Première Vision's International Observatory pinpoints emerging trends and gathers exclusive data on new lifestyles around the world. The International Observatory also offers fabric producers and manufacturers a summary of the major trends detected among consumers and end-users by highlighting both important tendencies and niche opportunities. Eighteen months before retail window displays, the Fashion Department introduces the season's colors and fabric trends.

Première Vision also participates, along with Espace Textile and the Consejo Intertil Español, in European PreView, held twice a year in New York at the start of the season. European PreView is a Première Vision initative for the North American market exclusively. This "workshop" makes it possible, on one hand, for Americans to discover the earliest directions emerging from the 150 collections of Europe's most creative weavers, and for Europeans, on the other hand, to better understand the expectations of American designers and manufacturers.

European PreView visitors—designers, manufacturers, and textile stylists—also have access to a selection of the earliest samples of the collections on display. This enables them to establish product development programs with the weavers. Visitors can also attend a conference presenting the season trends, which is organized by Première Vision's Fashion Information Division.

The Jacob Javits Convention Center in New York is home to the International Fashion Fabric Exhibition.

INTERNATIONAL FASHION FABRIC EXHIBITION

The International Fashion Fabric Exhibition, held at the Jacob Javits Convention Center in New York City, attracts thousands of attendees from around the world. It is recognized as the number one fashion/fabric event in North America. This vital industry sourcing event features hundreds of textiles, Eurotex, a pavilion of European fabrics, trim, leather, CAD/CAM, color/trend services, and trade publication exhibitors.

The event, which is endorsed by the Textile Distributors Association (TDA), runs concurrently with the Designer Summit Seminar Series, which features twenty seminars led by industry experts. The Designer Summit Series is intended to keep apparel and textile professionals on top of current trends and critical industry issues. Seminar speakers include some of the industry's top professionals, and seminars to date have reached more than 60,000 attendees worldwide.

The following is a sample listing of topics and speakers from the 2002 presentations. (Tickets are required to attend seminars.)

seminar schedule

MONDAY

9:30 AM "Real: Spring/Summer 2002 Forecast."
The American Trend & Color Committee will present a comprehensive color and trend forecast, representing the opinions of over 25 industry experts. Lisa Mainardi, Director of the American Trend & Color Committee and Inprints NY, along with featured members of the Committee will provide valuable information on color, fabric and styling to help you make the right decisions for the Spring/Summer 2002 season.

11:00 AM "New Concepts in Cotton for Spring 2002."
Kathryn Gordy Novakovic, Director, The Cottonworks Fabric Library and Linda Bunning, Assistant Manager, The Cottonworks Fabric Library. Come see the new colors and innovations in cotton for Spring 2002!

12:00 PM "Spring 2001: The Edit."
Sharon Graubard, Vice President, Design Director, Ellen Sideri Partnership. A clear and concise edit of the Spring 2001 U.S. and European Collections focusing on the ideas, items, colors and fabrics that will impact Spring 2002.

1:00 PM "Peclers – Paris Spring 2002 Menswear Forecast."
Robert di Mauro, Vice President of Promotion and Communication, Ellen Sideri Partnership. Robert di Mauro will present the key Menswear trends for Spring 2002. This presentation will feature main themes with color, fabric and silhouette directions for the season.

2:00 PM "Spring 2002 Essentials."
Pat Tunsky, Creative Director, D3 Doneger Design Direction. Spring 2002 essentials including color fabric and trend forecasts will be presented.

3:00 PM "Spring 2002 Color & Lifestyle Direction: A California Approach."
Fran Tesser-Sude, Owner, Design Options. Join us as we explore the continuing fusion of the apparel and home fashion industries for a lifestyle approach to the retail environment and how it will impact your business.

4:00 PM "FashionFACTSfolio Spring 2002."
Ellen Campuzano, Editor, Publisher, fashionFACTSfolio The colours...the trends...the buzz...the reality... A look at the season's forecast and an analysis of what will probably really happen for Spring 2002 with a special focus on accessories.

TUESDAY

9:30 AM "Top Ten Trends."
David Wolfe, Creative Director, D3 Doneger Design Direction. Famed fashion forecaster presents ten major trends influencing future color, fabric, design, marketing, advertising, and lifestyle.

10:30 AM "Junior Street Scene: Europe and L.A."
Jamie Ross, Trend Analyst, Doneger Design Direction. A slide presentation of junior trends photographed on the streets of London, Paris, Barcelona, and Los Angeles. The focus will be Spring 2001 trends that will continue to influence Spring 2002.

11:30 AM "Fall/Winter 2002/03."
Tod Schulman, Director of Marketing – Textiles, Pantone Incorporated. Look for the latest trends in color harmonies and fabric for men's, women's, active, cosmetic and industrial design as Pantone showcases the newest looks in the PANTONE View Colour Planner for Fall/Winter 2002/03.

12:30 PM "Spring/Summer 2002."
Jayne Mountford, Senior Trend Consultant, Promostyl. Colors, fabrics and silhouettes for the Spring/Summer 2002 season will be presented.

1:30 PM "Demystifying Fashion Forecasting."
Neville Bean, Owner, Neville Bean. Does the process of figuring out where fashion is going seem shrouded in mystery and apparent only with those blessed with a "magic eye?" Find out from a forecaster how trends are tracked and how you can train your own eye to recognize fashion cycles and evolving silhouettes and colors.

2:30 PM "Spring 2002 Global Color & Trend Predictions with "An American Point of View."
Ben Gomes, Vice President of Creative Services, OPR/The Style Center. Spring/Summer 2002 color summary and fabric, print style and trend forecast. Including Autumn/Winter 2002/03 preview!

3:30 PM "Inprints NY Spring 2002 Print Trends Overview."
Lisa Mainardi, Director, Inprints NY and Director, American Trend & Color Committee. Lisa Mainardi presents the season's most directional and salable prints and textile surface design concepts from fifteen studios, representing over 50 international collections. A must see for anyone working with prints.

4:30 PM "MagicOnline: The Power of B2B!"
Edward Cortese, Fashion Domain Executive, MAGIConline and Joel Arndt, Fashion Domain Executive, MAGIConline. A discussion of the online B2B fashion experience and its growing role in global buying/selling/marketing strategies. Modeled on the exacting needs of real buyers in today's competitive arena, MagicOnline will provide the example of how a B2B partnership can increase sales, streamline order processing and extend brand awareness – and do it faster and more cost effective. Site navigation and screen demonstrations will be done via laptop projection. Presentation followed by an open Q & A forum.

WEDNESDAY

9:30 AM "Trends in Home Furnishings: Spring/Summer 2002."
Nancy Waites, Design Consultant, Candlar Archives; Member, Fashion Group International; Adjunct Assistant Professor, F.I.T., Parsons School of Design and L.I.M. Nancy will highlight trends in home furnishings including color, fabric, texture, embellishment and surface treatments for Spring/Summer 2002.

10:30 AM "Real: Spring/Summer 2002 Forecast." (encore presentation)
The American Trend & Color Committee will present a comprehensive color and trend forecast, representing the opinions of over 25 industry experts. Lisa Mainardi, Director of the American Trend & Color Committee and Inprints NY, along with featured members of the Committee will provide valuable information on color, fabric and styling to help you make the right decisions for the Spring/Summer 2002 season.

11:30 AM "Inprints NY Spring 2002 Print Trends Overview." (encore presentation)
Lisa Mainardi, Director, Inprints NY and Director, American Trend & Color Committee. Lisa Mainardi presents the season's most directional and salable prints and textile surface design concepts from fifteen studios, representing over 50 international collections. A must see for anyone working with prints.

12:30 PM "Principles of Color For Textiles."
Georgia Kalivas, Representing the office for Professional Training, The Fashion Institute of Technology. Designers and manufacturers of textiles and apparel need to understand some of the principles applied to color science – color perception, the different types of color mixing, the measurement of color, how to use the various color spaces and simultaneous contrast. These principles can enable you to better evaluate lab dips, and in turn give direction to dyers so that you can approve colors more quickly. Learn why certain color matching problems occur and how to avoid them. We will also discuss instruments used for color matching and new color technologies.

1:30 PM "Technology in Design to Market."
Holly Henderson, President H4 Design Technologies. Discover how the latest innovations in technology are being used by industry leaders to streamline the design to market process, its role in reducing operating costs and the positive impact on the bottom line profits of major manufacturers and retailers. We will look at the timeline & process required to more rapidly anticipate and respond to fashion trends and consumer demand, manage design images, distribute product information, business documents, sales and other data while examining software solutions, network requirements and the functionality that enables industry-trading partners to transact business, share information and interact worldwide. A panel of experts will present new discoveries in color management solutions, discuss 2D and 3D server-based and Internet technologies specific to textile development and marketing, driving sales in the rapidly expanding global marketplace. Designers, merchandisers, product developers and anyone involved in the sales and marketing of apparel and textile products should attend this most informative session.

A sampling of the seminars offered at the Designer Summit Series.

"Top Ten Trends": David Wolfe, creative director, D3 Doneger Design Direction. This famed fashion forecaster presented ten major trends influencing future color, fabric, design, marketing, advertising, and lifestyle.

"New Concepts in Cotton for Spring 2002": Kathryn Gordy Novakovic, director, The Cottonworks® Fabric Library, and Linda Bunning, assistant manager, presented new colors and innovations in cotton for Spring 2002.

"Real: Spring/Summer 2002 Forecast": The American Trend & Color Committee (AT&CC) presented a comprehensive color and trend forecast, representing the opinions of more than twenty-five industry experts. Lisa Minardi, director of the AT&CC, along with featured members of the committee, provided valuable information on color, fabric, and staying to help attendees make the right decisions for the upcoming season.

THE INTERNATIONAL FASHION FABRIC EXHIBITION'S AMERICAN TREND & COLOR COMMITTEE (AT&CC)

The AT&CC is a group of more than twenty industry experts from the international marketplace who bring to the table their individual color cards, already tested in the industry. The committee members have diverse levels of expertise in forecasting, from fiber to finished product—in specialized areas of women's, men's, children's, and active apparel, as well as home furnishings.

The committee meets to develop a color projection one year ahead of a season. The forecast for the International Fashion Fabric Exhibition includes six palettes of forty-eight colors specifically targeted to the American market.

MAGIC

Magic International, a subsidiary of Advanstar Communications, Inc., produces the International Fashion Fabric Exhibition and MAGIC trade shows, Femme and the International Kids Fashion Show.

MAGIC (Men's Apparel Guild in California) is the largest men's apparel trade show in the world, organized and produced by Magic International. MAGIC originated in Palm Springs, California, and relocated to Las Vegas, Nevada. The show is part of the MAGIC Marketplace, which comprises trade shows for the men's apparel market (MAGIC); the women's apparel market (WWDMAGIC); the children's apparel market (MAGIC kids); and the cutting-edge youth market (the EDGE). The August 2000 show broke all previous attendance records, attracting more than 100,000 attendees from 110 countries. The MAGIC Marketplace had more than 3,200 exhibiting companies and represented more than 5,500 fashion and accessory brands and 21,000 product lines.

To accommodate a market this size, MAGIC has grown to encompass multiple venues at the Las Vegas Convention Center and the Sands Expo & Convention Center. The exhibitor participation at the MAGIC Marketplace is extensive, including new designers with "up-and-coming" companies, as well as established companies representing globally recognized brands. The retail base is equally impressive, consisting of representatives from all classes of trade, from single-unit stores to large department stores and virtually every retail channel in between.

Attendees range from assistant buyers to chief executive officers, all seeking to discover new resources and the latest products. With MAGIC's ability to bring the industry leaders and decision makers together, fashion passes through Las Vegas on the way to the stores.

HOW TO SHOP A TRADE SHOW

First time visitors to a trade show may be initially bewildered by the vast arena of exhibitors. There are miles to walk and a seemingly endless number of exhibitor booths and designer pavilions. However, attending a trade show can be a most rewarding experience if you plan ahead to maximize your time and energy.

The Show Directory

Plan your visit wisely. Before you arrive at the trade show, highlight the hall location and the pavilion number of the exhibitors you plan to see for possible purchases. Plan to visit all the firms in a specific hall at the same time. Do not skip around from hall to hall; it will waste time.

Advance Notices

Most exhibitors send out notices about their location and booth number before the show. If you are already doing business with these exhibitors, stop by and say hello or shop the line.

- New Vendor Resources: Provide time to shop the lines of exhibitors whose product lines you are not familiar with.
- Trend Displays: Start your visit to the trade show in the trend display area, where samples from all the exhibitors are displayed in segments by color and fabric classifications. This overview will confirm the new trend direction for a season.
- New Sources: This is also a good way to source new product offerings, which will be displayed.
- Color Cards: If available, acquire color cards or trend brochures.
- Trend Seminars: Attend a trend seminar before the show in which trend direction given by industry professionals will confirm commonalities in color, fabric, or silhouette.
- Fashion Shows: Many trade shows present fashion shows highlighting selections from exhibitors' collec-

tions. Check the schedule so you can see the silhouette trends in advance before shopping the show.

- Buying Guide: The trade show is an opportunity to meet with established industry friends and to develop new ones. Remember to spend time with exhibitors in which you might have future interest. Buying decisions will not only be based on the current season, but project forward into future seasons.
- Pause and Pace: Trade shows are usually located in enormous exhibit halls. You may walk miles in one day. To get the most out of the day or days you spend at the show and keep up your enthusiasm and energy, it is important to pause and pace yourself. Treat yourself to a break in the hospitality area.
- Hospitality: Trade shows usually have a cafe area where you can purchase light meals, rest, and take time to review your notes.

Trade Terminology

Booth
Exhibitor
Organizer
Pavilion
Show directory
Sourcing
Trend preview
Trade show
VIP lounge

READING 10-1 | Searching for Trends at Shows BY KRISTIN LARSON

NEW YORK—Retailers shopping the Industry (212), Moda Manhattan and Annex trade shows here last week were looking for the next big trends for fall.

What they found were trends that were all across the board, said one retail executive at the Jacob K. Javits Convention Center, where the Industry and Moda shows took place May 4–6. Annex, a smaller version of Designers & Agents, staged its second Manhattan edition May 5–7 in a sunny loft space at The Starrett-Lehigh Center on West 26th Street.

"The Industry show was great for items, but I walked both shows looking for emerging trends. For instance, I really liked the cute T-shirts by Bella-Chic—they would be great with jeans. Just a really cute top," said Key Hunter, fashion forecaster at Macy's East. "At Moda, the theme seemed to be hats. Hats in different styles, felt hats with leather trims and in different shapes and not with traditional applications.

"Every show is different but it's very important to attend all of them to see what everyone is showing. You try to be prepared, but if the hottest rap artist wears something that's the next big thing—that can blow your six-month plan out of the water."

Store owner Patricia Timm of St. Tropez boutique in Virginia Beach, Va., was perusing the two Javits Center shows for sweaters and fall items with a "fresh" twist.

"My store is like a mini-department store," Timm said. "I do everything from denim to accessories and dress a customer 15 years to 50 years old. But I'm really going toward comfort clothing and items that are very casual and comfortable. Business has been good, though, so I can't complain."

Better sportswear line Kiko's sales representative, Terri Kurland, said bookings at the Industry (212) show were strong.

"There are just so many junior lines out there and the misses customer doesn't know where she fits in," Kurland said. "So we feature garment-dyed fabrics in styles designed to fit this woman. We call it 'lifestyle.' Business is up 40 to 50 percent from the last show."

Alec Izarov, designer at NY77, which showed at Moda Manhattan, said people were buying a lot of sweaters, tops and separates in shades of brown and black.

"Everybody who stops is buying, but it is slow," Izarov said. "We're doing really well with coats. Overall, we've done about $500,000 in volume. We won some new accounts and saw some old ones."

Meanwhile, a mixed array of 25 exhibitors showed at Annex, including hat designer Tracy Watts, T-shirt maker Christina Lehr, Dulce Bags and Balamani.

"It's been a great show," said Susan Eisenberg, vice president of sales at Calypso by Christiane Cello, which is known for its breezy, pastel-colored clothes. "Buyers love that it's open and airy. Overall, we booked close to $120,000 for the show."

D&A co-founders Ed Mandelbaum and Barbara Kramer said they are committed to producing a tightly edited show, featuring designers with a "point of view."

Mandelbaum said the show "could have been five times bigger," but the organizers "are committed to making sure the taste level and quality are up to our standards and we want people to walk away and say 'what a great show.'"

Kramer added that a lot of the companies don't have a New York showroom and use the D&A venue as a place to meet with retail representatives.

She added: "We want to make sure when buyers walk the show, like an art display, what they see is a clear and concise image."

Source: *Women's Wear Daily*, May 14, 2003, p. 7. Courtesy of Fairchild Publications, Inc.

READING 10-2 | Lyon Expected to Shine BY KARYN MOGET

NEW YORK—Despite the fear factor of terrorism compounded by the weak American dollar and strained Franco-American relations over the war in Iraq, the turnout of visitors and exhibitors at the Lyon, Mode City show in Lyon, France, is expected to be the strongest to date.

That's the word from Claire Jonathan, show director, who said a turnout of 20,000 visitors representing 95 nationalities is anticipated at the Sept. 6–8 lingerie, swimwear and Interfiliere textile fair based on preregistration figures. This will be a record turnout, with some 1,500 more attendees than a year ago, she said.

The overall theme at the 660,000-square-foot trade fair for fall-winter 2004–2005, will be a "fun attitude that reflects the exuberance" of five key lingerie segments in a fashion aisle display called The Lingerie Forum:

- Design & Freedom, a section dedicated to high-performance and active-inspired garments that have an innerwear-outwear look.
- Design & Dream, an environment created for status and megabrands.
- Creation & Exception, a space for intimates bearing designer names.
- Creation & Young Fashion, a platform for younger designers.
- Design & Discoveries From Abroad, an international melting pot of lingerie talent.

"Our aim is to make the show easier to shop, and we want the show to get younger and more energetic," said Jonathan, noting there will be an extra 10,000 square feet of exhibit space to accommodate new exhibitors, as well as expanded trend forums.

The trade fair will showcase 500 lingerie brands from 24 countries, 80 of which are exhibiting for the first time from Italy, France, Turkey and Eastern Europe. The breakdown of categories will be 30 percent women's sleepwear and at-homewear, 26 percent foundations and corsetry, 25 percent daywear, 12 percent men's underwear and at-homewear and 7 percent legwear.

New features at this year's edition will include:

- A Sport of Living bodywear forum that will highlight the cross-merchandising of lingerie, active separates and ready-to-wear looks.
- A seminar with a legal expert on the dangers of counterfeit merchandise.
- A larger forum of men's products from brands such as La Perla, Punto Blanco, Zimmerli and Bruno Bannani.
- An expanded swimwear section of 350 brands, 70 of which are showing for the first time, such as Nautica, Ungaro and Versace. Jonathan said a young contemporary section with labels like JLo Swim by Jennifer Lopez will be highlighted for tweens and teens.
- An Elevation trends forum for the most directional fabrics selected from 330 mills and manufacturers. A main focus will be high-performance fabrics that have features such as wicking applications and protection from ultraviolet exposure.
- A 10-minute video presentation twice daily of key trends and new concepts in the Gold Club buyers lounge.

"We have a tremendous amount of newness to offer visitors this year and we want Americans to feel welcome," said Jonathan, noting that turnout of major American retailers is expected to be strong. "The big important buyers for our exhibitors said they will definitely be attending because they have a lot of money to spend that they haven't spent in prior seasons."

Key U.S. retailers who have registered for the fair include Saks Fifth Avenue, Neiman Marcus, Federated Department Stores, Chico's, which will be opening several freestanding intimate apparel stores this year, and Dillard's Inc., which plans to buy fabrics for new private label innerwear programs, said Jonathan.

She noted that Eurovet, the show's parent, will host two events: a formal fashion show of intimates and swimwear on Lyon's Quai du Rhone on Sept. 6 and a gala dinner catered by international chefs for 250 guests at Lyon's landmark 18th-century city hall on Sept. 7.

Eurovet also will feature a Fabrics Forum called Move dedicated to fabrics that address the blurring of lines between lingerie, rtw and sportswear. The three themes will be Breathe, garments that are body-hugging yet nonrestrictive for comfort, flexibility and movement in natural, soft cotton blends with Meryl, Supplex and Seacell; Evolve, streetwear-inspired looks in solid and printed microfiber laces, net and mesh; and Move, apparel and underwear for extreme sports in a wide range of high tech, breathable and thermo-regulating fabrics.

Regarding young design talent showcased in the Expression Dessous area, vendors will include Active Line Lingerie, Asia, Bas Bleu, Beau Bra, Dreamgirl, Elise Aucouturier, Emozioni Private, Emporiana, Endeanas, Eos, Eva Racheline, Fishbelly, Fleur T, Grazia Lliana, Guia, Le Monde d'Alba, Leg Avenue, Parakean, Pink Piranha, Sarah Fisk, Sophie Malagola, Sylvie Rost, Viamode, Zazi and Zedzz.

Source: *Women's Wear Daily*, July 14, 2003, p. 2. Courtesy of Fairchild Publications, Inc.

11

Fashion Show Production

Lights, music, action. Fashion show production is big business, and every designer's most important showpiece is the catwalk runway presentation of his or her collection.

ORGANIZING A FASHION SHOW

Once a new collection is designed and ready to be presented, the show producer goes into action. Backstage a team of dedicated and talented individuals, overworked assistants, hair and make-up artists, models, and public relations professionals converge on the show scene to realize the designer's vision. Putting one of these shows together is not much different than producing a Broadway play. Both require rigorous organization, dramatic sound and light effects, gorgeous models, and of course, beautiful clothes.

A fashion show lasts no more than thirty minutes, sometimes it is as short as twenty minutes, a fleeting moment in a designer's seasonal life. Unlike Broadway theatre, however, fashion shows do not have the luxury of tryouts in other venues, in another city. There are no trial runs. The show must go on with precision timing. It is a nerve-racking endeavor. The venue, the invitation, the show program, the models, the hair and makeup, must all present a unified image, as must the ambiance of the show and, most importantly, the music.

When the show goes on, the guests arrive at the Bryant Park tents during fashion week in New York City. The crowd surges forward to check in at the buyer or press desks. Industry groupies without invitations queue up in a separate line hoping to get into the show. The excitement mounts as fashionistas find each other, and in a frenzy of greeting one another, airborne kisses alight on the cheeks of fashion arrivals. Cameras click, television crews rush to capture the latest celebrity as she takes a front row seat reserved for the fashion cognoscente. It is all part of the fashion show ritual that takes place twice a year for Spring/Summer and Fall/Winter. Additional shows that highlight resort and holiday wear will also be held during the year.

The Show Producer

An effective designer show needs packaging, a venue to express ideas and reach the audience. There is one company that remains discreetly behind the scenes and makes the show process successful. That is the "Show Producer," a company, an individual, or production team that simultaneously directs all the physical aspects of the show from lighting to animated sound tracks, runway configurations to seating, and choreography to props for staged events.

Show producers tend to have nerves of steel, bringing calm to potential chaos. Many firms specialize in show production exclusively, but some public relations firms may also handle all the aspects of show production, including hiring the models, producing press kits, and liaising with the press.

Producing a show may take months. The designer may give the input for the theme saying, "This season I did Hawaii, rather than Tibet." At that point, the show producer, fashion director, or stylist must decide on the order in which to present the outfits. Because the garments are not ready at the planning stage of the project, the show producer may take two sets of color photos of each of the designer's creations with accessories, if available. One set of photos should be reserved for later use on each model's show chart, which will be placed at her dressing station to illustrate the garments she will wear in sequential order at the show.

SIDEBAR 11-1 Tools of the Trade: The Prop Kit

Every ground crew staffer is equipped with the following "must have" items to facilitate their work and handle unexpected necessities.

- A pair of scissors
- Pin cushion on a neck rope
- Shoe horn
- Double back scotch tape (a necessity to mend a hem)
- Masking tape (a modesty cover for see-through garments)
- Disposable razors
- A sewing kit
- A seam ripper
- Aspirin or Tylenol
- First aid kit
- Hand-held hole puncher to make holes in belts that are too small
- Shoe pads for shoes that do not fit
- Tissues
- Tampons
- Lint brush
- Static guard

The Ringbinder Technique

The main purpose of the photos, however, is as a pictorial reference of the show. Without the actual garments, the show can be coordinated in an ordinary ringbinder, by theme, scenes, and garment entrances. Each photo is mounted on a separate blank page in the ringbinder in the order of the run of show with cues for models, evocative lighting effects, and sound track.

The Ringbinder Format is ideal for planning and coordinating a show without the garments being immediately available. This is how it works for a 180-garment show with eighteen garments in each of ten scenes. Models' entrances will be assigned based on two, three, four, or even five models entering the runway at the same time. Groups of models may be brought out on the runway to emphasize a color, fabric, or silhouette message. At the same time, model groups make it possible to get 180 garments showcased in thirty minutes.

The elements of the ringbinder are:

- *Cover:* The cover identifies the name of the designer—in this case, the fictitious Bettina Ford. The theme name, "Hawaiian Fantasy," should also be on the cover. Each sequential scene will have a title that reflects the overall theme.
- *Page One:* Print the first scene's name, Scene I "Aloha," and list the music assigned for this scene.
- *Page Two:* (In the upper righthand corner, mark "1 of 4," which means that this is the first of four models entering the runway at the same time.) A photo of the first garment is mounted on the blank page with the name of the model assigned to wear it. Pertinent details include the model agency contact, accessories, and shoe size. The show producer will also include other instructions and may attach a small fabric swatch to check color accuracy from photo to garment.
- *Page Three:* (In the upper righthand corner, mark "2 of 4," which means that this is the second garment coming out in the group of four.) A photo of the second garment is mounted on the blank page with the name of the model assigned to wear it and pertinent details.
- *Page Four:* (In the upper righthand corner, mark "3 of 4," which means that this is the third garment coming out in the group of four.) Same information is added as recorded previously.
- *Page Five:* (In the upper righthand corner, mark "4 of 4," which means that this is the last garment in the set of four.) Pertinent information is recorded.

The show producer, fashion director, or stylist in charge of garment line up continues this process of mounting photographs on each blank page until all the remaining garments for Scene I, "Aloha," are similarly coordinated.

Using the same technique, the ringbinder will likewise identify Scenes II through X, and the order of the eighteen ensembles in each scene.

Translating Designer Vision

As a translator of the designer's mind, the show producer in charge of the physical set-up of the show must translate the message and the image of a collection and make the event a unique experience. Working one-on-one with each client, the show producer establishes the design of the space and the set. The fashion director's choice of the models, the hair, the makeup, and the music must mirror the designer's image. The styling of the garments and the specific direction given to the models must express the mood of the show.

The event must be special because along with the clothes, the show's main objective is to garner press coverage and sufficiently impress retailers who will decide what the consumer will want to wear for the new season. The show also contributes to a designer's reputation. The buzz in the fashion market among the fashion intelligentsia often refers to a designer's collection by the kind of show that launched it.

The Budget

While budgets are confidential, show producers concede that costs depend on the project, and how much money the designer has to produce the show, either through personal capital or through sponsorship. Young designers who cannot afford to invest in a major show may pay $50,000 to participate in a group show. Standard market week shows by an individual designer may start at $120,000 and increase substantially depending upon the elaborateness of the production.

The scale of the project may also be an incredible event, with a production on the level of a theatrical entertainment that may be held in the United States or in another country, costing up to $10 million.

The Show Producer's Worksheet

Producing a show takes into account many costly elements. An outline of the show producer's worksheet includes the following:

- *Theme:* Creating a theme for the show gives it a focus. For example, "Tulles of Seduction" is a theme that identifies with intimate apparel.
- *The Venue:* Represents the location in a hotel, public space like a center for the arts, museum, armory, retail store, Bryant Park tents.
- *Permits:* If the event is staged at a public location, a temporary permit is required to use the premises. Show producers must check ceiling height, access to elevators, electricity, and emergency exits.
- *Staging:* Installation of the physical set up of the show, including
  1. Runway size and catwalk can be constructed in configurations ranging from the traditional "T" to an arrow, square, or circular shape to accommodate a musical group in the pit.
  2. Décor and props may be used to illustrate and augment the theme.
  3. Lighting can manipulate the environment and become a major element of drama.
  4. Sound/Music: The music is critical to the show's success. The music has to work with the clothes on the runway and suggest an image. Music can evoke a pastoral mood, a cool, snappy attitude, or a contemporary spin.
  5. Seating: Important retailers, members of the press, and celebrities receive priority seating. Each seat is

assigned to indicate who sits in a specific section at the show. Company greeters may also assist guests as they enter the show arena.

6. Videotaping: A videotape of the show is an important tool that can be used as a point of critical reference after the show. When the tape is edited, it can be replayed in the designer's showroom during market week. The edited tape may also be used in a video press kit or as a merchandise training tool for salespeople at retail department stores.

- *Communication*
  1. Intercoms/walkie-talkies keep the production coordinators in touch with one another from backstage to the front of the house.
  2. Security guards are hired to secure the area and the merchandise.
- *Backstage Production Coordinator:* This person oversees the work of the following people:
  1. Stylist: This role is complex. A stylist can also set the mood for a collection. The stylist's input may range from suggesting how a designer might combine a jacket and skirt for a runway show to suggesting just the right shoes or accessories to finish off an outfit. Stylists help the designer complete their vision and set the mood for a collection. The stylist will also obtain accessories and shoes free of charge from firms, which consider the free runway publicity and credit in the show program well worth their participation.
  2. Hair & Makeup: Teams create the designer's point of view that will impact the look of the clothes. Before the show, the producer will ask the hair or makeup designer to do a test on a model for the designer's approval.

Most cosmetic companies provide cosmetics free of charge. The philosophy behind their generosity is a brand building opportunity to showcase products that will filter through to the consumer. The magazine and newspaper editors covering the shows validate the looks in editorials.

3. Models are hired who will represent the look, story, and vision of the designer. Today's models are work oriented and less diva-esque than those of previous years.
4. Dressers: They assist the models, dressing and accessorizing the outfits for the first run of the show. As the models return from the catwalk, the dressers also hang up the garments and bag the accessories.

- *Public Relations*: The PR firm usually creates the invitation and puts together the press invitation list. The firm also produces the press kit, which will be sent to major newspapers, magazines, and the electronic media, as well as television talk shows. The resulting publicity will boost the designer's image and spread the message about the collection throughout the broadcast and print media for months to come.

Musical Stylists

It is hard to believe that fashion shows were once parades of silent models walking to the beat of a commentator calling the style numbers. Runway fashion shows at the trade level have come a long way from those days. Today there is no commentary, but the sound beat of music rules the runways. Stirring up images and magical impressions, music is the master mix of sounds that contribute to the success of a collection.

The mere procession of outfits can be boring, but the right music not only sets the tone for a show, it evokes a mood that unifies a designer's fashion message. Most importantly the soundtrack can spark enthusiasm and inspire both the models and the audience.

The current breed of music man or woman is now highly regarded as a "runway musical stylist." Their attention-getting musical scores must be new, an original take on something that exists or on the work of an unknown talent. Musical stylists pay attention to what the young culture is listening to, what is very avant-garde, and what is very controversial. Music must make some kind of a statement. The star mix-masters select music that is memorable and motivating.

The first step in choosing music is to understand the philosophy of the designer's point of view and inspiration. When a designer is presenting a collection for the first time, music is the soundtrack that will drive the models down the runway and hype the press and impress the buyers. Fashion show organizers, therefore, must find the right music match to accentuate the show's theme and sequences.

The Models

The only people who work harder than the designer are the models. They have to look fabulous and gorgeous all the time, because they have to fit the image of the show and complement the designer's vision. New faces crop up each season, but the most important factor is the model's look as well as her magnetism and energy. For example, if you're putting on a show that has a young look, you would not book models who usually wear high fashion or couture.

The major agencies, such as Elite Model Management, Ford, and Wilhelmina represent some of the highest paid and most successful models, but other agencies such as Boss Models, Click Model Management, Marilyn Agency, and IMG Models are a rich source of established and newcomer talent.

Superstar models can command thousands of dollars for merely one turn down the runway. Standard fashion show runway models are paid by the hour or by the show and the rates differ depending on how the agency books the models. A novice model usually earns a modest fee, while a seasoned model with a runway track record garners a higher price. Prices may also vary depending upon the model's involvement with the show. For example, if the model is booked for a half or a whole day that price would be negotiated.

Because there is no rehearsal time, market week shows are very demanding on a model's ability to adapt and improvise. At show time, seasoned runway models may hear instructions like, "do a half runway and come back," or "take off the coat at mid center," or "wait for the other models in the group before leaving the runway."

Booking Models

Before engaging models for a fashion show, the show producer or the model coordinator on the production team may review the head sheet, look book, or composite cards from the different model agencies. The head sheet may feature all the models from the agency on one large poster size sheet. However, because an agency may represent hundreds of models, composite cards representing the statistics of a specific model may be used instead. The show producer/fashion director, therefore, must be model specific about the type of model required for the show.

The show's model coordinator calls the model agency and asks the booker, the person who books the models, to send in composite cards of fresh looking models or sophisticated professionals, depending on the type of show. The composite card shows the different looks of the model, his/her statistics, height, hair color, eye color, figure measurements, and shoe size.

The Go-See

After reviewing the composite cards, the model coordinator schedules a meeting with the models, a meeting called a go-see. The go-see stage of model selection is the initial procedure for interviewing both top models as well as new faces.

The go-see is important because it gives the show producer an opportunity to evaluate the model as "a fit" for a particular show's image. The model coordinator can also determine if the model has the right look and attitude for the show. Once the model has been selected, a confirmed booking should be made early, before each season's show, because many of the best models are scooped up by the top designers. At this point, the model coordinator and the booker at the agency agree on the rate, time, and location of the show. At the end of the show, the model coordinator on the show producer's team will sign the model agency's voucher, presented by the model, confirming the date, time, and rate for the show.

SHOW ORGANIZERS

There are many independent show producers and professional companies that specialize in show production. Presenting the collection in an organized and entertaining fashion show format may be of prime concern, but there are other considerations such as the designer's inspiration and vision.

Bureau Betak

Bureau Betak, a New York-based company, is among the most famous show producers. Bureau Betak provides the conception, direction, design, and production for fashion shows and special events of designers and design houses around the world. At the helm of Bureau Betak is Alexandre de Betak, a Frenchman, his partner Violaine Etienne, and their production managers, who produce shows for Donna Karan, Hussein Chalayan, Michael Kors, John Galliano, Victoria's Secret, and John Bartlett. The firm is known for turning staid fashion shows into an electrifying fashion event.

Betak says that client consultation is the start of the show design process. He and the designer always start with a story. For example, in presenting his new collection, John Bartlett had a vision of a woman touching down in her private jet.

INDUSTRY PROFILE 11-1 | Audrey Smaltz

Audrey Smaltz, one of the great success stories and most polished professionals in the fashion industry. In this photo, her style and dynamic personality jump out to the reader.

When you enter Audrey Smaltz' penthouse apartment, you immediately become aware that this is the home and work epicenter of a chief executive par excellence. A provocative administrator, engaging entrepreneur, and polished professional speaker, Audrey Smaltz could have invented the term "niche marketing." One of her companies, The Ground Crew, is a remarkable success story.

Ms. Smaltz is the driving force behind The Ground Crew, fashion's most indispensable backstage team and fashion show support system. She learned about sass and style in her native New York City and refined it in Paris, Milan, London, Tokyo, and Rome. Along the way she met and worked with world famous designers, stellar hairdressers, make-up artists, and supermodels, and she has also seen street-smart kids rise to the top of the fashion pack. By forming The Ground Crew, Smaltz created fashion's first professional backstage support organization. She single-handedly turned backstage creative chaos into a seemingly effortless production.

In 1982, the former Ebony Fashion Fair superstar began investigating business possibilities in an industry she had come to know and love. She wanted to create a company that would employ her expertise, provide a challenge, and expand her horizons. With more than 800 shows to her credit, she seized an opportunity. She demonstrated to designers that by hiring professionals instead of resorting to their standard practice of turning to friends and hangers on, the show would not just go on, but would go on flawlessly.

Creating The Ground Crew

"I called it The Ground Crew because a fashion show is like an aircraft, the designer is the pilot, but the show can't get off the ground without its support staff," says the dynamic Smaltz. She built a business that organizes, mends, pins and presses, and then dresses models, celebrities, and stars for runways, film, and photo sets. The Ground Crew also produces entire shows from concept to model selection, including hiring the dressers, makeup artists, hair designers, stylists, seamstresses, and backstage crew.

"Clients know that they can call us at 6 PM for a show the next day, and we'll send over a team during the night to steam all the clothes, and everything will be perfect for that show," Ms. Smaltz says.

Customized Work

All the work that The Ground Crew does is customized to the needs of the client. One client may need four dressers for a show, while another may need forty. The designer is totally involved with the show. The stylist's job is to put the personality of the designer into the show. To accomplish the designer's concept, the makeup and hair artists discuss the look the designer wants to portray. A rack is designated for each model, with garments lined up in the right order for the model's appearance on the catwalk.

"Facilitating the timeliness of a show takes professional know-how," notes Ms. Smaltz. "There are no try outs in another city, the show must go on with precision timing. A producer has one chance to get it right, and getting it right is how The Ground Crew has built its reputation."

Ms. Smaltz considers the behind-the-scene dressers one of the most important aspects of backstage production. Putting the models in the right outfit and totally coordinated, on time, is critical to the success of a show. Fastening hooks and eyes or zippers, making sure she is wearing the right belt is part of dressing each model. Ensuring that the right accessories and shoes complete the outfit is another way a professional dresser meets his or her responsibility with accurate coordination.

When the model returns from the runway, the dresser must quickly undress the model and get her set up in the next outfit. Garments which the model wore previously invariably end up on the floor. The dressers are constantly engaged with the clothes. Garments must be hung up and repackaged on the racks so that the designer's collection or loaned merchandise is returned as it was received. Nothing must be missing. Loaned accessories and shoes must also be neatly repackaged and returned.

"Two or three people we call runners take over a section of models, keep tabs on what garments the models are wearing, line them up, and cue them out on the runway," says Ms. Smaltz. "At the end of the show we line up the clothes again so the press can see the garments."

The Ground Crew staff, which swells to more than 100 during market weeks, handles some 300 events, including fashion shows, weddings, conventions, and corporate projects annually. Today, with a platinum client list from Sears Roebuck & Co. to Nordstrom and from Oscar de la Renta to Bill Blass, Donna Karan to Michael Kors, billing ranges from $500,000 to $l million.

The Fashion Diva

Audrey likes to say she was "born, bred, toasted, buttered, jellied and jammed and honeyed in Harlem." She also became beautiful, smart, and charming there. A head-turning model at age 15, she went on to greater accomplishments. Her talents began to ripen on stage as the single most unforgettable commentator in the history of the Ebony Fashion Fair. During her seven years with that organization, Smaltz learned about Haute Couture and Prêt-à-Porter in Europe, Japan, and the United States. Through the more than 800 shows she produced, she brought the best of international fashion to women across America.

Named to the "International Best Dressed List" three times, Audrey Smaltz is recognized as an intelligent, imposing, elegant, and savvy woman.

This idea resulted in fluorescent lighting that ran down the catwalk, like a landing strip.

The Garments

Production executive Violaine Etienne, vice president of Bureau Betak, says that when it comes to garment selection, there is a large range of possibilities. To narrow down the selection, photographs are first taken of each silhouette. Then the designer and stylists edit the looks on the photos down from one hundred shots to sixty-five silhouettes for the actual show. They create a story and work out the lineup for the show.

A team of collection coordinators (otherwise known as stylists) are there to work with the designer and his team on putting the pieces together, to theme them into specific looks or messages.

Model Selection

Prior to engaging the models, Bureau Betak calls the model agencies, sees all the models, and then sends them to the designer on a go-see. The designer approves the model selection and has each model try on some of the garments to assess the effectiveness of the look.

"Together with the designer, we finalize the bookings and negotiate the rate with the booker, the person who represents the models at the modeling agency," notes Ms. Etienne. "There are no rules on runway rates. However, we book at either an hourly rate or flat fee."

The Catwalk

The Cues by Bureau Betak book features now famous boards of direction originally created for the backstages of fashion shows for the world's top designers and design houses. There are many runway configurations ranging from the classic T shape to square, single catwalk entries.

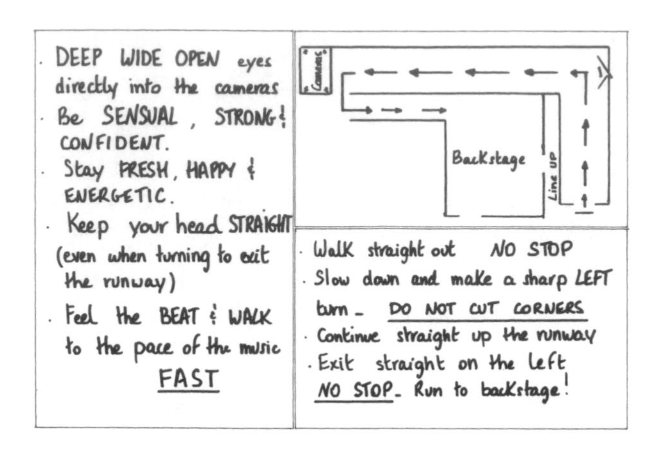

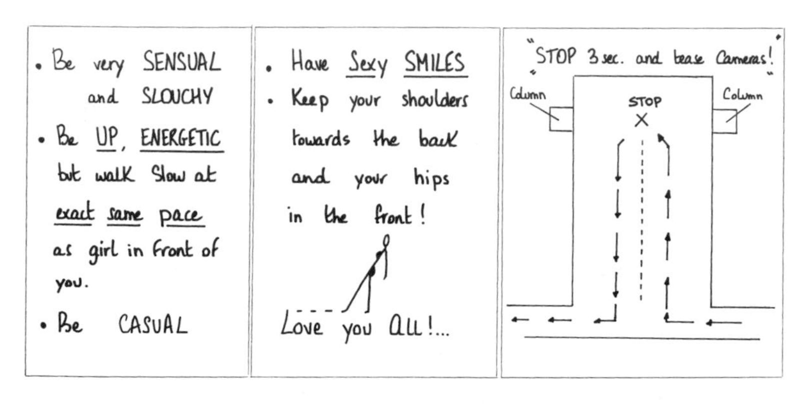

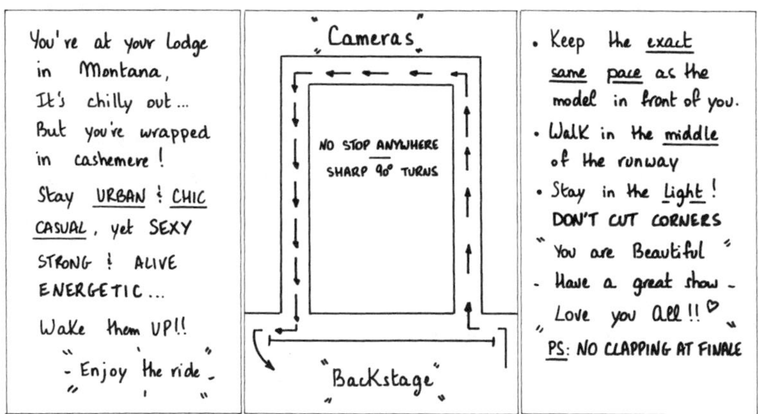

Bureau Betak's instructional board for the runway models for Donna Karan (top), Rifat Ozbek (center), and Michael Kors (bottom) from The Cues by Bureau Betak, *published in the Fall of 1999.*

These boards give the direction of the show, as well as the mood of the season to the models: "be sexy," "be strong," "be powerful," "be sensual," "be spiritual." These cardboard scripts are house rules for a successful show. Always graphic and funny, the boards combine pep talk cues with catwalk instructions that the models can easily follow. The messages capture the mood and attitude for a collection and help models build a character and create the right catwalk style. Setting the mood another script reads, "You're at your lodge in Montana, it's chilly out . . . but you're wrapped in cashmere! Say urban, chic, casual, yet sexy, strong, alive, and energetic. Wake them up!!! Enjoy the ride."

It is rare to do full dress rehearsals for an average market week show; therefore models are usually chosen with experience and know how.

Company Agenda

Company Agenda is a full-service public relations agency that coordinates marketing strategy, image management, event production, and press relations to create a unique and powerful image for their client's products and talents. Company Agenda works closely with each client to define, refine, and implement a client's strategic goals for maximum impact.

Fashion show production is a comprehensive package that involves the following:

Concept: Company Agenda develops a range of options that fulfill a client's expectations, from a standard runway fashion show to an alternative presentation.

Location: The specifics of a client's fashion show will dictate space, size, and location. The firm researches unconventional spaces, as well as securing space at traditional venues.

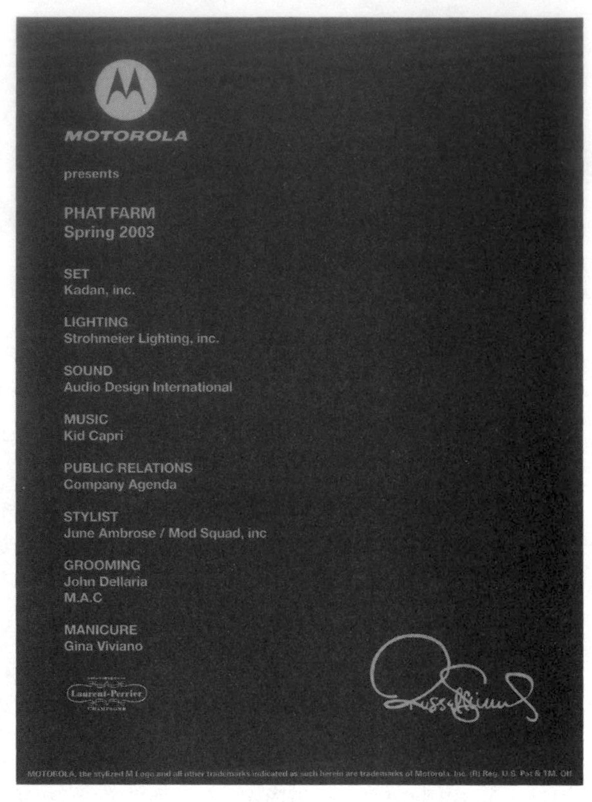

twinkle by wenlan

Spring 2004

Bryant Park, New York
Tuesday, September 16
5PM

RSVP
Company Agenda
212. 479. 7769

This page and opposite page: *Company Agenda's invitations to the Spring 2003 "Phat Farm" invitation* **(top)** *and to Wenlan's "Twinkle" exhibit at 7th on Sixth in Spring 2004* **(bottom)**. *Company Agenda also designs seating charts, as shown in this one for Mercedes-Benz Fashion Week in New York* **(opposite page)**.

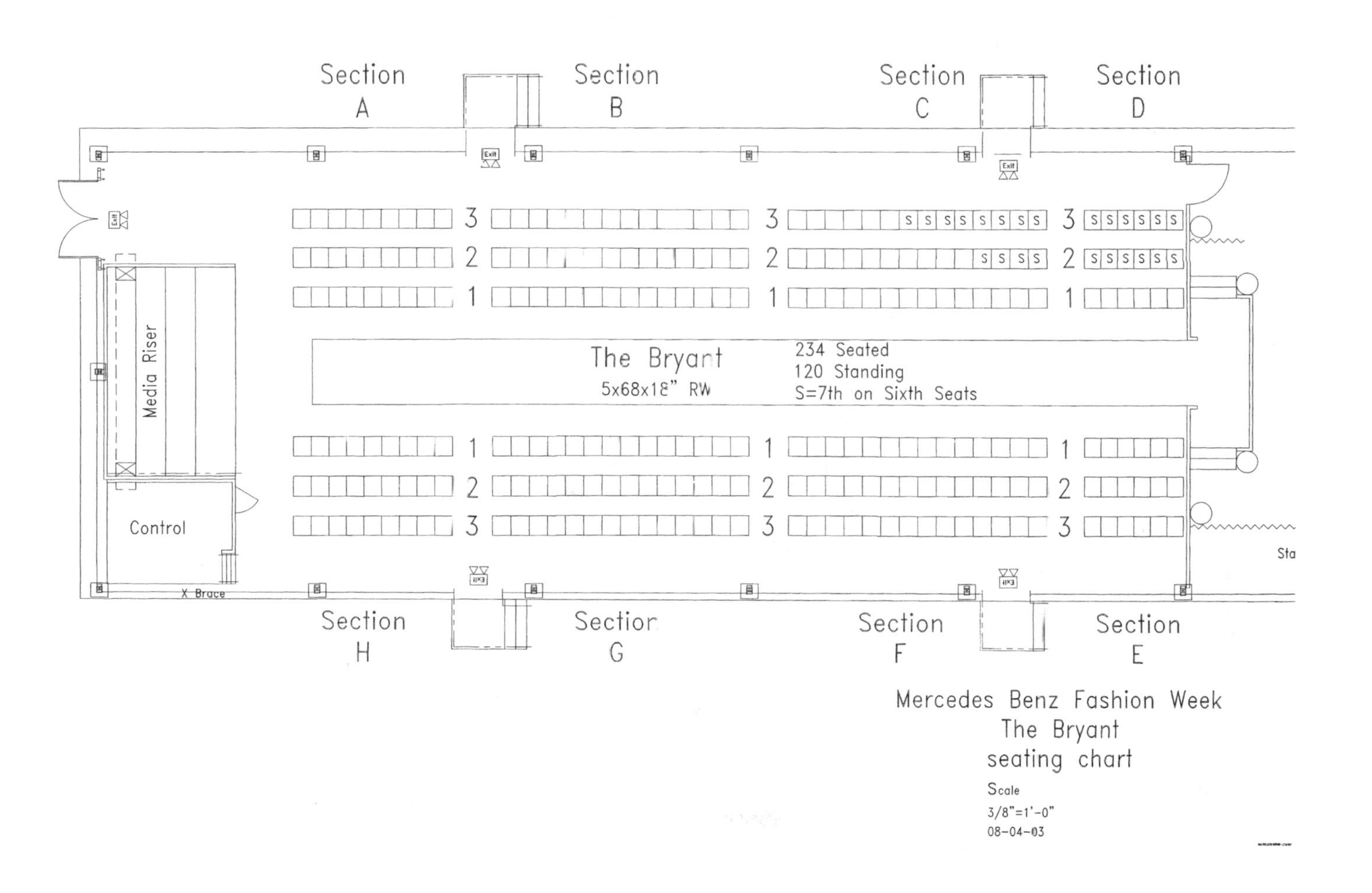
Section A
Section B
Section C
Section D
Exit
The Bryant
5x68x18" RW
234 Seated
120 Standing
S=7th on Sixth Seats
Media Riser
Control
X Brace
Section H
Section G
Section F
Section E
Sta
Mercedes Benz Fashion Week
The Bryant
seating chart
Scale
3/8"=1'-0"
08-04-03

Invitation: The invitation sets the mood and tone for the fashion show. Company Agenda will consult on an invitation design.

Timing: A prime slot in the seasonal fashion show agenda is always essential. Company Agenda works with the Fashion Calendar and 7th on Sixth to coordinate schedules. The Fashion Calendar is the industry calendar bible, to which press and buyers subscribe. It provides a complete listing of all shows and industry events, both in the United States and abroad.

Lighting: Top lighting specialists are hired to create the optimum setting for each fashion show.

Music: The firm works with a large pool of music artists and DJs and caters to the client's tastes and requirements.

Backstage: Backstage logistics are important and include hiring professional dressers and hair and make-up artists, arranging clothing transportation, organizing catering, checking in staff, and coordinating backstage photography and interviews.

Stylist: The stylist offers a fresh eye to the designer and can be influential in putting the garments together with appropriate accessories or props.

Program: The show producer conceives and produces the fashion show program, including quotations and sound bytes geared to press and retailers. Credits appear in the program as a "thank you" to accessories or cosmetic firms which have loaned or donated their products. The production team may also be listed, as will the music stylist.

Casting: Exciting and directional casting includes today's current model stars as well as presenting tomorrow's "it" girl.

Security: The show producer hires effective and discreet security teams to guard the merchandise and secure the area.

Fashion Show Press

The success of a show is also evaluated by the kind of press coverage the show receives in the print and electronic press. Considering the vast number of shows listed on the Fashion Calendar, attracting press coverage is paramount to the public relation firm's responsibility. Here is an example of the elements involved in working with the fashion show press:

- *Customization:* Company Agenda's extensive database is individualized to suit a client's fashion show, including a press list, which might include the following categories:

  National and international press

  Celebrities

  Electronic media

  Photographers

  Socialites
- *RSVPs:* An RSVP telephone line is dedicated for each show. Invitation requests are processed and seats assigned. At the event Company Agenda oversees meeting and greeting of guests and seat assignments.
- *Seating Chart:* Show seating is predetermined and approved by the designer before seating assignments are issued. Seating charts take into account important retailers, press and industry politics as well as personal relationships.
- *Press Strategy:* Press is coordinated before, during, and after the fashion show. Company Agenda will pitch

SIDEBAR 11-2 | Fashion Calendar

The Fashion Calendar is a valuable international industry resource. It features a complete listing of national and international events in the fashion and beauty industries. As an essential industry tool, the Fashion Calendar keeps industry professionals up to date on market weeks and serves as an important clearinghouse for scheduling dates and time slots for fashion shows. The publication also assists retailers and members of the press by giving them a detailed schedule of the date and time when the collections are shown. The calendar also lists fashion and beauty promotions, new store openings, book signings, and benefits. Subscribers are entitled to five listings throughout the year. Nonsubscribers may also place their event at a one line or three line-listing rate.

	FRIDAY FEB. 6	SATURDAY FEB. 7	SUNDAY FEB. 8	MONDAY FEB. 9	TUESDAY FEB. 10	WEDNESDAY FEB. 11	THURSDAY FEB. 12	FRIDAY FEB. 13	
9 AM				DANA BUCHMAN ELLEN TRACY PAUL HARDY (S)	REEM ACRA (A) THE GAP(9:30)	COSTUME INST. (7:30AM) VERA WANG (A)	JEFFREY CHOW (A)	RALPH LAUREN	9 AM
10 AM	KENNETH COLE (T)		TRACY REESE (S)	M. LHUILLIER (A)	GUSTAVO ARANGO (S) LUELLA BARTLEY	BAHAR KORCAN (S) DAVID RODRIGUEZ	ESTEBAN CORTAZAR (S)	RALPH LAUREN (PRESS) GEOFFREY BEENE (10-2)	10AM
11 AM	NAUTICA (P) TOCCA (11-3)	HANUK. (11-3)	ALICE ROI (P)	CAROLINA HERRERA (T)	DOUGLAS HANNANT (P) ARLEQUIN	MICHAEL KORS (T)	CHADO RALPH RUCCI (P)	RALPH LAUREN	11 AM
NOON	HARMON HEART TRUTH (S)	DIMMER/D'VRSI PATRIK RZEPSKI	IMITATION OF CHRIST	CYNTHIA STEFFE (S) KAPADIA VPL	BILL BLASS (T)	JOHN VARVATOS (P) YA-YA	CARMEN MARC VALVO (T)	ZANG TOI (S)	NOON
1PM	RON CHERESKIN (A)	RAIKA. D (A)	MARC BOUWER (A)	OSCAR DE LA RENTA (P)	CHAIKEN (A) LIBERTINE	VIVIENNE TAM J. MENDEL (A) JOHANNA HOFRING	PETER SOM (A)	MILLY (P)	1 PM
2 PM		ATIL KUTOGLU (S) CLOAK	YIGAL AZROUEL TESS GIBERSON	JILL STUART PALMER JONES	MAURICE MALONE (S) CHARLES ALEXANDER	PROENZA SCHOULER (S)	BEHNAZ SARAFPOUR (S)	RICHARD TYLER (A) PHI	2 PM
3 PM	PERRY ELLIS (P)	GARY GRAHAM RACHEL COMEY	CHANPAUL JACK MASCHARKA KEANAN DUFFTY	BETSEY JOHNSON	MARC BY MARC JACOBS	YEOHLEE ANTILIKA (3-7)	ROLAND MOURET MULTI BY BREE DARYL K (4-6)	DONNA KARAN	3 PM
4 PM	HONG KONG (S) GUIDO ALVIN VALLEY	REBECCA TAYLOR	CATHERINE MALANDRINO	DKNY VENA CAVA	SEBASTIAN PONS	LELA ROSE BENJAMIN CHO MICHAEL SOHEIL	JAMES COVIELLO (A) YOKO DEVEREAUX FAMURA	HAROUN + MOSQUEDA	4 PM
5 PM	VENEXIANA (A) NICCOLO (5-8PM)	MATTHEW EARNEST PIERROT (A)	NICOLE MILLER (S) LYNN PARK DEREK LAM	BADGLEY MISCHKA (P) DUCKIE BROWN	PAULA HIAN (A) MENICHETTI SHANNON STOKES	BABY PHAT H. FREDRIKSSON	CYNTHIA ROWLEY (P)	JACKIE ROGERS ATELIER COURVOISIER	5 PM
6 PM	BUCKLER (MEN)	Y & KEI (P) CAT SWANSON	DIANE VON FURSTENBERG	PAMELLA ROLAND (A) RUFFIAN	CALVIN KLEIN	CUSTO BARCELONA (P)	ZAC POSEN (T)	ELISA JIMENEZ	6 PM
7 PM	DOO. RI OLIVER HELDEN	SASS & BIDE (S) STEPHEN BURROWS(7-9PM)	TULEH (P)	BCBG (T) MARSHALL LEIGH AS FOUR (7:30)	NANETTE LEPORE (S) GENERRA	ANNA SUI (T)	FUSHA (S) UNITED BAMBOO	NICOLE ROMANO	7 PM
8 PM	EDWING D'ANGELO ALICE & OLIVIA	MARY PING	LUCA LUCA (T)	LLOYD KLEIN (S) GEOVA	NARCISO RODRIGUEZ (T) MARC ECKO (8-11)	MATTHEW WILLIAMSON (S) MIHO MIHO	TWINKLE (A)	YELLOW FEVER CIRCLE BY MARA HOFFMAN	8 PM
9 PM		JEREMY SCOTT HELEN YARMAK (10PM)	MICHAEL H. MACKAGE (A) CHRISTOPHER DEANE	MARC JACOBS	CARLOS MIELE (P) NOM D	JENNIFER NICHOLSON (A) BUILT BY WENDY	HEATHERETTE WRANGLER JEANS (9-midnight)	SYDNEY M & SARA CANT	9 PM

FASHION CALENDAR 153 EAST 87TH STREET NEW YORK, NY 10128 | (BRYANT PARK) A-ATELIER T-TENT S-STUDIO NOIR P-PROMENADE | TEL (212) 289-0420 FAX: (212) 289-5917

This page and opposite page: *Cover and one week in February from the Fashion Calendar for 7th on Sixth.*

and follow up with the national and international press, electronic media, photographers, and stylists.

- *Television Interviews:* Interview schedules are coordinated with the designer.
- *Front of House:* The company coordinates all necessary front of house staff, including door persons, ushers, security personnel, and team captains. It also oversees the meeting and greeting of press, retailers, and celebrities.

FASHION SHOW VARIETY

The Ebony Fashion Fair

When it comes to catwalk shows for public audiences, the Ebony Fashion Fair packs the house in every city it performs.

It is sponsored by local chapters of African-American charitable organizations, which in turn receive a portion of the proceeds from the show. The United Negro College Fund is a major beneficiary. Today, the show visits 179 cities and attracts more than 350,000 attendees annually. The total amount of funds raised by the Ebony Fashion Fair since it began in 1959 exceeds $50 million.

Part Broadway show, part haute couture, with sizzling music, dance, and catwalk moves, it is accompanied by commentary that is provocative repartee. In the grand finale, a bride resplendent in white, sometimes red, sometimes purple, wraps up the show.

Founded in 1958 by Ebony (Johnson Publishing Co.), the Ebony Fashion Fair is the world's largest traveling fashion show. From its beginning to the present, the Ebony Fashion Fair offers African-Americans a front-row seat to the best designs from Paris, Milan, London, and the United States.

Designs shown at the Ebony Fashion Fair included (below left) *a trendy ensemble designed by Gattinoni of Italy featuring striped pants with a black and ecru leather coat and* (below right) *a leaf-pattern fabric stole that complements a breathtaking gown with a leather panel front designed by Lancetti.*

The awesome splendor of the onstage fashion production is the result of the selection of more than 200 garments and accessories by Eunice W. Johnson, producer and director. She buys the designs in New York, London, Milan, and Paris from couture houses like Valentino, Yves Saint Laurent, and Christian Dior.

The 44th annual production of the Ebony Fashion Fair introduced a show entitled, "The Changing Trends of Fashion." The extravaganza was more like a celebration of fashion with designer garments that ran the gamut from sexy to sensational. The show was an extraordinary evening of entertainment and even included provocative vignettes that convey a romantic story.

Thousands of applications are received each year before the final model selection of ten beautiful women and two handsome men is made. The models travel from city to city with a skilled commentator, music director, stage manager, and business manager. Behind the scenes are four wardrobe assistants who maintain the exciting garments and accessories chosen by Ms. Johnson from the leading designers.

Trunk Shows

Trunk shows are typically two-day affairs during which designers hit the road to bring their collections directly to retail stores and shoppers. The store usually runs an advertisement in a local newspaper announcing the event, so the trunk show is open to anyone who wants to attend. The designer will also send an announcement to loyal customers, thus reinforcing attendance at the trunk show. When the designer makes a personal appearance, a trunk show can reap big profits, because customers want to meet the designer and express their views about the collection. When the designer's schedule does not permit a personal appearance at the store, the firm sends the fashion director or a qualified representative to present the collection.

The clothes represent the designer's entire collection, which is key to loyal customers, because the buyer of a store may not purchase the designer's complete range of garments. The clothes may be shown in a mini-fashion show, but customarily they are viewed on racks in an intimate setting in which customized orders are taken from customers.

Literally the designer's entire collection is in a trunk or trunks. Trunk shows take their name from the traveling salesmen who used to carry sample merchandise in trunks to show retailers around the country.

Trunk shows allow shoppers the luxury of reviewing and trying on a designer's entire collection in an uncrowded setting, but shoppers should realize that they may wait a couple of months for their garments to arrive. For the designer, it is an opportunity to get feedback from customers about fabric or style preferences. It is a one-on-one outreach to the customer that builds retail traffic in a "nonsale" event.

Macy's West Passport '01

According to the American Association for World Health 1998 World Aids booklet, "Every minute, five young people around the globe are infected with HIV." Responding to the continuing, global HIV/AIDS crisis, Macy's West Passport '01 took its unique blend of fashion and compassion to a new level as one of the single largest fund raisers for AIDS organizations among Western countries. The 19th annual Macy's West Passport '01, co-sponsored by American Express, dazzled Northern and Southern California audiences with the most exciting fashion theater.

The spectacular bash had models strutting for a good cause, with Fall fashions moving up and down the runway, wearing selections from DKNY, Joseph Abboud, Jessica McClintock, Armani Collezioni, and Dolce & Gabbana, to name a few. Star power gave the event even additional panache. Magic Johnson

This page and following page: *Macy's West Passport '01 was a splashy and touching event in which Macy's and American Express joined forces to raise money for AIDS organizations in Western countries. Major designers and high-profile celebrities participated in the event.*

VIVA

hosted a gala dinner auction benefiting the Magic Johnson Foundation. Other celebrity appearances included country music singing sensation Reba McEntire and Epic Records' recording artist Macy Gray, who performed. More than 3,000 guests attended the opening night gala, which included an exclusive VIP dinner and a cocktail and hors d'oeuvres reception. Passport is much more than a fashion show and because of it, millions of dollars raised were distributed among organizations that continue to provide support to those fighting HIV/AIDS.

RockOnColor Bra Show

Taking the fashion show to a trendy location hypes the event with theatricality and entertainment. Hosting a cocktail party and downtown Club Spa venue, Lily of France's fashion show introduced RockOnColor, a music-connected, fashion-inspired new collection of bras and panties in pulsating colors including hip hop pink, diva pearl, jammin' black, electric turq, orange strobe, coral jazz, and laser green.

Six of New York's top runway models and their bodyguards wore ensembles from up-and-coming young designer Margie Tsai. Each model evoked a different diva with colorful style as she opened her jacket or unbuttoned her shirt to reveal the RockOnColor bra.

Timing provides the venue with an additional attraction. The launch and party were timed around the Grammys, the MTV Awards, and the Oscars, because the target consumer, who is in the eighteen-to-thirty-four age range with a focus age of twenty-five, is "interested and involved with these events."

At the sizzling introduction of the RockOnColor event, Christine Royer introduced each girl as beefy "bodyguards" (hunky models from Wilhelmina) escorted her to the stage. These men in black with the requisite sunglasses to shield their eyes from the glare of paparazzi flashbulbs kept the crowd at bay as each girl posed on a series of staggered cubes.

Production talent included Graebar Productions for music; BLT Lighting for the light show; Wilhelmina Models for "divas (show models) and bodyguards"; supermodel Ingrid from Elite; styling and choreography by Christine Royer, CRC Consulting; hair by John Barrett; and makeup by Mac. Lori Zelenko, LSZ Communications, pulled the bash together and facilitated the press and public relations.

Quebec's Theatre Verité

With dramatic lighting, striking scenery, and a flair for spectacular fashion, Quebec Fashion Theatre, presented by the government of Quebec, highlighted twelve apparel and six avant garde home design manufacturers from Montreal. Quebec Fashion Theatre turned the tables on the traditional, run-of-the-mill fashion show by staging a theatre verité event through minidramas in twelve theater vignettes. When the curtain was raised, the collections were spotlighted in twelve captivating one-act plays. Each of the twelve apparel designers had their own stage on which to showcase representational garments from their Fall 2002 collections.

In most fashion events, the audience is seated while the models walk the runway. In this event, conceived by Sensation Mode of Montreal, the audience walks from stage to stage to review the Fall/Winter fashions that are presented through the staged minidramas. Thus, the twelve Montreal manufacturers of men's and women's apparel were simultaneously front and center in their own one-act plays. Two model/actors appeared in each manufacturer's vignette. Guests leisurely strolled from one vignette to the other and were captivated by each vignette's entertaining venue, as well as its fashion showcase. Select home fashion pieces from six creative companies were the backdrop to the action on stage.

The designers and companies included Shan for thoroughbred swimwear, Luk par Luc La Roche, concept designs for men, Margaret M suits and sportswear, Oscar Leopold for

In the Fall 2002, Quebec's Theatre Verité highlighted twelve clothing designers in a theater tableau setting. Audience members walked at their own pace from one vignette to another. In addition to apparel, each exhibit included home furnishings from six selected companies.

crafted leather, Mondor's massaging hose, Hilary Radley, outwear designer, and Louben's sophisticated career wear.

More than 300 guests attended this unique event, including retailers from the fashion and home design branches, trade and consumer press, and representatives from exhibiting companies.

Trade Terminology

Backstage logistics
Booker
Business manager
Catwalk
Collection coordinators
Customized orders
Designer appearance
Dressers
Electronic media
Entertainment vehicle
Fashion calendar
Fashion director
Fashion fund raiser
Fashion show stylist
Go-see
Hair designers
Makeup teams
Model agency
Music director
Music runway stylist
Press/public relations
Show producer
Stage manager
Star power
Trendy location
Trunk show
Venue
Wardrobe assistants

READING 11-1 The Trunk Show: Designers Take a Road Trip

BY ELIZABETH HAYT

NAPLES, Fla. It was perfect tennis weather at 11 a.m. on a recent Thursday, 80 degrees and sunny, but at Saks Fifth Avenue a dressing room was hard to come by. The Bill Blass spring 2002 trunk show was in town, with 62 sample dresses, suits and evening gowns, priced from $1,600 to $20,000, hanging on racks. A white-gloved waiter passed flutes of Champagne while sylph-like models in billowy ensembles shifted from one stiletto to the other, flamingo-style.

Lars Nilsson, a Swede given to banker's pinstripes and professorial eyeglasses, who took over the Bill Blass label last February, was selling his collection, one customer at a time.

"Try it with the petticoat to give that little picnic look," he told Elizabeth Star, handing over a red silk petticoat that she slipped on beneath a linen dress with awning stripes.

"If I invest in this," Ms. Star said, "no one else can have it in Naples. It's a small town." She wanted to avoid anything like a repeat of a scandalous incident two years ago, when two women appeared in the same gown at a charity gala.

"The store is keeping track of these things," Mr. Nilsson assured her.

Sue Lennane, who had canceled a trip to New Orleans to attend the trunk show, added her name to an order list, having decided on a gray flannel suit and platinum sequined slacks. "I buy 80 percent of my wardrobe at trunk shows," she said. "I get to see everything first."

Attention, trunk show shoppers: whether you live in Naples, New York City or Bala Cynwyd, Pa., stores and designers love you. They recognize that women who attend trunk shows are fashion-besotted, the kind of customers who follow runway news months before the clothes hit stores, and come in with checklists of must-haves.

And of course, they pay full retail.

"Customers are well versed; they print out Style.com," said the designer Michael Kors, who conducted a trunk show last week in Boca Raton, Fla. "We have a good customer in San Francisco. Last fall, she thought she had seen a shearling coat on the runway. She had bought a house in Idaho and wanted to wear it. She went to the trunk show in San Francisco and didn't see it because the sample was out on a shoot. She rearranged her schedule to come to New York to the trunk show, where she ended up buying it."

Contrary to popular perception, the shows are not invitation-only. Anyone can attend—announcements are mailed to stores' regular customers and sometimes supplemented by newspaper advertisements. Despite the name, no trunks are involved; designers' goods are displayed on racks, although the idea is much the same as when the Parisian couturier Paul Poiret toured Europe in 1911, visiting department stores with trunks of dresses that he displayed on mannequins. He invented the trunk show, said Alexandra Palmer, costume curator at the Royal Ontario Museum.

While the retail market in general is slouching toward a future of mass markdowns, trunk shows exhibit no signs of a slump. Because everything is full price, they attract people with money, and people with money have been immune so far to this recession, merchants say. By most reports, trunk show customers have bounced back from any hesitation engendered by the terrorist attacks of Sept. 11.

"Even in this difficult season, the trunk show and special-order business has continued to grow," said Ann Stordahl, senior vice president and general merchandise manager for women's apparel at Neiman Marcus. "The customer tends to be in our top level, and we didn't see any pullback with that customer."

For the fall and cruise collections sold last year, Neiman had a high double-digit increase in sales from its trunk shows compared with 2000. The Yves Saint Laurent boutique in New York recorded $1.1 million in spring trunk show orders, a 10 percent increase over its show for fall 2001. In early January, shoppers braved a wet snowstorm to visit the Chanel boutique on East 57th Street in Midtown in soggy mink coats and salt-stained leather boots, ordering $1 million of spring clothes and accessories.

Trunk shows drive 30 to 40 percent of Badgley Mischka's business. "Some of our biggest trunk shows are in Seattle and San Francisco," said Mark Badgley, who along with James Mischka designs for the label. "Some of our most elegant ones are in Detroit. We do big ones in New York, but in other communities they are more appreciative because they don't have the selection. There are women out there with a Ph.D. in trunk shows."

Suave salesmanship—sometimes from the designer in person—and the illusion of exclusivity help to move the merchandise. At the Saint Laurent show in New York, a sales associate told one shopper that a brown baby buffalo leather jacket, pierced and trimmed with tiny brass rings, was a steal at $2,995, and that only a few were available. A Vogue editor had already reserved one, the salesman let slip. The store received 48 orders.

"A trunk show is a chance to convince a client that if you don't buy it right now, you will never see anything so beautiful again," Boaz Mazor, a sales executive for Oscar de la Renta, said.

The smooth talk seems to work. Sixty percent of de la Renta's business comes from trunk shows. The company staged 162 around the country in 2001, three more than the previous year. Mr. de la Renta said that he had once known half the customers at his trunk shows at Bergdorf Goodman, but that last year he did not recognize a single woman—a sign that a new generation has discovered the trunk show and his label.

"She is not typical of the traditional customer," Mr. de la Renta said. "She is a professional, a psychologist or an executive. She will buy things that are more daring and extreme. You are dealing with a consumer who feels so much stronger about herself. You might have a fantastic top and suggest a pair of pants to them. They will say, 'No, I'm going to wear it with A/X jeans.' They are not bashful about how they will wear the item."

Trunk shows bring many customers a little closer to the experience of shopping directly from the runway. After the fall and spring catwalk shows, buyers and store owners view entire collections in designers' showrooms, either in New York or Europe. They make their selections based on what they think will sell well to their customers (bright colors for the South, neutrals for New York). But the merchandise is never shipped all at once.

The trunk show allows customers to view the breadth of a collection, and to see it weeks or months before garments arrive on the sales floor. (Trunk shows for spring clothing begin in October and extend through February; fall trunk shows start in April and continue through the summer.)

While many retailers maintain that trunk shows are profitable because there is a guaranteed taker for clothes at full price, that is not always the case. Department stores like Saks, Bergdorf Goodman and Neiman Marcus do not require prepayment for most orders, so if a customer never claims what she ordered, the store must place it on the racks and hope to sell it to someone else. To protect themselves, some smaller stores and specialty boutiques demand a deposit, which the shopper forfeits if she does not take the order—a situation that can make for trying customer relations.

For these reasons, Jeffrey Kalinsky, the owner of Jeffrey in New York and Atlanta, refuses to hold trunk shows. "I feel that asking for a deposit is taking advantage of the customer, and if you don't, you are taking a huge financial risk," Mr. Kalinsky said. "A lot of clients get caught up in the frenzy of the trunk show. It takes two to four months for the items to come in, and then they might not want them because they have been shopping between the time of the trunk show and the arrival of the merchandise. It is up to the salesperson to sell it for a second time."

"From my experience, a lot of trunk show business is phony business," he continued. "The client is being urged to say, 'Oh, I want it,' and then the store can say, 'Oh, I did this much trunk show business.' Then the piece comes in, and no one can enforce that the customer is going to take it. Or, sometimes a piece won't even make it to the store. As a merchant, I want to sell what is already in my store."

But the risk that high-priced clothes will go unsold is one most stores are willing to take. Robert Burke, the fashion director of Bergdorf Goodman, cited the example of a ruched black cotton blouse from Yves Saint Laurent, designed by Tom Ford for fall 2001, which was priced at $2,595. After seeing it on the runway, Bergdorf ordered five. Then at a trunk show in May, customers clamored for the blouse; 20 placed their names in an order book, with no money down. Expecting that not all would follow through, the store ordered nine of the blouses, for a total of 14. The store sold 12.

"Our customer travels a lot, has a few homes and doesn't know if she will be in town when the merchandise gets in," he said. "The only way to be sure to get it is to preorder it through a trunk show." The store holds 85 trunk shows of ready-to-wear a season, plus 105 trunk shows for jewelry and cosmetics.

While one might expect that designers, many of whom are now celebrities, might resent the time it takes to appear at trunk shows—not to mention having to push their clothes like lowly floor help—a number plunge right in.

Josh Patner, who, with Bryan Bradley, designs for Tuleh, relishes trunk shows for the feedback from customers. "Trunk shows are the most important market research a designer can do," he said. "A customer will tell you what she needs and has too much of. Collars too high! Button loop too short! Colors too harsh! We hear it all. I don't think you can be a good designer and not do trunk shows because if you don't, you are only concerned with the runway and not with the women who are paying for the clothes. It's like a chef who never tastes his own food."

READING 11-2 | Backstage with Makeup Artists

BY JULIE NAUGHTON, WITH CONTRIBUTIONS FROM ANDREA M. GROSSMAN, CASSANDRA CHIACCHIO, JENNY B. FINE, MATTHEW W. EVANS, LAURA KLEPACKI AND KRISTIN FINN

NEW YORK—It looked like a battle of the pretties.

Makeup looks on the New York ready-to-wear runways this season fell into two distinct camps: a dark-toned eye—often with a nude lip—or a classic red lip with very little on the eyes.

Diane Von Furstenberg's models fell in to the first camp, where makeup artist Ayako for Nars blended three shades of wine shadow to create offbeat cat's eyes. Bobbi Brown at Catherine Malandrino also embraced the dark eye—"But not too perfect. We wanted it too look like the model slept in and maybe had too much champagne," Brown said, smearing a greasy brown eye shadow from lid to browbone and finishing lips with a nude lipstick from her fall collection. Brown also did smoky, lined eyes in shades of charcoal, black and white at Nicole Miller.

The eyes at Christina Perrin weren't quite Elizabeth Taylor's in "Cleopatra," but they certainly were reminiscent of the 1963 film's look. Bold black lines curved out from the lid, something MAC's Ashley Ward termed "graphic." Ward also drew colors onto eyebrows with a new eye crayon called Spiked. Lips were a butterscotch color called Sis.

At Anne Klein, Tracy Murphy's centerpiece was an intense eye, using brown cream eye shadow from MAC on the eyelid and underneath the eye with Strobe Cream added to catch the light. Murphy rimmed the eyes with this season's twist on brown eyeliner: grayish kohl eye pencil. Murphy also chose smoky eyes at Badgley Mischka, where she drew the eyeliner out past the temples, then blended it, for a soft, blurry effect.

The smoke didn't clear elsewhere. At Bruce, Tom Pecheux used a mix of Shiseido's Goldleaf, a rich brown, and Silverscape, a grayish-blue, to completely cover the upper eyelid and to create a thick border underneath. A black pencil liner applied inside the eye created a stark outline "just to make it a bit more powerful," said Pecheux.

Linda Cantello aimed for "slightly decadent sexuality" at Carolina Herrera. Using her own eponymous cosmetics line, Cantello used silvery eye shadow and eyeliner, which she "smushed around," along with not-too-neat black mascara.

Teen brand Jane Cosmetics, in its first-ever Fashion Week appearance, provided fresh-faced simple looks for the MegaDenim show. Makeup artist Paige Smitherman and her team favored neutral lips using peaches and pinks and sheer browns. Cheeks got a dab of color on the apple.

"Henry and June meet Kiss," is how Charlie Green—who liked both smoky eyes and red lips—described the makeup look at Betsey Johnson. Pale skin served as a canvas for smoky gray eyes and matte, black-red lips. Cheeks were colored a rosy pink with Bourjois Blush Cendre de Roses Brune.

Miranda Joyce's lip choice at Matthew Williamson—MAC's true red Ruby Woo—popped straight off the runway, particularly since she chose to pair it only with a coating of black MAC mascara on the eyes. At Benjamin Cho, Shiseido's Miyako Okamoto also went very light around the eyes, saving her statement for the lips—where she used Shiseido's Strong Red, a brilliant crimson.

Sometimes the bright-red lip veered distinctly into berry territory, as at Cynthia Steffe, where Stila's Jeanine Lobell chose several lip shades, including a deep berry, from her upcoming long-wear lip color line, Demi Creme. Lobell also used a greenish-black eyeliner rather than black.

No matter what the season, there are always shows where you can count on minimalist makeup—like the classically elegant cosmetics looks always seen at Ralph Lauren and Calvin Klein. This season, Tom Pecheux joined the Upper East Side brigade at Chaiken, teaming pale skin with peach cheeks and sheer, pink lips. And, of course, there are always the wild cards—like Anna Sui, whose carnival of color included stripes of blue, peach and lavender eye shadow. At Bill Blass, Frances Hathaway for MAC used a bit of blackened teal and blackened plum on the eyes, while at Oscar de la Renta, Raphael Pita for MAC used deep metallic gray eye shadow, which graduated into a red loose pigment above and below, along with a blue-brown loose pigment placed on top with a light hand to create a "tapestry of color," said Pita.

But all of the looks had one thing in common: pretty, clear, natural skin, sending a clear message: If you don't have it already, start investing in treatment products. Add it to the list of reasons why retailers report that sales of treatment lines are booming.

Source: *Women's Wear Daily*, Feb. 15, 2002, p. 12. Courtesy of Fairchild Publications, Inc.

READING 11-3 | Rodriguez, Bergdorf Goodman Team Up for Early Trunk Show

BY ERIC WILSON

NEW YORK—Even before the last of the fall collections wrap up this week in Paris, Bergdorf Goodman is getting behind some of the clear stars of the season with an accelerated trunk show schedule, including a personal appearance with Narciso Rodriguez on April 2.

The store will host events to showcase several fall lines in the coming weeks, a few weeks ahead of the normal trunk show schedule, in an effort to create a more experimental atmosphere where designers can gain immediate customer reaction to their work, said Robert Burke, vice president and senior fashion director. The strategy is also designed to reinforce the image of Bergdorf Goodman as a retailer willing to quickly put its resources behind a designer of the moment.

"We have a very demanding customer who is extremely fashion savvy and aware of the collections," said Ron Frasch, chairman and chief executive officer of the store. "Narciso's was truly one of the best collections we had seen and we are very anxious to present it to our customers as soon as possible. This also continues to enhance our position in the marketplace as a store that takes a quick and decisive lead on getting collections first."

By moving up the trunk show schedule, which normally kicks off for the fall season in late April, designers also will have the opportunity to respond to the reactions of actual shoppers, rather than buyers or the press, Burke said.

"This will give them an immediate read on the collection and an opportunity to tweak the collection if they need to," he said.

Rodriguez's appearance will include a three-day trunk show through April 4, while BG is also in talks with other designers about staging similarly early events.

"It's great to do a trunk show so close to having shown," Rodriguez said. "The reaction you get from the press and retailers generates a lot of excitement, but the most important reaction you get is from your customers. When it's so fresh, it will make for a good experiment."

Trunk show sales are also an important ingredient in his estimated $20 million in annual wholesale volume.

As for any tweaking that might come out of the event, that might not fare as well. If a customer asked to change a look from red to purple, for instance, Rodriguez said the answer would be, "No."

Source: *Women's Wear Daily*, March 11, 2003, p. 2. Courtesy of Fairchild Publications, Inc.

12

Cosmetics and Fragrance Industry

The cosmetics and fragrance industry comprises two of the most important segments of the beauty business. Their product lines command strategic main floor retail, real estate space in department and specialty stores. Why? Because the beauty business is big business. It maintains its global market share by operating in a constant state of flux, reinventing itself with new product launches.

According to industry sources, department store sales in 2001 of prestige brands of color cosmetics, which grew faster than the skincare category, represented 32 percent of the market share, $2.3 billion worth of retail business. However, the total of makeup, skincare, sun, and body care products represented $7.1 billion at retail, while treatment lines garnered $1.8 billion, a 25 percent share of the market.

The women's fragrance market accounts for 26 percent of the market with $1.9 billion sales annually. The men's fragrance market stands at 14 percent of the market, with $1 billion annually at retail. Clearly the women's and men's fragrance markets are greater than even the market for color cosmetics.

With technology giving women control over their lives, customers are looking for high-tech and high-touch products. They want miracle ingredients and want to instantly comprehend what those products will do for them. As a result, customers seek out the best products to satisfy their needs, and product developers are challenged to create new solutions in hair, cosmetic, skin care, fragrance, and environmental aromatic products for the home.

SIDEBAR 12-1 | Industry Organizations

Cosmetic Executive Women, Inc. (CEW) is a not-for-profit trade organization of approximately 1,400 executives in the beauty, cosmetics, fragrance, and related industries. Based in New York City, CEW has associations in France and the United Kingdom. As a leading trade organization in the beauty industry, CEW helps develop the career contacts, knowledge, and skills of its members so that they may advance on both professional and personal levels.

In 1985 the organization expanded its mission to include education, philanthropy, and industry development. In addition to member services, CEW's charitable efforts include the Cosmetic Executive Women Foundation, a New York-based not-for-profit charitable organization that funds charities dedicated to benefiting women, including Women in Need (WIN), which serves homeless and underprivileged women and their children; and Cancer and Careers, an interactive resource and community for working women with any type of cancer.

Beauty Awards

This annual program recognizes outstanding product innovation in the following categories: Facial Skincare Product (cleanser or toner, eye treatment, mask, peel or scrub, moisturizer, problem-solving product); Women's and Men's Scents; Makeup Product (eye, face, lip, multipurpose, nail); Hair Product (hair care, hair coloring); Sun Product (sun protection, tanning, self-tanning, or after-sun product for face and/or body); Bath and Body Treatment (lotion, bath and shower gel, deodorant); and Home/Environment Scent (fragrances for the home including spray, candles, potpourri). Members vote to determine the finalists and the winner in each category.

Achiever Award

The Achiever Award was established in 1975 to honor a leading woman executive who has contributed significantly to the growth of the beauty industry and the advancement of women. Recipients for 2001 were Jean Hoehn Zimmerman, executive vice president fragrance & beauty, Chanel Inc., and Linda Wells, editor in chief, Allure. Past recipients included Bobbi Brown, chief executive officer of Bobbi Brown Professional Cosmetics, and Andrea Jung, president and chief executive officer of Avon Products, Inc. In 2002, CEW honored ten accomplished female executives who are innovators in their fields.

Career*Insights* Series

The Career*Insights* series, an exclusive benefit of CEW members, holds programs monthly, except for August and December. In a relaxed small-group setting, members have an opportunity to receive invaluable career advice from the most successful women in the industry.

In the cosmetics industry, the professionals who guide a firm into new product development are identified by various titles, including senior vice president corporate innovation, senior vice president product marketing worldwide, global product development, and senior vice president, marketing and product development. In the fragrance industry, titles include product category director, corporate fragrance developer, and creative fragrance director.

TRACKING TRENDS

The reality of all these titles is the fact that product developers are keen observers, investigators of customer needs and wants, and influential prognosticators and developers of skincare, makeup, hair, sun, bath, and body products, as well as home/environment scents and women's and men's fragrances. Leading marketers pay attention to trends that will impact the development of innovative products and drive launches into successful business. They sharpen their creativity by keeping tabs on everything from popular culture, entertainment, music, art, and theater to fashion and color forecasts, the Prêt, and the Haute Couture.

The study of demographics provides insights into population trends, income levels, and the state of the economy. Psychographic studies pinpoint the direction in which consumers' lifestyle preferences are emerging. New technology and analysis of the competition also contribute to new product development.

Forecasting Trends

Research in color, fashion, and consumer trends is among the key factors in product development. However, the product developer cannot take some trends too literally. For example, if green is fashion forward, what does that mean to beauty and fragrances?

Jeanine Recckio, beauty futurologist president of the firm Mirror Mirror and creator of the *Crystal Ball Beauty Trend Report*, says, "There are many excellent color forecasting services, but basically they are not cosmetic specific. If a trend is all about the ocean how do you translate it to a lipstick?"

Mirror Mirror's Crystal Ball Beauty Trend Report *is packaged to reflect the future. The CD-ROM label and insert are sleek and futuristic in design, with a clever use of light that lets the user know that he or she will be "illuminated" about trends in the beauty industry.*

To demystify trends, the *Crystal Ball Beauty Trend Report*, the first trend report to focus entirely on the beauty business, is an illuminating resource designed to fill the gap between the product developer and research and development. Compiled by the Mirror Mirror Imagination Group's team of global trend spotters and beauty futurologists, the *Crystal Ball Beauty Trend Report* helps companies "see into their future" and become the trendsetters. The report pinpoints futuristic predictions in a comprehensive array of beauty-focused areas, including makeup, skincare, fragrance, home fragrance, candles, spa, salon, hair, new packaging, ingredient ideas, in-store merchandising, and trends in the teen market.

Futuristic Predictions

According to Mirror Mirror, in the future your medicine cabinet will let you know that you will be out of foundation on Thursday. It will automatically order a refill through the Internet while you are at the office. Your cosmetic compact will talk to you. It will alert you when it is time to powder your nose and gloss your lips. New technology will create self-adjusting lipstick that will adjust to all lighting. The mirror in your purse will detect your mood, and it will release the appropriate fragrance aroma to change your mood while it plays music to entertain you and alter your aura. These are just some of the futuristic predictions the Mirror Mirror Imagination Group foresees in its beauty future-telling forecasts.

Provocative Ideas

To provoke and inspire new product ideas, clients who subscribe to the *Crystal Ball Beauty Trend Report,* twice a year receive a large see-through attaché-shaped box that actually lights up when you open it. It is filled with more than forty-five pages of futuristic forecasts, predictions, visions, and ideas in fashion, color, style, and consumer attitudes. Each customer receives a miniature crystal ball to ponder new ideas. A smaller box is filled with unique samples of beauty products and inspirational items from all over the world—all to tweak ideas for product development. Each month subscribers also receive monthly "readings" on emerging global trends. One month it is something unexpected, something special, something that takes your breath away, enabling your mind to think a little deeper. It could be a divine new essential oil from India or a copy of a food fusion menu from a trendy restaurant in London. A consummate trend spotter, Jeanine found inspirational books in an Asian bookstore. Each book was packaged in see-through vinyl and appeared to be floating in water, which could prove to be a cool trend for beauty packaging. Jeanine says, "If water is the trend what does it mean to fragrance, makeup, fashion, food, automobiles, and industrial products and packaging?"

Launching a New Product

Cosmetic firms take different paths in product development. No rigid rule governs the way product developers conceptualize ideas for new product launches.

ESTÉE LAUDER: IMAGINEERING

At Estée Lauder Companies Inc., however, Anne Carullo, senior vice president corporate innovation, is part of a team in the "Imagineering" group that provides a constant flow of ideas and concepts for all the brands of the organization. Brands under Ms. Carullo's direction include Prescriptives Estée Lauder and the Kate Spade line.

"This elite and diverse group is an efficient way to organize people from different disciplines within the company," notes Ms. Carullo. Individuals typically are invited to join the team, which includes a variety of individuals from different divisions of the company—from packaging to sales, advertising to public relations. "It provides a cross-fertilization of people and ideas for our 'ideation sessions' which create thought-provoking ideas that may lead to new product development."

Brainstorming Session

Visually monitored by a guide, the Ideation Session takes a journey into mind exploring inspiration. "We sometimes call it Mind Walking," says Ms. Carullo. The idea is to walk a person through their daily regimen and, from this path, find a menu of different techniques to envision and develop big and small product ideas.

Competition Evaluation

Another path to product development is to identify products in the market and evaluate what is missing from a firm's product line. This procedure involves looking at the competitive landscape and checking out the competition. Such an evaluation includes:

- Looking at the competitive field and evaluating what is in the market that the firm wants to reinvent.
- Brainstorming what is so good about the product.

INDUSTRY PROFILE 12-1 | Anne Carullo

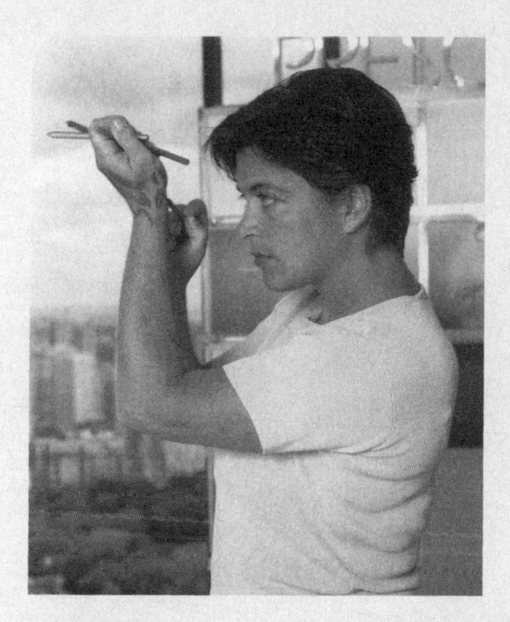

Anne Carullo, Prescriptives' senior vice president for marketing and product development, is constantly looking for new ideas for applying technology to cosmetics.

Affable, pert, and pretty, Anne Carullo, Prescriptives' senior vice president for marketing and product development worldwide, greets visitors with an effervescent enthusiasm. That's the kind of spirit that she infuses into her obsession with marrying technology to cosmetics.

Achieving a Goal

However, growing up with three brothers on Mulberry Street in New York City, Ms. Carullo openly admits that as a young girl she was not especially fascinated with makeup. One thing was certain, this future cosmetic executive did envision herself climbing the corporate ladder, wearing fashionable suits, and having an office and secretary.

That goal took a path through New York University and the Fashion Institute of Technology, where she graduated with a degree in marketing. Unabashedly, Ms. Carullo admits that she cheated on a typing test and landed her first job at Revlon. Ambitious and serious about her work, she was a keen observer of everything in the business. At one point, she saw an attractive woman from product development come through the office testing mascara and lipstick on coworkers. A spark of enthusiasm caught her imagination. "I decided I wanted to do that," recalls Carullo. With a job promotion from within the company, Ms. Carullo fulfilled her dream and moved into a product development position, which had become available.

She paid her dues, so to speak and worked at other firms including L'Oréal and Max Factor before joining Estée Lauder and later transferring to Prescriptives.

Today, Ms. Carullo splits her time between her New York office in Manhattan and regular visits to the Long Island laboratory of Prescriptives' parent company, Estée Lauder, where new ideas are tested and developed. As part of the innovation team, Ms. Carullo is a consummate idea person. On the wavelength of creativity she envisions extending existing lines and investigating new product ideas.

Sitting in her office she experiments with a new formula. The picture of the product developer/tester, she dabs some of the lotion on her hand and observes its performance by evaluations of content, blending, and drying time. "The most difficult aspect of achieving the right formula is that

Carullo was inspired to develop the Prescriptives product called "Magic," while traveling to work on the commuter train. Developing and marketing the concept was a carefully planned program.

the foundation must create an optical illusion of light emitting qualities and yet it must moisturize," she says. "The constant evaluation and testing process makes each day a challenge, but one that is met head on with renewed enthusiasm. Product development is an exciting field of study, one that is always reinventing, renewing, or giving birth to a new product."

Balancing a Career

Like many career women today, Anne Carullo balances the demands of a career and her personal life with considerable calm and dexterity. The mother of a seven-year-old son and wife of Louis, a neighborhood boy she met when she was eighteen, Ms. Carullo juggles her responsibilities with aplomb.

As for a career in the cosmetics industry Anne advises, "Get a college degree in marketing, promotion, or advertising, hone your skills, stay curious and inspired, and be prepared to work hard to reach your goal. Perseverance and determination can also serve to get you there."

- Discussing what can be changed, what improvements can be made.
- Evaluating what can be done to create a new product or to reinvent a product for a niche market.

Marketing Department

A request for new products can begin in the marketing department, which may identify what is missing in a company's product line. For example, market research indicators report that most women want to look natural when wearing foundation, as if they were not wearing makeup at all. While similar foundations may be core business, this information may encourage product developers to throw out everything used before and start with new ingredients to develop a product based on the market research department's findings.

Conceptual Development: One Product's Story

"Absolute accident can be another factor in conceptual development," admits Ms. Carullo. "A brilliant idea just comes to you in the most unlikely place." She cites an example of serendipitous inspiration, that resulted in the Prescriptives product called "Magic." "I was eight months pregnant at the time and as usual I was traveling to work on the Metro North train when I noticed a lovely woman sitting across from me who looked radiant and beautiful. I wondered why she looked better than I did. She looked fresh and glowing. I realized one of the major differences was that her skin looked unblemished and reflected light with a translucency that gave her skin a healthy glow. I wondered how a product could reflect light off the skin and create the same radiance. That was the beginning of an incredible journey into the research of light dancing materials that camouflaged imperfections and tricked light with optical raw materials that would enhance a radiant complexion."

A Working Model

The big idea had to be visualized so that upper management, the decision makers, could visualize the product. This required development of a working model, along with a complete presentation augmented with image boards. With the model, upper management would get the full impact of the product as it would be presented to the customer.

Research and Development

The next step involved opening a dialogue about the idea with the research and development (R&D) group, which began to find raw materials to create concept formulas. Breakthrough optics included the light dancing materials and prismatic textures designed by the New Venture Laboratory of Estée Lauder Inc. The result was a product to conceal visible lines, mask hyperpigmentation, and obscure imperfections. These synthetic, trilayered tints and clear prisms reflect and deflect light to impact a vision of translucent, radiant skin.

The first Magic products included Illuminating Liquid Potion, Illuminating Cream Potion, and Liquid Powder—all colorless substances with light-diffusing particles. Cooling Wand, a 70 percent water stick with blue-reflecting particles, was used around eyes to brighten and firm the skin.

The package design team was then brought into the picture to develop different bottles, jars, tubes, and wand shapes. The package designers created prototypes of container shapes in glass or plastic. The outside box to hold the containers was finalized in silver, reflecting light by its shiny surface.

Advertising/copywriters next developed the product's name and the wording to describe the product from the customer's point of view. The advertising department developed concept advertising in order to visualize how to present the product to the customer. Counter cards and other promotional aids were also considered at this stage.

The launch/public relations department suggested venues for the press launch in the cosmetic company's offices or at an outside venue.

Feasibility Development

Before a product goes into production, a product presentation is given to upper management. At this point, upper management is introduced to the complete developmental stages of the product, including all the steps from innovation to advertising and public relations. Feasibility development takes three to four months to evaluate the concept. The product development team waits for feedback from upper management, as many different points of view may need to be evaluated before the product gets the "go ahead."

Market Ready

When a product gets the "go" message, the product development team articulates the product so that it is market ready. The secondary strategy on the launch is critical. The product gets calendarized, so that the timetable for the product launch is met, and the brand new product is sold at the retail department store counters in eighteen months.

Lancôme's mascara, Amplicils, was developed through a seven-step process. This process, from brainstorming to launch, required input from a global team of experts.

According to the firm, in the initial launch stage, the Magic collection was launched with very little advertising, but did receive full-page editorial support by the beauty editors. The product line went from zero market share to a $14 million business.

LANCÔME: AN EXAMPLE OF GLOBAL TECHNIQUES

The technique utilized by cosmetic companies to merchandise products in the global marketplace starts with consumer research that includes evaluating consumer needs. That is the philosophy of Lancôme, the prestige department store brand owned by the French beauty behemoth, L'Oréal Group.

Lancôme marketing provides the following outline of techniques that were employed in product development for the Paris-based cosmetic giant's Panoramic Volume Mascara, called "Amplicils."

Global Product Launch

"It is important to look at the market areas that are growing and to look for a unique opportunity to satisfy a need," says Maeve Coburn, senior vice president of marketing, Lancôme-USA. "It all starts with the consumer, and establishing their needs. Lancôme works on global launches that follow an order of activity that begins with our global teams."

Lancôme's global product launches are based on the work of an international marketing team, called "Affaire de Marque" (business of the brand), which includes professionals from many disciplines.

- *Brainstorming:* The global teams meet four times a year and are in constant communication by telephone, fax, or e-mail to discuss creative ideas. As the industry leader in the prestige mascara category, the Lancôme global team agreed that what women want most is a mascara that provides intense volume for their lashes while it curls and separates.

- *Product Concept:* Recognizing that volume mascara is a key consumer need, a product concept is written to explain the unusual selling properties of a new mascara that would amplify lashes, both with volume and with curves, and at the same time separate lashes one by one for dramatic-looking expressive eyes.
- *New Vocabulary:* Establishing a new vocabulary for describing the intense volume properties of the mascara is another step toward identifying the new product.
- *Copywriters:* The internal copywriters brainstorm and establish a list of appropriate names. Many ideas come from the creative team, which creates a list of names that might be used to identify the mascara.
- *Consumer's Response:* At this point, Lancôme presents mascara product names to consumers through focus group sessions. Lancôme waits for feedback to determine which name would be a market fit.
- *The Juice:* Lancôme research goes into fast-forward mode while the R&D laboratories in France, Asia, and the United States work on "the juice," the term that refers to the ingredients that will go into the final mascara product.
- *Packaging:* The brush and juice need beautiful packaging. The package developers work in tandem with the juice makers to create the most effective mascara and container. The unique lash separating brush, which will be patented, is equally as important as the actual product. In addition, in any mascara product, the wiper, which controls the amount of product deposited in the brush, also plays a critical role

Blind Testing

When the product concept is perfected, an outside market research firm will conduct a product acceptance test outside the New York City area in two or three geographic areas in the

SIDEBAR 12-2 | Nonanimal Testing and Biodegradable Products

It is common knowledge that in recent years there has been strong consumer demand for no animal testing on cosmetic products. When this became a "cause célebre," women exercised their right to support the issue of no animal testing and were reluctant to purchase certain products. The power of the consumer proved effective, as changes occurred in testing and labeling. That is not to say that the beauty industry was not already tuned into consumer concerns, but cosmetic companies were clearly on the same wavelength and quickly responded with effective marketing that addressed the issue.

While testing of a new product before it is merchandised to the consumer is essential, cosmetic company labels today identify brands as consciously formulated products that are not tested on animals. Using the same philosophy, cosmetic companies also focused on socially responsible issues, such as the environment. As a result, bottles and jars are identified as recyclable and packages as biodegradable.

A Holistic Launch: Natural Ingredients

Sally Malanga is a visionary and founder of a socially responsible company called Ecco Bella Botanicals, a product line that was created in protest of animal testing and the use of many synthetic components prevalent in the cosmetics industry. Ecco Bella's 2002 launch introduced a new kind of flower power in FlowerColor Cosmetics. The product line features elegant new natural formulas made from high-quality essential oils, vitamins, and emollients.

Ms. Malanga called the company Ecco Bella because the expression means "behold beautiful" and embodies the firm's commitment to the natural products industry. The company logo is Botticelli's painting *The Birth of Venus.* An appropriate symbol, Venus is the Roman goddess of love and beauty.

Natural Ingredients

Ms. Malanga says, "We use flower waxes that come from flowers in nature, that are best known for their healing abilities: soothing and softening lavender and chamomile, sage and sunflower. Our philosophy is to provide women with a line that truly blurs the line between color cosmetics and skin care. It's very enticing to use all these natural ingredients in our products." She then adds, "Nature provides the most wonderful raw materials such as exotic extracts, cold-pressed herbs, and essential oils from magnificent flowers, they have a life-force that makes our products especially effective."

Ecco Bella's product line is extensive, ranging from Skin Survival Day Cream and Night Cream to pure and natural body lotion made of natural and organic ingredients combined in formulas to improve the skin. Holistic remedies also include a soft and soothing cleanser and toner, a purifying cleanser and toner, daily exfoliant, and Moisture-to-Go, a super moisturizer.

Packaging Concept

Package designer Joseph R. Messina designed Ecco Bella's luxe eco-paperback, portable compacts, which feature compartments to organize eyeshadow, eyeliner, and blush. Made of recycled corrugated heavy weight paper designed to last, each compact comes complete with mirror and space to insert different products and colors.

The single Paperback Face Powder compact contains an authentic Ecco Bella Flower-Color formula, based on flower wax coated with pigments and talc-free powder fortified with aloe, vitamin E, and green tea. According to Ms. Malanga, the flower wax enriched colors go on smoother, more evenly, leaving a dewy soft finish that lasts. Elegant, efficient, and ecological, the paperback compacts will gently biodegrade when they are ready to be recycled.

As a marketing strategy, Mr. Messina designed the lotion bottles to be flat, rather than round, with curved sides. "This shape gives the bottles better visual representation on shelf space at retail, and has an added advantage because more flat bottles can be displayed than round ones," notes Mr. Messina.

Commitment to Help

One of the most important aspects of Ecco Bella is Sally Malanga's commitment to helping others and teaching other people how to help as well. In 1986, she joined the board of directors of Friends of Animals, Inc., a Connecticut-based not-for-profit group that protects endangered species and actively promotes animal welfare.

Ms. Malanga continues to recognize our obligation to respect animals and the environment. Through her products, she educates consumers and raises money for a variety of causes. Free Ecco Bella products are donated to local women's shelters and physically disabled workers are given employment opportunities at Ecco Bella. "My company is truly committed to my beliefs," she comments. "Through Ecco Bella, we aim to do the right thing and really make a difference."

A Home-Based Start Up

Although large companies dominate the cosmetic industry, there is still room for new entrepreneurs. One such case is Ecco Bella Botanicals, which began in Sally Malanga's home, with a one-car garage/warehouse and two feline assistants. In the beginning, she sold, packed, and shipped all orders herself. She began sending free samples of her new products to health food stores. The response was positive, and today Ecco Bella products are sold in natural food stores and many salons nationwide. The all-natural Ecco Bella line has grown to include skin, hair, and beauty products, free from animal testing and holistic dermatologist recommended.

United States. The product will be presented in generic packaging, and it will not be identified by name. The mix of consumers at this test stage will consist of a good cross-section of prestige department store shoppers and non-Lancôme users.

At this point, the global creative team waits for feedback on the performance of the juice, the brush, and the satisfaction level of the product. This input will provide invaluable responses to a series of questions that Lancôme will utilize to tweak the product for full launch production.

Advertising Concepts

The advertising agency is briefed about the product and the R&D team prioritizes the product's benefits. The agency writes up a concept proposal for the advertising campaign, and a star spokesperson is chosen to endorse the product. For Amplicils, it is the model and actress, Uma Thurman.

The Photo Shoot

A photographer is selected to shoot many versions of beauty visuals, but he or she selects only the most outstanding photograph for submission. Management will accept the recommendation or ask to see other versions before making the final decision on the image that best expresses the Amplicils product.

Advertising Copy

The advertising agency works on a headline and selling line to hook the customer. More testing takes place. A marketing company performs a concept product test. Prototype advertisements are inserted in a standard magazine to ascertain clutter breakthrough and to see how the consumer recalls the product and brand name and what it does and whether she is interested in it. Based on these findings Lancôme will go into a full launch.

However, it is essential to have a local message and, depending on the culture, the advertising copy will communicate the product differently. For example, the French consumer has a more intellectual approach to product and wants more explanation, while the U.S. customer wants to know "what can the product do for me."

The Launch

As a general rule, Lancôme does not do big parties for every launch. However, a new model and a new face may be the catalyst for a huge party, at, for example, the Temple of Dendur at the Metropolitan Museum of New York.

Amplicils, however, had a public relations launch at Lancôme's executive offices. The support of the beauty editors who endorsed the product in editorials resulted in reams of publicity for months to come.

SALLY BEAUTY SUPPLY: BEAUTY FOR THE MASSES

To position its beauty supplies in the fashion arena, Sally Beauty Supply, touted to be the largest beauty supply company in the world, participated in the Mercedes-Benz Fashion Week in 2002 by providing makeup and hair looks for a youthful collection.

Bold color moved from fabric to face at the "Girls Rule!" Fall 2002 show in New York. Oliver Dow and Darren Greenblatt, show producers, had a vision to create a unique group show aimed at spotlighting the teen market and the young design talent responsible for creative teen fashions.

Sponsored by Sally Beauty Supply and *Teen Magazine*, "Girls Rule!" featured seven designer collections aimed at the junior market. The stars of the show were Chris Kirkpatrick of 'Nsync, who showed his FuMan Skeeto clothing line, and Darren Hayes, the voice of Savage Garden. Hayes opened the show singing his debut solo single. Kristi Fuhrmann, spokesperson for Sally Beauty Supply and makeup and hair key for MTV, designed brilliantly colorful makeup and hair for the young models who walked the runway.

While the clothes ranged from cutting-edge funk to fresh and frilly, the underlying theme of it all was feminine. Kristi took her cue from the feminine theme, creating hair with curls and color and faces with soft lips and colorful eyes. Kristi and her team used Manic Panic from Sally Beauty Supply to dye hair extensions brilliant blue, hot pink, bright purple, and sizzling orange. A cascade of ringlets and soft curls was created with "Gold 'n Hot 1" Curling Iron and a retro look of marcelled hair showed up in tiny waves created with a Helen of Troy Gold-Plated Crimper.

Eyes lit up the face with strong shadow that picked up the color of the hair. Ms. Fuhrmann and her team used Beautiful Eye Pencils in black to set off eyes and give them shape, then lavished on lots of mascara to make eyes look huge.

"Girls Rule!" is one of the hottest, most eagerly anticipated shows of Fashion Week, attracting more than 900 retailers and press members, as well as young celebrities.

COSMETICS AND FUND RAISING

Celebrity tie-ins with fund raising products give the cosmetics company a high-energy profile at both trade and consumer levels. Altruistic programs show the public that a company is socially responsible and also promotes corporate philanthropy.

THE FRAGRANCE INDUSTRY

Fragrances have had a fascinating allure through the history of scents, aromatic plants, and precious perfume bottles. Although the French "invented" the word perfume, they were not the first to use it. In fact, people have been aware of and have been using fragrance since prehistoric days. Early people were known to soak fragrant woods and resins in water and oil and then rub their bodies with the liquid. The first use of perfume!

Over the centuries, fragrance has defined sexuality and established status and social rank in society. Perfume has not lost any of its mystery or magic. A secret poison seduced the lovers in *Romeo and Juliet* to eternal sleep. Catherine de Medici was known for using perfumes, as well as poisons. Perhaps this is where the term "a killer fragrance" comes from! References

SIDEBAR 12-3 The Cosmetic, Toiletry, and Fragrance Association

As the national representative of the personal care products industry, the Cosmetic, Toiletry, and Fragrance Association (CFTA) provides a full range of services to support the industry's needs and interests in the scientific, legal, regulatory, legislative, and international fields. The association also takes a leadership role in coordinating public service, educational, and government affairs activities.

The association represents a highly visible industry. Its products are used every day by nearly everyone. In addition, the personal care products industry is also an important factor in the nation's economy, employing directly or indirectly more than two million people. CTFA has about 600 member companies, including manufacturers and distributors of personal care products.

Associate members include suppliers of ingredients, raw materials, and packaging services used in the production and marketing of finished products, as well as consumer and trade publications. Located throughout the United States and abroad, CFTA members market the vast majority of all personal care products sold in the United States. Trade sources estimate the industry's annual sales in 2001 exceeded $30 billion. CFTA's activities benefit the industry and consumers through the development of new scientific techniques, testing methods, and other discoveries that make continued marketing of sale and effect products possible.

The five day trade fair Cosmoprof, held in Bologna, Italy, according to *Women's Wear Daily* (March 15, 2002) attracted 129,827 visitors. Cosmoprof represents the opportunity for

This page and following page: *Cosmoprof's annual show offers exhibitors and visitors an opportunity to share trends and developments in the increasingly international beauty business. The five-day fair includes meetings, exhibits, and demonstrations of products.*

cosmetic industry professionals to keep pace with the fast internationalization of the beauty business and to have a global and multicultural vision of the latest trends and innovations. More than 1,700 exhibitors target international markets, including all sectors of the cosmetics industry: fragrances, makeup, professional beauty care, equipment, accessories, gift items, as well as packaging, machinery, raw materials, and services for the cosmetics industry.

Italy's Beauty Awards, the "Accademia del Profumo" are presented to best fragrance, best package, and best advertising communication in the male and female categories. The winner of the best fragrance award received the European FiFi award for Italy from Annette Green, the former president of the American Fragrance Foundation.

Cosmoprof Asia is held in Hong Kong, the capital of the beauty industry in the Asia Pacific area. Cosmoprof Cosmetica is held in São Paulo, Brazil.

to perfumes such as frankincense and myrrh are common throughout the Bible, an indication of how important fragrance was in everyday life. In ancient times, travelers plied their trade on the spice routes. Exotic spices and aromatics were highly prized as a source of barter as they were thought to enhance beauty, ward off disease, and dispel foul odors.

Today's fragrances and aromatics have not developed far beyond their ancient purpose. Fragrances, aromatherapy, and environmental scents are major product categories that not only enhance the lifestyles of men and women, but also satisfy the demand for emotional, spiritual, and sexual consumer needs.

SIDEBAR 12-4 | The Fragrance Foundation

The positive, global role of fragrances that not only make a fashion statement but also enhance the lifestyle and environments of men and women is largely the result of the dedicated efforts of The Fragrance Foundation (TFF), the not-for-profit, educational arm of the international fragrance industry. It was founded in 1949 by a group of industry leaders and is supported by membership categories including Active (manufacturers and suppliers), Associate (media, advertising and marketing agencies, financial service firms, consultants, package designers, etc.), and Retailers.

By the late 1950s, however, the organization had become defunct. In 1961, Annette Green was approved by an industry group trying to save TFF. At the time she headed up her own public relations/marketing agency, Annette Green Association. Although there were no funds available, Ms. Green agreed to join in the effort to rebuild the Foundation on a pro bono basis. It took her ten years to turn the organization around.

The FiFi Awards

Hollywood has its Oscars and the fragrance industry has the FiFi Awards. Considered the highest honor of the fragrance world, the FiFi Awards, held at formal ceremonies in June each year, are attended by celebrities and international members of the fragrance industry. Annette Green, former president of the Fragrance Foundation, conceived the idea of honoring the fragrance industry's creative achievements, and since its introduction, thirty-one years ago, the award has become an icon for the global fragrance industry.

In 1975, Pierre Dinand was commissioned by The Fragrance Foundation to design a crystal award. His creation, a crystal sculpture featuring two 12″ abstract columns embracing a droplet became an internationally acclaimed symbol. In 1989, the award was nicknamed FiFi by John Ledes, publisher of *Beauty Fashion* and *Cosmetics World* and has since been trademarked. The FiFi Award categories include:

- Fragrance Stars of the Year
- Bath and Body Star of the Year
- Best Packaging

- Best National Advertising Campaigns
- Technological Breakthrough
- The Most Original Magazine Feature

The "Fragrance Hall of Fame" award honors one men's or women's fragrance. Election to "Hall of Fame" honors a unique individual who is the personification of talent, which has distinguished the industry from the beginning.

The first women's FiFi award went to Chanel 19 in 1973. In 1975, Paco was awarded the first men's FiFi. Past recipients have included the fragrance by Sophia Loren, Obsession by Calvin Klein, Elizabeth Taylor's Passion, Polo by Ralph Lauren, Estée Lauder Pleasures, and Aqua Di Gio Pour Homme by Giorgio Armani.

The award has also become an icon for the global fragrance industry. In 1993, the first annual European FiFi Awards for the most successful men's and women's fragrances of the year were presented in the United Kingdom, France, Germany, Italy, and Spain.

National FiFi Week

National FiFi Week is celebrated in June, as part of the Foundation's celebration of the FiFi Awards. It has been conceived to celebrate the FiFi nominees, finalists, and past winners, and is a weeklong celebration of activities includes the opening ceremonies and the mayor's official recognition of National FiFi Week. Throughout the country, retail department stores feature the nominees in stores and in windows. The individual nominees and winners often plan special events.

The Annette Green Museum

In 1999, as a tribute to Ms. Green's contributions to the industry, the board of directors of the Foundation established the Annette Green Museum, the first in America devoted to the world of fragrance and its cultural, historical, and psychological impact on society. "It is the first of its kind, devoted solely to the joys and pleasures of the sense of smell, sight and touch," says Ms. Green. "Each exhibition was intended to give visitors a sense of how everything about a fragrance is conceived including name, color, packaging and advertising."

The first exhibition, "50 Years of Fragrance in America" featured a time capsule of 250 scents featured from 1950 through the 1990s, fragrance commercials from 1949 to the present, and vintage posters and vintage fragrance bottles. Special museum lecture series are organized in the Foundation's conference center and usually correspond to the current exhibition.

Fragrance Development

International Flavors and Fragrances Inc. (IFF), a leading creator and manufacturer of flavors and fragrances used in a wide variety of consumer products, holds a premier position in fragrances and is recognized as a worldwide leader in flavors. The

INDUSTRY PROFILE 12-2 | Vera Wang

Vera Wang, known for her bridal and evening wear, has used her romantic instincts and creative skills to develop her own fragrance.

"Fragrance provokes the senses and conjures up memories in inexplicable ways. The significance of a fragrance that captures all the emotion, dignity, and joy of a wedding is immeasurable. Incredibly intimate yet nearly imperceptible, a bride's fragrance remains with her long after the ceremony is over," says Vera Wang.

Capitalizing on her name, not just as a celebrity designer of bridal and evening wear, Vera Wang's bottled romance comes in a fragrance bearing her name that rang up an estimated $25,000 the day Ms. Wang appeared at Saks' Manhattan flagship store in February 2002. Obviously the power of Ms. Wang's name and reputation and the loyalty of her customers played a part in the successful launch. The beautiful juice and elegant packaging are other core elements that distinguish the fragrance, which is marketed to the estimated 2.4 million future brides, as well as women who are not walking down the aisle.

The diminutive Ms. Wang waxes poetic, saying, "My fragrance captures the emotion of desire. It's a modern concept, elegant and sensual." The department store fragrance is part of a larger licensing program by Ms. Wang to capitalize on her name. And why not, she has established herself as an arbiter of taste and style. Her bridal book, *Vera Wang on Weddings* (HarperCollins) covers everything from the bachelor party to the bouquet. And that is not all.

Ms. Wang has a built-in bridal audience and an image that tugs at the heartstrings of emotion and commitment to

Vera Wang's fragrance is packaged to convey romance, elegance, and femininity.

marriage. "My first fragrance symbolizes what weddings are all about," says Ms. Wang. "The inspiration for the fragrance combines three elements of joy, passion, and commitment."

The Inspiration

The scent is a modern floral bouquet developed by Firmenich. The "Flirtation" begins with Bulgarian rose, a timeless symbol of passion and utter femininity, and mandarin flower, the symbol of good luck. The "Kiss" consists of the passionate kiss of gardenia, a symbol of purity, lotus, a sacred symbol of innocence, and white stephanotis, a traditional symbol of marital happiness. The "Embrace" represents precious floral nectar, treasured for centuries because of its aphrodisiac qualities, and sheer musks, known for their sensuality.

Elements of Style

To carry through the theme of the elegant fragrance, it is housed in a frosted bottle with platinum-hued collars. Pure, white textured paper accented with the brand signature in rich nightshade brown wraps the fragrance collection. The uniquely feminine color of lavender lines the inside of the white cartons. The fragrance brand includes a collection of products devoted to the bath and indulgent body care.

Advertising

In keeping with the intense romantic and passionate emotions associated with the fragrance, Unilever Prestige's advertising campaign by Badger Kry & Partners in New York features dreamlike, impressionistic photographs of a misty veiled bride. In another advertisement a man and woman, perhaps a bride and groom, romantically embrace.

Ms. Wang's world extends far beyond the bridal and includes eyewear in conjunction with Oliver Peoples; Vera Wang china, stemware, and crystal, manufactured by Waterford Wedgwood, and a shoe collection under license to Stuart Weitzman. Future collections may include flatware and fine linens.

Beyond Bridal

Vera Wang embodies the spirit of the very modern woman who balances the demands of business and family, and like her fragrance which symbolizes commitment to marriage, she has a strong commitment to her husband Arthur Becker, a financier, and two daughters.

Her career began with a sixteen-year tenure as a senior fashion editor at *Vogue,* followed by a post as a design director at Ralph Lauren. In 1990, she went out on her own and opened a salon in the Carlyle Hotel in New York City to showcase her inaugural bridal collection. "My label quickly took off," notes Ms. Wang. "Although I had built a name as a bridal couturier and the core of my business flows through the bridal business, the idea to license came to me when I realized that I had nothing to sell the average person who could not afford a $4,000 wedding dress. Now with the unveiling of my fragrance, the average woman can afford to wear a Vera Wang creation and fulfill their own dream."

In addition, Wang designed the skating costumes for Olympic gold hopeful Michelle Kwan, who competed in the games in Salt Lake City.

fragrance division has three groups: Fine Fragrances, Personal Care, and Household Products and Fragrance Ingredients.

With more than seventy perfumers (referred to as "Noses") located in eleven creative centers worldwide, IFF's creative perfumery staff works together to create products that offer both a local and global appeal for a wide range of end uses.

A fragrance development group trainee learning to be a "Nose."

Creating a Fragrance

"Projects come in different ways," notes Sarah Friend, IFF's vice president for fragrance development. "The creative steps in developing a fine fragrance product are complex and time consuming. Foremost, it is important to understand the client's point of view."

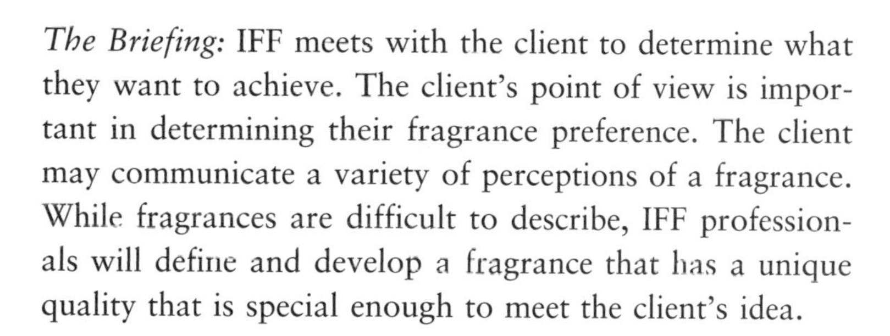

The Briefing: IFF meets with the client to determine what they want to achieve. The client's point of view is important in determining their fragrance preference. The client may communicate a variety of perceptions of a fragrance. While fragrances are difficult to describe, IFF professionals will define and develop a fragrance that has a unique quality that is special enough to meet the client's idea.

Creative Boards: IFF uses a variety of marketing tools, including creative boards mounted with images to show the client that IFF understands the client's needs.

Internal Teamwork: Teamwork is essential. A salesperson is assigned to work with the client, and "the Noses," the right perfumers for the project from the fragrance division are engaged. The perfumers are known as the "Noses" and have the rare ability to recognize many hundreds of ingredients, as well as to blend them with the greatest of artistry into an exquisitely harmonious fragrance.

Team Meeting: The IFF team assembles after a briefing to go over all the client's information and what it means in fragrance terms.

Women's fragrances traditionally exist in three forms: perfume, eau de toilette, and cologne. They are categorized into families: Citrus, Floral, Floriental, Oriental, Chypre, and Musk. The client might want something sweet. IFF asks, "Sweet like what? Sweet like vanilla or sweet like balsam?" The language of fragrance is complex and even more difficult to describe. Unlike a painting, which can be described in colors, tones, and shapes, fragrances cannot be discussed as easily.

Studies are made of marketing information. IFF studies commercial fragrances and asks what is selling and why are these fragrances popular?

Submission to the Client

Product development of a client's fragrance may take several routes. It is a long process, and the fragrance may go through many modifications before the scent satisfies the client's needs. IFF may be competing with other fragrance-producing companies, such as Givaudan or Firmenich. Sometimes a fragrance is coded and blind samples are presented to the client so they can make a fair evaluation of the fragrance. Other times the suppliers' names may be identified. Selection can also be based on a supplier's track record and ability to meet the customer's concept needs. Clients need to consider the following factors before making a decision.

The Name: Creating an appropriate name and fragrance description are also factors in the client's decision-making process.

SIDEBAR 12-5 | Cosmetics and Fragrance Marketing

Connected to the dynamic multibillion dollar cosmetics and fragrance industry, the Fashion Institute of Technology's (FIT) bachelor of science program in Cosmetics and Fragrance Marketing is the only one of its kind in the country. A strong core curriculum is offered in fragrance knowledge, cosmetics and fragrance marketing, product development, and product knowledge. Students study fragrance trends, conduct marketing analyses of cosmetic products, and engage in advanced work in product development from concept to finished product. They are also able to study in the first fragrance studio ever to exist on a college campus in the United States.

Students apply what they learn in required industry internships at such companies as Estée Lauder, Givaudan, Revlon, and Victoria's Secret. Industry members also act as mentors to senior students, ensuring their industry readiness. Graduates find positions with fragrance oil companies, finished goods manufacturers, private label manufacturers, retail organizations, beauty magazines, and cosmetics and fragrance marketing companies.

Market Ready: It takes approximately two months to a year for a supplier like IFF to be ready with a unique prestige fragrance that anticipates the market and meets a deadline so that the product is ready for sale to the customer.

Promotion: Tens of millions of dollars may be poured into the launch of a brand, including costs of the bottle design, package design, public relations, and advertising.

Home Fragrances

Fragrances and scents for the home and environment include a wide scope of product lines that tap into the consumers' desire to create an atmosphere, a safe haven, and a secure nesting place in a technology-driven society. Marketing futurists study the trends that evolve around the home, such as changes in home improvement and home decorating tastes. They study how consumers are reevaluating their lives and how they create their special home environment. Understanding seasonality, psychographics, current events, color trends, textiles, and the fashion world also play into the research and development analysis of trends. Ethnic preferences for certain fruits and spices inspire exotic nuances in mainstream fragrancing.

Knowing when to launch a product is essential to its success. For example, a rich heavy fragrance may not be effective in summer, but for holiday and winter it could be more appealing. Fragrances for home product classifications are quite diversified, ranging from air fresheners, candles, and soaps to fabric softeners, household cleaning products, shower gels, and hair care and styling products.

"There are a couple of pathways of how new products evolve," notes Debra Bornstein, business development manager at International Flavors and Fragrances' Creative Center in Hazlet, New Jersey. "Consumer trend interests are key indicators for product development. Research may tell us that comfort foods, like rich chocolate or caramel, represent the comfort food and security consumers seek in their everyday life. Therefore comfort in fragrance is a directional product theme for air fresheners and candles."

Fragrance Development Process: A New Candle

Ms. Bornstein further explains, "In the IFF Creative Center the account executives tell us what customers are looking for. We have a kick off meeting, a "Brainstorming Session" with a cross-reference of creative people including perfumers, fragrance evaluators, and marketing personnel. We track the market through primary and secondary consumer research. The team examines what's in the market and discusses how to make it better, more appealing to the customer. We map out a time line of how much time we need to accomplish a new product and meet market deadline."

"The creative team, which consists of the perfumers assigned to the project, are briefed and begin the process of developing new ideas. We establish a *benchmark* to work against, a standard to develop product that is better than what is on the market."

The fragrance evaluators go back and forth working with the perfumers to optimize their fragrance creations. The creative team develops a name for the candle product. The legal department will check to be sure that the name does not exist already and will possibly trademark it in advance. Before a product goes into production, it will go through technical testing and safety testing.

Consumer Research

Product testing with consumers is another important step in the creative process. In a central testing location, customers are brought into a facility where the product is presented and the scent is evaluated. Home testing can also be utilized to confirm if the product mix is optimal.

Partnering the right product with the right scent is critical to the success of a product. It is extremely expensive to get a new product on the shelves at retail. The package goods houses do not want to take any chances because package goods houses pay for the retail space to have their product on the shelves.

Trade Terminology

Aromatherapy
Benchmark
Blind samples
Body care
Brainstorming
Briefing
Calendarized
Crystal Ball Beauty Trend Report
Conceptual development
Concept formulas
Consumer research
Creative boards
Feasibility development
FiFi awards
Ideation session

Imagination team
Imagineering
The "juice"
Market ready
Mind walking
Package goods
Safety testing
Technical testing

READING 12-1 | Cosmoprof: Coming to America

BY ANDREA M.G. NAGEL AND STEPHANIE EPIRO

NEW YORK—Don't expect to find the Beauty and Barber Supply Institute trade show this July in Las Vegas. Cosmoprof North America is heading for the Vegas strip.

Cosmoprof, an Italian trade show that some consider to be the most well rounded and inclusive beauty event for the industry, has formed a partnership with BBSI and is bent on raising the bar with a complete beauty show that is designed to be more prestigious and easier to navigate than previous efforts.

In short, everything has changed.

Cosmoprof's reputation as the best-attended beauty trade show—its Bologna event is the world's largest—is helping garner exhibitors and attendees to its North American debut. Running from July 27–30 at the Las Vegas Convention Center, more than 600 exhibitors are expected to spread out over 190,000 square feet. Cosmoprof, which is organized by Italy-based SoGeCos SpA, has teamed up with BBSI, an association of salon distributors, the usual hosts of the summer show, for its North American debut. Cosmoprof also hosts annual shows in Asia and South America.

The most obvious changes to this year's event will be the clearly divided sections of cosmetics and toiletries, packaging, wellness, professional products and a demonstration forum.

"It is very important to know that Cosmoprof North America is not about hairdressers," said Laura Zaccagnini, a general director of Sogecos, referring to BBSI's show format, which catered exclusively to the salon industry.

Cosmoprof, on the other hand, targets nearly every role in the beauty industry from manufacturers, distributors, importers, exporters, manufacturer representatives to chain salons, salon owners, salon managers, hair stylists, nail technicians, estheticians, massage therapists, cosmetology school owners and students. Also scouting the aisles will be buyers from department stores, specialty stores and chain drug stores, such as Eckerd and Rite Aid. Kmart and Target buyers are expected to visit the show, too. And now each attendee will be able to easily navigate through the large floor plan, since each pavilion will be dedicated to specific product categories.

Pavilion A will feature international cosmetics companies, with businesses representing Spain, Germany, Israel, Italy and China, many of which are seeking U.S. distribution. On display will be a gamut of finished products from prestige department store fragrances to color cosmetics.

Cosmetic Lab, for example, a Paris-based company, is seeking a U.S. distributor to launch its Elyor skin care line, which is sold in France, Italy and Hong Kong. Elyor products target the upper segment of the market with upscale packaging and silky formulas that are comprised of fruits and plant extracts.

Pavilion A will also feature health products, hair accessories and home decor items.

In pavilion B, packaging, contract manufacturing and private label exhibitors will be found. Design agencies and packaging machines round out the pavilion's exhibitor list.

In pavilion C, wellness, professional skin care, spa products and equipment will be presented. Everything from suntanning lamps to electro-stimulation accessories and hydro-massage baths will be there, in addition to complimentary wellness education seminars. Featured speakers include Dr. Howard Murad, Amby Longhofer of DermaNew and Lydia Sarfati of Repechage Spa. A spa demonstration stage will also be in pavilion C, highlighting the newest product spa lines and spa treatments.

Everything needed to stock the shelves of a salon will be featured in pavilion D. Hair care, tools for hairdressers, professional clothing, scissors, razors and products for nail reconstruction will be offered there.

However, several key professional hair care companies, such as L'Oréal Professionel and Clairol Professional, will not be exhibiting.

Hair stylists will have an entire area, pavilion E, completely dedicated to them. There they will be able to see and learn the latest hair innovations at Looks Mainstage & Expo. Looks features international artists from the UK, Spain, Japan and the U.S. in 90-minute hair and fashion presentations.

Hair stylists will also be able to sit in on several complimentary hair education seminars. For example, stylists could learn the latest in Japanese hair straightening from Fernando Romero of Bio Ionic, a hair straightening company he founded.

Classes for nail technicians abound at Cosmoprof, with presentations by OPI, Creative Nail Design, NailCare and Seche, running throughout the day on Sunday and Monday.

Staying true to Cosmoprof's new layout, attendees and exhibitors will only be allowed to enter spaces according to what their badge permits.

"No hairdressers will be able to enter other sectors besides Looks, not because we don't like them, it's just that if you have the correct badge you will be able to access your area of your interest exclusively," said Zaccagnini.

Moreover, Italian style has been injected into the look of the exhibitor booths. First to be tossed aside was the old pipe-and-drape decor. "It looked dreadful," Zaccagnini said, adding that Cosmoprof was insistent companies take their raw space and build it into a prestige-type booth, or take one of Cosmoprof's turnkey booths with three 2.5-meter walls. Decor guidelines were also instituted to help differentiate one area from another.

Cosmoprof is also issuing advertising communications to promote and explain each area.

"This is not technical, it's marketing—it's the way you introduce your company and it's important," Zaccagnini said.

Zaccagnini said it took "months to make [BBSI's usual exhibitors] understand this concept." But other exhibitors, especially those familiar with Cosmoprof's flamboyant flavor, are used to the guidelines and are even looking forward to making a dramatic booth impression for their American debut.

Davide Bollati, founder and chief executive of Parma, Italy-based beauty company Davines Group, is spending nearly $300,000 on the construction of his 1,800-square-foot booth. He's hired architects Jacques Herzog and Pierre de Meuron of Basel, Switzerland, the recipients of the 2001 Pritzker prize, to construct the Davines booth.

"In Europe we are used to this type of investment," Bollati said. "This is a conference where you will meet with your best clients and distributors. And, because we are in cosmetics, I think [our image] is about a sense of beauty and aesthetics."

The booth will be constructed of embossed stretched metal and will feature a wellness, styling and shopping space. "Each area is a vision of the salon in the next five years," Bollati said.

The upscale feel of Cosmoprof is sure to take many of BBSI's usual attendees by surprise.

"It's not a BBSI event anymore," said Steve Sleeper, BBSI's chief executive and executive director. "A lot of members are excited about it and have embraced the new format. They knew our convention was diminishing and there was less and less need for a buyers conference. Some are grappling with the changes . . . but I am sure we will look back 10 years from now and be happy," Sleeper added.

Source: *Women's Wear Daily*, June 27, 2003, p. 10. Courtesy of Fairchild Publications, Inc.

READING 12-2 | Annette Green Takes a Look Back

BY CASSANDRA CHIACCHIO AND KRISTIN FINN, WITH CONTRIBUTIONS FROM LAURA KLEPACKI

It only took a moment at the microphone to end an era.

Annette Green, president of The Fragrance Foundation, announced her imminent retirement at Tuesday evening's FiFi ceremony. Green, who became visibly emotional during her speech, will step down at the end of the year and remain as a consultant to The Fragrance Foundation for the next two years.

The announcement, which came at the very end of the ceremony, stunned industry members, many of whom thought Green, who is in her late 70s, would never retire.

"No one has more love and infectious passion for fragrance than Annette Green," said Evelyn Lauder, senior corporate vice president of the Estée Lauder Cos. "No one has done more to establish American fragrances as major players with high worldwide reputations than Annette Green. She better not retire too far away from everyone in the fragrance world. We still need her."

Eric Thoreux, president of Coty Beauty Americas and third vice chairman of the board of The Fragrance Foundation, first met Green four years ago when he arrived in the U.S. to assume his current position. Green, he said, "helped him better understand the market.

"She is an extraordinary person who has dedicated her life to developing this fragrance business," he said. "She is a unique combination. She is a living memory of the past and a crystal ball for the future, and she has an incredible knowledge and intuition. With her incredible level of energy and curiosity, she really kept reinventing The Fragrance Foundation."

Green herself already has a game plan for the future. "I just spent 41 years as savior of The Fragrance Foundation and what I really want is to prepare the Foundation for the next 40 years," she said.

First on her list is finding her replacement. "There are a lot of qualities that are necessary—overall management and financial skills and a certain star quality—someone who can get up in front of 1,200 or 1,300 people," she said. "Most importantly, they must have a passion for fragrance, which I don't think you can learn."

As for the future of the Foundation, Green said she agrees with Foundation chairman Patrick Bousquet-Chavanne that the fragrance industry needs a generic television campaign, like the 'Got Milk?' advertising, but in the past, money has been an obstacle. "This is what is needed," she said. "Otherwise we're talking about bits and pieces."

Second on the list is to go back to her first love—writing. "I'd like to [write] a book about my experiences in the industry," said Green, who started her professional career as a reporter. She'd also like to write a book about career development for young people and, in the fiction arena, a children's book based on Elian Gonzales and his experiences with dolphins on his way from Cuba.

Green, who was born in Philadelphia and grew up in New Jersey, discovered her own passion for scent early on, first through her mother's love of fragrance and then later as a fledgling journalist in the Fifties. Green worked for American Druggist, where she was assigned a column to report on teen preferences. As research, she went to work in a local drugstore on the weekends. "I became fascinated with the psychological element of selling cosmetics and fragrances," she said.

Throughout the years, she never lost that fascination.

In 1961 Green, who by then had created her own public relations firm, became aware of industry executive Jack Mohr's quest to save The Fragrance Foundation, which was founded in 1949. "I had covered The Fragrance Foundation as a young journalist in the late Fifties," Green recalled. "I covered a television commercial they did. I was young and didn't know much, but I knew that commercial was awful. It showed a big clock and said 'Tick tock, wear fragrance around the clock.' "

Mohr, a former employer of Green's, brought her on board to save the foundation. "They told me they had no more money but had lots of files, and that if I wanted to try to save it I could. It was up to me."

Green, who never backed down from a challenge before, welcomed the opportunity.

"My main concern was to make it a membership organization, to get a board of directors, to make it legitimate," said Green, who worked pro bono for the first five years.

That meant generating more awareness.

"I was trying to think of something dramatic to do for the industry so we'd get a lot of press," she said. The result was the Costume Promenade Gala, a competition where companies created costumes that reflected fragrance. The idea was discontinued after two years. "People spent so much money on these costumes that they got very violent when they didn't win," laughed Green, who said she was actually pushed across the ballroom floor by an unhappy competitor. "I thought, 'You know, my life is in danger, I better think of something else.' "

Her next idea was The Fragrance Foundation Awards, which later came to be known as the FiFis. "This is a very creative industry and they deserve to be honored as much as people in the movies or the theater," said Green, who patterned the concept after the Oscars. "That first one, I had to beg people to come," she said. "It was in the ballroom at the Plaza—I managed to get 250 people to come. We had three or four categories and Chanel No. 19 was the winner that year.

The rest is FiFi history.

"My hope is that [the FiFis] get to be important to the public," said Green, who was elected president of The Fragrance Foundation in 1992. This year's FiFi award attendees totaled about 1,200 people, including 200 members of the general public.

Green's contributions to the industry are not just limited to the FiFis. Among other accomplishments, she introduced the "wardrobe of fragrance" concept, coined the term "aroma-chology," helped found the Sense of Smell Institute (formerly the Olfactory Research Fund), initiated the Cosmetic/Fragrance Bachelor's Program at FIT and co-authored a book, "Secrets of Aromatic Jewelry."

"Annette Green has singlehandedly been the driving force behind the growth of the fragrance industry, both in the U.S. and abroad," said Leonard Lauder, chairman of the Estée Lauder Cos. "She is a dynamo of energy and it's hard to imagine the fragrance business without her great presence."

Source: *Women's Wear Daily*, June 7, 2002, p. 14. Courtesy of Fairchild Publications, Inc.

READING 12-3 | No Sleeping Beauty BY HARLAND S. BYRNE

Howard B. Bernick likes to remind anyone who will listen that almost as long as he can remember, one Wall Street analyst or another has been predicting the demise of Alberto-Culver Co. True, concedes the company's 48-year-old CEO, Alberto-Culver was wobbly during its early years in the 'Fifties. But thanks partly to a strong and growing lineup of new products added to VO5, its best-known offering, the company's earnings the past 10 years have nearly quadrupled and sales have nearly tripled. Despite stiff competition in personal-care products, the company for years has posted solid gains, usually double-digit, for its shampoos, skin conditioners and related products, in good times and bad. And Bernick happily observes that most analysts now have Buy recommendations on the stock.

"Most people don't stop washing their hair or bathing during tough times," Bernick says. And at no time has his company's resistance to tough times been more noticeable than in the past fiscal year, ended September 30, and the just-completed first quarter of fiscal 2002, a stretch covering a recession and the general business disruption (though, for Alberto-Culver, short-lived) following the September 11 terrorist attacks. The company's stock took a quick dive after September 11, but quickly recovered to pre-attack levels and approached a record high.

In fiscal 2001, sales climbed 11%, to $2.49 billion, from $2.25 billion in fiscal 2000 as earnings rose close to 14%, reaching $110.4 million, or $1.91 a share, up from $97.2 million, or $1.72, the prior year, excluding an 11-cent-a-share nonrecurring gain.

And, last week, the company reported that in the current fiscal year's first quarter, ended December 31, Alberto-Culver exceeded the consensus of analysts' earnings estimates, as compiled by Thomson Financial/First Call, by a penny a share. On a sales increase of 8.9% from last fiscal year's first three months, the company earned 50 cents a share, diluted, versus 41 cents in the year-earlier span. Basic earnings ran 52 cents a share, versus 42 cents. The recent quarter's results included three cents a share from elimination of good-will amortization.

For fiscal year 2002, the consensus calls for earnings of $2.29 a share, including 12 cents from eliminating goodwill amortization, against the previous year's $1.91. And for fiscal 2003, the consensus is $2.55.

This fits Bernick's projection that in the next five years the company should keep up its brisk growth by doubling sales and more than doubling profits. Reflecting that optimism and the company's solid financial condition, directors last week raised the annual dividend on Alberto's common stock for the 18th consecutive year, to 36 cents a share from 33 cents. The new nine-cent-a share quarterly, which is the same for both classes of the company's common, will be payable February 20 to shareholders of record February 5.

Alberto-Culver's Class B shares, which are more than 40%-owned by founder Leonard H. Lavin and his family and which command 10 votes a share, have been trading recently at a premium of several dollars a share to the Class A shares, which carry only one vote each. Thus the Lavin family exercises voting control and has given no hint yet of plans to relinquish it.

The B shares also are in the Standard & Poor's 500 index, which makes them a required holding for institutions and other investors who pursue an indexing strategy based on the S&P. Both classes ended the past fiscal year slightly ahead of stocks in the company's peer group and the S&P 500.

The Lavin family not only has voting control of Alberto-Culver, it also has a firm grip on the company's day-to-day operations. Leonard Lavin, who started the company with the purchase of a small hair-care firm for $150,000 in 1955, today sits as chairman of the board. Wife Bernice is company secretary, and daughter Carol, who is married to CEO Bernick, plays a key role as head of North American operations.

Alberto-Culver's growth is all the more remarkable because of its many large and small rivals in the personal-care business.

The big competitors include Avon Products, Procter & Gamble and Gillette.

Over the years, Alberto-Culver has strengthened its position through acquisitions, the introduction of innovative and moderately priced products, focusing on a few strong brands (VO5, St. Ives and TRESemmé), and, most notably, by the steady buildup of a distribution network that is second to none in the industry.

The system consists of a chain of Sally Beauty Supply stores, more than 2,000 strong, and the Beauty Systems Group, with 300-plus outlets. The system's units now account for 70% of Alberto-Culver profits.

Last month Alberto disclosed that it had reached a definitive agreement to buy Armstrong-McCall, a beauty-products distributor and franchiser based in Austin, Texas. The acquisition of Armstrong-McCall, which does about $100 million in annual sales, extends the reach of the Beauty Systems Group throughout the South and Southwest and into Mexico. The purchase price wasn't disclosed.

Sally Beauty Supply stores are no-frills, low-cost, cash-and-carry operations, catering both to consumers and beauty-care professionals such as salon operators. They sell not only the popular retail brands, but also a line of products not usually found in drug, food and department stores and marketed under such brand names as Matrix, Paul Mitchell, Graham Webb and Sebastian.

The Beauty Systems Group concentrates solely on the lucrative professional trade, an effort that is bolstered by about 600 sales professionals who call directly on salons in the U.S. and Canada.

As things stand now in the industry, the distribution end of the business is clearly dominated by Alberto-Culver. Most other distributors have fallen short of the success of Sally Beauty and Beauty Systems, frequently giving up by selling out to Alberto-Culver.

Alberto-Culver's success could eventually make the company a takeover target for one of its giant competitors, although there are no indications that any such move is in the works or that the controlling shareholders would welcome it.

However, it must be noted that Procter & Gamble last year ponied up an eye-popping $5 billion for Clairol, a company with year sales far below Alberto-Culver's $2.5 billion. Based on that, the price that Alberto-Culver might fetch could be a real beauty.

13

Men's Wear

The male vanity boom has ushered in a new breed of male customers who want quality, luxury, and personal products that pamper their egos and evoke individualism. Why? Because men today are just as fashion conscious as women.

Although men's clothing has not changed drastically in the last 150 years, what the modern male wants goes beyond tradition to beautifully tailored suits, separates they can mix and match, tweeds and Scottish cashmere, sophisticated British men's wear fabrics, and rich signature details that identify "style." The new men's wear collections are about individualism and lifestyle, not fashion. As David Chu says, "What you wear says a lot about who you are."

The male customers themselves and their multifaceted and multidimensional lifestyles have fueled inspiration that has driven fresh ideas that create a wider selection of apparel that takes its cue from the vintage, military, and sports arenas. As men engage in a wide variety of activities, the basic needs for business, weekend attire, club apparel, and formal wear has expanded to include clothing categories for the outdoors, including rugged wear, biking, and extreme sports.

The total of vibrant color and conversational prints in underwear and sleepwear and personalized style in accessories—ties, socks, belts, suspenders, handkerchiefs, scarves, and small leather goods—all contribute to providing more options that satisfy the male vanity boom.

LICENSING: SPORTS/CELEB ENDORSEMENT

Men's fashions get a further boost from sports personalities, celebrity, and designer tie-ins through licensing agreements. Elegant new ranges are introduced by celebrities like Sean Combs, who delivers sophisticated styles for both high and mass market fashion. The designer, also known at various points during his career as Puffy, Puff Daddy, and P. Diddy, has climbed to the top of the fashion pyramid. He is considered "one of the top five designers in the world," and has been nominated for a (CFDA) Council of Fashion Designers Fashion Award in the men's wear category for the third year in a row.

Regis Philbin, the celebrity show host, lends his name to the Phillips–Van Heusen brand for both dress shirts and neckwear. The Regis name not only expands the Van Heusen presence with existing retail customers, but also penetrates additional retail doors. Oscar veteran Denzel Washington may wear heavy-hitting ensembles delivered by Perry Ellis, and bad-boy basic black by Donna Karan New York evokes Sean Penn's perfect combo of rebel and respectability. Russell Crowe, the Australian with an attitude, manages to create a strong sense of style by opting for a basic black suit by Giorgio Armani as a tough-guy alternative. Men's wear lines are also designer driven through licensing agreements with such key players as Bill Blass, Henry Grethel, Ralph Lauren, Marc Jacobs, Pierre Cardin, Perry Ellis, and Tommy Hilfiger.

Industry trend advisers and marketing professionals closely watch the men's wear industry. In fact, some of the men's wear ideas are so fashion forward they trend and eventually spill over into the women's wear sector.

FASHION FORECASTING

Creative forecast presentations that are specific to men's wear are an important source of color, trend, and silhouette information utilized by the press, fashion directors, and retailers. The fashion forecasting services produce a variety of products that forecast color and silhouette trends targeted to the men's wear industry.

For example, Pantone, the color registry system and forecast company, issues a color/trend report called *Let's Talk Color* that encapsulates trend and color information from the MAGIC trade show. "Color Me Spring!" talks about the color palettes, while the "'A' List of Style!" says, "For spring, the focus is on the individual and the items that update his wardrobe." The "Style Watch!" pinpoints the key silhouette trends.

In addition, major fiber producers provide men's wear–specific color, fabric, and trend predictions for the men's wear manufacturers and designers, private label, trade press, fashion directors, and retailers. James N. Siewert, men's wear fashion director at Celanese Acetate, is a prognosticator of both men's and women's wear trends, which are presented in the fiber giant's fabric library, the Celanese Acetate Global studios in New York City. The library serves as an important point of reference and gives a broad audience of men's wear producers and retailers a hands-on opportunity to review the fiber firm's brands, as well as new fabrics made exclusively in Celanese Acetate.

MEN'S WEAR RETAIL

As senior vice president for fashion direction at Bloomingdale's Kal Ruttenstein is an important figure in the men's and women's wear trades. He has orchestrated in-store extravaganzas for the chain for the past twenty-five years and, as head of Bloomingdale's Fashion Office, he is the store's major domo, the trend watcher and prognosticator who keeps in touch with all fashion trends. He also oversees the production of various men's wear products, including the *Strictly Confidential* men's fashion book, which provides themes and photos of key men's wear colors, trends, and fashions, a fresh way men will work and play with all the options. The fashion office, under his administration, produces high-profile, seasonal men's wear fashion catalogs. Mr. Ruttenstein received the (CFDA) Council of Fashion Designers Eleanor Lambert Award (2002) for his distinguished role as a longtime fashion director.

TRENDS IN MEN'S WEAR

American Custom-Made

The trend for custom-made men's wear has been enthusiastically embraced by affluent American customers who frequent the custom made-to-measure departments of major retailers such as Barneys New York, Brooks Brothers, Dunhill Tailors, and the Rome-based Brioni store in New York City. Prices may start as low as $2,000 but increase depending on choice of fabric and customization of fit.

Digitally Tailored Suits

These suits are a modern day answer to customization at Brooks Brothers, where a digital tailoring adviser scans a nearly naked customer's topography as he stands in a private booth. The data are translated into measurements that are transmitted, along with a customer's choices for fit, style, and fabric, to the retailer's suit factory outside Boston or the shirt factory in North Carolina. The result: three weeks later the customer receives a digitally designed suit. Traditionally custom suits at Brooks Brothers start at $1,000, but a digitally tailored suit is only $700. Digitally tailored custom shirts start at $90, trousers at $200 and a sports coat at approximately $500.

Savile Row

London's Savile Row is traditionally recognized as the quintessential center for classic, well-tailored, made-to-measure men's business suits. Companies on Savile Row have tailored suits for royals, celebrities, and captains of industry.

Richard James has infused a new, younger spirit into the Savile Row establishment with one of the largest corner shops in the area. It is light, airy, bright, and inviting. "This is a stark contrast from the old-fashioned dark wood and animal trophy heads adorning most shops, which modern customers perceived as out of date and not young people friendly," says Mr. James. "Instead the brighter environment appeals to the younger customer and so do our sales associates. When a young customer comes into the store, a younger sales associate will address their needs—someone who speaks their language and understands their lifestyles. Hugh Grant is among our regular customers. He also wore Richard James suits in the film, *Bridget Jones' Diary*. While flannels and gabardines are traditional men's wear fabrics, denim was the fabric of choice for another customer who wanted a finely tailored denim suit to wear to the opera."

Richard James has attracted a younger shopper to his establishment in London's traditional Savile Row.

James is also the first Savile Row tailor to open on Saturdays, which also attracts the avant garde and young executive customers, who appreciate not only the custom-made apparel, but also the Richard James men's ready-to-wear collection.

Andrew Bolton, associate curator of the Metropolitan Museum of Art's Costume Institute, talks about the joys of a well-tailored Savile Row suit from Richard James or Timothy Everest. In a column entitled "Bold Bolton" by Norah Zis in *Women's Wear Daily* (April 23, 2002), he says, "I love the Savile Row suits because there is detail only the wearer can appreciate." As a case in point, he describes his natty navy suit with lavender pinstripes and silk lining. "The cut of the jacket is longer with a double vent, along with flared cut and pinched waist," Bolton points out, just in case a visitor misses the fine point.

Men's tailored shirts, preferred by high-profile professional men from London's Turnbull & Asser, Harvie & Hudson, or Hilditch & Key, pricey at $125 to $175, represent the quintessence of custom fit and quality. Not to be outdone, Sulka, a venerable haberdashery store in New York City, is a major source of custom-made shirts as well as custom-made suits.

It is common knowledge that new trendy British designers are stepping up London fashion recognition in the men's wear genre, wooing designers such as Alexander McQueen to Paris. Hedi Slimane now designs the Dior Homme collection and Julien Macdonald, another Englishman, designs for Givenchy.

Custom Clothes

Italian tailors who produce handmade clothing are mainly based in Naples and Rome. Their wealthy and successful clientele includes modern-day movie stars, celebrities, and luxury connoisseurs, who represent the current market for handmade clothing. Prices can go as high as $15,000 for a suit. This is Italy's answer to the Paris couture, but the business is not regimented and has fewer operating requirements. The garments may require several fittings and take months to finish, but the result is personalization and exquisite fit.

MEN'S WEAR FASHION SHOWS

The men's wear catwalk shows create a monumental stir on the international runways, earning respect comparable to the limelight of the women's wear shows. In fact, men's wear designer shows scheduled on the Fashion Calendar are presented before the women's wear shows. That gives the men's wear industry a jump start on trends.

In Milan, Italy, the epicenter of men's wear fashion, the Fall/Winter men's wear catwalk collections hit the runway in January 2004 for the 2004/2005 Fall/Winter season. In June 2004 the Milan men's wear collections debut for Spring 2005. The men's wear shows continue in Paris and then the final destination is New York. In New York City the Fall men's wear shows are held in February, and the Spring men's wear shows are held in September.

INDUSTRY PROFILE 13-1 | Salvatore J. Cesarani

Salvatore J. Cesarani, "New York's Dean of Good Taste," builds his collections on American themes.

Dubbed "New York's Dean of Good Taste," Salvatore J. Cesarani creates a men's wear collection that is all about American style. Sculpted out of the finest Italian fabrics, the Cesarani collection is imbued with traditional Italian craftsmanship and the good breeding of English elegance.

Mr. Cesarani is an award winning American fashion designer and president of S.J.C. Concepts, Inc.®, an American fashion design house. The Cesarani® label has been a part of the fashion industry in the United States for more than twenty years.

Icons of Style

He creates a new fashion mix for his stylistic vision of the American lifestyle. The cinema was an opportunity for him to observe every detail of popular Hollywood icons, such as Cary Grant, Fred Astaire, Clark Gable, Tyrone Power, and Jimmy Stewart. To Cesarani, these actors were models of American culture.

Therefore there is something very familiar and very, very American in Cesarani's Fall/Winter 2002 men's wear collection. The collection is defined by an enhanced use of color and precisely matched patterns that are hallmarks of distinction in checks, glen plaids, and country weaves. The garments are created in luxury fabrications of merino wool, lambs wool, and cashmere blends.

A Couture Look

It is a nostalgic embrace of film star glamour that exudes refined tailoring and a couture look that is achieved through attention to details. Obvious details include hand pick stitching so a lapel lies properly, and hidden details include lightweight interlinings that provide super soft construction for regular suits or jackets. An extension waistband with inside button to hold pants securely at the waist is yet another example of couture work that distinguishes the Cesarani label.

MR magazine said of him, "Salvatore Cesarani, one of the members of the American tailored royal family, has developed a regal point of view and stuck with it. Through his extensive knowledge of fabric and cut, Sal consistently creates timeless staples for a man's wardrobe."

Cesarani's talent as an American men's wear designer may very well be linked to the fact that his parents were immigrant tailors from Italy who taught him the technical aspects of creating a quality garment. "Color is the number one factor essential to design," says Mr. Cesarani. "The important directional trend is toward clean, sophisti-

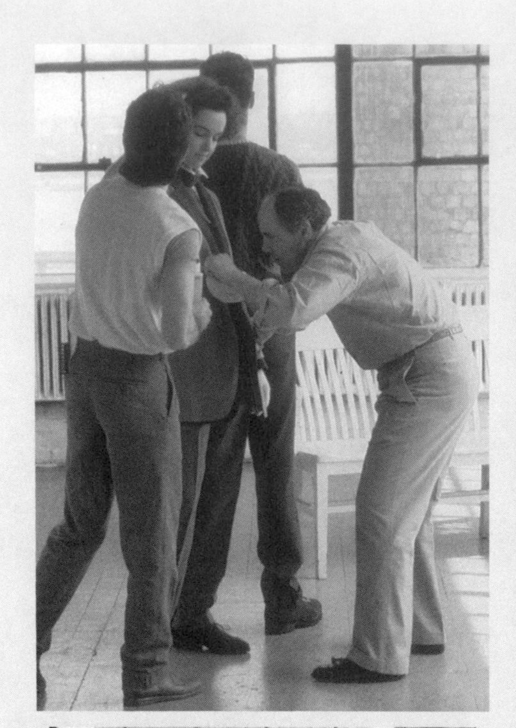

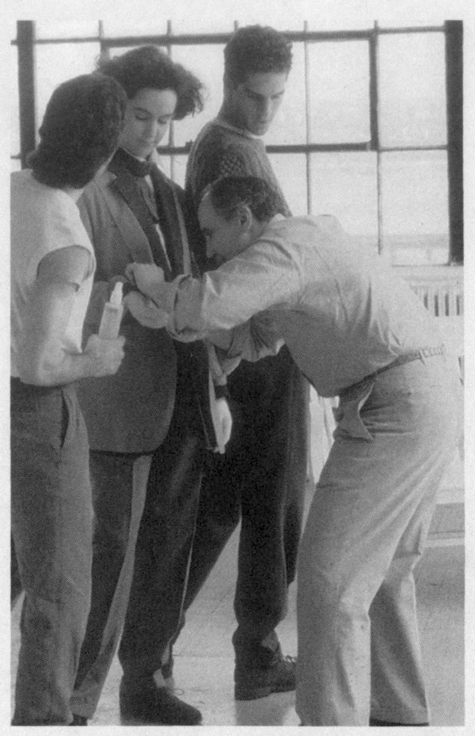

Cesarani's 2002 collection reflects nostalgia for the glory days of Hollywood movie stars. The colors, patterns, and luxury fabrics are expected of Cesarani, but this collection shows a remarkable attention to detail that creates a timeless yet regal appearance.

cated colors." For editors and buyers, he introduces the concept for the Spring collection on creative boards that are superimposed with top and bottom fabrics and color ranges that tell a thematic story.

For Spring/Summer 2002, Cesarani's colors were familiar and warm. Color ranges are designated by a theme name.

Poetic features watercolor neutrals, including sea salt, a sand color, sorbet rust, and banana cream. An azure blue accent in a glen plaid is both subtle and attractive.

The fabrics and colors relate in a range of distinct checks, basket weaves, Prince of Wales plaids, and flat donegals fashioned in pure silk, silk and wool, and silk and linen blends. The concept of the sport suit epitomizes the best of the collection, offering versatility though the pairing of sport jackets with finely tailored trousers.

Exuberance is the name of a bright and spontaneous color range. It is a heady mix of strong colors, goldenrod, aqua, red, and rusty orange, designated for shirtings and sweaters.

Provocative identifies a range of colors and linen fabrications in beet root, a deep maroon, cement gray and madras plaids, and sophisticated black.

The sport coat, now an essential jacket, has various influences exhibited in the Stadium coat with its suede trim and elbow patches or in the Kipling and Drawstring jackets in treated cotton twills, hombre plaids, and country checks.

The classics are the basic to every man's wardrobe. The navy jacket, the tattersall blazer, the white twill pants in dry ice white, deep-sea blue and squid ink navy all exude American style.

Made in Italy

"The entire collection is made in Italy of the purest and most elegant fabrics," notes Mr. Cesarani. "The trouser collection, for example, is offered in gabardine, calvary twills, whipcords, super flannels, and linen. These colors and patterns complement and enhance the jackets both for sport and elegant dressing."

After showing the collection at the Designers Collective and in the Cesarani showroom, retailers make their garment and fabric choices. To facilitate their selection and final order, the buyers from the finest specialty stores are given a line sketch affixed with a fabric swatch of the garment and the price. Three weeks lead time is required for orders and then every garment is cut to order in factories in Italy.

The Cesarani collection is presented to the trade as follows:

Spring/Summer Collection is previewed in June, sold in July and August, and gets into the stores in December and January.

Fall/Winter Collection is previewed in December, sold in January and February, and is in the stores during July and August.

Industry Recognition

Mr. Cesarani's astute sense of fashion trends, sharpened by his market research throughout Asia and Europe, have made him a valuable special consultant for several major fashion color forecasting groups and special projects. Mr. Cesarani is presently teaching "Fabric Selection and Design Styling Theory" at Parsons School of Continuing Education. He holds a seat on the Advisory Board of the Fashion Crafts Educational Commission of the High School of Fashion Industries. "I'm proud to say that I am a graduate of the High School of Fashion Industries and have an opportunity to serve on the board," says Cesarani. He is also a member of the Kent State University School of Fashion Advisory Board and an active member of the Council of Fashion Designers of America.

Awards recognizing his contribution to men's wear design include Special COTY Award for Menswear 1974, 1975; COTY Award for Menswear 1976; Fashion Group Award of Boston 1977; and COTY Return Award 1982.

Retail merchants, buyers, the fashion press, and the paparazzi all converge on the fashion capitals for the yearly ritual of the men's wear fashion shows to see and report about how the top designers will dress the nation in the coming season. With celebrities strategically seated in the front rows on the runway, reams of editorial publicity appear in major newspapers, magazines, and on electronic media worldwide. Further baiting the men's wear consumer are the editorial reports on the sports figures and celebrity endorsements associated with men's wear collections.

FOREIGN FASHION SHOWS

Milan Fashion Week

Milan Fashion Week takes center stage as the major location for the men's wear ready-to-wear collections which, like the French Prêt, fuel the coffers of the men's wear designers' empires. Traditionally associated with fine tailoring and hand craftsmanship, Italy is the country that produces and supplies most of the men's wear fabrics in the global marketplace. While known worldwide for their silks, jerseys, woolens, and worsted fabrics, the Italian mills constantly search for innovative fabric designs and are keen researchers and masters of customer service. That is why many American and French designers come to Italy for fabric sourcing and production.

In Milan, Valentino, the king of Italian haute couture, is a key presenter, as is the Japanese house Issey Miyake along with Fendi, Giorgio Armani, and Dolce & Gabbana. Major American designers who show in Milan include Ralph Lauren, who put his Purple label men's line on a runway for the first time in 2002. Referring to the importance of showing in Milan, John Bartlett said, "It's important to be there, to have a global presence, because buyers from all over the world make Milan their prime source for men's wear collections." While the designers are key players on the men's wear stage, the Ermenegildo Zegna Group and Loro Piana are turning textiles into luxury men's and women's wear brands.

INDUSTRY PROFILE 13-2 | The John Bartlett Studio

Every designer has his own private take on design inspiration and John Bartlett's rugged masculine style is no exception. Commenting on his Fall 2002 collection, Mr. Bartlett says, "I was inspired by a Pacific Northwest summer camping trip. My collection is more about a manly man, filtered through the lens of Sept. 11. I designed this collection in the two weeks following the attacks, and firemen were part of my research. The lumberjack is also such a great American icon and the collection included outdoorsy looks, thermals and quilted vests in velvet, denim, corduroy, and moleskin fabrics."

The home-bred collection was a strong departure from his past collections. In his Spring runway, Bartlett startled onlookers by presenting half-dressed models in prison cells while more than 1,000 guests walked around to view the off-beat presentation. The presentation was inspired by a quotation from Jean Gênet about "dreaming in darkness," and regardless of the intent, while stripes make sense in a prison setting, perhaps they also evoke the attitude that we are prisoners of fashion.

Getting serious, however, John Bartlett is a designer who is constantly motivated by everything and everywhere he ventures. Just watching old movies stirs an idea for a collection. For example, he was fascinated by the movie *Deliverance* and was inspired by how the star, Burt Reynolds, looked sexy in a scuba vest and black cargo pants. This idea fueled his imagination, and man versus nature became another theme, another collection.

John Bartlett's high-priced contemporary sportswear collections are designed in his studio/showroom in the trendy Chelsea meat market district of New York City. He also maintains a studio in Milan, which is considered the epicenter of the men's clothing industry.

"Italy is the center of men's wear because most of the fabrics are produced in the Italian mills, and therefore most of the men's wear lines are made in Italy," notes Mr. Bartlett. "Obviously, it is important to be there, to have a global presence, because buyers from all over the world, who may not come to New York City, make Milan their destination buying venue."

Mr. Bartlett's creative process begins with a preconceived idea of his next collection. A consummate researcher, he investigates many venues including the picture collection at the New York Public Library. He watches old and new movies, scans antique fashion and fabric books, and keeps a sketchpad with him wherever he goes. He finds inspiration everywhere. Then he builds a creative board with a collage of images that represent and define the collection's theme and fabrications.

At this point, the Italian fabric mills send him headers, samples of the season's fabrics, which he had already previewed at Première Vision. "It's a tight schedule," says the affable designer. "I now send the Italian factory, which produces my collection, the first round of sketches for the collection. This enables the factory to program production and to begin to look for distinctive buckles and buttons. For a Fall collection which will be shown in June, I meet with the factory the first week of April, define the fabrics and review the first garment prototypes. Then the collection goes into full production."

John Bartlett finds inspiration in literature, movies, and even the events of 9/11. His Fall 2002 collection startled its audience with its prison theme that included models with headbands covering their eyes and prison-striped tops and pants.

Mr. Bartlett points out that when planning a men's wear show for Milan's fashion week, one needs special practical pieces geared toward retail selling. "In merchandising a line, buyer research is a constant process," notes Mr. Bartlett. "We maintain and establish strong retail relationships. When the John Bartlett label hangs in the stores we have a global feel and presence."

The designer's diffusion line, John Bartlett Uniform, featuring more accessibly priced jeans, khakis, and basics, is rolled out to more retail doors.

Pitti Imagine Uomo

Pitti Imagine Uomo, a renowned men's wear show held in Florence, Italy, is a major men's wear trade event sponsored by the Centro de Firenze per la Moda Italiana in cooperation with the Ente Moda Italiana. An event of ever-greater international breadth, Pitti Immagine Uomo is increasingly regarded by the key centers of the men's wear clothing trade as the major reference exhibition. It presents a preview of collections of male clothing, brands, and accessories in January for the Spring/Summer season and in June for the Fall/Winter season of the next year.

The weeklong series of special events is designed to underscore the worldwide influence of Italian style on both tailored and casual men's wear. However, Pitti Uomo is also a showcase for international and American designers and manufacturers to present their collections with as many as 600 companies and more than 700 brands represented. Among the newcomers and reentries are Nautica, Pringle, Austin Reed, and Reebok, as well as Kenzo Sport, Versace Sport, Claude Montana, and Magnum Hi Tec.

Italian Fashion Week continues as journalists and buyers then proceed to Milan to view the Milano Confezioni Uomo collections. In 1999, the United States represented the third most important export market for the Italian fashion industry.

Paris Couture and Prêt-à-Porter

The third branch of Fédération Française, La Chambre Syndicale de la Mode Masculine, is composed of couture houses and fashion designers of men's ready-to-wear apparel. The Paris haute couture men's shows are held in January for the Spring/Summer season, and July for the Fall/Winter season. In lavish style, the various prestigious venues feature twelve Haute Couture Houses, ten "Membres Invites," and two "Membres Correspondants." The four "Membres Invites" are Carlo Ponti, Fred Sathal, Frederic Molenac, and Seredin & Vasiliev.

Approximately twenty-five collections are shown during five days with 810 journalists from thirty-eight countries covering the shows. Newcomer Nicolas Ghesquière chose this venue to introduce his first men's designs for Balenciaga for Fall 2002 (*Women's Wear Daily,* May 5, 2002). Ghesquière proposed a small "wardrobe" of pants, jackets, coats, knitwear, and other items. The French house, now controlled by Gucci Group, has sold classic men's tailored clothing under the Balenciaga label in its boutique for years, but Ghesquière designed none of it.

Mode Masculine

Mode Masculine is to men's wear what Prêt-à-Porter is to women's wear. The Spring/Summer 2002 designer collections, shown from June 30 to July 3, 2001, featured thirty-six catwalk shows and eighteen "viewing by appointment" over four days with 400 journalists from twenty-four countries viewing the collections. For the first time, Dominique Morlotti and Lacoste presented their men's collections and Ozwald Boateng returned to show in Paris. The Fall Mode collections are usually held in late January.

TRADE SHOWS

Casabo

Casabo takes place at the Carrousel du Louvre twice a year to coincide with the Paris men's wear catwalks, January for the Fall/Winter collections, July for the Spring/Summer collections.

Under white canvas marquees and inside spaces, the highly selective show brings designers from the men's wear and mixed collections of fashion and accessories sectors together from the worlds of design, objects, cosmetics, perfumes, and leisure goods in a multisector "lifestyle" event. International buyers representing department stores, upmarket, multilabel men's wear and mixed-wear retailers account for the majority of the visitors. Trainoi Homme is a concurrent show held at the Bourse du Commerce.

SEHM

SEHM, the Salon International de L'Habillcment Masculin trade show, is held each year in Paris at the Porte de Versailles, Parc des Expositions. SEHM enjoys a leadership position among international men's wear events and attracts international exhibitors from many countries who show their lines in casual leisure wear, sportswear, activewear, working clothes, townwear, leather, furs, knitwear, and accessories. Men's wear forecast and trend presentations augment the trade show's activities.

Additional Shows

Other trade shows that provide a rich source of men's wear trends and runway designer collections include:

Gaudi Hombre, Barcelona, Spain

International Men's & Boys' Exhibition, London, England

International Men's Week, Cologne, Germany

Scandinavian Men's Wear Fair, Copenhagen, Denmark

U.S. TRADE SHOWS

NAMSB WorldSource

NAMSB WorldSource, the show produced by the National Association of Men's Sportswear Buyers (NAMSB), is one of the most important trade shows in America. NAMSB currently sponsors four shows a year, in January, April, June, and October. For many years, the show was held at Show Pier 92 in New York City, the U.S. capital of apparel and textile sourcing, but in 1992 it moved to the Jacob Javits Convention Center. In October, the midseason New York Men's wear Show (NYMS) takes place with a focus on major classifications of men's wear.

The NAMSB WorldSource show gives international suppliers of apparel, accessories, textiles, and leather direct access to major U.S. buyers, including branded and designer apparel houses, corporate buying offices, resident buying offices, private label retailers, catalog companies, and other firms.

PUBLICATIONS

In addition to the shows, NAMSB publishes *NAMSB News,* the association's monthly newsletter. A membership service since the association's founding, it is an illustrated publication that analyzes trends in fashion and marketing.

The *NAMSB Fashion Futures* report is an annual illustrated trend projection for the print media. It has a counterpart for television, the semiannual package of men's wear Fashion Video News Releases, which reaches 20 million viewers each season.

The Collective

As owner of The Collective, Elyse Kroll, president of ENK International, has created America's most prestigious men's wear trade show, held twice yearly in New York City. It is one of the most anticipated events in the industry and launches New York's market week.

Exhibitors at NAMSB's 2002 show included (top) Tex Line Associates, (center) Gemelli (PTY) Ltd., and (bottom) Maral Overseas Limited.

ENK's The Collective includes invited exhibitors, guests, and media from the international world of mens' wear. In addition to collections from noted designers, The Collective offers opportunities for young designers to make their entrance on the fashion scene.

The show started out as a hotel boutique show, originally named Designers' Collective. Today, Kroll has the inside track on trade show development and has made Pier 94, in New York City, a major show venue showcasing every important category and price point in men's wear.

She has the final say on who gets in and who does not, as well as who gets those prime booths in the main aisle. Kroll screens the collections with a panel of retailers to qualify each men's wear applicant by the criteria of quality, craftsmanship, design point of view, and product category.

Men's wear companies from all over the world present their collections at The Collective to the most influential retailers and press from the United States and abroad. Kroll is known to have put more than one men's wear designer on the map and counts among her early finds Andrew Fezza, Paul Smith, and Makins Hats. Other prestigious brands at The Collective include Cole Haan, Marzotto, Kenneth Cole, and Tommy Bahama, along with the more edgy collections of Ted Baker, Etro, and Theory. To bring fresh new talent to the attention of the industry, The Collective annex introduces new young designers who are judged by originality, craftsmanship, and integrity of design.

The ENK International-produced shows also include Sole Commerce, a first-class shoe show, the Fashion Coterie, a prestige women's wear show, and the Accessories Circuit, Children's Club, Intermezzo Collections, and Pacific Champions.

MAGIC

MAGIC (Men's Apparel Guild in California) is considered the world's largest men's wear show. Formerly held in Palm Springs, California, for West Coast manufacturers, it is now held in Las Vegas, a city more ideally suited to attracting international exhibitors and retailers from all major areas of the United States and abroad.

Exhibitors display a wide breadth of merchandise, including the most innovative looks in young men's, activewear, denim, and streetwear. Women's apparel collections are also featured.

American Apparel & Footwear Association

The American Apparel & Footwear Association (AAFA) is the national trade association representing apparel, footwear, and other sewn products companies and their suppliers which compete in the global market. AAFA's mission is to promote and enhance its members' competitiveness, productivity, and profitability in the global market by minimizing regulatory, legal, commercial, political, and trade restraints.

AAFA's American Image Awards are held at a black tie event where luminaries and fashion insiders gather at a prestigious hotel each year to honor distinguished executives who have made a significant contribution to the men's wear industry through their dedication, professionalism, and generosity. The American Image Awards support the promotional efforts of AAFA. A share of the proceeds from the event are donated to the American Apparel Education Foundation and the Young Men's wear Association, which are dedicated to encouraging promising college students and graduates to pursue careers in apparel retailing, design, and manufacturing.

Other Trade Organizations

Other important trade organizations include the Clothing Manufacturers Association of the USA (CMA) and Men's wear Retailers of America (MRA), a national trade association representing independent men's and boys' wear specialty stores.

TOM JULIAN: THE TREND ANALYST

While the fashion industry has its forecasters, one of the most recognizable spokespersons for men's wear is Tom Julian. As

SIDEBAR 13-1 | Dallas, Texas: The International Menswear Mart

The International Menswear Mart, opened in 1982, adjoins the International Apparel Mart. The six-story building includes "The Territory," home to western apparel and tack showrooms. More than 750 western lines are represented, including all major manufacturers of boots, hats, and apparel. There are also important men's wear sectors in the apparel marts in Chicago, Atlanta, and Los Angeles.

TRENDS *Report*

NEWSFROMTOMJULIAN

Fall '02 Headlines from Italy
A Sensible Shift

The color palette was changing; the fabrics were softer as the menswear market officially began its shift to the sensible and familiar at the semiannual Pitti Uomo trade fair held in Florence, Italy in January. The coming fall season is looking cozy and comfy with warmer colors, richer fabrics, and winterized details. Antique is now good, while moderne looks synthetic. The old classics became new and natty as designers and manufacturers told their stories, in which outerwear and accessories gave way to a total style story. The lean millennium fashion statements have given way to looser and laundered sportswear. Leather and suede finishes ranged from the rugged to the vintage touch.

One of the strongest visual indicators at the show was the setting for the clothes and a singular recurring theme – the cabin. Many of the booths included fireplaces and backdrops reminiscent of a Saint Moritz ski chalet (for the deluxe) or the lodges at the Adirondacks (for the rugged). Wood, bark, leaves, and rustic furniture created from horns and antlers allowed the clothes to come to cabin life in all types of rooms, including the library, the bedroom, and the living room. The look and feel of the photo campaigns and marketing materials created a "home is good" mood. Several booths relied upon motorcycles and vintage cars to make the masculinity message stronger. Even Nissan contributed to the atmosphere: in a marketing outreach, the company lined the entrance to the show with their X-Terra SUVs for visitors' interaction.

The 61st Pitti Uomo trade fair was the first serious selling show since the events of September 11. This premiere show hosted over 640 companies and 730 brands from all over the world. Pitti Uomo continues to grow with new buildings and exhibitions, but still combines the right balance of old-world Italian craftsmanship with the emerging-world of directional brands and designers. During the first day of the show, there was a surprising surge in traffic; early reports from show officials indicated that it was the local buyers who helped increase attendance. Since the sale season in Italy kicked off earlier this January, some suspected that it allowed more opportunity for buyers to focus on the impending fall buy.

BUSINESS BUZZ

Sure, there were several retail groups and publishing companies from the States that were not represented, but the Americans did help to make global headlines at Pitti Uomo! John Varvatos (part of the publicly-held Nautica organization) led the effort with the international debut of his menswear. Some of his signature pieces: a 3-button roll to 2-button silhouette, luxe outerwear, limited-edition Converse sneakers, and Poor Boy sweaters. Heritage-driven Levi's presented for the first time their Red-Label (along with the oldest, most expensive jeans ever acquired on eBay) to pique European markets denim interest. Designer John Bartlett (no longer involved with Byblos) decided Pitti Uomo was the place for his Uniform collection of collegiate-themed, military-inspired value-priced sportswear. Brands like Timberland, Columbia, Nautica, Gant, and Converse felt right in step with the Pitti market and illustrated the power of American brands.

Tom Julian is one of the menswear industry's leading forecasters. His Trends Report for the Fall 2002 is an example of the depth of information his research and travels provide for his clients.

a leading trend analyst for the award-winning advertising agency Fallon Worldwide, Mr. Julian plays an integral role in building the agency's reputation for creative brand management for its Fortune 500 clients.

Adweek, the trade newspaper, recognized Tom Julian as having one of "coolest jobs" in advertising. He is a contributor for the nationally syndicated television show *Main Floor*, which began airing September 1994. Now in its tenth season, *Main Floor*'s coverage has expanded to include his men's wear and celebrity reports from the Milan and New York Fashion shows, as well as other international venues. His men's wear background also contributes to his apparel knowledge and retail analysis. He spent eight years as the spokesman for the Men's Fashion Association trade group, as well as a retail career with Gucci.

Tom Julian's work is multifaceted. In the pursuit of marketing and fashion news, his workdays are not typical. He is constantly on the road, and his travels take him not only to major U.S. cities, but on annual trips to Europe. He is the eyes and ears for the Fallon agency and as such he appreciates the fact that management understands, supports, and endorses what he is doing in the world of fashion, global retailing, and marketing. To further clarify his position as trend analyst, Mr. Julian says, "Advertising has become more than just a marketing campaign. Rather than being just a hot shop for advertising, Fallon is involved with creative branding and problem solving with a strong relevance to the bottom line. Trend analysis, therefore, is a major component of the Fallon Agency's diversified client services. Information is filtered in house, then expands throughout Fallon's global client community."

The Analyst's Strategy

A consummate researcher, Mr. Julian connects all the points of reference. When he is on the international travel circuit to review a trade show or fashion event, he expands his areas of trend tracking and exploration by engaging in diverse areas of investigation. His checklist includes the following.

- Determine what's happening at retail (specialty and mass market)
- Visit the local museum or the most significant cultural event
- Check Trade/Special Event/Activity other than fashion
- Observe or participate in social happenings
- Visit the local university's community center to observe trends and glean an insight into current youth attitudes.
- Visit an innovative supermarket to evaluate food preferences and emphasis on health
- Survey an off-the-beaten-path vintage or used clothing store; it may offer a unique opportunity to discover the next big item

Tom Julian also connects with the local people. He talks to everyone, including media contacts, taxicab drivers, the hotel concierge, and waiters in restaurants. Every person is treated as part of a focus group of information that will contribute to his analyses of trends, demographics, and lifestyles. He travels with a digital camera to record photo opportunities and picks up material, flyers, and brochures that he will read and digest as points of reference for his reports.

This combination of research fuels Tom Julian's ability to generate timely and futuristic trend information that has established his reputation as a significant trend analyst. National newspapers including *USA Today,* the *Wall Street Journal,* and the *Los Angeles Times,* as well as syndicates such as Copley, Bloomberg, and the AP wire service contact Mr. Julian on a regular basis seeking quotations on trends and retail news.

Mr. Julian recounts, "Many people say I have the ideal job. Yes, I do have the ideal job for my skill set. I am working for

SIDEBAR 13-2 | Margit Publications, Inc.

Margit Publications is a publication-driven trend company with an emphasis on customer relations. The creative team of experts attends the major international trade shows such as Première Vision, Indigo, and European Textile Collections. "All information gathered is then shared with clients through creative fashion presentations, reports, and company consulting," said Margit Zsedely, president. Margit Publications is now affiliated with The Doneger Group.

the ideal company that supports my work. However, the statistics are high for both parties. As one of the recognizable voices in the company everything has to be applicable, efficient, and economical."

He advises students that opportunity is everywhere. "Creative Fashion Presentations is an opportunity for branding your personality by continuous critique of yourself. It is critical to improve and continue to reevaluate one's performance. Wherever one works it is important to understand the corporate culture and the political process on the job and with clients. Honing your skills is a continuous learning process. Foremost learn how to excel in a competitive and changing environment."

IZOD: THE DESIGN PROCESS

Izod, Phillips–Van Heusen's sports-influenced brand, places its roots in active sportswear, but its successful expansion was implemented by subdividing the line into other garment classifications. Thus, pants, shorts, outerwear, woven sport shirts, and swimwear augment Izod's core business in sweaters, fleece, and knitwear. Each of the Izod categories is further subdivided into solids versus fancies, tops versus bottoms, and logo versus "unlogo." These are further subdivided into percentages of sales by color and sales by item.

The design team and decision makers evaluate each category. They lock heads and question the "business sense" of each garment. Does it fit a price range? Is it cost effective to produce? The designer today must have more technical knowledge and needs to understand how business is run. When these questions are satisfactorily answered, the product lines are calendarized and scheduled with production dates and the store delivery time frame.

The Design Team

When designing the line, the design team does not start from scratch, but begins each season with proven success styles. "The Izod crested polo shirt is an annuity sell," says Mark Weber, the affable president/chief operating officer of Phillips–Van Heusen. "We sell 3 million units per year in the United States alone. In this case, the design team may only need to recolor the polo shirt or the coordinating crest, according to the new seasonal ranges."

Origins of Creativity

The creative process is diversified, but there are calculated steps to take in the development of a theme for a line. Mark Weber says, "Suppose this year Izod wants to do an Hawaiian theme. This idea may come from the flow of fashion information or from instinct."

Mr. Weber points out that the theme name colors and line development are a collaborative effect among sales, merchandising, and the design team. The Izod professionals discuss the theme name, "Honolulu Surf," and the colors, soft medium pastels with a shot of color to pop the design. The debates on several issues continue concerning the line, and after final endorsement by all the team participants on the theme and the colors, the line goes to the next step. Every company has variations of the design process. However, at Izod, once Hawaiian is confirmed as a viable direction and theme, the design team takes the following steps.

This page and opposite page: *Two boards from Izod's Swimwear 2003 collection, entitled Honolulu Surf, are actually used as part of the sales campaign. Each garment is realistically portrayed in coordinated collections with features highlighted. The boards can be further enhanced for greater visual impact.*

1. Research can be conducted on several levels.
   - A. Define what Hawaiian actually means in terms of motif
   - B. Take a plane to Hawaii to get an authentic impression
     - a) Go to the library, check the references
     - b) Shop antique stores, look for unusual Hawaiian-like ideas
     - c) Check swatch houses for Hawaiian prints
     - d) Check color services for current and historical colors
     - e) Check yarn stores for texture and color
     - f) Shop retail in general and see what is out there
2. Color is the number one consideration.

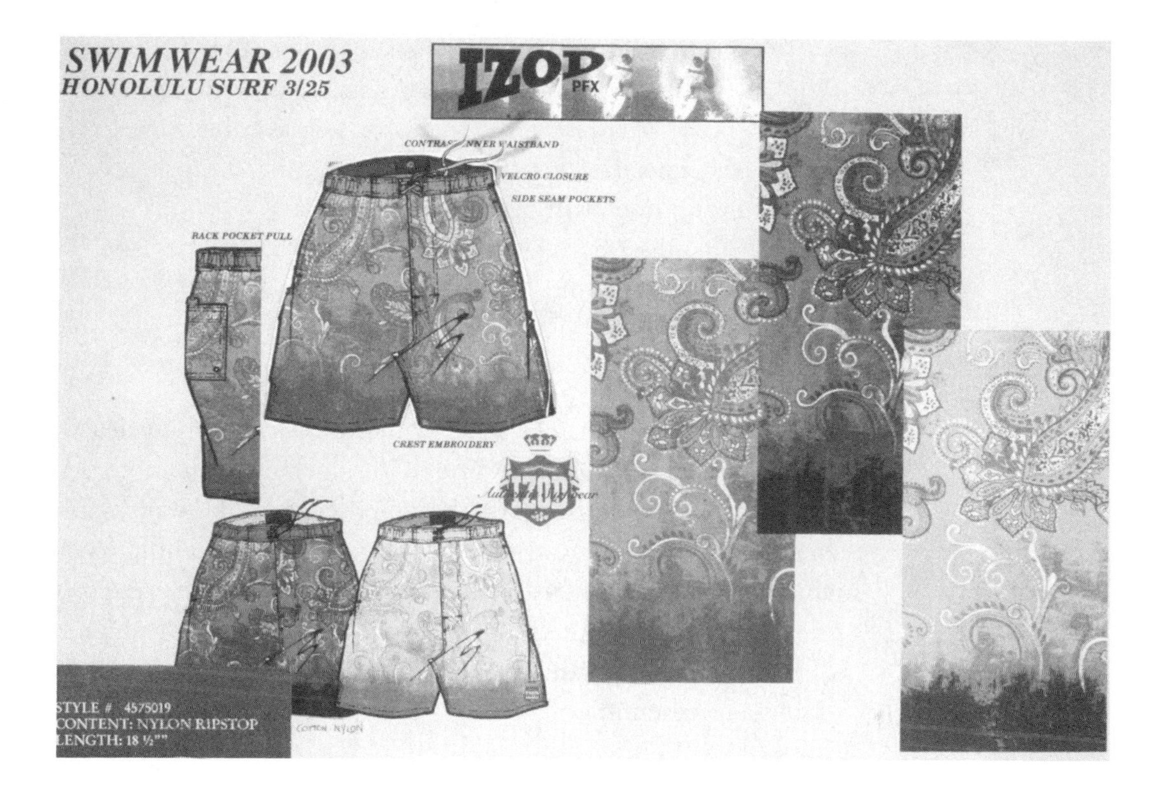

3. Fabric designs and fabric patterns are researched and secured.
4. Garment models and details are developed.

These four elements all come together in the form of story boards.

5. Creative story board presentations are developed.

   "Boards are critical to the firm's decision to invest in producing samples," notes Mr. Weber. "At collaborative meetings, management looks at the ideas. Rejections and acceptances of line development take place. Boards are the lifeblood of the company. They represent the completely coordinated classifications of the

Izod lines. These are low frill boards that tell the complete line story by color, fabric, and styles." The storyboards represent the final decisions on line development and the "go" to invest significant corporate funding that will be put into inventory.

6. Final edits represent the fine tuning of the lines and putting the samples into work.

Boards: A Sales Tool

A lot of companies may also sell from the boards, which clearly represent the coordinated line with garments in a three-dimensional perspective. All the color ranges and fabric assortments are also represented in a low-frills presentation, from which the firm takes customer orders. For customer presentations, various montage treatments, like coconuts and fruits for a Hawaiian theme, can theatricalize the boards for a more entertaining presentation.

NAUTICA

The Design Inspiration

"Evolution is at the heart of the Nautica concept. Since I founded Nautica in 1983, refining our signature modern classic design philosophy continues to be my top priority as we evolve into a truly global lifestyle brand," says David Chu. Chu is the Nautica founder and designer who has stayed true to his original concept of modern classics and has infused the spirit of Nautica with the color blue—the spirit of the sea and sky.

"I've always lived on islands, first Taiwan then Manhattan. I think the proximity to the sea has influenced my designs immeasurably. Being surrounded by water, I have always been drawn to and fascinated by the sea," says the designer. "This love of the sea is reflected in the name of the brand itself, 'Nautica,' derived from the Latin word for ship, *Nauticus*, and in the J-class spinnaker logo, a symbol of adventure, action, and classicism."

Beyond the metaphor of the sea as symbol of adventure and exploration, the practical side of sailing and life at sea has fundamentally influenced David Chu's designs for Nautica. He notes, "Seventy-five percent of the world has coastal lines, everyone understands nautical, it's a global, universal icon, as is the anchor emblem, which hasn't changed for over four thousand years." As you look around Mr. Chu's office, several objects evoke the symbols of the sea, including a magnificent crystal schooner. This represents a reminder that Nautica is the official designer for the high-performance outfits worn by the crew of "Stars and Stripes," the entry of the New York Yacht Club in the America's Cup Challenge.

David Chu, founder of Nautica, has always been influenced by the sea and the romantic adventures it offers.

Anchoring Inspiration

From a very early age, Mr. Chu has been fascinated with the utilitarian and functional aspects not only of architecture, but also of military uniforms, specifically those of sailors. An avid collector of military and antique men's clothing, he says, "When I design our apparel collections, I often find inspiration in the clean lines and functionality of military clothing. Historically, the fashion and style of military clothing has evolved, but what never changes is the overwhelming need for functionality. Utility and wearability are paramount. I always try to keep this simple concept in mind when I design for Nautica." Mr. Chu points out that design is a synergistic process in which he works closely with the design team in every product line. The dedicated staff, in this multifaceted lifestyle company, also anchors their inspiration in the nautical philosophy through the dominant color blue and fabric innovation.

Brand Expansion

Under David Chu's design direction, the Nautica concept has evolved from a collection of men's outerwear into a complete lifestyle brand with more than thirty-five different products in sixty-five countries in the global marketplace. At the core of the brand is Nautica Sportswear for men. From this line, the firm has expanded into tailored clothing that features greater comfort through softer technology and stretch materials. The line diversification also includes a full line of accessories, men's and women's sleepwear, jeans for men and women, and swimwear for women. David Chu has further expanded the Nautica concept into a complete lifestyle approach with the Nautica Home Collection, a complete line of bedding, bath linens, dinnerware, and furniture.

David Chu's achievements have garnered him many awards, and his philanthropic work includes his commitment to the River Keeper Organization, whose mission is to protect America's fresh water resources.

HARTMARX ENTERPRISES

In an industry where men's wear has traditionally been produced by huge conglomerates, one major player stands out, and that is Hartmarx. Long known and respected as America's foremost manufacturer of high-quality men's apparel in formal and casual collections, Hartmarx has expanded its position as a modern fashion apparel enterprise with a strong sportswear and women's wear presence. A variety of fashions, price points, branded, and designer products are created for an extensive range of retail channels and consumers.

Diversified Brands

In addition to the Hart Schaffner and Marx men's and women's apparel labels, the diverse brands include Hickey-Freeman, elegant men's tailored clothing, and sportswear apparel with a golf flavor under the Bobby Jones and the Nicklaus and Pringle of Scotland labels. The Ted Baker of London men's and women's introduction represents a dynamic, young fashion force and targets a younger customer.

Hartmarx has also expanded its leadership position with a significant licensed suit, sports coat, and slacks business under the Tommy Hilfiger, Kenneth Cole, Burberry, Claiborne, Evan-Picone, Austin Reed, and KM by Krizia labels. The Gieves & Hawkes brand brings its celebrated Savile Row quality and distinctively British styling to North America in a collection of tailored clothing.

The Designer Connection

Jorge Molina, Kenneth Cole's design director for tailored suits at Hartmarx, has the unique challenge of working with one of the most influential American designers today. In tandem with Hartmarx, Cole, the shoe mogul, has firmly established himself as an authority for men's wear designs that represent the sophistication of city life.

"A major aspect of the men's wear business is designer name driven," says Mr. Molina. "That's where most designers build their business and increase their profits." Thus, Molina and Cole have a syngergistic relationship as they engage in fabric sourcing and development of the collection. "We're running a business, and cost and quality are major considerations as well as every button, zipper, trim, and interfacing," notes Mr. Molina.

The Design Process

The creative process begins with establishing an identifiable taste level. Teamwork is a key factor between Kenneth Cole and the design team. Innovative fabrications can lend distinction. "An 1888 fabric swatch book with its vintage wool patterns, which I had acquired, serves as inspiration for new color

Kenneth Cole values teamwork in developing his classic lines of menswear.

ways and retro fabric design ideas," notes Mr. Molina. "Our fabrics are all exclusive to Kenneth Cole. We design the patterns and the weaves with Kenneth's direction. The fabrics and silhouettes are selected with versatility in mind. Men want to feel like they are buying something special, fashionable yet classic, trendy but wearable, and that's what the Kenneth Cole label delivers."

Mr. Molina points out that designing is not about creating a new silhouette, because a basic suit silhouette is the same as it was in the eighteenth century. However, in the Kenneth Cole designer line, there is not one dominant model; it is more about a sexier shape, with the jacket a bit closer to the body shown with a plain front pant. A best-selling silhouette features narrow lapels, slanted hacking besom pockets, and a high button stance. Shape suits have iridescent linings. The Kenneth Cole Reaction collection features separates and sportswear that reflect a younger point of view and is a more affordable line.

Cole's Spring 2002 collection is reflected in these five designs. They are more relaxed, yet sexier, with a comfortable look. With this collection, Cole is reaching out to a younger audience.

Line Introductions

New trends in marketing tailored men's wear suits, sold off the rack, have increased the line presentations schedule from twice a year to four times a year:

December for July delivery

February for October delivery

May for January delivery

August for May delivery

Sportswear traditionally shows four times a year and delivers four times a year.

Trade Terminology

AAFA'S American Image Awards
British influence
Celeb endorsement
Chambre Syndicale de la Mode Masculine
Custom-made
Designer name
Digitally tailored
Milan Fashion Week
MAGIC
NAMSB WorldSource
New York Fashion Week
Pitti Imagine Uomo
Prognosticator
Savile Row
The Collective
Trend analyst
Vanity boom

READING 13-1 For the Man With a 15.95-Inch Neck

BY DAVID COLMAN

Not since Yankee Doodle stuck a feather in his hat 225 years ago and called it macaroni—a derogatory reference to London's Macaroni Club, decadent young fops who had traveled in Italy and adopted its tastes—has Italian style held such sway in the wardrobes of American men.

The houses of Gucci, Armani, Prada, Versace and Dolce & Gabbana have raised the style ante over the last two decades, so that today's macaronis—myself, I admit, among them—would scarcely trade their Gucci loafers for Bass Weejuns or their Armani shirts for ones with button-down collars.

But I recently found myself in a bastion of men's style—some might call it a stick-in-the-mud—Brooks Brothers, which promised to put me in the smartest suit I could imagine.

On the third floor of the company's Madison Avenue flagship, I was handed a pair of neutral-gray boxer briefs, changed into them and was directed to stand semi-naked in a mahogany-paneled chamber. I grasped two handles, closed my eyes and squeezed the "on" buttons. Very bright lights flashed for about 10 seconds. I would soon be the first on my block with a computer-tailored suit.

The lights were scanners, and they plotted 200,000 topographical points on my body. A software program translated the data into 45 tailoring measurements—collar, biceps, drop from side of neck to chest—all within a hundredth of an inch.

Brooks Brothers transmits the measurements—along with a customer's choices for fit, style and fabric—to its suit factory outside Boston or its shirt factory in North Carolina, where a made-to-order wardrobe is produced in two to three weeks. Custom shirts start at $90, trousers at $200 and a suit is only $700, or $100 more than an off-the-rack model. (It can cost more, depending on fabric.) A sport coat is $500 made of a lightweight wool; in alpaca, $700.

Traditionally made custom suits at Brooks Brothers start at $1,050. At more exclusive suit makers in New York, London and Milan, prices for a custom suit run from $2,000 to $5,000. They can also require several fittings and take months to finish; the result can be the most exquisitely fitted garment imaginable.

Or not. "The whole custom-tailoring process usually takes too much time," said Montieth Illingworth, a public relations executive who had several suits made in New York in the mid-80's. "And my experience was that after all that, they didn't always get it perfectly right, whether it was the inseams, this measurement, that one."

Mr. Illingworth, one of the first customers for Brooks Brothers' digital tailoring service, introduced Nov. 4, ordered a black suit in an Italian worsted wool for $1,100, less a 30 percent discount offered during the first two weeks of the service. As he awaits his new clothes, he is anxiety-free. "Every tailor who ever measured me told me I had a 15½-inch neck," he said. "With the computer scan, I now know it's 15.95 inches—so already they're ahead."

The computer-aided system follows several other companies that offer to customize shoppers' purchases: Levi's lets you order tailor-made jeans, and Adidas will customize its sports shoes. But Brooks Brothers has inaugurated mass-customization's most comprehensive and perhaps ambitious service to date. It plans to install the digital scanners in its stores in other major cities, and it will offer customers the option of ordering over the phone with only a swatch book, said Joe Dixon, an executive vice president.

Since most customers expect to wait for alterations to an off-the-rack suit, Brooks hopes the service will eventually replace a good percentage of its suit sales, and relieve the financially struggling company of carrying a large inventory. After a major makeover a few seasons back—flat-front trousers and brightly colored shirts replaced staid styles—the company's owner, Marks & Spencer, is trying to sell it.

While the new service might seem to doom traditional custom tailors, Joseph Gromek, the company's president, disagreed. "This will affect the whole clothing business more," he said. "The off-the-rack business is much, much larger than the custom business, and there will always be people who want a true custom service." B. Joseph Pine 2nd, a business consultant and co-editor of "Markets of One: Creating Customer-Unique Value Through Mass Customization" (Harvard University Business Publishing, 2000), said that computer tailoring of suits had a better chance of success than the fads for custom-made jeans and footwear. Customers for ready-made jeans and shoes are used to taking them right home, but suit buyers are used to waiting for alterations.

By the time I had dressed, the computer had my body mapped with unnerving accuracy. It was bizarre to see my silhouette broken into hundreds of lines—both utterly abstract and oddly familiar.

I picked out the clothes I wanted made. I didn't need another suit, so I chose a sport jacket—a countrified houndstooth in alpaca that would run me $698. I ticked off my preferences: a slim three-button silhouette, fully lined, with two side vents, notch lapels, slant welt pockets, picked-stitched and finished sleeves with three buttons.

Fear not: all these were multiple-choice questions, and Brooks Brothers will make nearly all the choices for you if you defer to the house style.

But macoroni that I am, I wanted veto power on every detail.

Then, a shirt. Starting with an eccentric but bankerly blue-and-white-striped cotton, I ticked off my choices: French front, Ainsley collar, barrel cuffs, no pocket, side back pleats, no monogram. Again, fear not: I learned almost all of these terms on my visit.

A week later—I had asked for the items on a rush—I went back. The results, on a Macaroni Club scale of 1 to 10? The jacket was an 8: beautiful to behold, and since it had been fashioned exactly as I like it, it almost seemed as though someone had read my mind. But it fit a little loosely for my taste—the Brooks Brothers way. I asked the store to take in the sides a bit, but I have a feeling my own tailor might have to do a little extra lipo.

The shirt was a 9. The fabric was fantastic, the fit was very good, and it buttoned precisely around my neck (which is 14.88 inches around according to the scan, and that's the only measurement I'm revealing). But because of a computer glitch, two shirts were made: one in the fabric I had chosen and one in the fabric the salesman had preferred. While it was an error that cost me nothing, it was a reminder that even in the digital age there are ways for salesmen to slip their own tastes in.

The good news: as Nick Pollito, the store's digital tailoring adviser, pointed out, the computer would note my postproduction preferences, so next time ordering would be even smoother. Yes, I'll go back for more. Maybe even another scan. But first I'm going to get a good 1.37 inches off my waist: my own personal form of mass customization.

READING 13-2 Tailor Made: The Italian Reputation for Excellence in Tailoring Is Rooted in the Sartorial Art of Men's Wear

BY SAMANTHA CONTI

Ever wonder about the origins of the Armani slouch? The hand-sewn buttonholes on the Kiton suit? The hand-stitched collar on a Vestimenta jacket? The roots of Italian fashion are in tailoring—in particular, the tailoring styles developed by the Neapolitans and Romans, who over the centuries have turned the simple act of sewing into what many consider a form of art. Long before Giorgio Armani tore out the linings of the traditional suit and unleashed a fashion revolution, the Neapolitans and Romans were making jackets that—in the words of the Neapolitan tailor Cesare Attolini—felt like "cardigan sweaters, not armor."

The Neapolitans have been stitching seriously since the 14th century, when the first Aragonese kings arrived dressed to the nines and ready to rule what was then known as the Kingdom of Sicily. In the centuries that followed, the city's natives cut and sewed side by side with tailors from the Aragon, Bourbon and Hapsburg courts that ruled Naples into the 19th century.

"Our tailoring is a mix of the French, English, Spanish and Italian traditions. We took the best from everyone," said Antonio De Matteis, the commercial director of Kiton, the Neapolitan suit maker.

The Neapolitan sartorial jacket fits snugly: the armhole is high and small, and the sleeve, by comparison, is wide, allowing men and women to move their arms freely while their shoulders stay put. Lapels join the collar on the collarbone—a trick to lengthen those short Italian torsos—and the padding and underpinnings are minimal. Telltale details of the Neapolitan jacket are breast pockets that curve upward like half moons and hand-sewn eyelets, collars and armholes.

"The Neapolitan jacket has to move with the man," said Attolini, whose father, Vincenzo, dressed the Duke of Windsor and Clark Gable. Today, Attolini's client roster is as diverse as German Chancellor Helmut Kohl, Oliver Stone and Muammar al-Qaddafi. Both Kiton and Attolini have recently unveiled small women's collections bearing the same sartorial marks as the men's collections. Retailer Janet Brown described the jackets made in Naples as "art, not commerce. This is the height of luxury—without being conspicuous. You wait for them to be made, just like you wait for a Kelly bag or a Porsche."

ICA, whose factory is in the shadow of Naples' Capodichino airport, is the most industrial of all the Neapolitan tailors, and produces men's and women's wear for designers including Versace, Vestimenta, Joop and Nicole Farhi. Owner Michele De Simone said the company's strength is its ability to work closely with designers and offer a sartorial look and finishing at a variety of price points. De Simone's in-house tailors work with each designer's team to develop models, and his seamstresses travel to Milan each season to stitch into the wee hours before fashion shows. While part of ICA's product is done by machine, the company ensures that sleeves and shoulders, armholes, collars and buttonholes are all sewn by hand.

Another industrial company specialized in sartorial techniques is Herno, which manufactures men's and women's clothing for Giorgio Armani, Prada, Gucci and Louis Vuitton—in addition to producing an eponymous in-house line that's designed by Rebecca Moses. Buttonholes are hand-sewn, fabrics with patterns are cut by hand, and jackets are crafted with the utmost care.

"A jacket here takes double the time of one made industrially because it goes through at least 10 passages. Nothing is heat-fused, and every single layer is placed and sewn by hand," said Claudio Marenzi, whose family owns the company based in Lesa, on the shores of Lago Maggiore. Herno is one of Italy's few sartorial manufacturing companies based in northern—rather than southern—Italy.

Like their Neapolitan counterparts, the Romans wore the fine-tailoring traditions of foreign cultures into their suits. Rome's tailors made their name during Italy's postwar industrial boom, dressing swank tourists and American heartthrobs who were filming at Cinecitta—Rome's answer to Hollywood. Rock Hudson, Clark Gable, John Wayne and Kirk Douglas never left the city without a suit made by Brioni, Domenico Caraceni or Litrico—who were among the first generation of Roman tailors. Umberto Angeloni, CEO of the men's wear company Brioni, said the foreign invasion taught Roman tailors not to be provencial in their approach to fashion.

"They have always had to adapt to the demands and needs of an international clientele," Angeloni said.

Milanese tailoring is similar to that of the Roman school. Shoulders are straighter and more constructed and waists are a little narrower than in Naples. Mario Caraceni, whose father, Augusto, moved to Milan in 1946 after a 10-year-stint in Paris, said Milanese tailoring used to be "rigid and militaristic, like the old Savile Row style."

After World War II, the Milanese began to loosen up and follow the general trend of Italian clothing toward softer fabrics, lighter internal construction and comfort.

"It's part of the Italian character," said Mario Caraceni, whose clients include Austrian barons, Italian counts and Milanese millionaires. "We're gentle people, so it's only natural that—whether we're dressed by Neapolitans, Romans or Milanese—in the end, we're all wearing soft suits."

Source: *Italy, The Fashion Makers* (*WWD* supplement), February 2000, pp. 102–103. Courtesy of Fairchild Publications, Inc.

14

Toy Industry

> The toy market is benefiting not just from sales of play toys for kids, but more and more adults are buying toys as collectibles. After all collectibles are really only toys for adults.
>
> *Pam Danziger, Unity Marketing*

HISTORICAL REFERENCES

There would be no childlike faith, no poetry, and no romance if there were no toys to play with and stimulate children's intellect, imagination, and creativity. As children, many of us had a favorite toy. Whether it was a stuffed animal, building blocks, or a toy car, it inspired our creativity, could entertain us for hours, and was an outlet to explore the world around us. This need for discovery and love of play is a universal part of being a child. While all children have different needs, likes, and interests, the desire to play is a constant part of our social history. Children of every culture, from every corner of the globe engage in play—from the African boy who makes music with a hand carved plaything to the North American girl who cuddles a store-bought teddy bear.

As witnessed by the crude discoveries in archeological digs, dolls and toys have been expressions of childhood and adult memories since the dawning of civilization. Although play has existed since ancient times, only recently have we come to realize that it enables children to develop the physical, mental, social, emotional, and creative skills needed for life.

SIDEBAR 14-1 The American International Toy Fair

Government, trade, media, and consumers recognize the Toy Industry Association (TIA), formerly the Toy Manufacturers of America, Inc., founded in 1916, as the authoritative voice of the U.S. toy industry. The Association, headquartered in New York City, is the trade association for U.S. producers and imports of toys, games, and entertainment products for children and families

TIA's more than 280 members include manufacturers and importers of toys, games, and children's entertainment products. Regular members account for approximately 85 percent of total domestic sales. Associate members include toy testing laboratories, design firms, and professional inventors. TIA is governed by a board of directors that is comprised of a chairperson and up to five directors drawn from a wide range of TIA member companies.

American International Toy Fair

Toy Fair, as it is commonly known, is the largest toy trade show in the United States. Owned and managed by the Toy Industry Association, it is the premier marketing event of the year for the worldwide toy industry. Held annually since 1902, Toy Fair is recognized as the world's most important toy trade show, with exhibitors including manufacturers, distributors, importers, and sales agents from the United States and around the world, ranging in size from major multinational companies to entrepreneurial organizations. Nearly 2,000 exhibitors from thirty countries showcase their toy and entertainment products at Toy Fair. Products on display range from classic toys to interactive items and everything in between for the family entertainment market.

Toy Fair is held in New York City every February in display booths at the Jacob K. Javits Convention Center and in showrooms in Manhattan's West 23rd Street area. In the year 2002, fourteen seminars were open to Toy Fair attendees on such diverse topics as buying trends, retailing advice, and licensing updates.

In addition to Toy Fair and member services, TIA is involved with outside legal, logistics, and tariff/trade counsels and consultants on trade, legislative and communications matters. TIA established The American Toy Institute, Inc., in 1961 as a fund raising arm for children's charities and also to distribute educational brochures to institutions and the public. A current publication, *Fun Play, Safe Play,* is available in English and Spanish.

THE TWENTY-FIRST CENTURY

There has never been a greater array of toys available than today. At the core of play in the twenty-first century, as with every other aspect of our lives, technology has had a profound influence. This applies to the creation of toys, and talented designers and innovators are needed to fulfill the demand. The

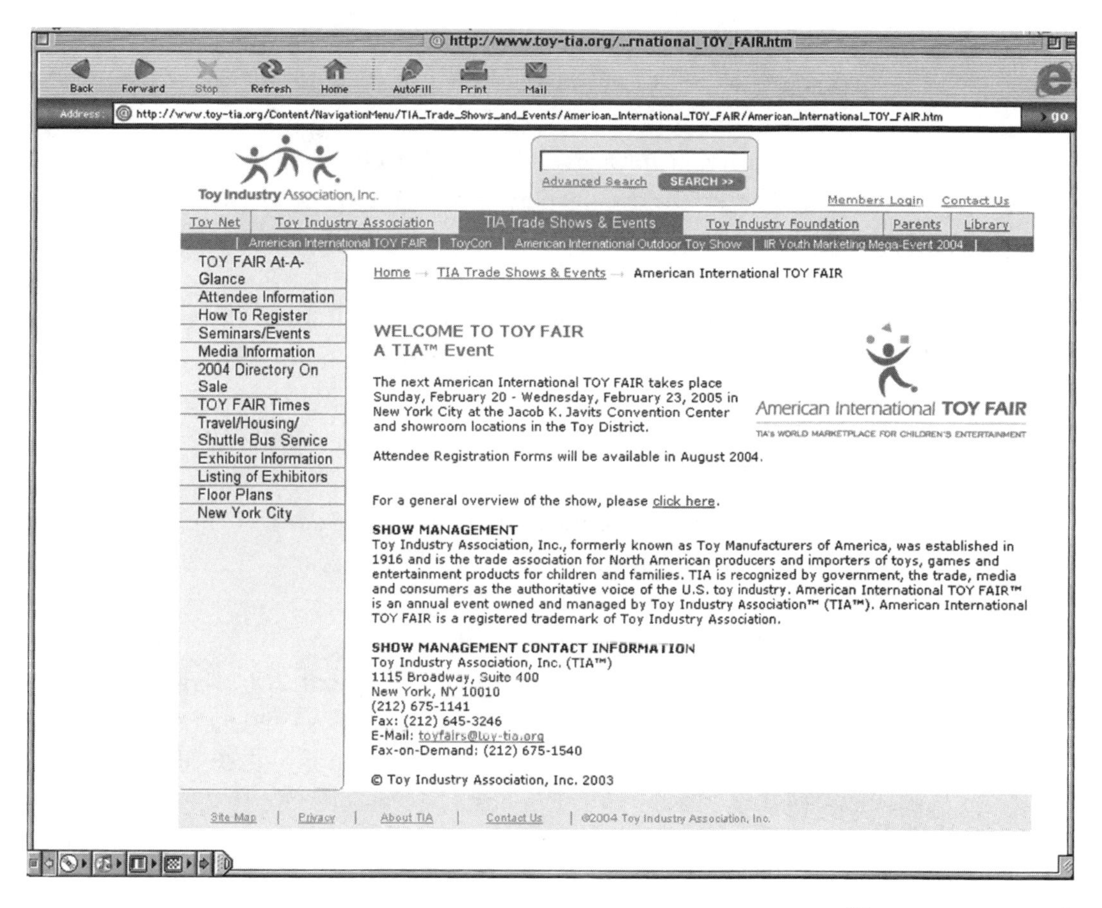

The announcement of the 2005 American International Toy Fair on the Web site of the Toy Industry Association. The number of venues and activities reflects the large number of exhibitors and buyers from all over the world.

so-called "smart toys" have now been phased into almost every toy category.

Peter Eio, chairman of the Toy Industry Association (TIA™), confirmed this fact in a powerful speech at the 2000 American International Toy Fair. He said, "The single, most important change affecting the industry, both from a business and creative viewpoint, is technology."

Youths today are the first generation to grow up in a digital world. They learn, play, communicate, shop, and even relate to each other differently than their baby boomer parents.

To meet these changing play patterns, toy manufacturers have incorporated an unusual blend of new and classic elements, as evidenced in the wide variety of dolls, plush animals, and toys that offer a new level of play for children today. The issue of toy safety and safe play remains, as always, a vitally important issue among American toy manufacturers.

As the *TIA Fact Book* report states, "To take an idea and transform it to a toy that allows a child to discover, wonder . . . and yes, make magic, is at the heart of the industry." TIA ought to know. It has represented the U.S. producers and importers of toys and holiday decorations since 1916. According to the TIA report, annual sales of toys since 1999 has been the strongest in a decade and are a leading source of entertainment and education for children (and adults).

TEDDY BEAR PHENOMENON

According to an article in the February 2002 edition of *Toy Fair Times,* the official TIA publication, in 1999 collectors in the United States purchased $441 million worth of teddy bears (Teddy Bear and Friends, Margarete Steiff Gmbh). Ganz, Gund, Dean's, Knickerbocker, Grisley Spielwaren, and Steiff are among those manufacturers who celebrate the 102-year-old icon, which was introduced in 1902. As *Toy Fair Times* writer Lisa Kelly tells: "Legend has it that Teddy Roosevelt was on hunting trip that produced no results. Fearing the President would go home disappointed his aides found a bear cub, tied it to a tree and offered it to the President. A true sportsman, he refused to shoot the helpless bear!"

The story might have ended there, but two days later a political cartoonist from the *Washington Post* named Clifford Berryman drew a cartoon depicting the incident. The story captured the hearts of animal lovers everywhere, including Morris and Rose Michtom, who created a stuffed "Teddy's Bear" to sell in their candy shop. The next year, the couple launched the Ideal Novelty and Toy Co., which specialized in producing the new phenomenon.

Meanwhile, in Germany, Margarete Steiff of the Steiff Toy Factory asked her nephew Richard Steiff to produce the first jointed bear, which was introduced in March 1903 at the Leipzig Toy Fair. Though the Michtoms and Steiff were working on bears at the same time, neither knew about the other's creation. This transatlantic coincidence was abetted by the fact that an astute American toy buyer, aware of the growing interest in "Teddy's bears" in the United States, ordered 3,000. This helped to propel the teddy bear to the position of preeminent toy of the century.

Trend Spotting

Gund has come a long way with staying power since 1898, when it was founded by Adolph Gund, as a toy and novelty company—which was one of the first to produce teddy bears in the early 1900s.

Always a trend setter, in the 1940s, Gund was the first to employ striped tiger and spotted leopard materials originally used in "fun furs" to create stuffed versions of those animals. With fun furs, the pattern was printed or woven into plush. Prior to that, animal markings had been sprayed on.

"We challenge ourselves to stay abreast of trends," notes Ms. Moritz. "When roses are strong, we put this motif into our teddy bears, or might embroider a rose on a toe pad of the foot or the bum. In order to anticipate trends the product development team immerses themselves in research. Ideas may cross over from fashion forecasting for apparel, from foreign magazines, everywhere and anywhere, research provides the design innovation. With butterflies or lady bugs, Gund is right on target with plush toy interpretations. Gund considers the ethnic preferences and pays close attention to skintones, clothing, coloring, and patterns.

The Design Process

Design team artists, who conceive characters in thumbnail sketches, create ideas for new products. Ms. Moritz meets with the creative group and they collectively discuss the following:

- The sketches
- The materials
- Feasibility of design and production
- Aspects of building a line (not just an item but a series)
- Naming the product

Uniqueness is a major consideration in character development, and the personalities must identify with Gund. It can not be just another puppy dog or teddy bear. Although teddy bears outsell all categories, in the last few years, according to Ms. Moritz, dogs are climbing up the sales ladder and are approaching teddy bears in popularity. Innovative materials from faux fur enhancements to fashion fabrics that heretofore had not been used in plush animals also build strong characters.

What's in a name? A lot when it comes to plush toys. "Names are an important part of the attraction, the sell of the product," notes Ms. Moritz. "Two of the company's most famous animals, Snuffles the bear and Muttsy the dog, were introduced in the 80s."

Licensing Products

Throughout the 1960s, Gund continued to be best known for its Disney plush toys. In the 1970s, its Winnie the Pooh exclusives for Sears and its Collectors Classic line were extremely popular, and its Luv Me Bear was its bestseller. In 1979, however, Gund launched the famous Gotta Getta Gund advertising campaign, which led to the company's recognition as a leading consumer brand. In September 1996, Puddles the pooch made the biggest splash yet, and the babyGund line was introduced in 1997. Gund is a company that does it all—from baby products to collectibles and licensed lines, the company has carved a special niche in the market.

POP-MUSIC TOYS: KARAOKE

Today's childhood fantasies revolve around the stage, and the playground culture has evolved into a high-tech experience. Recognizing the fact that most little girls want to be a star, toymakers are bringing the music celebrity experience even closer to home for the "tween" audience. Tween is industry jargon for children eight to twelve years of age. Now girls just pop in a videotape or cassette and sing their hearts out like Christina Aguilera while gyrating like pop-music stars.

Karaoke products are the catch-all industry categorization used to describe the hardware, accompaniment tapes, and CDs produced by a wide variety of recording companies that have penetrated the toy market with interactive pop-music toys. The entertainment aspect of karaoke makes it perfect for kids' parties and daycare, as well as for weddings, senior activities, and other social occasions. Everybody is an instant star as they pick up the microphone and start singing.

Sound Choice Accompaniment Tracks

The beat behind the Sound Choice Accompaniment Tracks is brothers Derek and Kurt Slep, who have teamed up to make Sound Choice, a karaoke powerhouse. "Although we never really liked the word 'karaoke,' we were using 'accompaniment' or 'sing-along' as a description, but karaoke won out as the identifiable icon," says Kurt Slep, vice president. At the firm's sprawling Charlotte, North Carolina, headquarters, literally thousands of sing-along tapes are produced each year. "The market for sing-along tapes is everyone from two to ninety-two," said Kurt Slep. "Who else in the music industry has a product that targets such a wide demographic?"

Sound Choice Accompaniment Tracks are arranged and produced to duplicate the original hit recordings, both with

Cover of the booklet that comes with the Children's Activity Songs recording.

and without the lead vocals. The firm's studio musicians, working in the same key and tempo as the original artist, record all songs. The diversified range of products is available on audiocassette and compact disc plus graphics (CDG) and videocassette formats. Some songs include background vocals of the original recording and lyrics are included for most songs. Each CDG in the Karaoke Spotlight Series features the performance version of 15 different songs. Lyrics appear on-screen when used with a karaoke machine with graphic capabilities connected to a television. Recognizing that not everyone has purchased a karaoke machine, the firm established the Party Pak Rental System for rentals.

In addition to the celebrity-based Karaoke Star Series, the product selection in the children's category includes Old-Time Favorites, Holiday Songs, Movie and Television hits, and campfire songs. The youngest singers in the firm's customer base are preschoolers who sing along with *B-Flat the Cat*. This cassette features children's favorite nursery rhymes, activity songs, and Sunday School songs. Sound Choice also offers sound tracks for senior citizens and music therapy programs.

Karaoke is a growing market and includes other major players, such as Toymax's VJ Starz's lunch-box-size toy that hooks up to a VCR and is a combination video camera and karaoke machine, and Hitclips produced by Tiger Electronics.

Children using the karaoke machine.

A DOLL'S LEGACY

While the world turns on the spin of a computer-driven society, one precious commodity continues the timeless tradition of handcrafting with pride—and that is Madame Alexander Dolls, one of the only remaining major manufacturers of handcrafted dolls.

Since 1957, the doll maker has occupied the former Studebaker factory on West 131st in Harlem in New York City. In 2002, the company celebrated its 79th anniversary. The Alexander Doll Company continues the tradition, elegance, and innovation of Madame Alexander® dolls, with a full line of quality, handcrafted collectible dolls, baby dolls, and play dolls.

Three examples of Madame Alexander dolls reflect the high standards and attention to detail for which this doll maker is noted. The fashions are as couture as the designs of Paris's fashion houses.

The Creative Process

The firm's reputation for handcrafted quality workmanship is evident in the many hand-applied details. Workers lovingly attach arms, legs, rouge cheeks, trim, and dresses, and apply the Lilliputian hats and shoes.

This buzz of activity begins with the Madame Alexander Design Team. Once the award-winning team creates the original prototype from head to toe, the dolls are executed by a creative team, which works in production stations using the Japanese business philosophy, Kaizen, or continuous one-piece flow system. Instead of individuals in different locations working on batches, centralized teams of workers now carefully assemble one doll at a time from body part assembly to dressing and packaging. The completed hand-made doll is packaged in the firm's famous blue-and-pink boxes.

"It's a synergistic process," said Daun Fallon, vice president of design. "Workers participate in the creative as well as production process and realize a pride-of-product relationship with each doll. The process is different for each project."

Limited Editions

Limited edition dolls have joined the ranks of collectibles that include the Alex doll line of 16-inch fashion dolls, which are created with attention to attractive characteristic details. Each doll is exquisitely attired in up-to-the-minute fashions or dressed in award-winning evening clothes.

Introduced with a charming story line Madame Alexander's Alex Fairchild Ford™, editor-in-chief of the hip fashion magazine *Elan,* takes her act on the road with a cross-country fashion show with the full support of entertainment editor Paris Williams™, an elegant African American doll. When Ford decided to relocate *Elan*'s New York office to a Soho loft, she chose award-winning architect Jadde Lee™, a perfect blend of American and Asian heritage, to redesign the space.

SIDEBAR 14-2 | Unity Marketing: Doll Report

According to a new market research report, *The Doll Report, 2002: The Market, The Competitors, The Trends,* published by Unity Marketing, "Consumers' passion for dolls remains strong today, as in the past year nearly one-fourth of American families bought dolls, either as gifts, for play or to collect.

While the doll market is following an upward trajectory because of positive demographic trends, including the 42.8 million U.S. households in the 25-to-44 age group, prospects are favorable for sustained growth in the doll market through 2020. Pam Danziger, Unity spokesperson, says, "Today the majority of dolls bought as gifts are the play-doll type, as a result they are destined to be given to a child. These dolls tend to be lower priced, loaded with play features and more likely to be bought in mass merchants or toy stores. Over the next decade the big opportunity in dolls is to exploit the gifting potential of dolls as a token of love and affection for both young and old, just like the plush industry has done with the 'teddy bear.' Tapping into nostalgia by adding finer detail."

Three new versions created by the firm's Artist Circle for the limited edition Cissy collection feature the 21-inch "classic haute couture" doll created by Madame Alexander in 1955. In 2002 Cissy takes a turn as a famed courtesan for Pompadour Cissy, wearing a historically accurate eighteenth-century costume; the Old West is brought to life as the legendary Baby Doe, which became a classic sportswoman for Equestrian Cissy. The doll maker holds licensing deals to make likenesses of other brands, such as Peanuts and the Wizard of Oz.

Olivia Doll and Trunk

Olivia, a doll based on Ian Falconer's best-selling children's books, is a recent arrival that was offered exclusively for two years through FAO Schwarz, the leading children's lifestyle and specialty chain, which had suggested the doll to coordinate with the book. Daun Fallon worked with the book's illustrator to determine the size of the doll and its target market as a collectible, play toy, and price point. "The physical development of the doll also involved creating different outfits which were packaged with the doll as a trunk set." The Olivia doll and trunk set includes an 8-inch vinyl Olivia with an assortment of outfits, including a lipstick red bathing suit, a red dress with a white sailor collar, and a red and white horizontal striped T-shirt. The popular Madame Alexander Doll Club, founded in 1964, is based in Illinois and sponsors an annual convention. Of its 12,000 members, 40 percent are male.

BOARD GAME CRAZE

It takes skill, a brilliant mind, and the ability to conceptualize childlike play and more fun than can be imagined to be a game designer. In the toy industry, creative people are rather brainy types who are always on the verge of designing something new to tweak the imagination of the game-playing public. What is more, they are referred to by some rather unusual names!

Take the makers of Cranium, the fastest selling independent board game that won the "Game of the Year" award at the annual Toy of the Year (T.O.T.Y.™) ceremony in New York in 2002. The Cranium board game is a merry mix of activities. It focuses on more than one skill and rewards such underappreciated talents as spelling words backward, humming tunes, sculpting clay, and drawing with your eyes closed.

"I'm thrilled! We know how fantastic our game is, but for Cranium to beat such splashy products as Xbox and Game Cube surprises even us," said Richard Tait, Cranium's Grand Pooh-Bah. (Pooh-Bah? That means he is the head honcho.) Cocreator and Chief Noodler Whit Alexander added, "We wanted to create a game that would let people connect with one another in a personal, creative, and meaningful way while having an outrageously fun time. And this year more than ever, Americans want to spend time having fun and discovering the talents of their friends and family."

Cocreators Tait, Alexander, and fellow Microsoft alums have also created Cranium Cosmo™, an outrageously fun office toy, and Cranium Cadoo, the award-winning kids game.

INDUSTRY PROFILE 14-1 | Robert Tonner

Robert Tonner's vinyl fashion dolls wear elegant garments created by the leading fashion designers and are now housed in part of the Louvre. He is responsible for many firsts in doll creation, including the full-figured Emme, as well as dolls for famous personalities in real life and fiction.

Paris may be synonymous with haute couture, but Robert Tonner, award-winning doll designer and Tonner Doll Company president, is to the doll world what Dior is to the world of fashion. Robert Tonner's forté of sculpting vinyl and porcelain dolls has set new industry standards. Also capturing the spotlight are Tonner's 20-inch vinyl fashion dolls. Wearing the most elegant outfits, these dolls strut in style wearing garments by current designers, such as John Galliano, Oscar de la Renta, Donna Karan, Badgley Mischka, and Issey Miyake. Tonner dolls are also the first dolls known to model hairstyles by internationally famous hair designer John Sahag.

Wearing such haute designer fashions, it was not long before Tonner dolls, so stylish and so fashionable, were invited to Paris. They are now in a permanent collection of the Museum of Decorative Arts at the Louvre Complex.

Big Is Beautiful Doll

Setting another first standard, Tonner's newest creation is the Emme doll, the first full-figured fashion doll that immortalizes the full-figure supermodel, Emme, otherwise known as Melissa Miller. The life-like Emme doll is a timely introduction in the doll market. It represents a celebration of women's bodies that come in all shapes, sizes, and colors.

"When I saw Emme on a talk show, I was swept away by the model's beautiful persona. I was also impressed that this plus size woman represented fashion. That's how the idea for a new fashion doll came about," says Tonner. "So I approached Emme with the idea of making a plus size doll and the synergy clicked. The doll's inspiration was the model's looks. I sculpted a beautiful woman in close consultation with its original and designed even the hands and feet with the integrity of plus-size proportion. In close collaboration with the celebrity and the Tonner design staff, we developed an ideal replica of the personality of Emme."

Currently the blond, blue-eyed Emme struts her ample frame wearing a black cocktail dress and platform sandals. Tonner plans other fashionable outfits for the doll, including satin pajamas, a denim jean/red jacket ensemble, and sheer paisley asymmetrical hem dress. The Emme doll will not be alone either, as some plus size sister dolls will also be introduced.

Emme was dubbed the "hottest" toy at the American International Toy Fair 2002. Tonner has also created dolls for some of the most famous celebrity personalities and iconic fiction characters. Among these are Orphan Annie, the Titanic Rose Doll, Demi Moore, Superman, Lois Lane, Wonder Woman, and fashion designer Edith Head.

A Dream Job

While millions dream of living out their fantasies, few ever have the opportunity. Tonner is an exception. He knew his dream job would be designing and sculpting dolls. However, he honed his skills and studied at the prestigious Parsons School of Design in New York City, which is located right in the heart of the garment district on Fashion Avenue. The artist fell in naturally with fashion and spent 15 years in the fashion industry, working eight of those years with the celebrated designer Bill Blass, where he designed the Blassport line.

"At the same time I was designing fashion, a friend introduced me to the doll show business," notes Tonner. "I was smitten and became interested in doll clothes and the sculpture process of creating beautiful heads. As I attended more doll shows my interest grew and I started sculpting dolls for various companies. Then, after mastering my sculpting technique and with my fashion background, I decided to turn my dream into a reality, and in 1991 I founded the Tonner Doll Company, Inc. in Kingston, New York."

The Design Process

Spend a day with Robert Tonner and get a behind the scenes look at his world. You will spend the morning sketching with Robert in the design room, where creativity is a synergistic relationship with the design team. The afternoon will be spent sculpting in the doll studio, where all his collections begin. The design process flow from sketch to reality is carefully engineered to produce fine quality dolls that are recognized worldwide. With his creative eye and a business savvy, Tonner has brought the doll industry to a higher standard, a collector's standard.

Playing the Game

The Cranium game includes the Cranium board, 800 Cranium cards covering thirty different subject areas, a ten-sided Cranium die, a tub of cool Cranium Clay, a sixty-second timer, four Cranium pads and pencils, and four funky Cranium play pieces. The game requires four or more players and takes about an hour to play.

The object of the game is to move clockwise around the board and into Cranium Central™, as the team completes its final activities to win. Players harness their collective brainpower to answer questions and complete the activities from all four decks as they advance around the board. Each player must successfully complete the activity described on the card, matching their board position before the timer runs out, in order to roll the Cranium die and move on. Cranium's activities are organized into four card decks:

- Creative Cat®: Creative Cat activities have the team sketch, sculpt with Cranium Clay®, and draw with their eyes closed.
- Word Worms®: Can you spell "asparagus" backwards? Word Worm activities have the player unscramble words, spell challenging ones, guess definitions, fill in the blanks, and spell backwards.
- Data Head®: Do you know how much water the human bladder can hold? Data Head activities stimulate the player's gray matter by testing their knowledge of uncommon information, provocative true/false queries, and challenging multiple choice questions.
- Star Performer®: Can you shake like Elvis? Star Performer activities have the team hum or whistle a tune, impersonate a celebrity, or act out a clue. Fun for the family, fun for all, the Cranium game brings a new meaning to togetherness.

CLASSICS AND RETRO TOYS

Old-time classics comprise a major component of favorite playthings. This is because people who were kids in those eras are now having kids of their own and play becomes an adult/child thing.

Schylling

Schylling, known for its nostalgic approach to toy making, introduced its retro Mickey line of toys and collectibles at Toy

Fair 2002. Included in this retro Mickey line are reproductions of the earliest Mickey Mouse© products. Other classics include Raggedy Ann & Andy©, Classic Pooh©, and Madeline©, as well as the first-ever felt dolls, wind-up celluloid figurines, tin toys, wooden toys, porcelain tea sets, and poseable vinyl dolls.

Lionel

Trains for play and as collectibles continue to drive sales. The Lionel brand, for one, is an American icon; the company is

Lionel trains have long been the leader in the manufacture of model trains. Three of the five models first shown at the 2002 Toy Fair were the 2-8-8-2, the Sante Fe, and the Virginian locomotives. The detail and craftsmanship reveal why Lionel's reputation is so dominant.

Richard Simmons with two dolls in the collection Goebel produces for him. (Left) a child attending the "First Day of School" and (right) Bridget in the "Memories of Childhood" line. Celebrity tie-ins give products additional recognition.

recognized as the quintessential toy train manufacturer. Since 1900, Lionel has been the master hobby maker of model train collectibles and accessories that stand for quality, innovation, and family togetherness. At Toy Fair 2002, Lionel unveiled two new 2-8-8-2 die-cast metal historic steam locomotives in a series of five special locomotives. John W. Brady, vice president of marketing, said, "They mark a significant advance in realism and performance of scale-sized, O-Gauge replicas of their real-life counterparts."

Celebrity Tie-Ins

GOEBEL

Celebrity tie-ins also drive the toy business. Goebel, world-renowned distributor of fine giftware and collectibles, produces world entertainer and fitness guru Richard Simmons' "Collection of the Masters"™ line. Newest additions feature six diminutive dolls exquisitely costumed with character, humor, and depth of expression. Talented artists meticulously reproduce the figures, selected from Richard's personal collection. Eighteen-inch Bridget is the latest piece from Cynthia Malbon's "Memories of Childhood" line, and a child representing school activities evokes nostalgia about bygone days in a 13¾-inch figure called "First Day of School," by Stephanie Cauley.

Marie Osmond's Little Miracles™ dolls reflect a child's view of the miracles of everyday life. Connections with entertainers give products caché and recognition.

MARIE OSMOND

Entertainment personalities with established name recognition and a celebrity persona also add prestige to toy and collectible collections. Take Marie Osmond, for example, an internationally known entertainer and collecting enthusiast, who is also the creator of her own collectible porcelain doll line and creator of Little Miracles™. She is also a children's advocate, mother, author, and cofounder/cohost of the Children's Miracle Network, a project of the Osmond Foundation.

According to Ms. Osmond, the Lilliputian "Little Miracles" fine porcelain figurines and accessories celebrate the every day "miracles" in life through the eyes of children. She created the line to remind us of the inspiration that children provide and that the simple joy of being young and innocent can still be felt at any age. The collection, created in conjunction with the Ashton-Drake Galleries and Gallery Marketing Group, also

SIDEBAR 14-3 | Industry Annual Sales Volume

Toy retail sales increased 2 percent between 2000 and 2001. The category representing the largest increase was action figure toys, which experienced a 36 percent increase in retail sales between 2000 and 2002. This category shows the continuing strength of licensing in the industry, with properties such as Star Wars, Toy Story 2, and World Wrestling Entertainment (WWE) demonstrating how toys and entertainment continue to be a winning combination.

Another category that reflected a healthy increase was the infant and preschool category, where retail sales increased by 14 percent. A substantial part of the increase came from the influence of technology, including the creative use of computer chips in preschool learning toys such as Vtech's AlphaBert and Leapfrog's LeapPad Learning Center.

Toy industry categories include the following classifications: Infant/Preschool, Dolls, Plush, Action Figure Toys, Vehicles, Ride-Ons, Games/Puzzles, Activity Toys, Video Games, and Miscellaneous Toys.

Foreign Production of U.S. Toys and Games

Like many aspects of the apparel manufacturing industry, toy production remains labor intensive, requiring, for example, painting, assembly, inspection, packaging, and detailing for authenticity. As the labor and social benefit cost per employee has risen steadily since 1945, as has the American standard of living, the cost of this type of production in the United States is often very high for the toy industry. As a result, like the apparel industry's global manufacturing outreach, American manufacturers have tried to significantly decrease costs since the 1950s by combining high value-added domestic operations with overseas production in developing countries where labor rates are low.

The Retail Challenge

It would be hard to discuss annual toy sales without addressing the changing face of toy retailing. Discount, warehouse, specialty, and e-commerce toy retailers are jockeying for market share. Wal-Mart remained the number one toy retailer in the United States during 1999, followed by Toys 'R Us at 15.6 percent.

While brick-and-mortar retailers battled for the largest share of toy sales, *Time Magazine*'s naming of Amazon's CEO Jeffrey Bezos as "Person of the Year" reflected the influence of e-commerce in America and the world. Following book sales, perhaps no industry was affected as immediately as the toy industry, with on-line toy sales catapulting from $45 million in 1998 to $425 million in 1999, according to the NPD Group, Inc., and Media Metrix, industry forecasters.

Category Trends

Although many expect technology to signal the demise of traditional toys, sales demonstrate quite the opposite. On the surface nothing much has changed about yo-yos since their commercial introduction in 1929. However, one need only look deeper to discover the successful marriage of technology and newly developed materials to contribute to the challenge and play value that continues to spark the interest of children—and adults—across the country.

The tidal wave of high-tech, interactive toy and game introductions is hyped by the fact that consumers are clamoring to discover the latest and greatest gizmo on the market. Front and center are kids (and parents) hoping to find the next "it" toy.

Mattel, the largest publicly held toy company, known for its Barbie and Elmo lines, offers Planet Hot Wheels, a car that comes with a code that lets children race on the Internet. Each time they win, they gain points and chances to win prizes. On the international circuit, Mattel snagged the rights to market figures for Yu-Gi-Oh!, based on a Japanese cartoon.

As even preschool children know how to use a mouse, smart toys are just a matter of smart business. Clifford and Hot Wheels, for example, have been injected with a high-tech component. Although it is common to associate boys with high-tech, girls are flocking to the computer as well. Thanks to Mattel's introduction of Barbie and Radica's GirlTech brands, girls continue to demonstrate their growing interest in the tech-toy phenomena, proving another shift in the paradigm of play.

As the popularity of video games increases and questions increase about how video-play influences behavior, the question of how to appropriately regulate content looms large throughout the interactive entertainment industry. As a result, the Entertainment Software Rating Board (ESRB) was established to independently review entertainment software.

represent a section of limited-edition collectibles also includes designs by Thomas Kinkade and Mel Odom (Gene).

TREND TRACKING

Trend tracking on the movement of consumer interests and even serendipitous ideas that derive from technology or nostalgia are major considerations for toy designers. According to industry experts, toys with movie tie-ins and retro toys will be successful product launches. Kids clamored for toys tied to the new installment of *Star Wars* and *Spiderman*. Then there was *Spy Kids 2*, *Scooby Doo*, and another Harry Potter flick. "I think there will be more toys sold with movie tie-ins in 2002/2003 than in the past five or six years," said Jim Silver, publisher of the trade magazines *The Toy Book* and *The Toy Report and Specialty Retailer*.

Why retro? Well, like the fashion industry's penchant for classic, nostalgic, and vintage clothes, retro toys from say the

1970s draw revival interest, because adults who grew up in the 1970s had fun playing with those toys and are having children of their own. Remember toys are not just for children.

Trade Terminology

Board game
Chief noodler
Cranium
Emme
Karaoke
Lilliputian
Lionel
Madame Alexander
Mattel
Pooh-Bah
Porcelain figures
Retro
Richard Tonner
Teddy bear
Toy fair
Toy Industry Association (TIA)
Trend spotting

READING 14-1 | Betcha Didn't Know

*. . . **that behind every** toy, there's a story as entertaining as the toy itself! These tales include how some toys were invented, how others got their name, how some famous companies began, and fun facts to enjoy and share. Anecdotes are listed alphabetically by company name. So let's see how much you know about the toy industry!*
—2002 Edition

Unusual Beginnings
BRIO Toys
BRIO Corporation
Named for the brothers Ivarsson of Osby, Sweden in 1884, BRIO started as a trading company by their father, Ivar Bengstsson. The brothers adopted a quality approach to innovative wooden playthings that support a child's natural development. More than 100 years later, BRIO toys are sold in more

than 35 countries and in 2002 BRIO Corporation celebrates 25 years of distributing these wonderful playthings in the United States.

Gooey Glitter Goo
Curiosity Kits, Inc.
Gooey Glitter Goo is an icky, squishy substance that also makes "big gross sounds." This additional feature was discovered quite by accident at Curiosity Kits' Hunt Valley, Maryland, product development lab. Once the product development personnel tested the formula and were satisfied with the invention, they tried to stuff the goo back into the jar. That's when the "squoinks," and "phlbbts" erupted, as did the laughter. During kid-testing later that summer, all the junior scientists delighted in the noises—and a selling feature was born.

Cybiko, Inc.
David Yang, physicist and inventor, took his knowledge of computer engineering and software development from the old Soviet Union and used it to work on something some physicists might consider too lighthearted. . . . toys! He founded Cybiko in 1999 with headquarters in Illinois and set out to develop the first handheld wireless communicator designed specifically for the teen market. It took 10 months to translate that concept into a real product, also called Cybiko, and gain U.S. shelf space. This was all made possible by a talented technology staff of 140 hardware, software and Web developers, mechanical designers, and RF scientists, and a laboratory in Moscow.

Endless Games
What started as a barstool game of make-believe turned into an exciting business venture for three friends. Brian Turtle and Kevin McNulty had made a habit of pretending they were someone else while drinking at their local watering hole. The object of their game was to be as outrageous as possible and keep their story going for as long as they could. One night after many drinks, they exhausted all their fantasy lifestyles and began to talk about setting out to create a real life fantasy—starting their own business. They talked through the night and by sunrise they decided to start a game company. Together with an old friend of Kevin's, they built Endless Games.

Fisher-Price, Inc.
Fisher-Price was founded in 1930 in East Aurora, New York, by three talented entrepreneurs: Herman Fisher, formerly involved in marketing games, Irving Price, a retired variety chain store executive, and Helen Schelle, owner and operator of a toy store in central New York. Today, backed by more than 70 years' experience, the Fisher-Price name is considered one of the most trusted brand names in America and one of the "top 10 brands of the decade" according to research company Equitrends.

Little People
Fisher-Price, Inc.
In 1950, two of Herman Fisher's key toy designers created the Looky Fire Truck with three little round-headed wooden firemen permanently attached to the toy. Nine years later, the little wooden figures gained their independence. With the introduction of the Safety School Bus, Little People as we know and love them today were born. The Safety School Bus included six little wooden peg figures that could be removed from the school bus. Only the driver, whose head turned while the bus rolled along, remained attached to the toy. Throughout the next four decades, over one billion Little People figures have been played with by millions of preschoolers around the world.

Rescue Heroes
Fisher-Price, Inc.
When Fisher-Price introduced Rescue Heroes in 1998 they faced a serious challenge. Rescue Heroes were the first team of action figures representing real-life heroes like firefighters, police officers, construction workers, mountain rangers and paramedics—there were no "bad guys" in the line. But that didn't stop them. Providing positive role models for kids and an alternative to the good guy vs. bad guy theme, Rescue Heroes beat the odds and more than 7 million Rescue Heroes figures have been sold to date. A special FDNY Rescue Heroes figure, all proceeds of which benefited the FDNY's Fire Safety Education Fund, was one of the hottest toys of the 2001 holiday season. It just goes to show, good guys rule!

View-Master
Fisher-Price, Inc.
View-Master was originally the brainchild of William Gruber, a piano tuner by trade and a stereo photographer by hobby. Mr. Gruber's idea was to use color transparency movie film in a hand-held viewing device that contained two eyepieces. This would help the observer combine the images of two photographs, taken from slightly different points of view, into one full-color, three-dimensional picture. Since Mr. Gruber's invention over 60 years ago, people around the world have delighted in peering through View-Master viewers and seeing 3-D images of their favorite cartoon characters, television stars and movie legends. There are scenic reels available at nearly every tourist spot in the world, and restaurants across the country let patrons view "daily specials" through a View-Master viewer.

Play-Doh
Hasbro, Inc.
When Play-Doh first debuted in 1956 it was available in only one color and size, an off-white, 1½ pound can. Introduced originally to schools, kindergartens and nursery schools it was first demonstrated and sold in the toy department of Woodward & Lothrop Department Store in Washington, D.C. Since that introduction more than 700 million pounds of Play-Doh have been sold. The formula for the original Play-Doh compound still remains a secret.

Candy Land
Hasbro Games
While Eleanor Abbott of San Diego, California, was recuperating from polio in the 1940s, she occupied herself with devising games and activities for youngsters who had polio. One of her inventions was called "Candy Land." Her young friends liked the game so much, she submitted it to Milton Bradley Company where it was immediately accepted. Since then, Candy Land has been recognized internationally as a "child's first game."

Cootie
Hasbro Games
Herb Schaper, a letter carrier for the U.S. Post Office, whittled the first Cootie out of wood in 1948. In the first year, Schaper built, by hand, 40,000 wooden Cootie games. Three years later, more than 1,200,000 were produced with the aid of machinery. By 1978, Cootie's 30th birthday, more than 30 million games had entertained children worldwide.

Lincoln Logs
K'NEX Industries, Inc.
Lincoln Logs were designed and developed in 1916 by John Lloyd Wright, son of one of America's most famous architects, Frank Lloyd Wright. The younger Wright conceived his idea for Lincoln Logs when he was traveling with his father in Tokyo and became inspired by the construction tech-

niques used in the foundation of the earth-quake-proof Imperial Hotel, which his father designed.

Lionel L.L.C.
The first electrical Lionel train was designed to beckon window-shopping New Yorkers using the power of animated display. Lionel was named from its founder's middle name: Joshua Lionel Cowen. Lionel has sold more than 50 million train sets since its humble beginning in 1900 and today produces more than 300 miles of track each year.

Little Kids No-Spill Bubble Tumbler
Little Kids, Inc.
The concept for Little Kids No-Spill Bubble Tumbler actually came from the Ooops Proof No-Spill Tumbler, a drinking cup specifically designed to keep toddlers from spilling their juice. It didn't take long for consumers and the trade to recognize the No-Spill Bubble Tumbler toy for its unique design that truly prevents bubble solution from spilling.

Magna Doodle
Mattel, Inc.
In 1974, four engineers at Pilot Pen Corporation of Japan began searching for a dust less chalkboard. What they found would eventually become one of the world's most popular drawing toys—Magna Doodle. More than 40 million have been sold to date. Magna Doodle also has a knack for showing up in some of the most unlikely places: Hal Hunter, offensive line coordinator for the Cleveland Browns, uses Magna Doodle on the sidelines to diagram his plays; hospital patients often use Magna Doodle when they cannot communicate vocally, and a high school Latin teacher uses Magna Doodle, dubbed "Magna Tabulae" or "large slates," to go over difficult Latin exercises with her first-year students.

Matchbox
Mattel, Inc.
The "birth of Matchbox" was marked in 1952, when Jack Odell created a brass prototype of a small Road Roller and put it in a matchbox-sized container so his daughter could take it with her to school. The first "Matchbox" series produced four different models. Now, almost 50 years later, the Matchbox line consists of 100 vehicles and each can still be purchased for under $1.

Neurosmith
Educational software designer John Sosoka was not surprised that his young son preferred playing with blocks on the floor to sitting at the computer desk. But he couldn't ignore the educational power of the computer. His solution? Combine the technology of a computer with a more child-friendly platform. Sosoka teamed up with co-worker Brooke Abercrombie to found Neurosmith, a toy manufacturer dedicated to combining state-of-the art technology with the latest cognitive research to create inspiring and interactive learning tools for young children.

Koosh
OddzOn, Inc. (Division of Hasbro, Inc.)
The Koosh ball is celebrating its 15th anniversary this year. Koosh has entertained people of all ages with its amazing versatility and tactile feel, but was actually invented to teach young children how to catch. In 1987, engineer Scott Stillinger found that his kids' small hands couldn't easily grasp balls during a game of "catch," so he tied rubber bands together to make a small, catchable ball that was easy for small fingers to hold onto. What to name the unusual toy? Listening to the "koosh" sound the ball made as it landed in his hand, the inventor realized this was the perfect name and the Koosh Ball was born! How many

rubbery strands does it take to create the energy-absorbent, porcupine-look of a Koosh Ball? The answer—approximately 5,000 fibers go into each ball!

Spin Pop, Laser Pop
OddzOn, Inc. (Division of Hasbro, Inc.)
Did you know that the candy craze that set the sweets industry spinning was invented in a country kitchen by two friends who worked together at the local post office? It all began on a Halloween night when they were greeted by a trick-or-treater wearing a neon glow-in-the-dark necklace. Wouldn't it be great if they could incorporate that kind of fun into a candy? Later that evening they tried shining a flashlight through melted clear candy and the idea of a light-up candy—the Laser Pop—was born. The Laser Pop and Spin Pop, a motion-accented candy they also developed, were introduced to the world in 1993 and their immediate, phenomenal success prompted the creation of a new category—interactive toy candy.

TriBond
Patch Products, Inc.
TriBond celebrates its 12th anniversary this year. Tim Walsh and two friends created the idea for the game at college, but they struggled to gain the respect from the toy industry. Going against the odds, they raised money from their families and friends to develop a prototype that they brought to Toy Fair 1990. The game that gets players to think in threes has quietly become an international success and has sold almost 2 million copies. Not bad considering that for the first four years Tim sold TriBond out of the back of his jeep!

**NSYNC Backstage Pass Game*
Patch Products, Inc.
The concept of this game is to have players answer personal, juicy questions about Justin, JC, Lance, Joey and Chris. Patch needed first-hand information about the guys, so they created unique questions for each of the heartthrobs. Peggy Brown, VP of Product Development at Patch, presented personal questionnaires to Joey's brother, Steve, on the *NSYNC tour bus. Steve made sure all the band members answered their questions and when it was completed the members of the band had a bit of fun quizzing each other with questions from the game.

Ant Farm
Uncle Milton Industries, Inc.
The idea for Ant Farm came about on July 4th, 1956, at a family picnic. Milton Levine couldn't help but notice a colony of ants marching, scavenging and generally wreaking havoc with the family's leisurely afternoon. The intrusive little creatures gave him the inspiration to develop a formicarium, or ant vivarium that could be mass-produced and sold to the consumer market, and thus the Ant Farm was created. After the Ant Farm sold out in its first year, the company realized they had a hit on their hands.

Fascinating Facts
Crayola Crayons
Binney & Smith, Inc.
Crayola products are sold in more than 80 countries from the Island of Iceland to the tiny Central American nation of Belize. They are packaged in 12 languages including Japanese, Finnish and Dutch. According to a Yale University study, the scent of Crayola crayons is among the 20 most recognizable to American adults. If all the regular size Crayola crayons made in one year were laid end to end on the Equator they would circle the earth six times.

Silly Putty
Binney & Smith, Inc.
Binney & Smith produces more than 1,500 pounds of Silly Putty each day—that's more

than 20,000 eggs. Over the years, Silly Putty has been put to some unusual uses; it was used at the zoo in Columbus, Ohio, to take hand and foot prints of the gorilla population as replica prints for educational purposes. The astronauts of the Apollo 8 mission carried Silly Putty into space with them, in a specially designed sterling silver egg, to alleviate boredom and to help fasten down tools during the weightless period. Silly Putty is recommended by several organizations that help individuals quit smoking. Smokers are encouraged to play with Silly Putty every time they get the urge to light up.

Cadaco, Inc.

As long ago as 2700 B.C. in ancient Egypt, magicians were fascinating audiences with tricks and illusions that seemed to defy the laws of nature. Over time, magicians have carefully guarded the secrets to their tricks, passing them down from one magician to another. With the help of world famous magician Marshall Brodien and master magician Lance Burton, Cadaco continues this age-old tradition by developing the largest line of magic products for people to perform at home. Cadaco magic products comprise 40 different sets and over 400 individual tricks and illusions.

Disguise Inc.

A manufacturer of the top selling costumes for the past three years, Disguise may specialize in kids' costumes but its line has made appearances on a few well-known big kids as well. On Halloween 2000, Diane Sawyer shocked her Good Morning America co-host, Charles Gibson, by wearing a Disguise-designed mask of him!

Tickle Me Elmo
Fisher-Price, Inc.

It's been more than five years since the original Tickle Me Elmo first took the country by storm and turned a little furry red muppet into a cultural phenomenon. Since then, he's walked and talked, played pretend and even had a stint as a rock 'n roll singer. Five years later and people still ask what's the next Tickle Me Elmo? In 2001, Fisher-Price heeded the call and created a special fifth anniversary Tickle Me Elmo full of surprises. . . . Five tickle spots instead of just one and Elmo's most ticklish spot changes every time kids play. Fisher-Price took the surprises one step further with the introduction of a whole new fun way to play that was activated on January 9th. On that day, five lucky people found out that they were winners in the Tickle Me Elmo Surprise Sweepstakes.

Power Wheels
Fisher-Price, Inc.

With driving still being the number one role-play fantasy of young children everywhere, motorized toy cars have been a favorite for more than 30 years. Since their introduction in 1984, Power Wheels has sold over 10 million vehicles and is the leader in the battery-powered ride-on category.

Easy-Bake Oven
Hasbro, Inc.

The Easy-Bake Oven had its "official" introduction at Toy Fair in February 1964. In its first year more than 500,000 units were sold. Easy Bake became a household word in the United States in the mid '60s with television advertising extending to all three networks and 130 local markets. In its 38 years, more than 19 million Easy-Bake Ovens have been sold and more than 130 million mix sets have been used.

Mr. Potato Head
Hasbro, Inc.

In 2002 Mr. Potato Head celebrated his 50th birthday. Mr. Potato Head was the first toy product ever advertised on television. Introduced in 1952, Mr. Potato Head took advantage of TV's explosive growth to gain access to tens of millions of newly plugged-in households. At the time, two-thirds of American televisions were owned by Baby Boom families with children under twelve, and the looney toy tuber grossed $4 million in his very first year.

Tonka Trucks
Hasbro, Inc.
Tonka celebrates its 55th birthday this year. More than 230 million trucks have been manufactured since 1947. It takes 119,000 pounds of yellow paint and 5.1 million pounds of sheet metal a year to make Tonka trucks and other Tonka vehicles.

Scrabble
Hasbro Games
This year marks Scrabble's 54th anniversary. Even though it's a word game, the real story about the Scrabble Brand Crossword Game is numbers. One hundred million sets have been sold worldwide and between one and two million are sold each year in North America. Of keen interest to the legions of passionate players, somewhere over 147,000 words can be used in their scoring arsenal.

Trivial Pursuit
Hasbro Games
Trivial Pursuit celebrated its 20th anniversary in 2002. Since 1982, it has made its way into more than half of all homes in this country. More than 30 million Trivial Pursuit games have been sold worldwide in 18 languages and 32 countries.

Funnoodle
Kidpower, Inc.
Funnoodle, the popular floating foam tubes for the beach and pool, made the headlines with a unique story this past summer. A 71-year-old grandmother from Tampa, Florida was caught in rough waters when a storm hit suddenly in Old Tampa Bay. The woman's daughter was able to throw two Funnoodles to her, which she wrapped around her chest and legs. Though not intended as life-saving floatation devices, the Funnoodles nevertheless helped her stay afloat while she waited in the raging surf for nearly two hours to be rescued!

My Own Baby
Lee Middleton Original Dolls, Inc.
These life-like dolls are used for therapeutic and teaching purposes. The Red Cross uses them for babysitting training, nurses use them to instruct new mothers, and others have used them to comfort people with Alzheimer's. Television producers have also been captivated by the lifelike appearance of the dolls and have used them on shows such as *ER, Touched by an Angel* and *The Bold and the Beautiful.*

Phonics Desk, Phonics Traveler
LeapFrog, L.L.C.
LeapFrog's teaching toys were developed with assistance from a major university and . . . a . . . nuclear weapons laboratory! When attorney Mike Wood was creating LeapFrog's award-winning Phonics Desk and Phonics Traveler, he turned to Sandia National Laboratories for technical assistance. Renowned for verifying weapon performance, the staff at Sandia's Electronics Prototype Laboratory worked with commercial suppliers to create three working prototypes of LeapFrog's toys that teach youngsters how to read.

LEGO Systems, Inc.
Two eight-stud LEGO bricks (of the same color) can be combined in 24 different ways. Three eight-stud LEGO bricks can be

combined 1,060 different says. Six eight-stud LEGO bricks can be combined in 102,981,500 different ways!

Barbie
Mattel, Inc.
Barbie celebrates her 43rd anniversary this year! Since 1959, more than a billion Barbie dolls and members of the Barbie family have been sold in more than 140 countries around the world. Every second, two Barbie dolls are sold somewhere in the world. Close to one billion fashions have also been produced since 1959 for Barbie and her friends. More than 105 million yards of fabric have gone into making Barbie doll and her friends' fashions, making Mattel one of the largest apparel manufacturers in the world.

See 'N Say
Mattel, Inc.
See 'N Say toys have kept kids listenin', laughin' and learnin' for more than 30 years. This line of talking toys has taught kids the basics, everything from identifying animals to primary colors and counting. From its early pull string, followed by its famous pull lever and classic preschool themes, See 'N Say has helped entertain and teach generations of children.

Etch A Sketch
The Ohio Art Company
After four decades, the same ingredients still make Etch A Sketch one of the world's favorite drawing toys: the bright red case, glass screen, aluminum powder, plastic beads and two knobs that help control the movement of the stylus. Besides a minor switch from brass to larger plastic knobs, the classic Etch A Sketch hasn't changed; only for a period of time in the '70s were pink- and blue-framed models made available. What's more, five of the toy's original assemblers from 1960 still dedicate their "magic" handwork to making Etch A Sketch today.

Playmobil, USA, Inc.
At just under three inches high, Playmobil figures are proportioned exactly for the hand size of children. If all the Playmobil figures in the world stood in a row, they would circle the earth more than one and a half times. Playmobil manufactures approximately three million individual parts every day.

Radio Flyer, Inc.
The Classic Little Red Wagon model #18 has become such an American icon that the actual shape has been trademarked. This classic wagon has been in continuous production for more than 70 years—a toy industry record. The exact color of red used on the Original Little Red Wagon is a closely guarded trade secret. 'Radio Flyer Red' is custom mixed and prepared using a proprietary formula developed by company founder Antonio Pasin.

Rokenbok Building System
Rokenbok Toy Company
The Rokenbok System, an innovative building system that features interactive play with state-of-the-art radio control technology, was designed and developed by a team of individuals with no toy industry experience whatsoever. The original Rokenbok Toy Company team includes an ex-president of a computer video projection company, a computer scientist, inventory and electrical engineer, an industrial designer and a high performance super computer scientist and inventor.

Safari Ltd.
Here's proof that Safari snakes are truly realistic looking. A customer put a large snake

in her shrubs to keep the birds from eating the berries. The yardman saw it and called the security guard—the security guard shot it three times before it was discovered to be one of Safari's model snakes.

Sport Fun, Inc.
Sport Fun, the California-based sporting goods and outdoor toy manufacturer, holds the record for the longest, continuous manufacturing of skateboards, which debuted in 1963 and have been in the company's line ever since. Skateboarding came of age in 1975, a year when Sport Fun produced up to 10,000 units each day! Today, the company is taking skateboarding to a whole new level as the first company to bring entertainment licensing to the skateboard industry.

Tootsietoy
Strombecker Corp.
Tootsietoy is America's oldest toy company, dating back to 1876, and created the world's first die-cast metal toy car in 1910, when the Dowst Brothers Company of Chicago made a miniature Model T Ford. The early vehicles were called Tootsietoys, named after one of the Dowst Brothers' granddaughters, "Toots." Today, Strombecker, the maker of Tootsietoys, produces over 40 million cars per year. It is also the leading manufacturer of bubble solution and bubble toys in the world with more than 50 million bottles of Mr. Bubbles bubble-blowing solution sold each year. These Tootsietoy bubbles have been used on the Lawrence Welk Show, at the Ice Capades, and on the Mississippi riverboat *Delta Queen*.

Creepy Crawlers
Toymax Inc.
It would take a platoon of National Guard soldiers four years to stamp out all of the bugs produced by Creepy Crawler sets thus far.

Supersonic Ear
Wild Planet Toys, Inc.
The Supersonic Ear has had some unusual uses as reported by some very satisfied consumers. The Supersonic Ear was once used to determine if a cat had fallen into a well. When the "faint meow" was picked up by the directional microphone, Tabby's presence was confirmed, and she was plucked from the well in one piece. One gentleman used the Supersonic Ear to locate a family of skunks that had taken up residence under his floorboards. Rather than tear apart the entire floor, this clever man used the Supersonic Ear to locate the exact position of the skunks, saving him time, money and a lot of hard labor!

A Toy by Any Other Name
Crayola Crayons
Binney & Smith, Inc.
The Crayola brand name is recognized by 99 percent of Americans and is ranked 51st of all world brands in terms of the brand's recognizability and consumers' esteem for the brand.

Jenga
Hasbro Games
As a child Leslie Scott, creator of Jenga, lived in Africa and for some years Swahili was her first language. This is how she came up with the name for her game. Jenga is a Swahili word, meaning, "to build."

Yahtzee
Hasbro Games
Yahtzee was invented in 1956 by a Canadian couple aboard their yacht. When friends were invited aboard, they were taught how to play their "Yacht Game." Eventually they approached Edwin S. Lowe, who made his fortune selling Bingo games in the 1920s, and asked him to print up a

few games as gifts. Lowe liked the game so much he offered to buy all the rights. The couple was not interested in receiving royalties, and they signed away their rights in exchange for a few copies of the game. Lowe changed the name of the game to Yahtzee and enjoyed great success with this classic dice game.

LEGO Systems, Inc.
The word "LEGO" is formed from the Danish words "leg godt," which means, "play well." Later it was discovered that LEGO means, "I put together" in Latin.

Hot Wheels
Mattel, Inc.
This year marks the 35th anniversary of Hot Wheels. The success story starts with one man's idea to speed up the industry. In 1967 Elliot Handler, one of the original founders of Mattel, decided to add axles and working wheels to the static wheel diecast model cars of the times. What was developed was a prototype gravity-powered car that could run at a record-breaking scale speed of 300 mph downhill. The secret to such high performance racing action was low-friction wheels made of styrene that were hung on torsion bars and soon to be patented by Mattel. Handler took one look at this new, ultra-fast car, and exclaimed—"Wow, those are hot wheels"—thus, also naming the new product.

Source: Toy Industry Association web site. Compiled by the Toy Industry Association, Inc. (TIA) in 2002. www.toy-tia.org.

READING 14-2 | Training Players for the Toy Business

BY POLLY GUÉRIN

In this computer-driven world, how does a creative person become a doll designer, and why?

That's the question I asked Amanda Van Holt, who now designs dolls for infants at PlaySkool, Inc., Pawtucket, R.I.

With girlish glee, she says, "You have to know how to play like a child, and still have the wonder of discovery to become a doll designer."

Amanda is a graduate of the world's first college program in toy design, initiated in 1989, at the New York City-based Fashion Institute of Technology (F.I.T.), a part of the State University of New York.

F.I.T.'s toy design department, which offers a baccalaureate degree in toy design, grew out of a special project sponsored by Mattel, working with industry advisors and consultant George Dunsay, president of Total Toys.

Among the unique aspects of the program is the fact that many industry leaders from toy and doll companies teach the courses. Department faculty members are industry professionals with expertise in toy and doll design, child psychology, and the marketing, advertising and promotion of toys.

In addition, students have the opportunity to intern in toy companies and industry think tanks across the country.

Child's-Eye View

Judy Ellis, Toy Design chairperson at F.I.T., echoes Amanda's sentiments. "Students enrolled in the toy design program at F.I.T. have a child's-eye view of the world; they are playful, bright and curious, and they know a good toy when they see one. In addition to the curriculum, in our school, the student designers have play sessions, where they play with their toys, meet inventors and talk about how their ideas developed. These young people go out to their jobs as savvy professionals, and are much sought after by the $9.2-billion-per-year toy business."

Industry Standards

Students like Amanda worked out their dreams in a 4,400-square-foot, state-of-the-art facility modeled after a Hasbro shop. The space enables students to produce professional-quality work. In fact, the program gained national attention when plush characters, designed and constructed by students, were honored during a Jim Henson Productions competition.

Amanda, for one, takes a watchdog approach on trends. From fashion to industrial influences, everything serves to inspire new designs. "Right now, I'm designing in the infant group, mostly soft toys.

"The shop at school is the same as the shop at PlaySkool, so from the moment I arrived, I felt at home."

She points out that being a toy designer is more than just a job. "It's a 24-hour occupation that's fun and satisfying. Most of all, it's exciting to see the development of a prototype from concept to sketch to sculpted 3-D model to actual product."

Oh, Boy! What a Job!

Women do not hold an exclusivity on jobs in the doll world. David Voss is a designer for the Hot Wheels group at Mattel, Inc., El Segundo, Calif. He's busy creating fast-action, 18″ doll-like figures for boys, like Jack Slater and Arnold Schwarzenegger.

David's training in fine arts and his associate degree in toy design have served him well in his current profession. "I do a lot of drawings and quick prototypes. We work as a team, and these people are incredibly talented. In fact, I'm working side-by-side with the people who taught me at school."

David is quick to add, "It's not a 9-to-5 job; if you love the work, you're thinking about it all the time."

"F.I.T.'s program is really geared toward what the actual job situation's going to be like," says graduate Michael Montalvo, whose toy design was included in Hasbro's line. "I try to invent toys that remind me of things I wanted as a kid. I think about what I liked and work with that."

A Fashionable Doll

Experience as a clothing designer in the children's wear business gave Terry Richardson an excellent jump start on designing garments for dolls. "All the technical knowledge I learned in the industry applies" she says. "From pattern making, to fittings and sewing, and following the fashion trends, methods of doll decoration—it's the same expertise one needs to apply to designing doll clothing."

Terry rounded out her training in F.I.T.'s toy design program, where she complemented training techniques with her expertise in clothing design. She is currently affiliated with Meritus Industries in Livingston, N.J. "Creating the total picture is important," urges Ms. Richardson. "You need to take into consideration face design and hairstyle, too. It's all interrelated in doll design."

Making It in the Doll World

Many designers enter doll designing through other glamorous doors.

Since winning her first sewing contest at age 11, Janet Goldblatt's dream was to design extravagant showgirl-style gowns and headdresses. After gradation from the New England School of Art, Janet headed for Hollywood with high hopes of designing fabulous costumes for the stars.

Although she did not break into show-biz, so to speak, Janet spent 10 years instead designing fashion apparel. Then one day she answered a job advertisement, and to her surprise it was Mattel Toys. On her first interview, she was asked to take a Barbie® doll home and design an original ensemble. Janet created not one, but three different outfits and was hired on the spot.

For almost two decades, the glitz, the glamour, the sequins and the sensation of haute couture have inspired the creations she identifies with the doll legend. "There's never a dull moment in my life," says Janet. "Designing fashions allows me the freedom to work in a wide variety of different looks, from evening wear to sportswear and even lingerie."

Qualifications

A doll designer may have a background in several disciplines of study from art, in both sketch and sculpture media, to costume and fashion studies, advertising or production capabilities.

However, most of all, according to F.I.T.'s Judy Ellis, "A good designer is always on the cutting edge, perhaps a step or two ahead of the industry. Students must study past design movements, as well as today's developments in the areas of product, design, graphics, fashion, textile development, computer, sound technology and robotics."

If you have talent, the magic of childhood in your heart, and the desire to work toward a creative and rewarding career, F.I.T.'s bachelor of fine arts degree program in toy design may just be the way you'll fulfill your dreams in doll design.

Source: *Doll World*, pp. 24–25.

15

Internet

E-COMMERCE MERCHANTS

In the beginning of the Web site phenomenon, E-commerce merchants approached the Web with unprecedented enthusiasm. Designers, manufacturers, and upscale luxury brands launched Web sites to reap the benefits of Internet shopping. However, the downside to the launch of new sites was precipitated by companies that jump started their sites without adequate conceptual design or navigation content.

As a result Web sites hawked everything from pet food to a plethora of fashion on-line shops and just assumed that the Internet shopping population would materialize and demand would fulfill itself. The dot.com bust is old news. All-too-many E-tailers had not separated themselves from the pack by creating Web design format and content that would entice people to log on and remain loyal customers.

After the initial surge of Web site use fell off, fashion apparel and auxiliary entrepreneurs started to rethink the design process.

TWO MERCHANDISING PHILOSOPHIES

Web sites in the fashion industry can be classified into two categories: (1) informational/educational or entertaining and (2) commerce oriented. The bottom line for firms using informational sites is to provide on-line users with product or company information and to allow companies another marketing platform via the Internet. Commerce-oriented Web sites provide on-line information platforms that

SIDEBAR 15-1 Driving Traffic to Your Web Site

So your new Web site is completed, and you are ready to have people start visiting. This means getting your Web site listed on the search engines that direct Internet traffic. But what if you do not have the budget to pay an Internet promotion company to get your Web site listed on the search engines? Fortunately, all hope is not lost. You can submit your Web site to the search engines yourself and save money in the process.

Submitting your Web site to the search engines is really quite simple, but you should take a moment to familiarize yourself with how sites are indexed by the search engines before you start the submission process. If you understand how to structure your Web pages for optimal search engine indexing, you will get more action and will have more chance of being listed when you submit your service. Let us first learn how search engines access Web sites on the Internet.

Spiders and Robots

The World Wide Web is constantly being updated and indexed by the Internet's search engines with the use of programs called "spiders" and "robots." When the robot or spider visits a Web page it reads the page's HTML text, which can include such things as Meta tags, page titles, HTML text, image alt tags, comments, and links. It is important to remember that not all of the search engines look at all of these criteria. Because it varies from search engine to search engine, develop a Web site that utilizes all types of HTML text, in particular, the Meta tags and page titles.

Robots and spiders index pages in your site by traveling through your Web page's links and also accessing outside Web sites through the use of external links. External links are also how search engines initially crawl onto your site. This is why it is so important to have external links leading to and from your Web site. This is especially important if you would like to have your site indexed and updated quicker and more frequently.

Another thing to keep in mind is robots and spiders are not particularly fond of Web sites that use frameset technology. When they index a frameset, they may not be able to leave the frameset because that HTML page of the parent frameset most likely does not provide any links. This is often the case when pages are brought up in search results individually and not displayed in conjunction with the other HTML pages in the frameset. This can be a real nightmare if you want search engine traffic to be able to navigate your Web site.

One last thing that can be a hindrance to search engines accessing your site is creating a Web site that uses technologies that do not utilize HTML links. Technologies such as Macromedia Flash will not allow the text portion of the page developed in Flash to be indexed. There are creative ways around this, however, such as ensuring your pages have a title, the use of Meta tags, and use of navigation links in HTML at the bottom of each page so the robots and spiders will have access to other pages in your site.

Preparing Individual Web Pages

How do you get the individual HTML pages ready for the robots and spiders? It is done with the use of page titles, Meta tags, HTML text, HTML links, comment tags, alt tags, page headers, and subheaders. The following is a short description of the main points.

The Page Title Tag

Ensuring that all your HTML documents have a page title is extremely important. The document title is the one thing that all search engines see eye-to-eye on and will be used when indexing your Web page. The page title is located in your HTML code in between the header tags in your document. If you look in your source code and you see, *Untitled Document*, you have no page title. Web page titles should be descriptive and state the name of your business. Here are a few examples/explanations of page titles.

Pinnacle Decision Systems: This is the bare minimum a title should be. It helps to be more descriptive than just offering the name of the company. It also helps individual pages achieve ranking if they have unique page titles describing what that particular page has to offer, rather than giving a general page title to the whole site.

Pinnacle Decision Systems, Home: This again is pretty minimalist for a page title. It adds a bit more description, but home really should be replaced with more descriptive words.

Microsoft Gold Certified Partner, Internet/Intranet development, information systems, computer consultant, Microsoft technologies, application development: This example is certainly descriptive and uses keywords in the title but it is too long. Page titles should be short and descriptive.

Pinnacle Decision Systems-Microsoft technologies, computer consultant, application development: This is what you want to aim for. This title gives the name of the company and a few key descriptive words for the page. The descriptive words can and should change to reflect the page content.

Meta Tags

There are three key Meta tags that you want to be concerned with as you prepare your individual pages for the search engines: description, keyword, and robot indexing Meta tags.

The Description Tag

This is the Meta tag that tells the search engine about the site. It is also the explanation that is displayed when Internet users are viewing search results. Your description tag should be 20 to 30 words long and should contain your Web site's company/business title, geographic location (if important), and key descriptive words and phrases utilized in such a way that search engine Internet users recognize quickly what your Web page has to offer.

Here is an example of a page description tag:

⟨Meta name= "description" content= "Pinnacle Decision Systems, Connecticut first Microsoft Gold certified Partner, is a professional services and software development company. Pinnacles' business consulting and development offerings include E-commerce, portals, and other Internet/Intranet sites; decision support and business intelligence systems; legacy transformation and migration; and Internet deployment of legacy applications. We manage all aspects of the project development life cycle to analyze, design and build complete, creative software applications"/⟩

The Keyword Tag

This is used by the search engines to locate your site when a user submits a particular search. It is important to keep in mind that keywords should be potential words or phrases that a search engine user might type into a search form to find your site. These keywords and phrases should reflect the content of your Web site and its objectives and intentions to your target audience.

To get a diversity of keywords for your Web site and to help your search engine ratings, use different keywords on different pages. Also, use a variety of keywords that reflect each individual page's content and reinforce the most important keywords and phrases on all pages. It is a good idea to do your own search of similar types of sites and see what keywords they are using. This can help you brainstorm for your potential keywords.

Remember that repeating words does not mean you will get listed better or faster. However you should combine keywords in your use of key phrases such as if someone searches for "gymnastics school" you can use the word "gymnastics" and follow it up with the phrases "gymnastics school," "gymnastic lessons," or "gymnastics classes." All of your keywords and phrases should be separated by commas and your list of words and phrases should be between 25 and 30 keywords long.

Here is a good example of a keyword Meta tag

⟨Meta name= "keyword" content= "All American Gymnastics Academy, gymnastics gym, gymnastics lessons and classes, Acrobatics, Gymnastics Team, Springfield, Massachusetts, tumbling, preschool physical exercises, children, birthday parties, cheerleading, USGF, Gymnastics School, Summer Camp, Sports Camp, fun, trampoline, preschool, after school"/⟩

The Robot Tag

This is a tool that you can use to make sure that a search engine does not list a particular page on your site. You can also use a robot tag to tell the crawlers how often they should come back and update the information.

To get the robots and spiders to index your Web pages, you need this tag:
⟨Meta name= "robots" content= "INDEX"/⟩

To instruct the crawlers how often to reindex the site, you would use the following tag. Remember, the tag should directly reflect how often you update the information on your site with new information that would need indexing. If your Web site is not constantly changing its content, this particular tag is not required, given that a one-time search engine index is enough.

⟨Meta name= "revisit-after" content= "30 days"/⟩

And if it is ever the case that you do not want a search engine to index a particular page, here is the code needed to deflect the robot.

⟨Meta Name= "robots" content= "NOINDEX"/⟩

HTML Text

Most search engines will use the HTML content text, header text, link text, image alt tags, and even comment tags text to predetermine how a Web site will be indexed and how it is ranked. Some simple tricks that you can use to place more indexable HTML text into your pages are: (1) Whenever possible use HTML text in place of graphic text, (2) label image names that can be indexed, (3) use straightforward alt tags with images, and (4) use descriptive link names. Once you have your site all coded and have all of your tags in place, the next step is to get the search engines to come to your site so they can index it. There are really two ways to do this.

Internet Directories

Internet directories use human editors who review sites submitted to them. They are looking for sites that are rich in original content and that are relevant to the work, leisure, and home lives of busy people. In particular, editors prefer sites that are high-quality, reliable and up-to-date, accurate, easy to use, fast, interactive, unique in content, interesting, visually appealing, and useful to consumers. Directories usually charge a fee to be listed in them.

One of the best Internet directories which is free to submit to is DOMZ, a.k.a. the Open Directory Project. DOMZ was formerly started by Netscape and provides search sources for major search engines such as Netscape, Lycos, and Hotbot. This is also the case with many various search engines that utilize Internet directories to obtain their resource information.

Search Engines

Engines use programs to crawl through the Internet indexing Web site URLs. The process starts once you have submitted your URL to a search engine, or when a crawler accesses your site via an external link to your Web site. When this happens, the crawler indexes the HTML and various tags on your site and places them in its database. But all search engines are not created equal. In fact, the information indexed by the various search engines differs from one to another. This is why it is important to cover all your bases and ensure the use of proper technologies (i.e., Meta tags, page titles, and HTML text) to achieve the best results with search engines. One good aspect of search engines is many have merged or enlisted the services of other search engines to pool their databases. This means being listed on one site can help you get listed on other sites.

For best results here is a list of search engines worth submitting to. These particular search engines and directories are responsible for providing information to other search engines.

1. DOMZ
2. Inktomi
3. Direct Hit
4. Google
5. Overture
6. Looksmart
7. Fast

Search Engines

Because the search engines and directories are in a constant state of flux, information is not provided on the top search engines for fear that this information might be out of date. Instead a link is provided to an on-line document that gives updated information on the major search engines and links:
http://www.bruceclay.com/searchenginechart.pdf

Courtesy of Mary Elges, Web Master, Pinnacle Decision Systems, 100 Roscommon Dr., Suite 310, Middletown, CT 06457 Tel: 860-632-7766 Fax: 860-632-8811 E-mail: info@pinndec.com Internet: www.pinndec.com. Pinnacle Decision Systems provides complete, creative IT solutions for information management needs.

sell a company's diversified merchandise, offering anything from fashion apparel to accessories and gift products. The revenue garnered from an effective Web channel of distribution is the catalyst that boosts the company's financial coffers.

UPDATING WEB DESIGN

Older Web sites that remain active can look outdated. If a Web site has not been updated or redesigned in more than two years, it should be carefully evaluated. In an article in *Women's Business New York* (June 2002), Mary Elges, a Web designer at Pinnacle Decision Systems, confirms this fact, "In business, you should be doing all you can to separate yourself from the pack. Companies with old Web sites are falling behind their competition."

To meet today's Internet standards, Elges recommends the following:

Clear Look and Feel: Today, the standard requires Web sites to have a clean, understandable, and consistent look and feel. Companies must make sure that their Web site looks professional and less "techy."

INDUSTRY PROFILE 15-1 | Mary Elges

Mary Elges brings her experience and expertise to Web design. She advises aspiring Web site designers to acquire skills in graphic design, code development, and new media design on both PC and Mac platforms.

Mary Elges has been working as a Web design professional for more than five years. She formally studied graphic arts at Springfield Technical Community College in Springfield, Massachusetts. She is an Adobe Certified professional and has been published in numerous articles in various publications. Mary Elges currently works on an IT developmental team as a Web designer at Pinnacle Decision Systems in Middletown, Connecticut, where she designs and develops Internet/Intranet sites, software applications, multimedia presentations, and Media for Print. When I asked Mary Elges what it takes to be a Web design professional here is what she had to say:

"To appreciate this unique professional, an understanding of the history behind Web design and the Web designer career is a must. The field of Web design is a relatively new line of work brought about by the establishment of the Internet in the 1980s. The first generation of Web pages lacked the visual stimulation generated in other mediums such as TV and print ads. This opened the doors for the graphic artist to build on their skills and enter a new market. The career path of a Web designer is finally formalizing in many colleges and universities. It has evolved several times over the last few years, and the job description of a Web designer varies from company to company."

History of the Web Designer's Role

Earliest to arrive in the role of the Web designer were the code developers. They understood the HTML language that is used to format text, color, positioning, and graphics into a Web page. But the code developers lacked the creative aspects that can be seen on the more fashionable Web pages of today. Clients could see the value in the functionality being created by the developers, but they were less than thrilled with the visual aspects of the sites being created. Something was missing.

With the release of software like Adobe's Go Live and Macromedia's Dreamweaver, graphic designers were able to step into the picture and design Web pages with little or no hand coding. Today, advanced Web designers have an excellent understanding of both the more difficult coding techniques and tools such as HTML, Cascading Style Sheets, JavaScript, and site development tools and the way to brand and build a visually stimulating site. This includes understanding the best strategies for site navigation, site structure, browser compatibility/resolution, testing, development for a specific target audience, branding, and the best tools for developing the site.

These advance designers also have a background in graphic arts, and today, more and more designers must understand "new media design." New media design is a form of visual communication that uses software such as Macromedia Flash and Adobe Premier to animate and stream video across the Web.

Streaming video and sites developed in Flash have become increasingly popular as a result of the improvements in both modem speed and high-speed connections such as T1 lines and DSL. The path I recommend to any aspiring Web designer is to major in graphic design. This will provide a solid background in visual communication, a key skill required by any Web designer. Early in your graphic art education it is a good idea to take an HTML course, as this will be a Web designer's main development tool.

As one pursues a graphic arts degree, pay close attention to information that applies to creating output for the Web as an end medium. It is also imperative to understand the RGB color space that is utilized by a computer's monitor. Become an expert in the areas of file format, resolution, and image optimization for Web pages, and keep in mind this will differ from print designation work, which is still the predominant output media taught in most graphic art programs.

I would also stress that being familiar with both the PC and Mac platforms will increase your marketability to employers. Although most web development is PC based while graphic design is not, it is important to understand both platforms, as both are popular within the industry. Keep up with the latest developments in your software design tool, get certified whenever possible, and participate in a coop/internship to gain some real experience.

Lastly, create sites for friends and family, this is always the best method for learning.

What Does It Take to Be a Web Designer?

- The **Web** in Web designer is the ability to understand, develop, and manipulate HTML code (Hypertext

Markup Language) on the World Wide Web. A Web designer must gather and develop a list of best practices for Web page development. This includes understanding usability within a site and simple, concise navigation concepts.

- The **designer** in the term Web designer is the skill set gained as a graphic artist. These skills would include knowledge of visual design, an understanding of the creative process, and well developed skills in the use of tools/software available within the graphic art industry.
- The final skill, which a Web designer should have, is a good understanding of the overall business and marketing that surrounds Web site development. A solid Web site development methodology needs to be in place.

The Web designer needs to understand the client's overall goals for the site in terms of audience, branding, technology limitations or requirements, and navigation needs. The designer must be creative in design and problem solving!

Tools/Software Used:

Intel Pentium 3 processor, 1 GHZ Dell PC

Adobe Photoshop 7.0

Adobe Illustrator 9.0

Macromedia Dreamweaver Ultra Dev 4.0

Macromedia Flash MX

Microsoft Visual Studio.Net

Adobe Premier 6.0M

Timeliness: Content should be updated at least quarterly. One of the worst mistakes is to allow your site to be static with no change. When someone in your target market visits your site and sees that the information remains unchanged, chances are they will not come back a third or fourth time. To create a professional Web site, you need to show your visitors what you are doing today.

Simple Navigation: On-line users are now accustomed to a certain style of navigation, and they depend on a site structure that allows easy access to information on the site. Gone are the days when visitors would put up with clever, but difficult, navigation.

Not Just Text: You need a hook to keep visitors entertained and coming back for more. Technologies such as Macromedia Flash, rotating graphics, frequently updated company highlights, and news feeds can help. Companies can also incorporate databases into Web sites, so visitors can do things such as on-line ordering, maintain customer information, and view order status. Companies that incorporate a database on their Web site gain advantages, because the database eases workload, aids with inventory, and increases the customer base.

Interactivity: The days of static Web sites are over. You may think "interactive" means "maintenance," but there are ways to provide interactivity while keeping maintenance simple. An example of interactivity would be a member log-in area on the Web site. Once logged in, members can sign up for newsletters, view news forums, enter member-only chat rooms, upload and download documents, and even view schedules of events.

Search Engines: One of the most important parts of Web site design is the structure of the Web site's Meta data and HTML content. By formatting content and using your source code's Meta tags efficiently, you will attract traffic to your site via the search engines. The search engines utilize small programs called spiders or robots, which crawl through the World Wide Web indexing information on Web sites and then process the information to be displayed during on-line searches. To obtain high rankings companies should pay special attention to their site's Meta information and the structuring of key words within the content of the site.

Budget: Before starting the redesign, you need to figure out how much money you want to spend. The size, complexity, multimedia design, and any additional functionality to your Web site will increase the cost.

Audience: If your site is designed for the general public, you need to make sure it looks and functions consistently in all of the major Internet browsers. It should also be reasonably fast enough to be downloaded by the slowest of modems.

In the real world of fashion merchandising, the key players face off with innovative merchandising. Similarly, fashion Web sites face considerable competition and combat the challenge with a variety of enticements, including dramatic graphics and storylines, chat rooms, E-mail, games, and wardrobe advice.

Maintenance: Sites can be designed to let companies maintain the content through Content Management Interfaces. This is something that needs to be determined prior to site construction.

THE ON-LINE CUSTOMER

To capture the elusive consumer dollar, E-tailers have to keep women happy, satisfied with product, and entertained. However, one of the problems facing women who shop on-line is that they cannot feel the fabric and try an item on for size or appearance. To address these issues, some E-tailers have chosen high-tech tools, such as virtual dressing rooms.

Lands' End, for one, offers the quickest and easiest way to capture a customer's fit points. Their Web site features three-dimensional personal body scanning, combined with virtual modeling, for a precise body replica. In time, the virtual fitting room may replace the actual store fitting room and take shopping from spending hours in the mall to just a few minutes on line.

SIZING UP A WEB SITE

Customers size up Web sites based on several elements.

- *Ease of navigation:* The ability to get around the site with relative ease.

SIDEBAR 15-2 | New Membership Registration Letter for a Luxury Web Site

Dear Mary Jones:

Welcome to Fabulousgifts.com. Putting together the Fabulousgifts.com collection represents luxury, and our desire for the best is only surpassed by our desire for the unique or the rare or simply the beautiful. That is our merchandise philosophy.

We also recognize that you are the kind of individual who knows how to reward yourself with the transcendent experience of owning or giving something truly special. Therefore, we feel privileged to register you with Fabulousgifts.com. Our luxury products go beyond mere necessity. They transport you to a status place in the ownership of precious items and products unparalleled by any other.

Visit Fabulousgifts.com often. We are constantly offering new ideas and ways to enrich your shopping experience.

Sincerely,
Julie Cameron
Vice President
Customer Service

- *Ease of registration:* New customer registration made simple and easy to log on to the site and establish an account.
- *Customer service:* Greeting for new customers, a thank you e-mail. Special packaging, gift wrap, ability to respond instantly to customer questions.
- *Delivery:* On time ability to deliver the goods, multiple mailings.
- *Delivery method:* UPS, overnight, next-day delivery.
- *One-stop shopping:* Variety of products easily accessed and purchased all at the same time.
- *Gift registry and gift certificates:* Providing customers too busy to shop the convenience of sending a gift certificate. Gift registry policy for bridal and other gift giving. For example, a Web site could contain the fol-

lowing message: "Too busy to shop? Why not send a thoughtful Fabulousgifts.com gift certificate. Your every gift need for holidays, birthdays, special occasions, and weddings can be instantly gratified by selecting from our unique repertoire of exclusive gifts gleaned from the global marketplace."

- *Easy return policy:* Uncomplicated instructions and easy return of merchandise.
- *Product information:* Concisely written details and description of items.
- *Check order status:* Ease with which customers can cruise through a site with the order confirmation number and track an order. A Web site could contain the following statement: "Each order received by Fabulousgifts.com comes with an Order Confirmation Number that enables you to track the status of your order. Just go to our Order Status page and enter your Order Confirmation Number to check the shipping status of each item in your order. It will also give you each item's tracking number so you can click on this tracking number and go directly to the FedEx Web site for up-to-the-minute shipping status."
- *Method of payment:* Credit cards or company's Web site credit card?
- *Privacy policy:* Protection of customer's personal and credit information. For example: "At Fabulousgifts.com we respect and value our customers and are committed to protecting their privacy with the highest ethical standards. However, we automatically collect customer information mainly to communicate with our customers and to personalize their shopping experience with product updates, services, and upcoming events, and to enhance the Fabulousgifts.com Web site content. Please note the Privacy Policy information."

- *Access to account:* Ability to access account information including order history, returns, and exchanges.

As Web sites become more and more sophisticated, E-tailers are continually revving up the cybervolume with loads of new information and a clean, streamlined, or entertaining look.

RETAILING ON-LINE

"Women's adoption rates of E-tailing are growing at a faster rate than men's adoption rates." That's the prognosis stated in the *Lifestyle Monitor*™, a weekly update on consumer attitudes and behavior based on ongoing research from Cotton Incorporated, which appears on Thursdays in *Women's Wear Daily*.

The population of women is growing more rapidly than the on-line population overall, and apparel and accessories rank much higher as purchases among women than men. In the first quarter of 2000, for example, the number of women on-line surpassed the number of men for the first time ever, with women edging out men at 50.4 percent versus 49.6 percent.

"What everyone has seen is the first time that E-commerce made an impact on traditional retailing," said Mark Goldstein, president of Impulse! Buy Network (www.impulsebuy.com), a company that licenses e-tailing technology to retailers and portal sites such as Women.com. "Looking forward into the twenty-first century, retailers are realizing that they have to take E-commerce seriously and not (view it) as a stepchild."

"A lot more retailers are going on-line," says Scott Silverman, director of Internet Retailing for the National Retail Federation (NRF). "In most cases, the 1998 holiday season is what drove the decision. A lot of retailers used the holiday season to find out what works and doesn't work, and throw out what doesn't," noted Silverman.

Brick-and-mortar retailers such as JCPenney.com, Macys.com, Nordstrom.com, and Sears.com are current leaders in E-tailing. Bloomingdales.com's navigating tools make shopping on-line faster, fun, and similar to shopping at Bloomingdale's stores. In addition to showcasing the store's top categories and labels, the retailer's Web site offers tips on wardrobing or decorating a bedroom or bathroom, views of the store's Lexington Avenue window displays, and items in the windows that can be bought on-line.

Catalogs

Most of these retailers not only have a Web site that sells product, but many have a catalog as well. Traditional stores performing best on-line are those that already have fulfillment capability through a catalog operation, such as JC Penney, Nordstrom, and Macy's. Catalogs and the Internet have become highly compatible mates. Companies often use their catalogs to lure buyers to Web sites, and Web shoppers often request catalogs. Catalogs still offer superior photo quality, portability, and a live customer service representative, which is still important to many customers.

WEB SITE DIFFERENTIATION

Filene's Basement, for example, is famous for its great close-outs. According to Goldstein of Impulse! Buy Network, Filene's planned its site carefully, and used what they are known for best.

"On the other hand, the Gap's strength is the quality of the shopping experience. So the company thought through TheGap.com, put a lot of time and money into it, and really integrated its on-line presence with its stores. For example, say a local Gap is out of a customer's jean size. She can buy on-line while she's in the store, and it will be shipped to her home without shipping charges. The Gap's on-line presence benefits

its stores, and vice versa. Live Picture is a company whose technology is used on the Gap and other sites. It allows the customer to zoom in on the product without any degradation of resolution (in fact, the resolution improves as you zoom). Rebecca Weill, Gap's spokesperson, says, "Our site is about making shopping easy for customers."

Personalized technologies are another plus in e-tailing. Land's End's "my virtual model" allows you to build a model of yourself and try on different outfits.

A Community for Women

Building a Web site that caters to plus size women by factoring in a celebrity tie-in proves another successful way that E-tailing draws customers to a site. Take Lane Bryant, for example. With more than 500,000 unique visitor hits per month, the Lanebryant.com site has attracted quite a following. Why? Because customers like the feel of the site and its hip spokesperson, Queen Latifah, who represents the celebrity tie-in with Lane Bryant clothing.

"The Web has been the single greatest tool we've brought in," says Chris Hansen, executive vice president of marketing. In addition to browsing the latest in-store offerings, visitors to the site can take part in a "Chick Chat" session on fashion, beauty, and body types, get advice on outfits, or view a Webcast Lane Bryant fashion show.

Luxury Web Sites

Upscale firms are also joining in the Web site race. A standalone site, such as Hermes.com, offers a selection of silk scarves and ties, as well as fragrances. In keeping with Hermes' equestrian image, customers enter the site through a signature orange page featuring a galloping horse. Best of all the company promises next-day delivery in the signature orange Hermes packages.

Upscale firms that do not have stand-alone sites are represented in the luxe sector by various portals, such as eLuxury.com. In the final analysis, however, no matter how creative or entertaining the Web site, the thing that really drives sales is great merchandise.

THE WEB CHALLENGE

Web watchers would think that a lot more fashion brands would have their own Web site selling direct to consumers online. Not so! Many style-driven labels do not want to do it themselves or do not have the capabilities to create a site. These companies rely on Web portals or Web consultants to do it for them.

Fashion industry firms, therefore, look for a creative Web shop that has the technical and creative savvy to construct the site and maintain it.

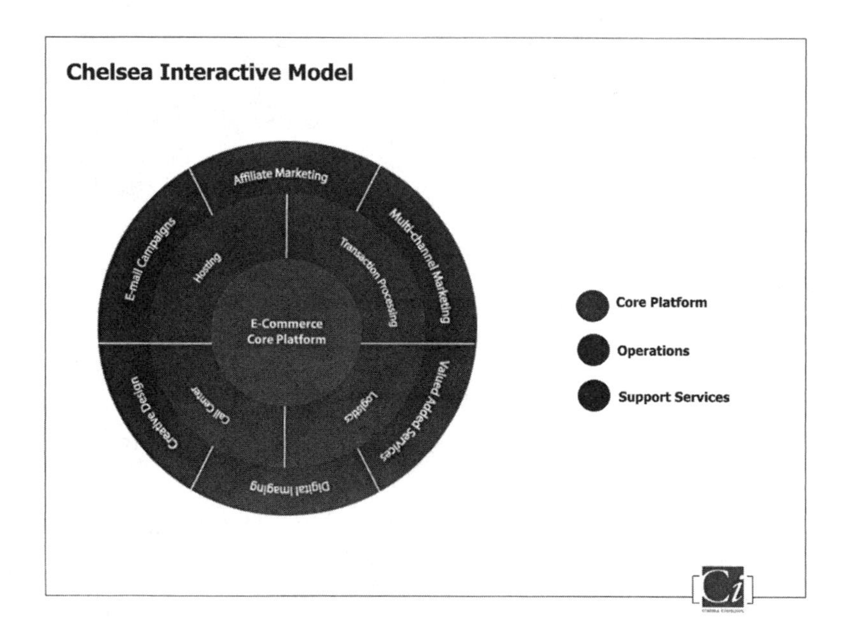

This page and opposite page: *Web pages from Chelsea Interactive offering services to retailers, designers, and manufacturers who want to establish on-line stores.*

@ Chelsea Interactive, an affiliate of Chelsea ...

Address: http://www.chelseainteractive.com/br/index.html

ci brands

Chelsea Interactive is dedicated to providing a customized e-commerce platform that helps premium brands create online stores. Each brand retains control over all aspects of its online store's products, prices and image. The quality of a brand's site will always match the allure of its label, and brand equity is based on the brands themselves.

ci brands

- Polo.com
- Elisabeth
- Timberland
- Cole Haan
- Maidenform
- Liz Lange
- Ulta.com
- Intershoe

ci solutions

ci platform

ci links

POLO.COM
RALPH LAUREN

Polo has long believed in a multi-channel approach to their customers. Last year, Polo extended its reach through Polo.com's very successful entry into e-commerce. This year, they chose to migrate Polo.com onto the Chelsea Interactive platform to enable the continued growth and evolution of their business. Chelsea Interactive's unique model allows Polo to leverage our enterprise-class technology platform while lowering and stabilizing their costs. Polo retains complete creative control and has access to continued Chelsea Interactive enhancements and upgrades.

ELISABETH
BY LIZ CLAIBORNE

"Elisabeth.com is a key element in our ongoing effort to learn as much as we can about the Internet as a shopping medium for better apparel. Our vision is to be where our consumers shop. To be responsive to today's consumers, who want to purchase products anywhere at anytime, we need to understand firsthand the dynamic between the shopper and the Internet."

- Paul R. Charron, Chairman and CEO of Liz Claiborne, Inc.

Timberland

"After reviewing many alternative strategies, we concluded that Chelsea Interactive's model offered us both a world class experience for our consumers as well as a great value for our shareholders. Our strategy is designed to leverage the Internet as a vehicle for consumer insight. Our ability to experiment and learn how consumers interact with the brand in such a data-rich environment will provide learnings that we expect will benefit us across all our channels of distribution."

Chelsea Interactive

Chelsea Interactive (CI) is an example of an E-commerce consultant and service provider that delivers customized E-commerce solutions to world-class retail brands. Liz Claiborne's plus size collection, Elisabeth.com, Maidenform's online store, Liz Lange Maternity, Cole Haan, Timberland, and Via Spiga Nickels are typical E-commerce clients.

CI Solutions services include Web site design and development, business intelligence, order fulfillment and logistics, customer service call center, and inventory management. Brands can also track customer behavior, analyze it, and act on real E-commerce and Web traffic trends.

CI builds, operates, and maintains a common E-commerce technology platform so that world-class retail brands may sell product direct to consumers over the Internet, through catalogs and other channels. As a result, CI allows retailers to do what they do best: design the high-quality products their customers expect from world-class brands while having total control over product, price, and image. The quality of a brand's site always matches the allure of its label, and brand equity is based on the brands themselves.

Chelsea Interactive's core allows each brand to work with tools that enable even nontechnical users to keep site content current, accurate, and engaging.

NicoleMiller.com

Nicole Miller was one of the first designers to have a Web site. When her firm first put up the Web site, it was thought of as more information oriented than commerce oriented. However, with an Internet consumer population of more than 150 million browsers, a lot of traffic was generated. As a result, Nicole Miller revamped its Web site, converting it into a full-blown E-commerce network.

Nicole Miller accessories—handbags, totes, umbrellas, ties, and socks—are all offered, along with sleepwear and select outerwear, such as leather jackets. Eyewear and fragrances are also available online.

The home page of the revamped Nicole Miller on-line destination, complete with a South-Beach inspired color palette and cartoon Nicole Miller Emcee, are engaging visual enticements. In two on-line departments, "Hot Looks" and "Big Night Out," select outfits are displayed. Clicking on a given item will reveal its style number and product description, as well as a listing of stores where the item is available. Bridal shoppers can order the Nicole Miller bridal catalog directly from the site and even download it and print it out.

The Nicole Miller Web site is continually updated with the latest fashion and product information.

Donegermarketplace.com

Donegermarketplace.com is an on-line community for the fashion industry presented by The Doneger Group. Drawing on more than fifty-six years of experience in retail consulting, Doneger Marketplace is a secure business-to-business Web site that provides a platform for retailers and manufacturers to communicate and conduct business.

Doneger considers itself a service center that caters to retailers, connecting them with resources that are right for their business. Manufacturers can create a powerful on-line presence in their own Virtual Showroom, where retailers log on everyday. Exhibitors can store styles in a fully searchable database that allows retailers to find product easily. Retailers can shop the market when it is convenient—anytime, anywhere—stay up to speed on fashion and business trends, find new resources, comparison shop across lines, and initiate orders using E-mail.

GET THE DAILY FIX

Fashion Wire Daily

Executives and decision makers from companies like Gucci to The Gap and Ogilvy & Mather to the *New York Times* sub-

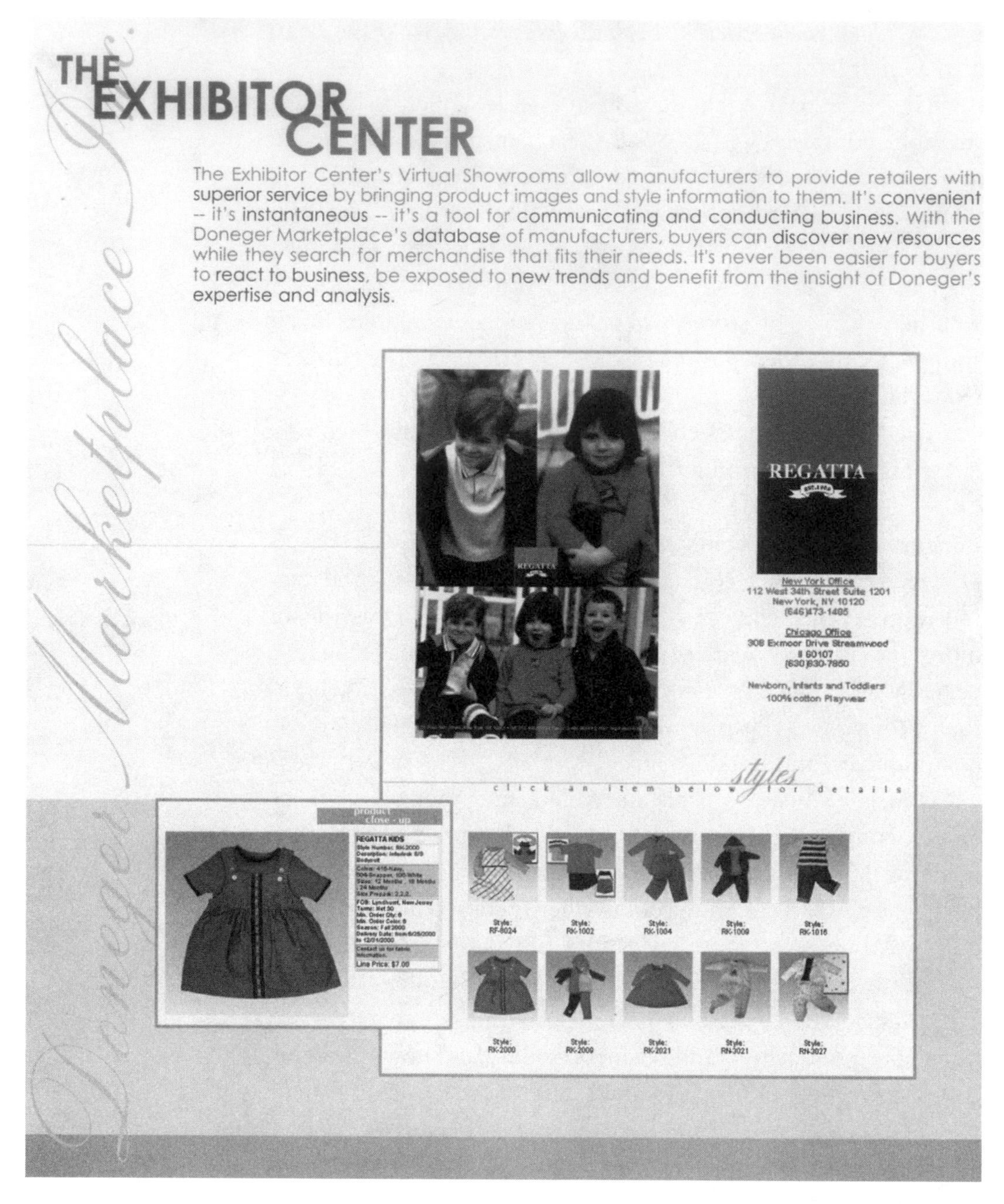

Doneger's "Exhibitor Center" offers manufacturers and retailers virtual showrooms with product images and trend information. Never has information been so up to date.

An ad page for Fashion Wire Daily, a wire service devoted to stories on fashion, trade shows, and runway productions.

scribe to Fashion Wire Daily news services for their daily must-have coverage of fashion news, features, events, and photos.

Why? Because Fashion Wire Daily (www.fashionwiredaily.com) is the world's first and only syndicated newswire service devoted to fashion news, trends, and worldwide runway show coverage. FWD posts an average of ten stories and fifty photos each day, filed by reporters and photographers located in

SIDEBAR 15-3 | Cyberspace Conversation

HTML (Hypertext Markup Language): Code that formats text, graphics, and multimedia and is rendered by a browser to be displayed as a web page.

Browser (Web browser): A software application used to locate and display Web pages. The two most popular browsers are Netscape Navigator and Microsoft Internet Explorer.

Cascading Style Sheet (CSS): This gives Web site developers more control over how pages are displayed and reduces maintenance by referencing the CSS in html pages. Thus, CSS developers only need to make site style changes by editing one file.

Content Management Interface: A Web based interface that allows individuals to edit, create, and delete Web page content by just filling out a Web-based form.

Database: A collection of information in such a way that a computer program can quickly select, sort, and store desired pieces of data. You can think of a database as an electronic filing system.

E-tailer: Retailer sites that use the Internet as a cyberspace method of selling and distribution.

Meta Tag: A tag (that is, a coding statement) in the Hypertext Markup Language (HTML) that describes some aspect of the contents of a Web page.

Modem: A device or program that facilitates a computer to transmit data over telephone, DSL, or cable lines.

Web Master: Professional who constructs Web pages.

Web Content Editor: Professional who writes the Web text.

the key fashion, beauty, and celebrity capitals of New York, Paris, London, Milan, and Los Angeles.

Current content includes insider access and full coverage of the Oscars, Golden Globes, Grammy Awards, Emmys, Sundance awards, VH-1 Fashion Awards, Cannes Film Festival events, and celebrity parties. The coverage is presented in:

- Interviews with major film and television celebrities
- Trend reports and style guides
- Celebrity profiles and designer interviews
- Extensive runway coverage
- Full access to FWD's archives, containing more than 80,000 photos and 10,000 articles.

Style.com

The Style.com E-commerce component shop was the first site to tie editorial content from *Vogue* and *W* magazines to an opportunity for customers to view the latest trends chosen by Style.com merchandisers and Neiman Marcus buyers. In this partnership, Style.com is cobranded with Neiman Marcus, which handles orders, inventory, shipping and returns, and pays a commission to Style.com.

READING 15-1 | Web Designer, Web Master, or Both?

BY HALEY WOOD & MARK ROESSLER

There are a wide variety of software options available these days that allow just about anyone to assemble a website. The results can vary. As with any other medium, hiring a designer or editor can add a level of creativity and clarity that your cousin just cannot. Finding and selecting the right person or people to help you develop a site requires an understanding of what you want the site to accomplish.

Whatever the ultimate goal for the site, there are three basic tasks that need to be covered: a design that involves a navigation scheme, someone to assemble the site and make it operational, and an editor to maintain and refresh the site. Large sites employ a fleet of editors, writers, interface designers, illustrators, animators, programmers and web masters. There are plenty of freelancers and smaller firms who can both create content, and help you to assemble your own information.

Web Designer and Web Master

In general, the above tasks boil down to those of a web designer and a web master. While it is important to find a designer whose visual taste is not completely foreign to yours, a good designer needs to be foremost an efficient organizer and communicator. It is not good to have your visitors lose their way in a pretty site. People need to know where they are and be enticed to look further. They need to be able to quickly return where they left off.

When researching sites and reviewing those of possible design firms you might hire, do not just glimpse at the graphics. Read the content. It might be as uninteresting to you as yesterday's weather report, but remember that not everyone will be familiar with your message initially. Try to make certain you understand what the site is trying to convey. Try to read every page of the site without getting lost. Make certain you understand the function of every button on a page.

Besides building attractive, clear navigation and expressing your ideas effectively, a good designer also needs to be able to prepare his/her work so that it can be edited by other people. Even if the designer will also maintain the site, your site is much less valuable to you if only the designer can make changes. If the site is going to be maintained by anyone else, the content needs to be well organized and documented.

Mastering a site . . .
The most frequently visited websites are those that change and are updated regularly. Many designers are happy to hand their work over to you or an employee to edit and maintain. Whoever manages the digital files that make up the site becomes the web master. Given the importance of good organizational skills, a good designer builds a template for the site that is flexible. You need to make sure your designer can build a system that the master can learn.

With this in mind, no matter who you hire (designer or master), it is important to know how many people worked on the sites you admire. Did they create them alone, or as part of a team? Is the site frequently maintained, and how obvious are the additions to the overall fabric of the site?

There are generally two extremes amongst web masters—those who excel in creating and building interesting, content filled sites, and those who build sites with tremendous functionality. Depending on what you need to accomplish, you will need to assess each candidate for how he/she blends these tasks. A crafts catalog, looking to sell artwork on-line, will need to manage email correspondences, accept credit cards and have a web designer who can convey a sense of the craftspeople's style. But a company's newsletter might require someone who can write and edit articles, archive content libraries, and possibly manage a database.

A web master does not need to be a programmer, but it is best if he/she understands how to work with them. Forms that people can fill out on-line that are sent to you as an email can be created by hosting services for a few hundred dollars, and the resulting code can then be made to work seamlessly by a savvy designer.

Keep in mind . . .
Above all, any good website is clear. If you're new to building a website, hiring a designer or a web master ought to help make things easier. If he/she cannot make the process more understandable to you, then be wary of how your message will be communicated.

Source: *Women's News*, August 2001, p. 6 Courtesy of Hayley Wood and Mark Roessler.

READING 15-2 | Just a Click Away BY JULEE GREENBERG

NEW YORK—Teens are heading to their computers with a mouse in one hand and a credit card in the other.

In an economy where dot-coms are not making as much money as they once were, teen girls are surely keeping e-commerce alive. According to Rob Callender, trend manager at Teenage Research Unlimited, teens are most comfortable with modern technology and still look to the Internet regularly for advice, fun and shopping. Teens, he said, go online even more often today than they did before.

A study conducted by the company in the spring revealed that 37 percent of teens have made a purchase on the Internet at one point or another, a higher percentage than in the past. However, that number was dominated by purchases made by teen boys rather than girls. Of the items purchased, apparel came in at number one with 25 percent of the vote, CDs were second at 19 percent and sports equipment and books were tied at 10 percent.

"If the site is providing a service to them, it will be successful," he said. "As for the sites that only sell clothes and are not providing any other exciting features, I am sure they are not doing as well."

Teens see shopping as a social event, he noted. They go to the mall with friends or their parents, look at magazines, play video games and shop for clothes. So, Callender said Web sites should model their entertainment value as a small world and provide a variety of services on the site. He used gadzooks.com as an example.

"It has a store, but also information about music, contests, movies and horoscopes," he said. "These are all things that motivate the customer."

Jane Rinsler Buckingham, president of Youth Intelligence, agrees.

"Teens tend to go to sites through word of mouth," she said. "They go there if their friends go there. As for shopping, they tend to browse the stores online that they already know and then purchase at the store."

At Delia's, orders placed on the delias.com site and through the catalog account for $83.7 million or 61 percent of the company's sales. The company offers many services on the site. For example: once the customer shows interest in a particular product, there is a service to recommend other pieces to complete the outfit.

Also, Delia's has recently made it easier for the customer to shop the catalog online by showing the exact catalog she received in the mail. They also send e-mail alerts to frequent buyers to inform them of what's new on the site.

"The Web is where our customer chooses to shop," said Evan Guillemin, chief operating officer. 'It's where she spends her time and her money."

Guillemin insists that teens find a way to pay for the products they want and if they are under 18, the credit card comes from the parents.

"We have a database of about three million buyers who gave us their credit card numbers and it has never been a problem, said Hilary Chasin, executive vice president of marketing at Delia's. "They take their time on the site, look for what they want and then get mom in the room for the purchase."

Delia's also uses its Web site to gather information about the customer and find out what she is looking to spend. For example, when the company was looking to revamp its offerings for the home collections, a survey was sent out to find out how they would like to decorate their rooms.

At Alloy Inc., a media, direct-marketing and marketing services company targeting generation Y, the Internet is a major part of business. It's Web site, alloy.com, was launched in 1996 and according to Jim Johnson, president and chief operating officer, there has been "strong growth every year since the launch."

"The site accounts for about 30 or 40 percent of the business," he said. "Our theory is that when teens go shopping, they are going to the mall to do more than just shop, so we added these areas to the site much like a mall would have."

New York-based Alloy said major revenue gains for the first quarter ended April 30 led to net income of $3.1 million, reversing a year-ago loss of $7.4 million. Total sales spiked 78.6 percent to $50.4 million, with merchandise revenues jumping 30.9 percent to $31.1 million, while sponsorship and other revenues kicked in a more than fourfold increase to $19.4 million.

Junior clothing makes are also finding the Internet useful for business. Candie's launched a Web site in November that sells the company's clothes, shoes and accessories. It also uses the Web to showcase the Candie's Foundation, which raises awareness for teenage pregnancy. The foundation sells T-shirts with the phrase: "Be Sexy: It doesn't mean you have to have sex," which have been big sellers on the site.

"We sold more of the 'sexy' shirts online than we did in the stores," said Ken Ruck, director of interactive for Candie's, who pointed out that the site gets anywhere from 15 million to 25 million hits per month. "Teens head to the Web more than any other age group."

Ruck said customers also look to the Candie's site for information about the retail locations. When they find there is no Candie's store in their immediate area, they buy merchandise from the site.

"They use the site to look at what we have in the stores and then go to the stores to purchase," he said.

For Los Angeles-based Rampage, the company has seen a large increase in teen Net surfers stopping at its site, but Web sales are still not a large part of the business.

"It's successful, but not wildly successful," said Francheska Anderson, vice president of Rampage.com. "It accounts for about 1 percent of the business."

Still, Rampage advertises the site in all of its print ads, as well as on hang tags. It has found prom seasons to be its most successful on the site.

"So many parents placed orders for their daughters' prom dresses," she said.

For Los Angeles-based junior denim brand Tyte, the Internet site is used as a magazine. According to owner Alden Halpern, it no longer sells products online.

"We used to, but it became too difficult and not very cost effective," he said. "It's more for the kids to see a company profile and for us to get feedback from the customer. It gives fashion advice and trend information as it changes, so there is a reason for her to come back later."

Halpern said the biggest benefit of having the site has been the ability to reach the customer and find out what they want from the brand.

"We learned a lot about our customer through the site," he said. "They really do live on the Web."

Source: *Women's Wear Daily*, July 25, 2002, p. 23. Courtesy of Fairchild Publications, Inc.

READING 15-3 | Luxe E-Tailers Seen Wasting Millions

BY VALERIE SECKLER

New York—Virtual baubles appear to be leaving the online luxury customer base.

E-tailers aiming at affluent cybershoppers, or those with liquid assets of $1 million or more, had best not pin their hopes on the offer of exclusive designer fashions or extravagant jewels, let alone Flash-animation features of whiz-bang multimedia extravaganzas, according to a report released last Wednesday by Internet consultant Forrester Research Inc.

"These affluent people have specific demands when they shop online that are different from what they are looking for when they shop offline," advised Ekaterina O. Walsh, a senior analyst at Cambridge, Mass.-based Forrester, in an interview Wednesday. "Upscale e-tailers are wasting millions of dollars. They're all focused on the things that don't work: exclusivity, extravagance, completely unusuable Web site features."

What is working at Web sites appealing to cypershoppers with wide-ranging income levels, Forrester found, is simple: convenience, control and confidence. "Affluent shoppers are a critical consumer segment because they set the pace for e-commerce adoption," Walsh noted. "They have been buying online longer, feel more comfortable doing so, buy more frequently, and, of course, spend more online than anyone else. At the same time, they buy online for the same reasons as all online shoppers do; they care about price and positive experiences as much as the less-wealthy."

"Despite their readiness to purchase everything from prestigious cosmetics to designer clothes," Walsh added, "the affluent have held back from buying luxury goods online because they are not getting what they want. Sites like armaniexchange.com, eLuxury.com and Boo.com are all focused on things that don't work."

Informed of Forrester's findings, the chief executives of both Boo.com and eLuxury.com agreed that it's vital to make their Web sites easy to use—and contended they have done so and are continuing to refine those efforts. (Armaniexchange.com officials did not return calls for comment). At eLuxury, for example, a number of changes have recently been made, or are soon upcoming on the site.

"Particularly for luxury sites—but for any Web site—you need to make them easy to use," offered Barbara Wambach, chief executive officer of eLuxury.com, the San Francisco-based joint venture between LVMH and Europatweb, the Internet development vehicle of LVMH chairman and CEO Bernard Arnault. "The luxury customer is more demanding than others. Speeding page-load times and making navigation easier are things we've been working on.

"It's a challenge to sell at high price points online," Wambach acknowledged. "You want to show the product clearly, but you don't want to overwhelm the [technology]. Most people in the U.S. are still using 56K modems."

Ben Narasin, chief executive officer of Fashionmall.com Inc., the portal that acquired various assets of Boo.com last May, said of the Forrester advisory: "I think it's dead-on right, but she's referring to the old Boo.

"The original Boo.com was a whiz-bang techno site with all-out Flash, and some extreme exclusives, like Jil Sander Pumas. We've made some fundamental changes at Boo, broadening the merchandise focus from so much footwear, especially athletics. We've added and expanded a lot of categories," he noted, citing apparel, accessories, home goods, and style-driven gifts. "We've hired style scouts to try to identify what products people want."

However, neither Wambach nor Narasin necessarily agreed with the word from Forrester that designer exclusives and extravagant merchandise are not tasty lures for the luxe crowd online.

"Some of the things our users want are very pricy," Narasin said. "At Boo.com, for $27,000, you can buy a floating home for six, to be used outside a lake house. You can also buy everything from a modestly priced MP3 player to a Ducati. What our users want is something different. And the something different isn't price."

Offered eLuxury's Wambach: "I would just disagree with [the notion] that designer exclusives and extravagant merchandise do not appeal to the luxury customer online. It is normal for retailers to differentiate with various labels, whether it's Target's proprietary brands or exclusives on designer goods, like Louis Vuitton and Christian Dior handbags, which can be found at eLuxury."

Nonetheless, the picture surfacing from Forrester's research, Walsh insisted, is one of an Internet where luxury merchants are engaged in a misguided, futile attempt to recreate the world of offline luxury shopping on the Web.

"Online purveyors of luxury goods should quit trying to recreate an offline shopping experience," Walsh counseled. "Channels aren't different funnels through which identical experiences can be poured."

Making matters worse, most Web sites appealing to luxury customers, Walsh said, are unwittingly erecting technical barriers to convenient shopping, like bandwidth-intensive interfaces; links that are broken; features that require plug-in devices, and "error" messages, which can be confusing.

"By understanding and responding to the demands of affluent online shoppers," Walsh concluded, "retailers will be poised to fulfill expectations of non-affluent customers, who are right behind them."

Source: *Women's Wear Daily*, March 19, 2001, pp. 2, 14. Courtesy of Fairchild Publications, Inc.

Appendix A

Examples of Employment Opportunities in the Fashion Industries

JOBS WITH CREATIVE VISUAL BOARDS

Baby Togs.
Childrenswear
Girl's Dress Designer
Immediate Position Available
Excellent Opportunity

We are looking for a Senior Girl's Dress designer for size ranges newborn - 6x. This position will have a strong emphasis on Holiday and Social dresses. The candidate must be a creative and motivated individual and will be responsible for the product design process including market research, mood board creation, designing, sketching and fit. Conduct fit sessions and responsible for final approval for sample fit.

Please e-mail your resume to:
or fax:
Please no telephone calls. EOE

Baby Togs.
Childrenswear
Girls Dress Designer
Childrenswear

A leader childrenswear manufacturer has an excellent job opportunity for a girls dress designer for sizes toddler-16. This candidate must be a creative and motivated individual and will be responsible for the product design process including market research, mood board creation, designing, sketching, and fit, conduct fit sessions and responsible for final approval for sample fit.

Please e-mail your resume to
or fax to
Please no telephone calls. EOE

Graphic Design Assistant
cK CALVIN KLEIN JEANS,
division of Warnaco Inc.

cK Calvin Klein Jeans has an exciting opportunity in our Graphic Design Department. We are seeking a highly creative Graphic Design Assistant who will help in illustration, typography exploration, library research, factory and presentation templates, tech packs, direct applications, trims, disk preparation, filing, color copying, preparing concept boards, presentation boards, organizing samples and conducting market research. Qualified candidates must be proficient in Mac software/Adobe Illustrator and Photoshop. Illustration skills a plus. BFA in Graphic Design preferred.

Please fax resume along with salary requirements to or e-mail as an MS Word attachment to

Please reference Graphic Design Position in subject field of your email.

PLAYBOY

Asst. Product Designer

Playboy brand, one of the world's fastest growing consumer fashion brands is seeking a talented, fashion savvy, dynamic recent Fashion Designer graduate.

SKILLS/RESPONSIBILTIES

- Must have strong portfolio demonstrating understanding of street fashion and retail marketplace
- Develop seasonal graphics and patterns for men & women's markets. Must have experience in PhotoShop and Illustrator.
- Flat technical drawing and concept board development
- Responsible for the design of retail signage, packaging and branding tools
- Oversee design lay out of Playboy style guides
- Develop and maintain archive "library" in order to better assist team in research.
- Bachelor degree from leading Fashion/Art College

Send/fax/email resume and salary requirements to:
Playboy Enterprises, Inc.
Attn: HR -
730 Fifth Avenue New York, NY 10019
Fax:

RETAIL BRAND ALLIANCE

ADRIENNE VITTADINI BROOKS BROTHERS CAROLEE CASUAL CORNER GROUP

Retail Brand Alliance is home to some of the most prominent brand names in the industry including: Adrienne Vittadini, Brooks Brothers, Carolee and Casual Corner Group. We are currently seeking an experienced designer to join our Northern Connecticut design studio.

DESIGNERS

- Develop existing and emerging concepts and trends across multiple brands
- Create flat sketches, illustrations and specifications for samples
- Present product line to merchant and production teams

Requirements:

- 3+ years design experience in Sweaters, Knits or Wovens
- Strong flat sketching and illustration skills needed
- CAD experience a plus

We offer bonus potential every 6 months, a comprehensive benefits package including 401(k) and pension plans, a generous merchandise discount and relocation assistance. Submit resume and salary requirements to: **Retail Brand Alliance;** Attn: Recruiter, Human Resources; 100 Phoenix Ave., Enfield, CT 06082; Fax: ; Email: EOE.

JOBS IN FASHION FORECASTING

dollhouse®

DESIGN DIRECTOR

Seeking creative self motivated individual with a passion for clothing and the ability to lead a very talented design team. You need to be fast, aggressive and result oriented. Extensive knowledge of denim and denim related styling is a must.

Pls fax resume to:
Or E-Mail to:

HOT JUNIOR URBAN COLLECTION

New junior urban line seeks creative, energetic senior sportswear designer to lead a team. MAC computer skills & foreign travel required. Trend, spec & production knowledge needed. 5 years experience necessary. Excellent salary & benefits. E.O.E. Pls fax resume to: Attn: HR

MAKE A SMART MOVE

Gap, Inc. is a global company with three distinct brands - Gap, Banana Republic and Old Navy. We have the following career opportunity in **San Francisco, CA**.

Fashion Director/Marketing: Provide styling POV for the brand as determined at NY Product presentation. Develop key partnerships with design, merchants, marketing and visual merchandising. Min. 8 years senior level fashion styling experience, 5 years experience in retail and 4 years managing people.

Interested? Email your resume to fax Please reference **AA-307106 & NEW-WWD**. Or visit www.gapinc.com.

JOBS AT THE FIBER/FABRIC AND LEATHER/FUR LEVELS

JONES APPAREL GROUP

WOVEN/KNITWEAR ASSOCIATES NEEDED

A division of Jones Apparel Group Inc, is currently looking for highly motivated, and organized team players with 3-5 years experience, who thrive in an upbeat and fast paced environment. Must have technical knowledge of specing, experience with lab dips, flat sketching, layouts and worked with agents and mills in Asia. Must be computer literate, and AI knowledge preferred.

Jones Apparel Group, Inc. offers an excellent benefits package and an exciting work environment. EOE.

For confidential consideration, please fax or e-mail resume with salary requirements to:

Knitwear Design Assistant

cK CALVIN KLEIN JEANS, division of Warnaco Inc.

cK Calvin Klein Jeans has several opportunities in both our Womens and Mens Design Departments for talented knitwear designers who possess 1 - 3 years of related apparel experience working with sweater or knitwear lines. Qualified candidates will work closely with all members of the design team to develop seasonal lines. Candidates must demonstrate a high taste level combined with a great sense of color and style. A demonstrated ability to produce flat sketches along with solid organization and computer skills (e.g. PDM, Photoshop, etc...) are necessary for success in this team-oriented environment. Basic experience with fabric and trim is a big plus.

Please fax resume along with salary requirements to or e-mail as an MS Word attachment to

KNIT TECHNICAL DESIGNER

TSE

- Strong knitwear and fully fashioned background
- Extensive spec experience
- Aptitude to interpret designer's ideas, concepts and sensibilities from sketches
- Ability to conduct fitting
- Extensive technical knowledge of all aspects of knitwear construction
- Strong computer skills
- Excellent communication, organizational and follow up skills
- Proven track record with solid industry references

Candidates should fax resume and cover letter, including salary requirements to or email to

Artist

TEXTILE ARTIST

Expanding Design Studio seeks Talented & Experienced Artist to work in-house in gouache, watercolor, and dyes. Knowledge of colorways & layouts is essential. Excellent opportunity to join the professional team of artists in our Busy Textile Design Studio specializing in Home Furnishings & Fashion. Please Fax or E-mail resume in confidence to at:

baby phat

LEATHER DESIGNER

Superhot jr.urban line seeks creative, energetic person. Must have 3+ yrs. exp. in leather/outerwear. MAC computer skills and foreign travel required. Knowledge of trends, fit samples, production approval samples needed. Excellent salary & benefits. E.O.E. Pls fax resume to: Attn:HR

GOSSAMER WINGS

SANTE FE

SAMPLEMAKER

Relocate to Santa Fe, New Mexico! Couture house of suedes & leathers needs professional level samplemaker. Minimum of 5 years experience.

Please fax resume to:

Production Coordinator

Men's & Ladies' Leather Outerwear Co. seeks detail oriented individual responsible for pre-production process including SPL tracking, fittings, pattern corrections, comments & daily overseas follow-up w/factories. Computer sketching a must (CorelDraw Preferred). 1-2 years exp. w/leather outerwear a +. Fax resume to at:

JOBS AT THE MANUFACTURER LEVEL

Merchandising

Head Merchandiser
(Children's Wear)

Hartstrings, LLC., wholesale manufacturer of high-end children's sportswear located in the beautiful mainline western suburbs of Philadelphia, has an excellent opportunity for a talented senior level, creative Merchandiser to work with Design staff to develop and execute merchandising plan for our 5 product lines. Ideal candidate will have 15+ years experience, preferably in children's market. Responsibilities include Product Development, including seasonal calendar, lkeading product development meetings, profitability and SKU analysis of all product lines, providing product assortment and planning direction to design staff. Also responsible for analyzing wholesale and retail business and developing seasonal merchandising plans; working with production on margin opportunities and goals; and working with marketing/design/production on final costing process.

This position will report directly to the Chief Operating Officer and is an outstanding opportunity for the candidate who meets our criteria. Hartstrings offers a comprehensive compensation and benefits package, including excellent salary and bonus package, health/dental/life insurance, 401k plan and much more. (Hartstrings is located in the beautiful mainline western suburbs of Philadelphia.)Qualified candidates, please fax or email resume with salary requirements to:
[illegible]
or [illegible], attn: MM0303. EOE

Associate Designer

Jacques Moret, Inc., a major apparel co., is seeking an Associate Designer with 3-5 yrs. activewear exp. in both Knits & Wovens. Responsibilities will include: design development, board presentations, market research, color & sample line development, lab dips, technical skills for fittings, an awareness of current trends & knowledge of garment construction, fabrics & trim. Candidate must be creative, organized, detail - orientated & a team player. A BA/BS degree in fashion design & strong computer skills in Mac Illustrator & Photoshop are required.

We offer a unique environment with competitive salaries & comprehensive benefits. Send resume with salary history to: Jacques Moret, Inc. 1411 Broadway 8th floor, NY, NY 10018 or Email to: [illegible]

We will only contact those candidates for further consideration.
Equal Opportunity Employer

Merchandiser- Socks

Jacques Moret Inc., a major activewear intimates & sock company, is seeking a Sock Merchandiser to handle our private label & licensed products. In this newly created position, a minimum of 5 yrs. experience is required, preferably in women's & kids socks.
We are looking for a team - player who is creative and an experienced line-builder & line planner. Good analytical & communications skills & computer skills in Word & Excel are needed. Responsibilities will include: overall seasonal trend direction, key item development & a strong understanding of the mid-tier & mass - market business is essential.
We are a leader in our industry and offer a unique culture with competitive salaries & comprehensive benefits. Please send resume with salary history to:
Jacques Moret Inc, 1411 Broadway
8th Floor, NY, NY 10018
or email to [illegible]

We will only contact those candidates under further consideration.
Equal Opportunity Employer

Product Development and Design Manager

Provider of corporate and career apparel to business clients seeks an experienced product development/designer. The successful candidate must be proficient in the establishment and control of garment specifications, first samples, pre-production and size set samples, fabric lab dips and first article trim samples. The candidate must have a design background in men's and women's tailored and non-tailored apparel. Working with contract designers, manufacturing, pattern development and size grading specifications, fabric and trim resources essential. This position requires the ability to prepare and present design presentations to major customers and prospects.

Salary commensurate with ability. We offer a full benefit package including health and dental insurance and 401(k) plan. Please send resume to:

LION APPAREL
6450 Poe Avenue, Ste. 300
P.O. Box 13576, Dayton, Ohio 45413-0576
Fax: [illegible] / E-mail: [illegible]
An Equal Opportunity Employer

liz claiborne
KIDS

MERCHANDISER

Leading childrenswear mfr seeks a Merchandising Planner. Candidate should have extensive collection and classification exp. Will develop Style/Sku plans, determine price strategy, develop & maintain merchandise line plans for each season. Individual will be resp for providing all depts w/ retail & market feedback & prepare info needed for Market (incl line sheets, final prices, assortments & key trends), issuing style numbers & color codes and analyze selling from all major accts. Should have extensive infant thru size 16 exp.

Send resumes to: [illegible]
or fax: [illegible]. No calls please. EOE.
A Division of Baby Togs, Inc.

Product Development

JONES NEW YORK INTIMATES
Division of Madison Intimate Brands

ASSISTANT MERCHANDISER

Responsible for all administrative functions in Product Development Dept. Must possess the ability to develop and edit line plans, establish and follow-up on time/action calendars, schedules, budgets. Requires extremely strong skills with computers (Excel with formulas, spreadsheets; Outlook), and communications- both written and oral. Must be accurate, organized, have excellent follow-through, and ability to think in a fast-paced environment. Min 3 yrs prior experience in Product Development/ Merchandising. Competitive salary and benefits.

For immediate consideration, email resume with Subject Header: Asst. Merchandiser- Your Name, to:
[illegible]

MERCHANDISER MANAGER

Established Manhattan-based company seeks a Merchandiser for Ladies Apparel. Must possess the ability to develop and execute to assortment plan as determined by current customer base, market needs, and sales history; to include balanced product mix and hit targeted price points. Responsible to create / maintain / meet Designer's time / action calendar; liaison between design, production, sales. Minimum 7 years management experience, with proven track record. Outstanding communication /presentation skills, proficiency with computers; are musts. Some travel required. Competitive salary and benefits package. All resumes held in strictest confidence. Email resume to:
[illegible]

JOB IN FASHION SHOW PRODUCTION

JOHN HARDY

John Hardy, a luxurious brand for jewelry and home products, seeks dynamic and motivated individuals to support the next stage of its rapid growth in the following positions:

TRUNK SHOW COORDINATOR - exp coordinating calendar for seasonal trunk shows, liaison role to the sales exec and operations with regards to scheduling, billing and follow-up. Proficient with Excel to create and track via spread sheets.

We offer competitive salaries and benefits.
Please send your resume in confidence to:

No telephone calls please.

JOBS AT THE RETAIL LEVEL

CREATIVE RETAIL ADVISORS WTD.

New modern lifestyle concept boutique opening in the heart of Chelsea is seeking truly creative sales advisors. Must have at least 2 yrs. experience within the following backgrounds. High end apparel, cosmetics and accessories. Advisors must be willing to work and able to be trained in all these fields and more. An artistic background would also be a bonus but not a requirement. Full-time as well as part-time positions available so please specify.
Please email all resumes to:

Qualified candidates will be contacted for interviews.

QUIKSILVER/ROXY

Roxy Accessory and Footwear Division is seeking a sales professional for the Midwest Region. Candidate must have 3 - 5 years sales experience handling specialty stores within the territory. Qualified applicants please e-mail resume to

MERCHANDISING EXECUTIVE

Starcrest Products of California, Inc., a major Retailer located in Southern CA is seeking someone to manage our very unique merchandising environment. Due to our continued growth, we need an experienced merchant for our fast paced merchandising department within our national mail order distribution company.

Major Responsibilities include responsible for appropriate quantity of merchandise including product re-ordering, inventory turn, vendor communication and managing of up to 4 supervisors and a staff of 40 employees.

If you are a savvy professional who enjoys working in a fast paced, deadline oriented environment, possess strong negotiation and communication skills and think quickly on your feet this is the job for you!

Candidate must have 10+ years in merchandising with Retail/Buying experience. Excellent negotiation, analytical, interpersonal and leadership skills required. Ability to define problems collects data, establish facts, and draw valid conclusions. Must be polished, professional, and savvy

Starcrest offers comprehensive benefits and is an equal opportunity employer with a diverse workforce providing a drug & smoke free environment.

Please email resume to
w/salary history & expectations, or mail resume, salary history & expectations to:
Starcrest Products of California, Inc.,
3660 Brennan Avenue, Perris CA 92571

Appendix B

Examples of Color and Fashion Trend Forecasting Services

COLOR FORECASTING SERVICES

Color Association of the United States (CAUS)
315 West 39th Street, Studio 507
New York, NY 10018
Tel: 212-947-7774
Fax: 212-594-6987
www.colorassociation.com

Color Box
29 West 38th Street, 9th Floor
New York, NY 10018
Tel: 212-921-1399
Fax: 212-868-3130

Color by Design Options
10 East 9th Street, Suite B731
Los Angeles, CA 90079
Tel: 213-622-9094
Fax: 213-622-9050
www.design-options.com

Color Marketing Group
5845 Richmond Highway, Suite 410
Alexandria, VA 22303-1864
Tel: 703-329-8500
Fax: 703-329-0155
www.colormarketing.org

Color Portfolio, Inc.
P.O. Box 794447
Dallas, TX 75379
Tel: 866-876-8884
Fax: 972-447-0095
www.colorportfolio.com

Committee for Colour and Trends (CCT), Inc.
60 Madison Avenue, Suite 1209
New York, NY 10010
Tel: 212-532-3355
Fax: 212-447-1628
www.color-trends.com

Huepoint
39 West 37th Street, 18th Floor
New York, NY 10018
Tel: 212-921-2025
Fax: 212-730-2320

The International Colour Authority (ICA)
33 Bedford Place
London, WC1B 5JU
England
Tel: 011-44-20-7637-2211
Fax: 011-44-20-7637-2248
www.internationalcolourauthority.com

Pantone Inc.
590 Commerce Boulevard
Carlstadt, NJ 07072-3098
Tel: 201-935-5500
Fax: 201-896-0242
www.pantone.com

Trend Curve Colors™
14850 Scenic Heights Road, Suite 155
Eden Prairie, MN 55344
Tel: 952-893-1245
Fax: 952-893-1264
www.trendcurve.com

FASHION TREND FORECASTING SERVICES

Doneger Creative Services
The Doneger Group
463 Seventh Avenue
New York, NY 10018
Tel: 212-564-1266
Fax: 212-560-3699
www.doneger.com

Ellen Sideri Partnership
(Represents Peclers Paris, Jenkins and FM Decifer, both from London)
12 West 37th Street
New York, NY 10018
Tel: 212-629-9200
Fax: 212-629-0040
www.esptrendlab.com

Here and There
104 West 40th Street, 11th Floor
New York, NY 10018
Tel: 212-354-9014
Fax: 212-764-1831
OR
West Coast Office:
127 East 9th St., #410
Los Angeles, CA 90015
Tel: 213-622-5001
Fax: 213-622-2701
www.hereandthere.net

Margit Publications
(A Division of The Doneger Group)
463 7th Avenue, 3rd Floor
New York, NY 10018
Tel: 212-302-5137
Fax: 212-944-8757
www.mpnews.com

Promostyl Trend Office, Ltd.
250 West 39th Street, 16th Floor
New York, NY 10018
Tel: 212-921-7930
Fax: 212-921-8214
www.promostyl.com

Studio Edelkoort (View on Colour & Trend Union)
30 Boulevard Saint Jacques
75014 Paris
France
Tel: 011-33-01-4331-0589
Fax: 011-33-01-4331-7791
OR
New York Office:
90 Riverside Drive
New York, NY 10023
Tel: 212-724-3824

Tobé
501 Fifth Avenue, Suite 1208
New York, NY 10017
Tel: 212-867-8677
Fax: 212-867-8662
www.tobereport.com

The Trend Curve (Published by Marketing Directions, Inc.)
7215 Ohms Lane, Suite 175
Minneapolis, MN 55439
Tel: 952-893-1245 or 800-531-6614
Fax: 952-893-1264
www.trendcurve.com

Worth Global Style Network, Ltd.
157 Edgware Road
London W2 2HR
England
Tel: 011-44-20-7785-7700
Fax: 011-44-20-7258-3666
www.wgsn.com

There are many other forecasting services that specialize in trend information for women's wear, men's wear, and children's wear, as well as books on accessories, knits, and fabrics. For a complete listing, contact: Overseas Publishers Representatives, Inc. (OPR) at 252 West 38th Street, 4th floor; New York, NY 10018. Tel: 212-564-3954; Fax: 212-465-8938; www.oprny.com; Email: sales@oprny.com.

Appendix C

Selected Trade Associations and Industry Organizations

American Apparel and Footwear Association (AAFA)
1601 North Kent Street, Suite 1200
Arlington, VA 22209
Tel: 800-520-2262
Fax: 703-522-6741
www.apparelandfootwear.org

Chambre Syndicale de la Couture Parisienne
45 rue Saint Roch
75001 Paris
France
Tel: 011-33-01-4261-0077
Fax: 011-33-01-4286-8942

Clothing Manufacturers Association
730 Broadway, 10th Floor
New York, NY 10003
Tel: 212-529-0823

Cosmetics, Toiletries, and Fragrance Association
1101 17th Street NW, Suite 300
Washington, D.C. 20036-4702
Tel: 202-331-1770
Fax: 202-331-1969
www.ctfa.org

Cotton Incorporated
488 Madison Avenue
New York, NY 10022
Tel: 212-413-8300
Fax: 212-413-8377
www.cottoninc.com

Council of Fashion Designers of America (CFDA)
1412 Broadway, Suite 2006
New York, NY 10018
Tel: 212-302-1821
Fax: 212-768-0515
www.cfda.com

The Fashion Center
249 West 39th Street
New York, NY 10018
Tel: 212-764-9600
Fax: 212-764-9697
www.fashioncenter.com

Fashion Footwear Association of New York, Inc. (FFANY)
1414 Sixth Avenue, Suite 203
New York, NY 10019
Tel: 212-751-6422
Fax: 212-751-6404
www.ffany.org

Fashion Group International, Inc. (FGI)
8 West 40th Street, 7th Floor
New York, NY 10018
Tel: 212-302-5511
Fax: 212-302-5533
www.fgi.org

Fragrance Foundation
145 East 32nd Street
New York, NY 10016
Tel: 212-725-7255
Fax: 212-779-9058
www.fragrance.org

Fur Information Council of America (FICA)
8424 A Santa Monica Boulevard #860
West Hollywood, CA 90069
Tel: 323-848-7940
Fax: 323-848-2931
www.fur.org

Igedo Company
Messeplatz
D-40474 Düsseldorf
Germany
Tel: 011-49-21-1439-6387
Fax: 011-49-21-1439-6345
www.igedo.com

International Fashion Fabric Exhibition (IFFE)
One Park Avenue, 2nd Floor
New York, NY 10016
Tel: 917-326-6267
Fax: 917-326-6168
www.fabricshow.com

International Management Group (IMG)
7th on Sixth
22 East 71st Street
New York, NY 10021
Tel: 212-253-2692
Fax: 212-772-0899
www.7thonsixth.com

Intimate Apparel Council (IAC)
(a division of American Footwear and Apparel Association)
1601 North Kent Street, Suite 1200
Arlington, VA 22209
Tel: 800-520-2262
Fax: 703-522-6741

Italian Trade Commission
33 East 67th Street
New York, NY 10021
Tel: 212-980-1500
Fax: 212-758-1050
www.ice.it

Jewelry Information Center
52 Vanderbilt Avenue, 19th Floor
New York, NY 10017
Tel: 646-658-0240
Fax: 646-658-0245
www.jic.org

Leather Apparel Association
Creative Marketing Plus
19 West 21st Street, Suite 403
New York, NY 10010
Tel: 212-727-1210
Fax: 212-727-1218
www.leatherassociation.com

Leather Industries of America
1900 L Street NW, Suite 710
Washington, D.C. 20036
Tel: 202-296-4806
Fax: 202-296-7892
www.leatherusa.com

Masters of Linen
15, Rue du Louvre Boite 71
75001 Paris
France
Tel: 011-33-01-4221-0683
Fax: 011-33-01-4221-4822
OR
U.S. Representative
P.O. Box 1630
New York, NY 10028
Tel: 212-734-3640
Fax: 212-719-4301

Men's Apparel Guild in California (MAGIC)
6320 Canoga Avenue, 12th Floor
Woodland Hills, CA 91367
Tel: 818-593-5000
Fax: 818-593-5020
www.magiconline.com

Millinery Information Bureau
302 West 12th Street
New York, NY 10014
Tel: 212-627-8333
Fax: 212-627-0667

Mohair Council of America
233 W. Twohig
P.O. Box 5337
San Angelo, TX 76902
Tel: 915-655-3161
www.mohairusa.com

National Association of Men's Sportswear Buyers (NAMSB)
309 Fifth Avenue, Suite 307
New York, NY 10016
Tel: 212-685-4550
Fax: 212-685-4688
www.namsb.org

National Retail Federation (NRF)
Stores Magazine
325 7th Street NW, Suite 1000
Washington, DC 20004
Tel: 202-783-7971
www.nrf.com

Prêt à Porter
5 rue de Caumartin
75009 Paris
France
Tel: 011-33-1-4494-7000
Fax: 011-33-1-4494-7004
www.pretaporter.com

Toy Industry Association, Inc.
1115 Broadway, Room 400
New York, NY 10010
Tel: 212-675-1141
www.toy-tia.org

UNITE (Union of Needletrades, Industrial and Textile Employees)
275 Seventh Avenue
New York, NY 10001
Tel: 212-625-7000
www.uniteunion.org

The Woolmark Company
1230 Sixth Avenue, 7th Floor
New York, NY 10020
Tel: 646-756-2535
Fax: 646-756-2538
www.woolmark.com

Young Men's Wear Association (YMA)
47 West 34th Street
New York, NY 10001
Tel: 212-594-6422
Fax: 212-594-9349

MERCHANDISE MARTS

AmericasMart—Atlanta
240 Peachtree Street NW, Suite 2200
Atlanta, GA 30303
Tel: 404-220-2833
Fax: 678-686-5207
www.americasmart.com

Chicago Apparel Center
350 North Orleans
Chicago, IL 60054
Tel: 800-677-6278
Fax: 313-527-7779
www.merchandisemart.com/apparelcenter/

Dallas Market Center
2100 Stemmons Freeway
Dallas, TX 75207
Tel: 214-655-6100
www.dallasmarketcenter.com

California Mart
110 East Ninth Street
Los Angeles, CA 90079
Tel: 213-630-3600
www.californiamart.com

Picture Credits

Chapter 1

Pages 4–5: Reproduced from Pantone® View Colour Planner, published by Metropolitan Publishing BV, Amsterdam; 8: Courtesy of Neville Bean Designs.

Chapter 2

Page 19: Courtesy of the Trend Curve™; 24: Courtesy of Promostyl; 25: Courtesy of Promostyl; 26–27: Courtesy of Promostyl; 29: Courtesy of *The Tobé Report*, Robert Melendez, 2003. Illustrations from *The Tobé Report* by Robert Melendez; 34: Courtesy of The Doneger Group; 35: Courtesy of The Doneger Group; 39: Courtesy of Worth Global Style Network (WGSN).

Chapter 3

Page 50: Courtesy of the Color Association of the United States; 52–53 Huepoint® and Huepoint Color™ are registered trademarks of Huepoint, Inc. All rights reserved; 55: Courtesy of The Color Box™; 57–59: Reproduced from Pantone® View Colour Planner, published by Metropolitan Publishing BV, Amsterdam.

Chapter 4

Pages 78–79: Courtesy of Rachel Herbst; 80–81: Courtesy of Melissa Moylan; 84–85: Courtesy of Chatain & Thomas for Milliken & Company.

Chapter 5

Page 93: Courtesy of the Italian Vegetable Tanned Leather Consortium; 94–95: Courtesy of Faina Golub.

Chapter 6

Page 114: Courtesy of INVISTA (formerly DuPont Textiles & Interiors); 116–118: Courtesy of Roseann Forde; 124–125: Courtesy of Tencel; 127: Courtesy of Dorlastan's Trendvision 2004 by Bayer Faser GMBH, Germany (left); Courtesy of Dorlastan's Trendvision 2005 by Bayer Faser

GMBH, Germany (right); 129: Courtesy of Masters of Linen; 131: Courtesy of Cotton Inc.; 134–135, 137: Courtesy of Cotton, Inc.; 139: Courtesy of Masters of Linen; 145: Courtesy of Darlington Fabrics, a Moore Company; 147: Courtesy of Fortune International Ltd.; 148–149: Courtesy of Darlington Fabrics, a Moore Company; 153: Courtesy of Sag Harbor; 155: Courtesy of Alfred Dunner, Inc.

Chapter 7
Pages 173–177: Reprinted with the permission of Lord & Taylor; 179: Photos ©Patrick McMullan, April 19, 2001, Bloomingdale's; 186: Photo by Patrick Demarchelier. Courtesy of Saks Fifth Avenue.

Chapter 8
Pages 202–203: Courtesy of Ogan Dallal; 208: This photo is from the 7th on Sixth Spring 2002 Tulles of Seduction Runway Show, sponsored by the Intimate Apparel Council, a division of the American Apparel & Footwear Association; 211: Courtesy of Anand Jon; 212: C. Weber/CM; 214: Courtesy of Simon Ward; 220–221: Courtesy of Quebec Government House; 229: Courtesy of Agenda Venues.

Chapter 9
Page 235: Courtesy of Fairchild Publications, Inc.; 242: Courtesy of *Women's Wear Daily*, March 1, 2004.

Chapter 10
Page 252: Courtesy of *Women's Wear Daily*, May 28, 2003; 254: Courtesy of Igedo International Modemesse, Kronen FmbH u. Co. KG, Messeplatz, 40474 Düsseldorf, Germany; 260: International Fashion Fabric Exhibition, AdvanStar Communications, Inc.

Chapter 11
Page 279: Courtesy of Audrey Smaltz; 282: Courtesy of Bureau Betak; 284–285: Courtesy of Company Agenda; 288–289: Courtesy of Fashion Calendar/International; 290: Courtesy of Ebony Fashion Fair; 293–294: Photos courtesy of Berliner Studio/BEImages (top left) and ©Bruce Forrester, 2001 (all others); 297: Copyright ©Martin Rondeau.

Chapter 12
Page 308: Courtesy of Mirror Mirror Imagination Group; 311–312: Courtesy of Estée Lauder; 316: Courtesy of Lancôme; 323–324: Courtesy of Cosmoprof; 327: Courtesy of Unilever Cosmetics International; 329: Courtesy of International Flavors and Fragrances Inc.

Chapter 13
Page 345: Courtesy of Purple PR; 347: Courtesy of Salvatore J. Cesarani; 348: Courtesy of Salvatore J. Cesarani; 352: ©Jerry Kean; 357: Courtesy of National Association of Men's Sportswear Buyers, Inc.; 358: Courtesy of ENK International; 361: Courtesy of Tom Julian; 366–367: Courtesy of Phillips-Van Heusen Corporation; 369: Courtesy of Nautica Enterprises Inc.; 372: Photographer: Timothy Greenfield-Sanders. Courtesy of Kenneth Cole Productions, Inc.; 373: Photographer: Dan Lecca. Courtesy of Kenneth Cole Productions, Inc.

Chapter 14
Page 381: Courtesy of the Toy Industry Association; 386: Courtesy of Sound Choice Accompaniment Tracks; 387: Courtesy of Sound Choice Accompaniment Tracks; 388: Courtesy of Alexander Doll Company; 392: Photo supplied by Storm Photo, Kingston, N.Y. ©Tonner Doll Company, Inc.; 395: Images courtesy of Lionel LLC; 396:

From Richard Simmons Collection of the Masters. Artists: Stephanie Cauley ("First Day"), Cynthia Malbon ("Bridget"); 397: ©The Ashton-Drake Galleries.

Chapter 15

Page 418: Courtesy of Mary Elges; 428–429: Courtesy of Chelsea Interactive; 432: Courtesy of The Doneger Group; 433: ©FWD Fashion Wire Daily.

Color Insert

Color Plates 1 and 4: Courtesy of Cotton, Inc.; 2: Courtesy of Rachel Herbst; 3: Courtesy of Melissa Moylan.

Index